本成果受到中国人民大学"985 工程"的支持

孟广林◎主编

西方历史
文献选读
（古代卷）

**Selected Readings of
Historical Documents in the West
（Ancient Times）**

王大庆 ╱ 选编
米辰峰

社会科学文献出版社
SOCIAL SCIENCES ACADEMIC PRESS (CHINA)

前　言

　　五卷本《西方历史文献选读》(*Selected Readings of Historical Documents in the West*)，由中国人民大学历史学院世界史专业教师团队历时 5 年集体攻关完成。作为"九八五工程"子课题项目的成果，这套丛书共分"古代卷""中世纪卷""近代卷""现代卷""当代卷"，精心遴选西方重要的历史文献，力图多层次、全方位地显现西方各个历史时期在经济、政治、军事、思想文化、社会生活诸方面的基本状况与特征，从中透显出西方历史的演进脉络、流变趋向乃至发展规律。这些篇目，或对文献全文收录，或截取其中核心部分，在文献后编者运用马克思主义唯物史观依据相关历史背景对之作一解读，以期帮助读者阅读、理解。此外，还开列了一些与文献所反映的问题相关的研究著作，供有兴趣的读者延伸阅读，作进一步的深入探究。

　　我们之所以要设计这一课题并尽力完成，其主旨在于为世界史学科建设搭建一个基础性的学术平台，进一步提升本科生与研究生教育的教学水平。

　　众所周知，历史文献资料是历史研究的基础与出发点，同时也是史学人才培养的重要素材。改革开放前，由于语言、信息乃至经费等方面的限制，我国史学界在选编历史文献参考资料上基本采用了外文中译的方式，老一辈的史学家为此呕心沥血，成果凸显。周一良、吴于廑主编的《世界通史资料选辑》，齐思和、刘启戈主编选译的《中世纪初期的西欧》《中世纪中期的西欧》《中世纪晚期的西欧》，齐世荣主编的《当代世界史资料选辑》以及诸多的国别史、断代史乃至编年史、历史名著的编译等，涉及各个历史时期各主要地区、国家的经济、政治、军事、思想文化、社会生活等各个方面的原始资料，对于史学人才的培养发挥了十分重要的作用。自改革开放以来，随着国际学术交流的日益扩大和学术研究的不断拓展，依赖于汉译历史资料进行教学逐渐显示出其明显的局限性，这不仅使学生难以熟悉相关的各种名称、典故与术语，而且对相关历史现象的理解也有着诸多的文化隔膜感。为了克服这一困境，一些大学专门编选专业外语教材并设置相关的课程，一些教师径直开列外文书目让学生研习。这些举措虽然收到了一定效果，但不足以形成良好的长效机制。专业外语教材的历史资料编选常常显示出明显的研究热点的偏向性与历史时空的跳跃性，难以明晰地彰显长时段的历史过程与纷繁复杂的历史现象，很难与世界通史的基础性课程有机整合起来。同时，径直给学生（特别是本科生）开列外文参考书目在当下也难以收效，主要缘由是国内大多数高校的外文藏书数量十分有限，难以满足学生的借阅需求。在此情况下，的确应该结合基础性课程系统地编选一整套外文历史文献资料，来强化相关的教学需要。

我们的历史文献编选之所以聚焦在西方，主要有两个缘由。其一是团队力量有限。要编选整个世界通史课程的基础性文献，涉及众多的国家、地区，而我们团队又几乎都从事西方历史的教学与研究，要大跨度地涉历非西方的历史文献资料，不仅精力有限，而且学力不逮。而更重要的另一个考虑，则是旨在引导学生更多地关注西方历史。这些年来，中国的世界史取得显著的发展，但客观地说，西方历史是国内学者多为关注的学术领域。一段时间以来，国内史学界曾大力提倡世界史研究领域的均衡性，呼吁多关注非西方的国家和地区的历史，有的甚至将之提升到打破"西方中心"论之学旨高度。为了推动这一理路，一些高校教材在编写时，大幅度地压缩西方历史的内容，扩充非西方的国家和地区的历史内容。应该说，这类主张的出发点是好的，无可非议的。但应该指出，在现阶段乃至今后很长的一段时期，片面地强调世界史教学与研究的均衡性也是欠妥当的。西方历史之所以为国内大多数学人所看重，自然有着深层次的思想根源，与近代西方的崛起及其对世界的巨大影响、与中华民族近代的命运与探索、与当代中国社会主义现代化建设进程的曲折和拓展密切关联。可以毫不夸张地说，从关照中国的历史、现实与未来予以考量，西方无疑是一个最重要的历史参照坐标。不可否认，西方史学界的"西方中心"论的确包含着西方人"种族优越"论、"殖民征服合理"论的社会达尔文主义的谬论，但近代以来，对非西方国家、地区的传统社会而言，西方在世界历史发展潮流中的引领地位乃是客观的历史存在，也就是说，西方人借助资本主义工业化的张力，推动了世界各个地区的一体化。西方人的殖民主义侵略，客观上也刺激了非西方地区与国家告别传统、迈向现代的历史进程。直到十月革命发生后，特别是中国革命胜利后和中国改革开放所逐渐建构的中国社会主义现代化模式初步显现后，"西方中心"论才逐渐失去了"经验事实"的支撑。作为东方大国崛起的中国的历史与现实，必须更多地要在与西方历史的对称性参照中获得自我身份的理解、获得历史经验教训的借鉴。任意冲淡、压缩西方历史的做法，无疑是不明智的、非历史主义的。如果学者不去重点研究它，学生不去重点学习它，对它知之不多乃至知之甚少，又如何去突破"西方中心"论？事实上，当下史学界对西方历史的一些观点，仍旧深陷在西方史学界的传统诠释模式中而不能自拔，诸多学生对西方历史的不少理解仍然是西方学者曾经曲解乃至任意打扮的东西。在此情况下，重点研习西方历史的意义不言而喻。

正是基于以上缘由，我们编选了这套西方历史文献集。其中既有大量的原始资料（Primary Sources），也有不少当代权威史家整理、编译的第一手资料（Printed Primary Sources）。我们深知，研究西方历史，参考诸多语言种类的原始文献资料极其重要。然而，在当下的世界史教学中，由于学科起步较晚，语言训练欠缺，我们只能依照实际现状选编适用性普遍的英文历史文献来进行教学。"不积跬步，无以至千里。"在国内尚无这类书籍的情况下，我们相信这套书的出版，将填补我国世界史专业教学教材方面存在的重要空白，大大提升世界史专业本科生乃至研究生层次基础课程教学的质量，有力促进我国世界史学科的建设。

孟广林

2015 年 5 月于中国人民大学

目　　录

古希腊史文献选读

003 ‖ Homer: The Iliad

荷马《伊利亚特》节选

026 ‖ Hesiod: Works and Days

赫西俄德《工作与时日》节选

038 ‖ Aristotle: Athenian Constitution

亚里士多德《雅典政制》节选

062 ‖ Plutarch: Lycurgus

普鲁塔克《莱库古传》节选

095 ‖ Herodotus: Histories

希罗多德《历史》节选

119 ‖ Thucydides: The History of the Peloponnesian War

修昔底德《伯罗奔尼撒战争史》节选

131 Xenophon: Economics

色诺芬《经济论》节选

143 Aristophanes：Plutus

阿里斯托芬《财神》节选

172 Demosthenes：Third Philippic

德摩斯提尼《第三篇反腓力演说》

古罗马史文献选读

195 Polybius: The Histories

波利比乌斯《世界通史》节选

217 T. Livy: The History of Rome

李维《罗马通史》节选

245 M. T. Cicero: On the Republic

西塞罗《论共和国》节选

255 Julius Caesar: The Gallic War

凯撒《高卢战记》节选

269 Virgil: Aeneid

维吉尔《埃涅阿斯纪》节选

294 Ovid: Metamorphoses

奥维德《变形记》节选

319 Appian of Alexandria: Histories of Rome

阿庇安《罗马史》节选

331 P. C. Tacitus: The Annals

塔西佗《编年史》节选

359 Suetonius: Lives of the Caesars

苏维托纽斯《凯撒传》节选

385 后　记

古希腊史文献选读

Homer: The Iliad *

Now the goddess Dawn went up to high Olympus, to announce the light to Zeus and the other immortals, but Agamemnon bade the clear-voiced heralds summon to the place of gathering the long-haired Achaeans. And they made summons, and the men gathered full quickly. But the king first made the council of the great-souled elders to sit down beside the ship of Nestor, the king Pylos-born. And when he had called them together, he contrived a cunning plan, and said: "Hearken, my friends, a Dream from heaven came to me in my sleep through the ambrosial night, and most like was it to goodly Nestor, in form and in stature and in build. It took its stand above my head, and spake to me, saying: 'Thou sleepest, son of wise-hearted Atreus, the tamer of horses. To sleep the whole night through beseemeth not a man that is a counsellor, to whom a host is entrusted, and upon whom rest so many cares. But now, hearken thou quickly unto me, for I am a messenger to thee from Zeus, who, far away though he be, hath exceeding care for thee and pity. He biddeth thee arm the long-haired Achaeans with all speed, since now thou mayest take the broad-wayed city of the Trojans. For the immortals that have homes upon Olympus are no longer divided in counsel, since Hera hath bent the minds of all by her supplication, and over

* 荷马《伊利亚特》节选。本文选自该书的第 2 卷第 48~440 行、第 18 卷第 368~617 行。

the Trojans hang woes by the will of Zeus. But do thou keep this in thy heart.' So spake he, and was flown away, and sweet sleep let me go. Nay, come now, if in any wise we may, let us arm the sons of the Achaeans; but first will I make trial of them in speech, as is right, and will bid them flee with their benched ships; but do you from this side and from that bespeak them, and strive to hold them back."

So saying, he sate him down, and among them uprose Nestor, that was king of sandy Pylos. He with good intent addressed their gathering and spake among them: "My friends, leaders and rulers of the Argives, were it any other of the Achaeans that told us this dream we might deem it a false thing, and turn away therefrom the more; but now hath he seen it who declares himself to be far the mightiest of the Achaeans. Nay, come then, if in any wise we may arm the sons of the Achaeans." He spake, and led the way forth from the council, and the other sceptred kings rose up thereat and obeyed the shepherd of the host; and the people the while were hastening on. Even as the tribes of thronging bees go forth from some hollow rock, ever coming on afresh, and in clusters over the flowers of spring fly in throngs, some here, some there; even so from the ships and huts before the low sea-beach marched forth in companies their many tribes to the place of gathering. And in their midst blazed forth Rumour, messenger of Zeus, urging them to go; and they were gathered. And the place of gathering was in a turmoil, and the earth groaned beneath them, as the people sate them down, and a din arose. Nine heralds with shouting sought to restrain them, if so be they might refrain from uproar and give ear to the kings, nurtured of Zeus. Hardly at the last were the people made to sit, and were stayed in their places, ceasing from their clamour. Then among them lord Agamemnon uprose, bearing in his hands the sceptre which Hephaestus had wrought with toil. Hephaestus gave it to king Zeus, son of Cronos, and Zeus gave it to the messenger Argeïphontes; and Hermes, the lord, gave it to Pelops, driver of horses, and Pelops in turn gave it to Atreus, shepherd of the host; and Atreus at his death left it to Thyestes, rich in flocks, and Thyestes again left it to Agamemnon to bear, that so he might be lord of many isles and of all Argos.

Thereon he leaned, and spake his word among the Argives: "My friends, Danaan warriors, squires of Ares, great Zeus, son of Cronos, hath ensnared me in grievous blindness of heart, cruel god! seeing that of old he promised me, and bowed his head thereto, that not until I had sacked well-walled Ilios should I get me home; but now hath he planned cruel deceit, and bids me return inglorious to Argos, when I have lost much people. So, I ween, must be the good pleasure of Zeus, supreme in might, who hath laid low the heads of many cities, yea, and shall yet lay low, for his power is above all. A shameful thing is this even for the hearing of men that are yet to be, how that thus vainly so goodly and so great a host of the Achaeans warred a bootless war, and fought with men fewer than they, and no end thereof hath as yet been seen. For should we be minded, both Achaeans and Trojans, to swear a solemn oath with sacrifice, and to number ourselves, and should the Trojans be gathered together, even all they that have dwellings in the city, and we Achaeans be marshalled by tens, and choose, each company of us, a man of the Trojans to pour our wine, then would many tens lack a cup-bearer; so far, I deem, do the sons of the Achaeans outnumber the Trojans that dwell in the city. But allies there be out of many cities, men that wield the spear, who hinder me mightily, and for all that I am fain, suffer me not to sack the well-peopled citadel of Ilios. Already have nine years of great Zeus gone by, and lo, our ships' timbers are rotted, and the tackling loosed; and our wives, I ween, and little children sit in our halls awaiting us; yet is our task wholly unaccomplished in furtherance whereof we came hither. Nay, come, even as I shall bid, let us all obey: let us flee with our ships to our dear native land; for no more is there hope that we shall take broad-wayed Troy." So spake he, and roused the hearts in the breasts of all throughout the multitude, as many as had not heard the council. And the gathering was stirred like the long sea-waves of the Icarian main, which the East Wind or the South Wind has raised, rushing upon them from the clouds of father Zeus. And even as when the West Wind at its coming stirreth a deep cornfield with its violent blast, and the ears bow thereunder, even so was all their gathering stirred, and they with loud shouting rushed towards the ships; and from beneath their feet the dust arose on high. And they called each one to his fellow to lay hold of the ships and draw them into the bright sea, and they set themselves to clear the launching-ways, and their shouting went up to heaven, so fain were they of their return home; and they began to take the props from beneath the ships.

Then would the Argives have accomplished their return even beyond what was ordained, had not Hera spoken a word to Athena, saying: "Out upon it, child of Zeus that beareth the aegis, unwearied one! Is it thus indeed that the Argives are to flee to their dear native land over the broad back of the sea? Aye, and they would leave to Priam and the Trojans their boast, even Argive Helen, for whose sake many an Achaean hath perished in Troy, far from his dear native land. But go thou now throughout the host of the brazen-coated Achaeans; with thy gentle words seek thou to restrain every man, neither suffer them to draw into the sea their curved ships." So spake she, and the goddess, flashing-eyed Athene, failed not to hearken. Down from the peaks of Olympus she went darting, and speedily came to the swift ships of the Achaeans. There she found Odysseus, the peer of Zeus in counsel, as he stood. He laid no hand upon his benched, black ship, for that grief had come upon his heart and soul; and flashing-eyed Athene stood near him, and said: "Son of Laërtes, sprung from Zeus, Odysseus of many wiles, is it thus indeed that ye will fling yourselves on your benched ships to flee to your dear native land? Aye, and ye would leave to Priam and the Trojans their boast, even Argive Helen, for whose sake many an Achaean hath perished in Troy, far from his dear native land. But go thou now throughout the host of the Achaeans, and hold thee back no more; and with thy gentle words seek thou to restrain every man, neither suffer them to draw into the sea their curved ships." So said she, and he knew the voice of the goddess as she spake, and set him to run, and cast from him his cloak, which his herald gathered up, even Eurybates of Ithaca, that waited on him. But himself he went straight to Agamemnon, son of Atreus, and received at his hand the staff of his fathers, imperishable ever, and therewith went his way along the ships of the brazen-coated Achaeans.

Whomsoever he met that was a chieftain or man of note, to his side would he come and with gentle words seek to restrain him, saying: "Good Sir, it beseems not to seek to affright thee as if thou were a coward, but do thou thyself sit thee down, and make the rest of thy people to sit. For thou knowest not yet clearly what is the mind of the son of Atreus; now he does but make trial, whereas soon he will smite the sons of the Achaeans. Did we not all hear what he spake in the council? Beware lest waxing wroth he work mischief to the sons of the Achaeans. Proud is the heart of kings, fostered of heaven; for their honour is from Zeus, and Zeus, god of counsel, loveth them." But whatsoever man of the people he saw, and found brawling, him would he smite with his staff; and chide with words, saying, "Fellow, sit thou still, and hearken to the words of others that are better men than thou; whereas thou art unwarlike and a weakling, neither to be counted in war nor in counsel. In no wise shall we Achaeans all be kings here. No good thing is a multitude of lords; let there be one lord, one king, to whom the son of crooked-counselling Cronos hath vouchsafed the sceptre and judgments, that he may take counsel for his people." Thus masterfully did he range through the host, and they hasted back to the place of gathering from their ships and huts with noise, as when a wave of the loud-resounding sea thundereth on the long beach, and the deep roareth. Now the others sate them down and were stayed in their places, only there still kept chattering on Thersites of measureless speech, whose mind was full of great store of disorderly words, wherewith to utter revilings against the kings, idly, and in no orderly wise, but whatsoever he deemed would raise a laugh among the Argives. Evil-favoured was he beyond all men that came to Ilios: he was bandy-legged and lame in the one foot, and his two shoulders were rounded, stooping together over his chest, and above them his head was warped, and a scant stubble grew thereon. Hateful was he to Achilles above all, and to Odysseus, for it was they twain that he was wont to revile; but now again with shrill cries he uttered abuse against goodly Agamemnon. With him were the Achaeans exceeding wroth, and had indignation in their hearts.

Howbeit with loud shoutings he spake and chid Agamemnon: "Son of Atreus, with what art thou now again discontent, or what lack is thine? Filled are thy huts with bronze, and women full many are in thy huts, chosen spoils that we Achaeans give thee first of all, whensoe'er we take a citadel. Or dost thou still want gold also, which some man of the horse-taming Trojans shall bring thee out of Ilios as a ransom for his son, whom I haply have bound and led away or some other of the Achaeans? Or is it some young girl for thee to know in love, whom thou wilt keep apart for thyself? Nay, it beseemeth not one that is their captain to bring to ill the sons of the Achaeans. Soft fools! base things of shame, ye women of Achaea, men no more, homeward let us go with our ships, and leave this fellow here in the land of Troy to digest his prizes, that so he may learn whether in us too there is aught of aid for him or no—for him that hath now done dishonour to Achilles, a man better far than he; for he hath taken away, and keepeth his prize by his own arrogant act. Of a surety there is naught of wrath in the heart of Achilles; nay, he heedeth not at all; else, son of Atreus, wouldest thou now work insolence for the last time." So spake Thersites, railing at Agamemnon, shepherd of the host. But quickly to his side came goodly Odysseus, and with an angry glance from beneath his brows, chid him with harsh words, saying: "Thersites of reckless speech, clear-voiced talker though thou art, refrain thee, and be not minded to strive singly against kings. For I deem that there is no viler mortal than thou amongst all those that with the sons of Atreus came beneath Ilios. Wherefore 'twere well thou shouldst not take the name of kings in thy mouth as thou protest, to cast reproaches upon them, and to watch for home-going. In no wise do we know clearly as yet how these things are to be, whether it be for good or ill that we sons of the Achaeans shall return. Therefore dost thou now continually utter revilings against Atreus' son, Agamemnon, shepherd of the host, for that the Danaan warriors give him gifts full many; whereas thou pratest on with railings. But I will speak out to thee, and this word shall verily be brought to pass: if I find thee again playing the fool, even as now thou dost, then may the head of Odysseus abide no more upon his shoulders, nor may I any more be called the father of Telemachus, if I take thee not, and strip off thy raiment, thy cloak, and thy tunic that cover thy nakedness, and for thyself send thee wailing to the swift ships, beaten forth from the place of gathering with shameful blows."

So spake Odysseus, and with his staff smote his back and shoulders; and Thersites cowered down, and a big tear fell from him, and a bloody weal rose up on his back beneath the staff of gold. Then he sate him down, and fear came upon him, and stung by pain with helpless looks he wiped away the tear. But the Achaeans, sore vexed at heart though they were, broke into a merry laugh at him, and thus would one speak with a glance at his neighbour: "Out upon it! verily hath Odysseus ere now wrought good deeds without number as leader in good counsel and setting battle in army, but now is this deed far the best that he hath wrought among the Argives, seeing he hath made this scurrilous babbler to cease from his prating. Never again, I ween, will his proud spirit henceforth set him on to rail at kings with words of reviling." So spake the multitude; but up rose Odysseus, sacker of cities, the sceptre in his hand, and by his side flashing-eyed Athene, in the likeness of a herald, bade the host keep silence, that the sons of the Achaeans, both the nearest and the farthest, might hear his words, and lay to heart his counsel. He with good intent addressed their gathering and spake among them: "Son of Atreus, now verily are the Achaeans minded to make thee, O king, the most despised among all mortal men, nor will they fulfill the promise that they made to thee, while faring hitherward from Argos, the pasture-land of horses, that not until thou hadst sacked well-walled Ilios shouldest thou get thee home. For like little children or widow women do they wail each to the other in longing to return home. Verily there is toil enough to make a man return disheartened. For he that abideth but one single month far from his wife in his benched ship hath vexation of heart, even he whom winter blasts and surging seas keep afar; but for us is the ninth year at its turn, while we abide here; wherefore I count it not shame that the Achaeans have vexation of heart beside their beaked ships; yet even so it is a shameful thing to tarry long, and return empty. Endure, my friends, and abide for a time, that we may know whether the prophecies of Calchas be true, or no."

" For this in truth do we know well in our hearts, and ye are all witnesses thereto, even as many as the fates of death have not borne away. It was but as yesterday or the day before, when the ships of the Achaeans were gathering in Aulis, laden with woes for Priam and the Trojans; and we round about a spring were offering to the immortals upon the holy altars hecatombs that bring fulfillment, beneath a fair plane-tree from whence flowed the bright water; then appeared a great portent: a serpent, blood-red on the back, terrible, whom the Olympian himself had sent forth to the light, glided from beneath the altar and darted to the plane-tree. Now upon this were the younglings of a sparrow, tender little ones, on the topmost bough, cowering beneath the leaves, eight in all, and the mother that bare them was the ninth, Then the serpent devoured them as they twittered piteously, and the mother fluttered around them, wailing for her dear little ones; howbeit he coiled himself and caught her by the wing as she screamed about him. But when he had devoured the sparrow's little ones and the mother with them, the god, who had brought him to the light, made him to be unseen; for the son of crooked-counselling Cronos turned him to stone; and we stood there and marveled at what was wrought. So, when the dread portent brake in upon the hecatombs of the gods, then straightway did Calchas prophesy, and address our gathering, saying: 'Why are ye thus silent, ye long-haired Achaeans? To us hath Zeus the counsellor shewed this great sign, late in coming, late in fulfillment, the fame whereof shall never perish. Even as this serpent devoured the sparrow's little ones and the mother with them—the eight, and the mother that bare them was the ninth—so shall we war there for so many years, but in the tenth shall we take the broad-wayed city.' On this wise spake Calchas, and now all this is verily being brought to pass. Nay, come, abide ye all, ye well-greaved Achaeans, even where ye are, until we take the great city of Priam." So spake he, and the Argives shouted aloud, and all round about them the ships echoed wondrously beneath the shouting of the Achaeans, as they praised the words of godlike Odysseus.

And there spake among them the horseman, Nestor of Gerenia: "Now look you; in very truth are ye holding assembly after the manner of silly boys that care no whit for deeds of war. What then is to be the end of our compacts and our oaths? Nay, into the fire let us cast all counsels and plans of warriors, the drink-offerings of unmixed wine, and the hand-clasps wherein we put our trust. For vainly do we wrangle with words, nor can we find any device at all, for all our long-tarrying here. Son of Atreus, do thou as of old keep unbending purpose, and be leader of the Argives throughout stubborn fights; and for these, let them perish, the one or two of the Achaeans, that take secret counsel apart—yet no accomplishment shall come therefrom—to depart first to Argos or ever we have learned whether the promise of Zeus that beareth the aegis be a lie or no. For I declare that Cronos' son, supreme in might, gave promise with his nod on that day when the Argives went on board their swift-faring ships, bearing unto the Trojans death and fate; for he lightened on our right and shewed forth signs of good. Wherefore let no man make haste to depart homewards until each have lain with the wife of some Trojan, and have got him requital for his strivings and groanings for Helen's sake. Howbeit, if any man is exceeding fain to depart homewards, let him lay his hand upon his black, well-benched ship, that before the face of all he may meet death and fate. But do thou, O King, thyself take good counsel, and hearken to another; the word whatsoever I speak, shalt thou not lightly cast aside. Separate thy men by tribes, by clans, Agamemnon, that clan may bear aid to clan and tribe to tribe. If thou do thus, and the Achaeans obey thee, thou wilt know then who among thy captains is a coward, and who among thy men, and who too is brave; for they will fight each clan for itself. So shalt thou know whether it is even by the will of heaven that thou shalt not take the city, or by the cowardice of thy folk and their witlessness in war."

Then in answer to him spake the king, Agamemnon: "Aye verily once more, old sir, art thou pre-eminent in speech above the sons of the Achaeans. I would, O father Zeus and Athene and Apollo, that I had ten such counsellors; then would the city of king Priam forthwith bow her head, taken and laid waste beneath our hands. But the son of Cronos, even Zeus that beareth the aegis, hath brought sorrows upon me, in that he casteth me into the midst of fruitless strifes and wranglings. For verily I and Achilles fought about a girl with violent words, and it was I that waxed wroth the first; but if e'er we shall be at one in counsel, then shall there no more be any putting off of evil for the Trojans, no not for an instant. But for this present go ye to your meal, that we may join battle. Let every man whet well his spear and bestow well his shield, and let him well give to his swift-footed horses their food, and look well to his chariot on every side, and bethink him of fighting; that the whole day through we may contend in hateful war. For of respite shall there intervene, no, not a whit, until night at its coming shall part the fury of warriors. Wet with sweat about the breast of many a man shall be the baldric of his sheltering shield, and about the spear shall his hand grow weary, and wet with sweat shall a man's horse be, as he tugs at the polished car. But whomsoever I shall see minded to tarry apart from the fight beside the beaked ships, for him shall there be no hope thereafter to escape the dogs and birds." So spake he, and the Argives shouted aloud as a wave against a high headland, when the South Wind cometh and maketh it to swell—even against a jutting crag that is never left by the waves of all the winds that come from this side or from that. And they arose and hasted to scatter among the ships, and made fires in the huts, and took their meal. And they made sacrifice one to one of the gods that are for ever, and one to another, with the prayer that they might escape from death and the toil of war. But Agamemnon, king of men, slew a fat bull of five years to the son of Cronos, supreme in might, and let call the elders, the chieftains of the Achaean host, Nestor, first of all, and king Idomeneus, and thereafter the twain Aiantes and the son of Tydeus, and as the sixth Odysseus, the peer of Zeus in counsel. And unbidden came to him Menelaus, good at the war-cry, for he knew in his heart wherewith his brother was busied. About the bull they stood and took up the barley grains, and in prayer lord Agamemnon spake among them, saying:"Zeus, most glorious, most great, lord of the dark clouds, that dwellest in the heaven, grant that the sun set not, neither darkness come upon us, until I have cast down in headlong ruin the hall of Priam, blackened with smoke, and have burned with consuming fire the portals thereof, and cloven about the breast of Hector his tunic, rent with the bronze; and in throngs may his comrades round about him fall headlong in the dust, and bite the earth."

So spake he; but not as yet would the son of Cronos grant him fulfillment; nay, he accepted the sacrifice, but toil he made to wax unceasingly. Then, when they had prayed and had sprinkled the barley grains, they first drew back the victims' heads and cut their throats, and flayed them; and they cut out the thigh-pieces and covered them with a double layer of fat, and laid raw flesh thereon. These they burned on billets of wood stripped of leaves, and the inner parts they pierced with spits, and held them over the flame of Hephaestus. But when the thigh-pieces were wholly burned and they had tasted of the inner parts, they cut up the rest and spitted it, and roasted it carefully, and drew all off the spits. Then, when they had ceased from their labour and had made ready the meal, they feasted, nor did their hearts lack aught of the equal feast. But when they had put from them the desire of food and drink, among them the horseman, Nestor of Gerenia, was first to speak, saying: "Most glorious son of Atreus, Agamemnon, king of men, let us now not any more remain gathered here, nor any more put off the work which verily the god vouchsafeth us. Nay, come, let the heralds of the brazen-coated Achaeans make proclamation, and gather together the host throughout the ships, and let us go thus in a body through the broad camp of the Achaeans, that we may with the more speed stir up sharp battle."

......

On this wise spake they one to the other; but silver-footed Thetis came unto the house of Hephaestus, imperishable, decked with stars, preeminent among the houses of immortals, wrought all of bronze, that the crook-foot god himself had built him. Him she found sweating with toil as he moved to and fro about his bellows in eager haste; for he was fashioning tripods, twenty in all, to stand around the wall of his well-built hall, and golden wheels had he set beneath the base of each that of themselves they might enter the gathering of the gods at his wish and again return to his house, a wonder to behold. Thus much were they fully wrought, that not yet were the cunningly fashioned ears set thereon; these was he making ready, and was forging the rivets. And while he laboured thereat with cunning skill, meanwhile there drew nigh to him the goddess, silver-footed Thetis. And Charis of the gleaming veil came forward and marked her—fair Charis, whom the famed god of the two strong arms had wedded. And she clasped her by the hand, and spake, and addressed her: "Wherefore, long-robed Thetis, art thou come to our house, an honoured guest, and a welcome? Heretofore thou hast not been wont to come. But follow me further, that I may set before thee entertainment."

So saying the bright goddess led her on. Then she made her to sit on a silver-studded chair, a beautiful chair, richly-wrought, and beneath was a footstool for the feet; and she called to Hephaestus, the famed craftsman, and spake to him, saying: "Hephaestus, come forth hither; Thetis hath need of thee." And the famous god of the two strong arms answered her: "Verily then a dread and honoured goddess is within my halls, even she that saved me when pain was come upon me after I had fallen afar through the will of my shameless mother, that was fain to hide me away by reason of my lameness. Then had I suffered woes in heart, had not Eurynome and Thetis received me into their bosom—Eurynome, daughter of backward-flowing Oceanus. With them then for nine years' space I forged much cunning handiwork, brooches, and spiral arm-bands, and rosettes and necklaces, within their hollow cave; and round about me flowed, murmuring with foam, the stream of Oceanus, a flood unspeakable. Neither did any other know thereof, either of gods or of mortal men, but Thetis knew and Eurynome, even they that saved me. And now is Thetis come to my house; wherefore it verily behoveth me to pay unto fair-tressed Thetis the full price for the saving of my life. But do thou set before her fair entertainment, while I put aside my bellows and all my tools." He spake, and from the anvil rose, a huge, panting bulk, halting the while, but beneath him his slender legs moved nimbly. The bellows he set away from the fire, and gathered all the tools wherewith he wrought into a silver chest; and with a sponge wiped he his face and his two hands withal, and his mighty neck and shaggy breast, and put upon him a tunic, and grasped a stout staff, and went forth halting; but there moved swiftly to support their lord handmaidens wrought of gold in the semblance of living maids. In them is understanding in their hearts, and in them speech and strength, and they know cunning handiwork by gift of the immortal gods. These busily moved to support their lord, and he, limping nigh to where Thetis was, sat him down upon a shining chair; and he clasped her by the hand, and spake, and addressed her: "Wherefore, long-robed Thetis, art thou come to our house, an honoured guest and a welcome? Heretofore thou hast not been wont to come. Speak what is in thy mind; my heart bids me fulfill it, if fulfill it I can, and it is a thing that hath fulfillment."

And Thetis made answer to him, shedding tears the while: "Hephaestus, is there now any goddess, of all those that are in Olympus, that hath endured so many grievous woes in her heart as are the sorrows that Zeus, son of Cronos, hath given me beyond all others? Of all the daughters of the sea he subdued me alone to a mortal, even to Peleus, son of Aeacus, and I endured the bed of a mortal albeit sore against my will. And lo, he lieth in his halls fordone with grievous old age, but now other griefs are mine. A son he gave me to bear and to rear, pre-eminent among warriors, and he shot up like a sapling; then when I had reared him as a tree in a rich orchard plot, I sent him forth in the beaked ships to Ilios to war with the Trojans; but never again shall I welcome him back to his home, to the house of Peleus. And while yet he liveth, and beholdeth the light of the sun, he hath sorrow, nor can I any wise help him, though I go to him. The girl that the sons of the Achaeans chose out for him as a prize, her hath the lord Agamemnon taken back from out his arms. Verily in grief for her was he wasting his heart; but the Achaeans were the Trojans penning at the sterns of the ships, and would not suffer them to go forth. And to him the elders of the Argives made prayer, and named many glorious gifts. Then albeit he refused himself to ward from them ruin, yet clad he Patroclus in his own armour and sent him into the war, and added therewithal much people. All day long they fought around the Scaean gates, and on that selfsame day had laid the city waste, but that, after the valiant son of Menoetius had wrought sore harm, Apollo slew him amid the foremost fighters and gave glory to Hector. Therefore am I now come to thy knees, if so be thou wilt be minded to give my son, that is doomed to a speedy death, shield and helmet, and goodly greaves fitted with ankle-pieces, and corselet. For the harness that was his aforetime his trusty comrade lost, when he was slain by the Trojans; and my son lieth on the ground in anguish of heart."

Then the famous god of the two strong arms answered her: "Be of good cheer, neither let these things distress thy heart. Would that I might so surely avail to hide him afar from dolorous death, when dread fate cometh upon him, as verily goodly armour shall be his, such that in aftertime many a one among the multitude of men shall marvel, whosoever shall behold it." So saying he left her there and went unto his bellows, and he turned these toward the fire and bade them work. And the bellows, twenty in all, blew upon the melting-vats, sending forth a ready blast of every force, now to further him as he laboured hard, and again in whatsoever way Hephaestus might wish and his work go on. And on the fire he put stubborn bronze and tin and precious gold and silver; and thereafter he set on the anvil-block a great anvil, and took in one hand a massive hammer, and in the other took he the tongs. First fashioned he a shield, great and sturdy, adorning it cunningly in every part, and round about it set a bright rim, threefold and glittering, and therefrom made fast a silver baldric. Five were the layers of the shield itself; and on it he wrought many curious devices with cunning skill. Therein he wrought the earth, therein the heavens therein the sea, and the unwearied sun, and the moon at the full, and therein all the constellations wherewith heaven is crowned—the Pleiades, and the Hyades and the mighty Orion, and the Bear, that men call also the Wain, that circleth ever in her place, and watcheth Orion, and alone hath no part in the baths of Ocean.

Therein fashioned he also two cities of mortal men exceeding fair. In the one there were marriages and feastings, and by the light of the blazing torches they were leading the brides from their bowers through the city, and loud rose the bridal song. And young men were whirling in the dance, and in their midst flutes and lyres sounded continually; and there the women stood each before her door and marvelled. But the folk were gathered in the place of assembly; for there a strife had arisen, and two men were striving about the blood-price of a man slain; the one avowed that he had paid all, declaring his cause to the people, but the other refused to accept aught; and each was fain to win the issue on the word of a daysman. Moreover, the folk were cheering both, shewing favour to this side and to that. And heralds held back the folk, and the elders were sitting upon polished stones in the sacred circle, holding in their hands the staves of the loud-voiced heralds. Therewith then would they spring up and give judgment, each in turn. And in the midst lay two talents of gold, to be given to him whoso among them should utter the most righteous judgment. But around the other city lay in leaguer two hosts of warriors gleaming in armour. And twofold plans found favour with them, either to lay waste the town or to divide in portions twain all the substance that the lovely city contained within. Howbeit the besieged would nowise hearken thereto, but were arming to meet the foe in an ambush. The wall were their dear wives and little children guarding, as they stood thereon, and therewithal the men that were holden of old age; but the rest were faring forth, led of Ares and Pallas Athene, both fashioned in gold, and of gold was the raiment wherewith they were clad. Goodly were they and tall in their harness, as beseemeth gods, clear to view amid the rest, and the folk at their feet were smaller. But when they were come to the place where it seemed good unto them to set their ambush, in a river-bed where was a watering-place for all herds alike, there they sate them down, clothed about with flaming bronze. Thereafter were two scouts set by them apart from the host, waiting till they should have sight of the sheep and sleek cattle. And these came presently, and two herdsmen followed with them playing upon pipes; and of the guile wist they not at all.

But the liers-in-wait, when they saw these coming on, rushed forth against them and speedily cut off the herds of cattle and fair flocks of white-fleeced sheep, and slew the herdsmen withal. But the besiegers, as they sat before the places of gathering and heard much tumult among the kine, mounted forthwith behind their high-stepping horses, and set out thitherward, and speedily came upon them. Then set they their battle in array and fought beside the river banks, and were ever smiting one another with bronze-tipped spears. And amid them Strife and Tumult joined in the fray, and deadly Fate, grasping one man alive, fresh-wounded, another without a wound, and another she dragged dead through the mellay by the feet; and the raiment that she had about her shoulders was red with the blood of men. Even as living mortals joined they in the fray and fought; and they were haling away each the bodies of the others' slain. Therein he set also soft fallow-land, rich tilth and wide, that was three times ploughed; and ploughers full many therein were wheeling their yokes and driving them this way and that. And whensoever after turning they came to the headland of the field, then would a man come forth to each and give into his hands a cup of honey-sweet wine; and the ploughmen would turn them in the furrows, eager to reach the headland of the deep tilth. And the field grew black behind and seemed verily as it had been ploughed, for all that it was of gold; herein was the great marvel of the work. Therein he set also a king's demesne-land, wherein labourers were reaping, bearing sharp sickles in their hands. Some handfuls were falling in rows to the ground along the swathe, while others the binders of sheaves were binding with twisted ropes of straw. Three binders stood hard by them, while behind them boys would gather the handfuls, and bearing them in their arms would busily give them to the binders; and among them the king, staff in hand, was standing in silence at the swathe, joying in his heart. And heralds apart beneath an oak were making ready a feast, and were dressing a great ox they had slain for sacrifice; and the women sprinkled the flesh with white barley in abundance, for the workers' mid-day meal.

Therein he set also a vineyard heavily laden with clusters, a vineyard fair and wrought of gold; black were the grapes, and the vines were set up throughout on silver poles. And around it he drave a trench of cyanus, and about that a fence of tin; and one single path led thereto, whereby the vintagers went and came, whensoever they gathered the vintage. And maidens and youths in childish glee were bearing the honey-sweet fruit in wicker baskets. And in their midst a boy made pleasant music with a clear-toned lyre, and thereto sang sweetly the Linos-song with his delicate voice; and his fellows beating the earth in unison therewith followed on with bounding feet mid dance and shoutings. And therein he wrought a herd of straight-horned kine: the kine were fashioned of gold and tin, and with lowing hasted they forth from byre to pasture beside the sounding river, beside the waving reed. And golden were the herdsmen that walked beside the kine, four in number, and nine dogs swift of foot followed after them. But two dread lions amid the foremost kine were holding a loud-lowing bull, and he, bellowing mightily, was haled of them, while after him pursued the dogs and young men. The lions twain had rent the hide of the great bull, and were devouring the inward parts and the black blood, while the herdsmen vainly sought to fright them, tarring on the swift hounds. Howbeit these shrank from fastening on the lions, but stood hard by and barked and sprang aside. Therein also the famed god of the two strong arms wrought a pasture in a fair dell, a great pasture of white-fleeced sheep, and folds, and roofed huts, and pens.

Therein furthermore the famed god of the two strong arms cunningly wrought a dancing-floor like unto that which in wide Cnosus Daedalus fashioned of old for fair-tressed Ariadne. There were youths dancing and maidens of the price of many cattle, holding their hands upon the wrists one of the other. Of these the maidens were clad in fine linen, while the youths wore well-woven tunics faintly glistening with oil; and the maidens had fair chaplets, and the youths had daggers of gold hanging from silver baldrics. Now would they run round with cunning feet exceeding lightly, as when a potter sitteth by his wheel that is fitted between his hands and maketh trial of it whether it will run; and now again would they run in rows toward each other. And a great company stood around the lovely dance, taking joy therein; and two tumblers whirled up and down through the midst of them as leaders in the dance. Therein he set also the great might of the river Oceanus, around the uttermost rim of the strongly-wrought shield. But when he had wrought the shield, great and sturdy, then wrought he for him a corselet brighter than the blaze of fire, and he wrought for him a heavy helmet, fitted to his temples, a fair helm, richly-dight, and set thereon a crest of gold; and he wrought him greaves of pliant tin. But when the glorious god of the two strong arms had fashioned all the armour, he took and laid it before the mother of Achilles. And like a falcon she sprang down from snowy Olympus, bearing the flashing armour from Hephaestus.

一 文献出处

Homer, *The Iliad*, with an English translation by A.T. Murray, Cambridge, M.A.: Harvard University Press; London: William Heinemann, Ltd., 1924.

二 文献导读

《荷马史诗》包括《伊利亚特》和《奥德赛》两部，是古希腊文学宝库中的明珠。《荷马史诗》不仅是希腊人最早的文学作品，还是古希腊后来的戏剧、雕塑等艺术形式得以产生的一块沃土，在希腊人的社会和文化生活中占有至高无上的地位，是百科全书式的作品，相当于希腊人的"圣经"，对希腊乃至整个西方的思想产生了极其深远的影响。正如马克思所言，希腊的艺术和史诗至今"仍然能够给我们以艺术的享受，而且在某些方面来说，还是一种规范和高不可及的范本"。

对于历史研究者来说，《荷马史诗》不仅是文学名著，还是极为重要的历史资料，尤其是人们了解和研究荷马时代唯一的文献资料，因为其直接或间接地反映了迈锡尼时代以及荷马时代的社会生活状况。但是，由于其创作时间十分久远，长期处于口头流传的状态，从开始传唱到形成文字的定本经过了数百年时间，再加上缺乏相应的记载，因此，学术界对《荷马史诗》的作者是谁、创作过程如何以及史诗所反映的是哪一个历史时代等问题长期充满争议，从而在古典学界形成了所谓"荷马问题"。

相传《荷马史诗》的作者是小亚细亚附近开俄斯岛的盲诗人荷马。关于荷马其人唯一的记述来自据称也是出自荷马之手的《阿波罗神颂歌》的结尾部分：

> 无论什么时候，在旅途中疲惫了的人来到这里，询问你们："少女们啊，请告诉我，……谁的歌声你们最喜欢？"那时候，你们一定要用你们优雅的言辞，众口同声地回答："住在开俄斯岛上的盲歌人。"

对于荷马是史诗的创作者，古典时代的希腊人深信不疑，包括希罗多德、修昔底德在内的很多希腊作家皆信此说。到了希腊化时代，面对两部史诗中所表现出的矛盾和差异，亚历山大里亚的学者开始对史诗是否出自同一个作者产生怀疑。近代以来，学者们开始对史诗的作者及创作时间和过程进行全面的辨析和研究，形成了众多的流派和观点，大致分成两派：一派仍然坚持传统观点，认为史诗具有统一的艺术风格和特色，为荷马一人所作；另一派则认为如此宏伟和完美的史诗不可能是一人一时创造出来的，史诗中许多前后矛盾、不相一致的事实正说明了这一点。在双方争执不下的情况下，美国学者帕里（Milman Parry，1902—1935）另辟蹊径，从史诗的语言特点入手，对《荷马史诗》中大量出现的词组、短语和句组的"重复现象"进行了量化分析并做出了令人信服的解释，这项研究使"荷马问题"取得了突破性进展。帕里发现，史诗具有一套极其广泛复杂而又经济节约的程式化语句，也就是说，史诗不是诗人简单地运用一个个字或词创作出来的，而是由大量重复使用的程式化词组和句子结合而成的。这些程式化用语十分符合配乐吟唱的古希腊诗歌所特有的韵律要求，也便于在没有文字的条件下口头传诵和即兴创作。帕里由此得出结论，如此大量而固定的程式化用语显然不可能出自一个诗人的创作，而是经过很多代民间歌手不断积累、选择、口头相传而约定俗成的。正是由于帕里的研究，我们对《荷马史诗》的创作过程有了一个比较清晰的认识。

特洛伊战争结束后不久，多利亚人入主希腊，迈锡尼文明遭到毁灭。从公元前 12 世纪晚期开始，希腊境内开始出现一些专门以传唱特洛伊战争故事为业的游吟诗人，从而开启了荷马史诗的最初创作，不过这一时期的史诗只是作为供人传唱的口头文学作品。公元前 8 世纪前后，荷马史诗进入了统一加工和整理阶段，荷马既是一位游吟诗人，也是整理者之一，可能对传唱已久的史诗进行了统一的加工和提炼，这既是一项编辑的工作，又不失为一种创作。但这时史诗仍然没有被写成文本，直到公元前 7 世纪，小亚细亚才出现了职业的荷马史诗朗诵者，说明这一时期开始出现了史诗的抄本。到公元前 6 世纪，荷马史诗正式被编订成文本，出现在很多朗诵比赛上。虽然有了文本，但由于抄本颇多，良莠不齐，到公元前 3

世纪，亚历山大里亚的学者对现存的史诗抄本进行了最后的编辑、考订和分卷，按照所述事件的先后顺序加以组织，总称"史诗组诗"，其中有关特洛伊战争的共有八部，称"特洛伊组诗"，但是，除了《伊利亚特》和《奥德赛》，其余六部均已失传，只有内容提要和个别诗句存留。

《伊利亚特》分为24卷，共有15693行诗句，讲述的是希腊联军攻打特洛伊的战争进行到第十年，特洛伊城最终被攻陷之前五十多天内发生的事情，可以说是特洛伊战争高潮阶段的一个精彩片断。史诗以希腊联军大将阿喀琉斯受到主帅迈锡尼王阿伽门农的不公正待遇而发怒，既而愤然离开战场作为开端，由此，"阿喀琉斯的愤怒"成为全诗的一条主线。阿喀琉斯走后，希腊联军节节败退，阿伽门农万般无奈只好派人前去求情，请他返回战场，但却屡遭拒绝，阿喀琉斯的愤怒难以平息。就在希腊人眼看大势已去之时，阿喀琉斯的战友和部下帕特洛克卢斯借了阿喀琉斯的盔甲杀入敌营，特洛伊人都以为阿喀琉斯回来了，闻风丧胆，开始撤退，帕特洛克卢斯得意忘形，竟然忘记了阿喀琉斯临行之前的嘱咐，追击敌人直至特洛伊城下，结果中了埋伏，惨遭特洛伊主将赫克托尔的杀害。得知好友的死讯，阿喀琉斯万分悲痛，决定重回战场，为朋友报仇。同时，在希腊联军另一员大将奥德修斯的劝说下，阿喀琉斯和阿伽门农也终于言归于好，至此，阿喀琉斯的愤怒才基本上得以平息。阿喀琉斯投入战斗后，特洛伊人全线崩溃，死伤枕藉，战局得到很本扭转。史诗的高潮是阿喀琉斯与赫克托尔的决战，阿喀琉斯在众神的帮助下，杀死了赫克托尔。全诗的最后一幕是特洛伊年迈的老王普里阿摩用重金从阿喀琉斯手里赎回了儿子的尸体，举办国葬，整个特洛伊城淹没在一片绝望和痛苦的哭嚎声中。

《奥德赛》有24卷，共12110行诗句，讲述的是特洛伊战争结束后希腊联军将领伊大卡国王奥德修斯历经十年漂泊重返家乡的故事。诗人以神明决定让奥德修斯返乡为起点，围绕两条线索展开叙述。一条是在奥德修斯家中，在奥德修斯被阿伽门农征召前往特洛伊参战之后，前线不断传来奥德修斯战死的传闻，因此，很多地方贵族不断前来向奥德修斯美丽而贤惠的妻子佩涅罗珀求婚。他们索性就住在奥德修斯家中，每天宴饮，耗费他的家财。佩涅罗珀深信丈夫总有一天定会归来，但儿子年幼，母子俩形单影只，一时无法摆脱求婚者的无礼纠缠，就想出一些办法拖延时间。奥德修斯一去就是十年，儿子特勒马库斯长大成人后，在雅典娜女神的感召下，外出探询父亲的音讯。史诗的另外一条主线就是奥德修斯的返乡之路，途中充满了各种各样的艰难险阻，既有丧命的危险，也有迷人的诱惑，但是这些困境都被勇敢而富有智慧的奥德修斯一一战胜。在经过将近十年的漂泊之后，他终于踏上了故乡伊大卡的土地，特勒马库斯也寻父归来，两条线索会合。父子见面，二人设计报复了那些向佩涅罗珀求婚的贵族，一家人终于重新团圆。

两部史诗虽然写的都是特洛伊之战的片断故事，但在叙述风格和内容上确实存在很大差异。如果说《伊利亚特》讲述手法单纯，以战争场面的平铺直叙为特色的话，那么《奥德赛》的情节则颇为曲折、巧妙，充满了传奇和浪漫的色彩。此外，两部史诗在使用奴隶的记述、神人关系的亲疏等内容上都存在着比较明显的差异，甚至还有一些前后矛盾之处。不过，与史诗的创作者和创作过程相比，作为了解荷马时代的唯一的文献史料，我们更关心的是史诗能够在多大程度上反映荷马社会的真实情况。

从1870年开始，德国考古学家施里曼在小亚细亚和希腊本土进行了一系列考古发掘，发现了包括特洛伊古城、迈锡尼古城在内的多座荷马史诗所描述的王国的遗址，从而向世人证明了《荷马史诗》所描述的特洛伊战争的历史真实性。虽然学术界在特洛伊战争爆发的具体时间上还存在较大的分歧，但有一点是得到共识的，那就是史诗记录和反映了迈锡尼时代晚期和荷马时代的很多社会情况。实际上，史诗所描述的既不是单纯的迈锡尼时代，也非纯粹的荷马时代，而是两个时代的混合，是历史、现实和想象相互结合的产物。史诗虽然讲述的是迈锡尼时代晚期的战争，但却形成于荷马时代，对战争的叙述就不免带有追忆甚至想象的性质，与此同时，会自然而然地把诗人所生活的荷马时代的很多社会情况写到史诗里面去，这是所有历史题材文学创作的"滞后性"通病。因此，我们在把史诗用作历史研究的资料时需要十分谨慎，要结合考古资料和相关文献进行具体分析。比如，史诗中关于那些强大的王国所拥有的坚固的城池、豪华的宫廷、精良的手工艺品的描述显然与迈锡尼时代有关，而不可能属于荷马时代，关于这一点，考古学可以提供证明。同样，史诗中所提到的铁器的使用、氏族部落的组织和军事民主制度的政治形态，显然属于荷马时代。

以上内容选自《伊利亚特》中的两个段落，前一段描述的是阿伽门农召开全体大会的情形，反映了荷马时代包括王权、贵族和氏族部落组织在内的政治状况；后一段描述的是"阿喀琉斯的盾牌"，上面的浮雕全面而生动地反映了荷马时代的农业生产和各种社会生活的场景。

三　延伸阅读

Cairns, Douglas L., *Oxford Readings in Homer*'s *Iliad*, Oxford University Press, 2001.

Finley, M.I., *The World of Odysseus*, London: Penguin Books, reprinted, 1991.

Fowler, Robert, ed., *The Cambridge Companion to Homer*, Cambridge University Press, 2004.

Lang, Andrew, *The World of Homer*, London: Longmans, Green, and Co., 1910.

Morris, Ian, & Parry Powell, eds., *A New Companion to Homer*, Leiden & New York: E. J. Brill, 1997.

Murray, Gilbert, *The Rise of the Greek Epic*, 4th ed., Oxford University Press, 1934.

Osborne, Robin, *Greece in the Making*, London: Routledge, 1997.

Parry, Milman., ed., *The Making of Homeric Verse: The Collected Papers of Milman Parry*, Oxford University Press, 1971.

Snodgrass, A.M., *The Dark Age of Greece*, Edinburgh University Press, 1971.

Hesiod: Works and Days[*]

More hands mean more work and more increase. If your heart within you desires wealth, do these things and work with work upon work. When the Pleiades, daughters of Atlas, are rising, ^① begin your harvest, and your ploughing when they are going to set. ^② Forty nights and days they are hidden and appear again as the year moves round, when first you sharpen your sickle. This is the law of the plains, and of those who live near the sea, and who inhabit rich country, the glens and hollows far from the tossing sea, —strip to sow and strip to plough and strip to reap, if you wish to get in all Demeter's fruits in due season, and that each kind may grow in its season. Else, afterwards, you may chance to be in want, and go begging to other men's houses, but without avail; as you have already come to me. But I will give you no more nor give you further measure. Foolish Perses! Work the work which the gods ordained for men, lest in bitter anguish of spirit you with your wife and children seek your livelihood amongst your neighbors, and they do not heed you. Two or three times, may be, you will succeed, but if you trouble them further, it will not avail you, and all your talk

---

* 赫西俄德《工作与时日》节选。本文选自该书的第 383~694 行，以下皆为英文译本原书注释。

① Early in May.

② In November.

will be in vain, and your word-play unprofitable. Nay, I bid you find a way to pay your debts and avoid hunger.

First of all, get a house, and a woman and an ox for the plough—a slave woman and not a wife, to follow the oxen as well—and make everything ready at home, so that you may not have to ask of another, and he refuse you, and so, because you are in lack, the season pass by and your work come to nothing. Do not put your work off till to-morrow and the day after; for a sluggish worker does not fill his barn, nor one who puts off his work: industry makes work go well, but a man who puts off work is always at hand-grips with ruin. When the piercing power and sultry heat of the sun abate, and almighty Zeus sends the autumn rains, ① and men's flesh comes to feel far easier, —for then the star Sirius passes over the heads of men, who are born to misery, only a little while by day and takes greater share of night— then, when it showers its leaves to the ground and stops sprouting, the wood you cut with your axe is least liable to worm. Then remember to hew your timber: it is the season for that work. Cut a mortar ② three feet wide and a pestle three cubits long, and an axle of seven feet, for it will do very well so; but if you make it eight feet long, you can cut a beetle ③ from it as well. Cut a felloe three spans across for a wagon of ten palms' width. Hew also many bent timbers, and bring home a plough-tree when you have found it, and look out on the mountain or in the field for one of holm-oak; for this is the strongest for oxen to plough with when one of Athena's handmen has fixed in the share-beam and fastened it to the pole with dowels. Get two ploughs ready and work on them at home, one all of a piece, and the other jointed. It is far better to do this, for if you should break one of them, you can put the oxen to the other. Poles of laurel or elm are most free from worms, and a share-beam of oak and a plough-tree of holm-oak. Get two oxen, bulls of

---

① In October.

② For pounding corn.

③ A mallet for breaking clods after ploughing.

nine years; for their strength is unspent and they are in the prime of their age: they are best for work. They will not fight in the furrow and break the plough and then leave the work undone. Let a brisk fellow of forty years follow them, with a loaf of four quarters① and eight slices② for his dinner, one who will attend to his work and drive a straight furrow and is past the age for gaping after his fellows, but will keep his mind on his work. No younger man will be better than he at scattering the seed and avoiding double-sowing; for a man less staid gets disturbed, hankering after his fellows.

Mark, when you hear the voice of the crane③ who cries year by year from the clouds above, for she gives the signal for ploughing and shows the season of rainy winter; but she vexes the heart of the man who has no oxen. Then is the time to feed up your horned oxen in the byre; for it is easy to say: "Give me a yoke of oxen and a wagon," and it is easy to refuse: "I have work for my oxen." The man who is rich in fancy thinks his wagon as good as built already—the fool! he does not know that there are a hundred timbers to a wagon. Take care to lay these up beforehand at home. So soon as the time for ploughing is proclaimed to men, then make haste, you and your slaves alike, in wet and in dry, to plough in the season for ploughing, and bestir yourself early in the morning so that your fields may be full. Plough in the spring; but fallow broken up in the summer will not belie your hopes. Sow fallow land when the soil is still getting light: fallow land is a defender from harm and a soother of children. Pray to Zeus of the Earth and to pure Demeter to make Demeter's holy grain sound and heavy, when first you begin ploughing, when you hold in your hand the end of the plough-tail and bring down your stick on the backs of the oxen as they draw on the pole-bar by the yoke-straps. Let a slave follow a little behind with a

---

① The loaf is a flattish cake with two intersecting lines scored on its upper surface which divide it into four equal parts.

② The meaning is obscure. A scholiast renders "giving eight mouthfuls" ; but the elder Philostratus uses the word in contrast to "leavened."

③ About the middle of November.

mattock and make trouble for the birds by hiding the seed; for good management is the best for mortal men as bad management is the worst. In this way your corn-ears will bow to the ground with fullness if the Olympian himself gives a good result at the last, and you will sweep the cobwebs from your bins and you will be glad, I think, as you take of your garnered substance. And so you will have plenty till you come to grey [1] springtime, and will not look wistfully to others, but another shall be in need of your help.

But if you plough the good ground at the solstice, [2] you will reap sitting, grasping a thin crop in your hand, binding the sheaves awry, dust-covered, not glad at all; so you will bring all home in a basket and not many will admire you. Yet the will of Zeus who holds the aegis is different at different times; and it is hard for mortal men to tell it; for if you should plough late, you may find this remedy—when the cuckoo first calls [3] in the leaves of the oak and makes men glad all over the boundless earth, if Zeus should send rain on the third day and not cease until it rises neither above an ox's hoof nor falls short of it, then the late-plougher will vie with the early. Keep all this well in mind, and fail not to mark grey spring as it comes and the season of rain. Pass by the smithy and its crowded lounge in winter time when the cold keeps men from field work, — for then an industrious man can greatly prosper his house—lest bitter winter catch you helpless and poor, and you chafe a swollen foot with a shrunk hand. The idle man who waits on empty hope, lacking a livelihood, lays to heart mischief-making; it is not a wholesome hope that accompanies a needy man who lolls at ease while he has no sure livelihood.

While it is yet midsummer command your slaves: "It will not always be summer, build barns." Avoid the month Lenaeon, [4] wretched days, all of them fit to skin an ox, and the frosts which are cruel when Boreas blows over

---

[1] Spring is so described because the buds have not yet cast their iron-grey husks.

[2] In December.

[3] In March.

[4] The latter part of January and earlier part of February.

the earth. He blows across horse-breeding Thrace upon the wide sea and stirs it up, while earth and the forest howl. On many a high-leafed oak and thick pine he falls and brings them to the bounteous earth in mountain glens: then all the immense wood roars and the beasts shudder and put their tails between their legs, even those whose hide is covered with fur; for with his bitter blast he blows even through them, although they are shaggy-breasted. He goes even through an ox's hide; it does not stop him. Also he blows through the goat's fine hair. But through the fleeces of sheep, because their wool is abundant, the keen wind Boreas pierces not at all; but it makes the old man curved as a wheel. And it does not blow through the tender maiden who stays indoors with her dear mother, unlearned as yet in the works of golden Aphrodite, and who washes her soft body and anoints herself with oil and lies down in an inner room within the house, on a winter's day when the Boneless One [1] gnaws his foot in his fireless house and wretched home; for the sun shows him no pastures to make for, but goes to and fro over the land and city of dusky men, [2] and shines more sluggishly upon the whole race of the Hellenes. Then the horned and unhorned denizens of the wood, with teeth chattering pitifully, flee through the copses and glades, and all, as they seek shelter, have this one care, to gain thick coverts or some hollow rock. Then, like the Three-legged One [3] whose back is broken and whose head looks down upon the ground, like him, I say, they wander to escape the white snow.

Then put on, as I bid you, a soft coat and a tunic to the feet to shield your body, —and you should weave thick woof on thin warp. In this clothe yourself so that your hair may keep still and not bristle and stand upon end all over your body. Lace on your feet close-fitting boots of the hide of a slaughtered ox, thickly lined with felt inside. And when the season of frost comes on, stitch together skins of firstling kids with ox-sinew, to put over your back and to keep

---

[1] I.e.the octopus or cuttle.
[2] I.e.the dark-skinned people of Africa, the Egyptians or Aethiopians.
[3] I.e.an old man walking with a staff(the "third leg" —as in the riddle of the Sphinx) .

off the rain. On your head above wear a shaped cap of felt to keep your ears from getting wet, for the dawn is chill when Boreas has once made his onslaught, and at dawn a fruitful mist is spread over the earth from starry heaven upon the fields of blessed men: it is drawn from the ever-flowing rivers and is raised high above the earth by windstorm, and sometimes it turns to rain towards evening, and sometimes to wind when Thracian Boreas huddles the thick clouds. Finish your work and return home ahead of him, and do not let the dark cloud from heaven wrap round you and make your body clammy and soak your clothes. Avoid it; for this is the hardest month, wintry, hard for sheep and hard for men. In this season let your oxen have half their usual food, but let your man have more; for the helpful nights are long. Observe all this until the year is ended and you have nights and days of equal length, and Earth, the mother of all, bears again her various fruit. When Zeus has finished sixty wintry days after the solstice, then the star Arcturus [①] leaves the holy stream of Ocean and first rises brilliant at dusk. After him the shrilly wailing daughter of Pandion, the swallow, appears to men when spring is just beginning. Before she comes, prune the vines, for it is best so.

But when the House-carrier [②] climbs up the plants from the earth to escape the Pleiades, then it is no longer the season for digging vineyards, but to whet your sickles and rouse up your slaves. Avoid shady seats and sleeping until dawn in the harvest season, when the sun scorches the body. Then be busy and bring home your fruits, getting up early to make your livelihood sure. For dawn takes away a third part of your work, dawn advances a man on his journey and advances him in his work, — dawn which appears and sets many men on their road, and puts yokes on many oxen. But when the artichoke flowers, [③] and the chirping grass-hopper sits in a tree and pours down his shrill song continually from under his wings in the season of wearisome heat, then goats are plumpest

---

① February to March.

② I.e.the snail. The season is the middle of May.

③ In June.

and wine sweetest; women are most wanton, but men are feeblest, because Sirius parches head and knees and the skin is dry through heat. But at that time let me have a shady rock and wine of Biblis, a clot of curds and milk of drained goats with the flesh of a heifer fed in the woods, that has never calved, and of firstling kids; then also let me drink bright wine, sitting in the shade, when my heart is satisfied with food, and so, turning my head to face the fresh Zephyr, from the everflowing spring which pours down unfouled, thrice pour an offering of water, but make a fourth libation of wine. Set your slaves to winnow Demeter's holy grain, when strong Orion [1] first appears, on a smooth threshing-floor in an airy place. Then measure it and store it in jars. And so soon as you have safely stored all your stuff indoors, I bid you put your bondman out of doors and seek out a servant-girl with no children;—for a servant with a child to nurse is troublesome. And look after the dog with jagged teeth; do not grudge him his food, or some time the Day-sleeper [2] may take your stuff. Bring in fodder and litter so as to have enough for your oxen and mules. After that, let your men rest their poor knees and unyoke your pair of oxen.

But when Orion and Sirius are come into midheaven, and rosy-fingered Dawn sees Arcturus, [3] then cut off all the grape-clusters, Perses, and bring them home. Show them to the sun ten days and ten nights: then cover them over for five, and on the sixth day draw off into vessels the gifts of joyful Dionysus. But when the Pleiades and Hyades and strong Orion begin to set, [4] then remember to plough in season: and so the completed year [5] will fitly pass beneath the earth.But if desire for uncomfortable sea-faring seize you when the Pleiades plunge into the misty sea [6] to escape Orion's rude strength, then truly gales of

---

[1] July.

[2] I.e.a robber.

[3] September.

[4] The end of October.

[5] That is, the succession of stars which make up the full year.

[6] The end of October or beginning of November.

all kinds rage. Then keep ships no longer on the sparkling sea, but be sure to till the land as I bid you. Haul up your ship upon the land and pack it closely with stones all round to keep off the power of the winds which blow damply, and draw out the bilge-plug so that the rain of heaven may not rot it. Put away all the tackle and fittings in your house, and stow the wings of the sea-going ship neatly, and hang up the well-shaped rudder over the smoke. You yourself wait until the season for sailing is come, and then haul your swift ship down to the sea and stow a convenient cargo in it, so that you may bring home profit, even as your father and mine, foolish Perses, used to sail on shipboard because he lacked sufficient livelihood. And one day he came to this very place, crossing over a great stretch of sea; he left Aeolian Cyme and fled, not from riches and substance, but from wretched poverty which Zeus lays upon men, and he settled near Helicon in a miserable hamlet, Ascra, which is bad in winter, sultry in summer, and good at no time.

But you, Perses, remember all works in their season but sailing especially. Admire a small ship, but put your freight in a large one; for the greater the lading, the greater will be your piled gain, if only the winds will keep back their harmful gales. If ever you turn your misguided heart to trading and wish to escape from debt and joyless hunger, I will show you the measures of the loud-roaring sea, though I have no skill in sea-faring nor in ships; for never yet have I sailed by ship over the wide sea, but only to Euboea from Aulis where the Achaeans once stayed through much storm when they had gathered a great host from divine Hellas for Troy, the land of fair women.Then I crossed over to Chalcis, to the games of wise Amphidamas where the sons of the great-hearted hero proclaimed and appointed prizes. And there I boast that I gained the victory with a song and carried off a handled tripod which I dedicated to the Muses of Helicon, in the place where they first set me in the way of clear song. Such is all my experience of many-pegged ships; nevertheless I will tell you the will of Zeus who holds the aegis; for the Muses have taught me to sing in marvellous song. Fifty days after the solstice, ① when the season of wearisome heat is come to an end, is the right time for men to go sailing. Then you will not wreck your ship, nor will the sea destroy the sailors, unless Poseidon the Earth-Shaker be set upon it, or Zeus, the king of the deathless gods, wish to slay them; for the issues of good and evil alike are with them. At that time the winds are steady, and the sea is harmless. Then trust in the winds without care, and haul your swift ship down to the sea and put all the freight on board; but make all haste you can to return home again and do not wait till the time of the new wine and autumn rain and oncoming storms with the fierce gales of Notus who accompanies the heavy autumn rain of Zeus and stirs up the sea and makes the deep dangerous.

Another time for men to go sailing is in spring when a man first sees leaves on the topmost shoot of a fig-tree as large as the foot-print that a crow makes; then the sea is passable, and this is the spring sailing time. For my part I do not praise it, for my heart does not like it. Such a sailing is snatched, and you will hardly avoid mischief. Yet in their ignorance men do even this, for wealth means life to poor mortals; but it is fearful to die among the waves. But I bid you consider all these things in your heart as I say. Do not put all your goods in hollow ships; leave the greater part behind, and put the lesser part on board; for it is a bad business to meet with disaster among the waves of the sea, as it is bad if you put too great a load on your wagon and break the axle, and your goods are spoiled. Observe due measure: and proportion is best in all things.

一 文献出处

Hesiod, *Works and Days*, translated by Hugh G. Evelyn-White, Cambridge, M.A.: Harvard University Press; London: William Heinemann Ltd., 1914.

---

① July-August.

二 文献导读

赫西俄德是荷马之后古希腊最早的诗人，以长诗《工作与时日》和《神谱》而闻名于世。与传说中《荷马史诗》的创作者盲诗人荷马不同，赫西俄德是一个真实的历史人物。诗人的生卒年月不详，历史上的记载也存在较大的出入，但近代以来，学者们根据《工作与时日》所反映的社会风貌和发展状况推测，赫西俄德生活和创作的年代在公元前8世纪上半叶，也就是希腊的古风时代初期，这一点基本上得到了学界的一致认可。

赫西俄德出生在中希腊彼奥提亚的一个农民家庭。他的父亲原来是小亚细亚爱奥尼亚殖民城市库麦人，种田之外常常驾船出海经商，后来迁居到彼奥提亚的阿斯克拉村，在这里继续过着耕种土地和偶尔外出经商的生活，靠着勤劳和节俭积攒了一定的财富，建成一个小康之家，并在这里有了两个儿子，即赫西俄德和佩尔塞斯。父亲去世后兄弟俩分割了遗产，佩尔塞斯靠着贿赂当地的王爷（巴塞勒斯）得到了较大的一份，但却由于他的好逸恶劳而家境日益破落，以致伸手向赫西俄德求取救济。《工作与时日》正是在这样的背景下创作出来的，赫西俄德想以此劝诫兄弟勤勉持家。赫西俄德很少远足，在家乡过着一种勤劳朴素的乡村生活。有关他生平的其他事迹鲜有记载，只知道他曾经去欧玻亚的查尔基斯参加过安菲达马斯的葬礼运动会，在诗歌比赛中获奖，得到一只三角鼎作为奖励。根据修昔底德的《伯罗奔尼撒战争史》的记载，赫西俄德死于阿哥里斯的尼米亚。

赫西俄德生前创作了大量的诗歌，现在通行的赫西俄德作品集包括以下篇目:《工作与时日》《鸟卜》《天文》《喀戎的格言》《大工作》《伊得的长短格诗》《神谱》《名媛录及欧荷欧》《赫拉克勒斯之盾》《克宇刻斯的婚姻》《大欧荷欧》《爱基密俄斯》和《米兰浦底亚》等。其中，按照内容，这些诗歌可以大致分为两类，一类以《工作与时日》为中心，主要是生产技术上的指导和道德训诫；另一类以《神谱》为中心，主要追溯诸神的世系和名门望族的始祖。不过，在这些作品当中，只有三部完整地保留至今，即《工作与时日》、《神谱》和《赫拉克勒斯之盾》，其余均只剩下残篇。对于这些作品是否全部出自赫西俄德的笔下，从希腊罗马时代就有不同的看法，今天这些作品虽然都归在赫西俄德的名下，但仍然存在争议。从内容上判断，《工作与时日》写成的时间最早，可信度也最高，包括《神谱》在内的其余各篇很可能是赫西俄德之后的一些生活于彼奥提亚的诗人创作的。更为重要的是，《工作与时日》以现实主义的创作手法对诗人所生活时代的希腊的经济、政治、社会生活以及希腊人的宗教、幸福和道德观念进行了细致的记录和展示，因而也就成为人们研究和认识古风时代不可多得的珍贵的历史资料。

《工作与时日》共有 828 行，从内容上可以划分为五个部分：（1）1~10行。可以看作是序曲，表达了对万能的天神宙斯的赞美。（2）11~382 行。通过两个"不和女神"的比喻和"鹰和夜莺"的寓言故事谴责暴力与不公，劝勉人们要勤劳和谨慎，点出了全诗的主旨。（3）383~694 行。这部分重点在于生产知识上的指导，围绕农业生产、家畜饲养和海上航行，一方面生动地反映了早期希腊的农村经济生活，另一方面也真实地记录了当时希腊人已经掌握的天文、气象以及农业生产方面的知识。（4）695~764行。这部分大多是关于家庭日常生活的格言，重点是教导人们要虔敬神灵，事事谨慎。（5）765~828 行。可以看作是第四部分的进一步展开，论述某些生产活动一定要挑选吉日进行。全诗最重要的部分无疑是第二部分和第三部分。

作为公元前 8 世纪唯一的一部写实主义的文学作品，《工作与时日》向我们透露出很多希腊城邦形成时期的社会发展的真实状况。从经济上看，虽然远远不能够和繁荣的古典时代相比，但这个时期的希腊社会已经开始逐步走出落后和倒退的"荷马时代"，这主要表现在两个方面：第一，居民虽然仍然以农业和牧业作为主要的谋生手段，但手工业，尤其是商业已经有了明显的发展，诗中记述的小农在农闲季节常常出海经商就是一个十分值得注意的现象；第二，在贫富分化加剧的同时，奴隶制也逐步发展起来，这主要表现在奴隶在数量上有了明显的增加，使用方式上也逐步从家务性劳动和辅助性劳动的家长制奴隶向主要从事生产的奴隶类型过渡。

这些都预示了一个繁荣的古典时代即将到来。从政治上看,《工作与时日》记述了当时作为最高统治者的"巴塞勒斯"的种种权力和职能,尤其是根据习惯法对各种民事纠纷进行裁决和审判,从中反映出当时国家已经产生,但国家机器处于不发达状态的政治状况。从思想观念上,诗人从一个小农的角度和口吻,以十分形象和生动的语言,在表达了对当时出现的以强凌弱的不公正的社会现实的强烈不满的同时,呼唤社会的公正,倡导勤劳致富和谨慎持家,从而揭示了当时的希腊人对幸福和快乐的看法。尤其值得一提的是,诗歌的第二部分所描述的人类生活的五个时代,成为希腊历史哲学最初的萌芽,也可以看作是希腊文献中对人性问题的最早探讨,深刻地影响了古典时代的哲学思想。

上文即选自《工作与时日》的第三部分,主要内容是有关小农经济生活的描述。

三 延伸阅读

Edwards, G.P., *The Language of Hesiod*, Oxford, 1971.

Hall, Jonathan M., *A History of the Archaic Greek World*, Blackwell Pub., 2007.

Murray, O., *Early Greece*, London, 1980.

Shapiro, H.A., ed., *Cambridge Companion to Archaic Greece*, Cambridge University Press, 2007.

Snodgrass, A.M., *Achaic Greece*, London, 1980.

Starr, C.G., *The Economic and Social Growth of Early Greece 800-500 B.C.*, New York, 1977.

West, M.L., *Hesiod: Works and Days*, Oxford, 1978.

Aristotle: Athenian Constitution [*]

Such being the system in the constitution, and the many being enslaved to the few, the people rose against the notables.

The party struggle being violent and the parties remaining arrayed in opposition to one another for a long time, they jointly chose Solon as arbitrator and Archon, and entrusted the government to him, after he had composed the elegy that begins:

"I mark, and sorrow fills my breast to see,

Ionia's oldest land being done to death, —"

in which he does battle on behalf of each party against the other and acts as mediator, and after this exhorts them jointly to stop the quarrel that prevailed between them.

Solon was by birth and reputation of the first rank, but by wealth and position belonged to the middle class, as is admitted on the part of the other authorities, and as he himself testifies in these poems, exhorting the wealthy not to be covetous:

"Refrain ye in your hearts those stubborn moods,

Plunged in a surfeit of abundant goods,

---

* 亚里士多德《雅典政制》节选。本文选自该文的第 5~22 小节。以下皆为英文译本原书注释。

And moderate your pride! We'll not submit,

Nor even you yourselves will this befit. [①] "

And he always attaches the blame for the civil strife wholly to the rich; owing to which at the beginning of the elegy he says that he fears

"Both love of money and overweening pride—,"

implying that these were the causes of the enmity that prevailed.

Solon having become master of affairs made the people free both at the time and for the future by prohibiting loans secured on the person, and he laid down laws, and enacted cancellations of debts both private and public, the measures [②] that are known as 'the Shaking-off of Burdens,' meaning that the people shook off their load. In these matters some people try to misrepresent him; for it happened that when Solon was intending to enact the Shaking-off of Burdens, he informed some of the notables beforehand, and afterwards, as those of popular sympathies say, he was outmaneuvered by his friends, but according to those who want to malign him he himself also took a share. For these persons borrowed money and bought up a quantity of land, and when not long afterwards the cancellation of debts took place they were rich men; and this is said to be the origin of the families subsequently reputed to be ancestrally wealthy. [③] Nevertheless, the account of those of popular sympathies is more credible; for considering that he was so moderate and public-spirited in the rest of his conduct that, when he had the opportunity to reduce one of the two parties to subjection and so to be tyrant of the city, he incurred the enmity of both, and valued honor and the safety of the state more than his own aggrandizement, it is not probable that he besmirched himself in such worthless trifles. And that he got this opportunity is testified by the disordered state of affairs, and also he himself alludes to it in many

---

① 'Nor shall ye possess what ye have now without decrease' (Edmonds).

② Their actual provisions are quite uncertain.

③ Apparently certain well-known families, but not alluded to elsewhere.

places in his poems, and everybody else agrees with him. We are bound therefore to consider this charge to be false.

And he established a constitution and made other laws, and they ceased to observe the ordinances of Draco, except those relating to homicide. They wrote up the laws on the Boards ① and set them in the Royal Colonnade, and all swore to observe them; and the Nine Archons used to make affirmation on oath at the Stone ② that if they transgressed any one of the laws they would dedicate a gold statue of a man; owing to which they are even now still sworn in with this oath. And he fixed the laws to stay unaltered for a hundred years. And he arranged the constitution in the following way:

He divided the people by assessment into four classes, as they had been divided before, Five-hundred-measure man, Horseman, Teamster and Laborer, and he distributed the other offices to be held from among the Five-hundred-measure men, Horsemen and Teamsters—the Nine Archons, the Treasurers, ③ the Vendors of Contracts, ④ the Eleven⑤ and the Paymasters, assigning each office to the several classes in proportion to the amount of their assessment; while those who were rated in the Laborer class he admitted to the membership of the assembly and law-courts alone. Any man had to be rated as a Five-hundred-measure man the produce from whose estate was five hundred dry and liquid measures jointly, ⑥ and at the cavalry-rate those who made three hundred, —or as some say, those who were able to keep a horse, and they adduce as a proof the name of the rating as being derived from the fact, and also the votive offerings of the ancients; for there stands dedicated in the Acropolis a

---

① Three-sided (or perhaps four-sided) structures of wood (or perhaps stone) revolving on pivots; set up in the Stoa Basilike, the court of the King-Archon, on the west side of the Agora.

② Perhaps the altar of Zeus Agoraios.

③ See Aristot. Ath. Pol. 47.1.

④ See 47.2.

⑤ See Aristot. Ath. Pol. 52.1.

⑥ i.e. measures of corn and of wine and oil amounting in all to five hundred.

statue of Diphilus ^① on which are inscribed these lines:

"Anthemion Diphilus's son dedicated this statue to the gods

...having exchanged the Laborer rating for the Cavalry—"

and a horse stands beside him, in evidence that 'cavalry' meant the class able to keep a horse. Nevertheless it is more probable that the cavalry were distinguished by their amounts of produce as the Five-hundred-measure men were. And men had to be rated in the Teamster class who made two hundred measures, wet and dry together; while the rest were rated in the Laborer class, being admitted to no office: hence even now when the presiding official asks a man who is about to draw lots for some office what rate he pays, no one whatever would say that he was rated as a Laborer. ^②

For the offices of state he instituted election by lot from candidates selected by the tribes severally by a preliminary vote. For the Nine Archons each tribe made a preliminary selection of ten, and the election was made from among these by lot ^③ ; hence there still survives with the tribes the system that each elects ten by lot and then they choose from among these by ballot. ^④ And a proof that he made the offices elective by lot according to assessments is the law in regard to the Treasurers that remains in force even at the present day; for it orders the Treasurers to be elected by lot from the Five-hundred-measure men. Solon, therefore, legislated thus about the Nine Archons; for in ancient times the Council on the Areopagus used to issue a summons and select independently the person suitable for each of the offices, and commission him to hold office for a year. And there were four Tribes, as before, and four Tribal Kings. And

---

① 'Of Diphilus' is probably a mistaken insertion; presumably the statue was of Anthemion himself.

② Apparently the property qualification was ignored, without being formally repealed.

③ i.e. nine were taken by lot out of forty elected by vote by the four tribes; whereas in the writer's day the preliminary election was also by lot and produced one hundred from the ten tribes.

④ i.e. by lot again.

from each Tribe there had been assigned three Thirds and twelve Ship-boards ①
to each, and over the Ship-boards there was established the office of Ship-
commissioners, appointed for the levies and the expenditures that were made;
because of which in the laws of Solon, which are no longer in force, the clauses
frequently occur, 'the Ship-commissioner to levy' and 'to spend out of the
Ship-commission Fund.' And he made a Council of four hundred members,
a hundred from each tribe, but appointed the Council of the Areopagus to the
duty of guarding the laws, just as it had existed even before as overseer of the
constitution, and it was this Council that kept watch over the greatest and the
most important of the affairs of state, in particular correcting offenders with
sovereign powers both to fine and punish, and making returns of its expenditure
to the Acropolis without adding a statement of the reason for the outlay, and
trying persons that conspired to put down the democracy, Solon having laid
down a law of impeachment in regard to them.

And as he saw that the state was often in a condition of party strife, while
some of the citizens through slackness were content to let things slide, he laid
down a special law to deal with them, enacting that whoever when civil strife
prevailed did not join forces with either party was to be disfranchised and not to
be a member of the state.

This then was the nature of his reforms in regard to the offices of state. And
the three most democratic features in Solon's constitution seem to be these: first
and most important the prohibition of loans secured upon the person, secondly
the liberty allowed to anybody who wished to exact redress on behalf of injured
persons, and third, what is said to have been the chief basis of the powers of the
multitude, the right of appeal to the jury-court—for the people, having the power

① The Naucrariae were forty-eight administrative districts into which the country was divided
for taxation, each having to defray the equipment of one battle-ship. Their presidents were
Naucrari. Every four Naucrariae formed a Trittys, of which there were three in each Tribe.

of the vote, becomes sovereign in the government. And also, since the laws are not drafted simply nor clearly, but like the law about inheritances and heiresses, it inevitably results that many disputes take place and that the jury-court is the umpire in all business both public and private. Therefore some people think that Solon purposely made his laws obscure, in order that the people might be sovereign over the verdict. But this is unlikely—probably it was due to his not being able to define the ideal in general terms; for it is not fair to study his intention in the light of what happens at the present day, but to judge it from the rest of his constitution.

Solon therefore seems to have laid down these enactments of a popular nature in his laws; while before his legislation his democratic reform was his cancellation of debts, and afterwards his raising the standard of the measures and weights and of the coinage. For it was in his time that the measures were made larger than those of Pheidon, [①] and that the mina, which previously had a weight of seventy drachmae, [②] was increased to the full hundred. The ancient coin-type was the two-drachma piece. Solon also instituted weights corresponding to the currency, the talent weighing sixty-three minae, and a fraction proportionate to the additional three minae was added to the stater [③] and the other weights.

When Solon had organized the constitution in the manner stated, people kept coming to him and worrying him about his laws, criticizing some points and asking questions about others; so as he did not wish either to alter these provisions or to stay and incur enmity, he went abroad on a journey to Egypt, for the purpose both of trading and of seeing the country, saying that he would not come back for ten years, as he did not think it fair for him to stay and explain

---

① King of Argos, probably early 7th century B.C., see Aristot. Pol. 1310b 26. His standard of coinage and weights and measures came to prevail through most of Greece.

② i.e. seventy of the new drachmae; the drachma coin was also enlarged, so that seventy of the new equalled one hundred of the old; and see note on 4.1.

③ The weight of a fiftieth part of a mina.

his laws, but for everybody to carry out their provisions for himself. At the same time it befell him that many of the notables had become at variance with him because of the cancellations of debts, and also that both the factions changed their attitude to him because the settlement had disappointed them. For the people had thought that he would institute universal communism of property, whereas the notables had thought that he would either restore the system in the same form as it was before or with slight alteration; but Solon went against them both, and when he might have been tyrant if he had taken sides with whichever of the two factions he wished, he chose to incur the enmity of both by saving the country and introducing the legislation that was best.

That this is how it happened is the unanimous account of everybody, and in particular Solon himself in his poetry [1] recalls the matter in these words:

"For to the people gave I grace enough,

Nor from their honor took, nor proffered more;

While those possessing power and graced with wealth,

These too I made to suffer nought unseemly;

I stood protecting both with a strong shield,

And suffered neither to prevail unjustly."

And again, when declaring about how the multitude ought to be treated:

"Thus would the people with the chiefs best follow,

With neither too much freedom nor compulsion;

Satiety breeds insolence when riches

Attend the men whose mind is not prepared."

And again in a different place he says about those who wish to divide up the land:

"They that came on plunder bent were filled with over-lavish hope,

---

① See Aristot. Ath. Pol. 5.2 n.

Each and all imagining that they would find abundant wealth,

And that I, though smoothly glozing, would display a purpose rough.

Vain and boastful then their fancies; now their bile against me is stirred,

And with eyes askance they view me, and all deem me as a foe—

Wrongly: for the things I promised, those by heaven's aid I did,

And much else, no idle exploits; nothing did it please my mind

By tyrannic force to compass, nor that in our fatherland

Good and bad men should have equal portion in her fertile soil."

And again about the cancellation of debts, and those who were in slavery before but were liberated by the Shaking-off of Burdens:

"But what did I leave unachieved, of all

The ends for which I did unite the people?

Whereof before the judgement-seat of Time

The mighty mother of the Olympian gods,

Black Earth, would best bear witness, for 'twas I

Removed her many boundary-posts ① implanted:

Ere then she was a slave, but now is free.

And many sold away I did bring home

To god-built Athens, this one sold unjustly,

That other justly; others that had fled

From dire constraint of need, uttering no more

Their Attic tongue, so widely had they wandered,

And others suffering base slavery

Even here, trembling before their masters' humors,

I did set free. These deeds I make prevail,

Adjusting might and right to fit together,

And did accomplish even as I had promised.

---

① i.e. posts marking mortgaged estates.

And rules of law alike for base and noble,

Fitting straight justice unto each man's case,

I drafted. Had another than myself

Taken the goad, unwise and covetous,

He'd not have held the people! Had I willed

Now that pleased one of the opposing parties,

And then whatever the other party bade them,

The city had been bereft of many men.

Wherefore I stood at guard on every side,

A wolf at bay among a pack of hounds!"

And again in his taunting reply to the later querulous complaints of both the parties:

"If openly I must reprove the people,

Never in the dreams of sleep could they have seen

The things that they have now . . .

While all the greater and the mightier men

Might praise me and might deem me as a friend;

for had another,"

he says,

"won this office,

He had not checked the people nor refrained,

Ere he had churned and robbed the milk of cream;

But I as it were betwixt their armed hosts

A frontier-post did stand."

Accordingly Solon make his journey abroad for these reasons. And when he had gone abroad, though the city was still disturbed, for four years they kept at peace; but in the fifth year after Solon's archonship because of party strife they did not appoint an archon, and again in the fifth year after that they enacted a suspension of the archonship for the same cause. After this at the same interval of time Damasias was elected Archon, and held the post for two years and two months, until he was driven out of the office by force. Then because of the civil strife they decided to elect ten Archons, five from the nobles, three from the farmers and two from the artisans, and these held office for the year after Damasias. This shows that the Archon had very great power; for we find that they were always engaging in party strife about this office. And they continued in a state of general internal disorder, some having as their incentive and excuse the cancellation of debts (for it had resulted in their having become poor), others discontented with the constitution because a great change had taken place, and some because of their mutual rivalry. The factions were three: one was the party of the Men of the Coast, whose head was Megacles the son of Alcmaeon, and they were thought chiefly to aim at the middle form of constitution; another was the party of the Men of the Plain, who desired the oligarchy, and their leader was Lycurgus; third was the party of the Hillmen, which had appointed Peisistratus over it, as he was thought to be an extreme advocate of the people. And on the side of this party were also arrayed, from the motive of poverty, those who had been deprived [1] of the debts due to them, and, from the motive of fear, those who were not of pure descent; and this is proved by the fact that after the deposition of the tyrants the Athenians enacted a revision of the roll, because many people shared the citizenship who had no right to it. The different parties derived their names from the places where their farms were situated.

Peisistratus, being thought to be an extreme advocate of the people, and having won great fame in the war against Megara, [2] inflicted a wound on himself with his own hand and then gave out that it had been done by the members of the opposite factions, and so persuaded the people to give him a bodyguard, the resolution being proposed by Aristophon. He was given the retainers called Club-bearers, and with their aid he rose against the

---

① i.e. by Solon's legislation.

② Perhaps the hostilities that ended in the Athenians' capture of Nisaea about 570 B.C.

people and seized the Acropolis, in the thirty-second year after the enactment of his laws, in the archonship of Comeas. It is said that when Peisistratus asked for the guard Solon opposed the request, and said that he was wiser than some men and braver than others—he was wiser than those who did not know that Peisistratus was aiming at tyranny, and braver than those who knew it but held their tongues. But as he failed to carry them with him by saying this, he brought his armor out [1] in front of his door and said that for his part he had come to his country's aid as far as he could (for he was now a very old man), and that he called on the others also to do the same. Solon's exhortations on this occasion had no effect; and Peisistratus having seized the government proceeded to carry on the public business in a manner more constitutional than tyrannical. But before his government had taken root the partisans of Megacles and Lycurgus made common cause and expelled him, in the sixth year after his first establishment, in the archonship of Hegesias. In the twelfth year after this Megacles, being harried by party faction, made overtures again to Peisistratus, and on terms of receiving his daughter in marriage brought him back, in an old-fashioned and extremely simple manner. Having first spread a rumor that Athena was bringing Peisistratus back, he found a tall and beautiful woman, according to Herodotus [2] a member of the Paeanian deme, but according to some accounts a Thracian flower-girl from Collytus named Phye, dressed her up to look like the goddess, and brought her to the city with him, and Peisistratus drove in a chariot with the woman standing at his side, while the people in the city marvelled and received them with acts of reverence.

In this way his first return took place. Afterwards, as he was expelled a second time in about the seventh year after his return—for he did not maintain his hold for long, but came to be afraid of both the factions owing to his unwillingness to live with Megacles' daughter as his wife, and secretly withdrew—; and first

---

① Apparently, for some younger man to use.

② Hdt. 1.60.

he collected a settlement at a place near the Gulf of Thermae called Rhaecelus, but from there he went on to the neighborhood of Pangaeus, from where he got money and hired soldiers, and in the eleventh year went again to Eretria, and now for the first time set about an attempt to recover his power by force, being supported in this by a number of people, especially the Thebans and Lygdamis of Naxos, and also the knights who controlled the government of Eretria. Winning the battle of Pallenis, [1] he seized the government and disarmed the people; and now he held the tyranny firmly, and he took Naxos and appointed Lygdamis ruler. The way in which he disarmed the people was this: he held an armed muster at the Temple of Theseus, and began to hold an Assembly, but he lowered his voice a little, and when they said they could not hear him, he told them to come up to the forecourt of the Acropolis, in order that his voice might carry better; and while he used up time in making a speech, the men told off for this purpose gathered up the arms, [2] locked them up in the neighboring buildings of the Temple of Theseus, and came and informed Peisistratus. He, when he had finished the rest of his speech, told his audience not to be surprised at what had happened about their arms, and not to be dismayed, but to go away and occupy themselves with their private affairs, while he would attend to all public business.

This was the way, therefore, in which the tyranny of Peisistratus was originally set up and this is a list of the changes that it underwent. Peisistratus's administration of the state was, as has been said, [3] moderate, and more constitutional than tyrannic; he was kindly and mild in everything, and in particular he was merciful to offenders, and moreover he advanced loans of money to the poor for their industries, so that they might support themselves by farming. In doing this he had two objects, to prevent their stopping in the city

---

[1] The deme Pallene, dedicated to Athena Pallenis, lay just N.E. of Athens.

[2] The citizens had piled their arms when Peisistratus began to make a speech, and left them behind when they went up the hill.

[3] Aristot. Ath. Pol. 14.3.

and make them stay scattered about the country, and to cause them to have a moderate competence and be engaged in their private affairs, so as not to desire nor to have time to attend to public business. [1] And also the land's being thoroughly cultivated resulted in increasing his revenues; for he levied a tithe from the produce. And for this reason he organized the Local Justices, [2] and often went to the country on circuit in person, inspecting and settling disputes, in order that men might not neglect their agriculture by coming into the city. For it was when Peisistratus was making an expedition of this kind that the affair of the man on Hymettus cultivating the farm afterwards called Tax-free Farm is said to have occurred. He saw a man at farm-work, digging mere rocks, and because of his surprise ordered his servant to ask what crop the farm grew; and the man said, "All the aches and pains that there are, and of these aches and pains Peisistratus has to get the tithe." The man did not know who it was when he answered, but Peisistratus was pleased by his free speech and by his industry, and made him free from all taxes. And in all other matters too he gave the multitude no trouble during his rule, but always worked for peace and safeguarded tranquillity; so that men were often to be heard saying that the tyranny of Peisistratus was the Golden Age of Cronos; for it came about later when his sons had succeeded him that the government became much harsher. And the greatest of all the things said of him was that he was popular and kindly in temper. For he was willing to administer everything according to the laws in all matters, never giving himself any advantage; and once in particular when he was summoned to the Areopagus to be tried on a charge of murder, he appeared in person to make his defence, and the issuer of the summons was frightened and left. Owing to this he remained in his office for a long period, and every time that he was thrown out of it he easily got it back

---

[1] This policy will be found expressed in general formulae in Aristot. Pol. 1311a 13, Aristot. Pol. 1318b 6, Aristot. Pol. 1319a 30, Aristot. Pol. 1320b 7.

[2] See Aristot. Ath. Pol. 26.5, Aristot. Ath. Pol. 53.1.

again. For both the notables and the men of the people were most of them willing for him to govern, since he won over the former by his hospitality and the latter by his assistance in their private affairs, and was good-natured to both. And also the laws of Athens concerning tyrants were mild at those periods, among the rest particularly the one that referred to the establishment of tyranny. For they had the following law: 'These are the ordinances and ancestral principles of Athens: if any persons rise in insurrection in order to govern tyrannically, or if any person assists in establishing the tyranny, he himself and his family shall be disfranchised.' [1]

Peisistratus, therefore, grew old in office, and died of disease in the archonship of Philoneos, having lived thirty-three years since he first established himself as tyrant, but the time that he remained in office was nineteen [2] years, as he was in exile for the remainder. Therefore the story that Peisistratus was a lover of Solon and that he commanded in the war against Megara for the recovery of Salamis is clearly nonsense, for it is made impossible by their ages, if one reckons up the life of each and the archonship in which he died. When Peisistratus was dead, his sons held the government, carrying on affairs in the same way. He had two sons by his wedded wife, Hippias and Hipparchus, and two by his Argive consort, Iophon and Hegesistratus surnamed Thettalus. For Peisistratus married a consort from Argos, Timonassa, the daughter of a man of Argos named Gorgilus, who had previously been the wife of Archinus, a man of Ambracia of the Cypselid family. This was the cause of Peisistratus's friendship with Argos, and a thousand Argives brought by Hegesistratus fought for him in the battle of Pallenis. [3] Some people date his marriage with the Argive lady during his first banishment, others in a period of office.

Affairs were now under the authority of Hipparchus and Hippias, owing to

---

① The genuineness of section 10 may be questioned.
② Aristot. Pol. 1315b 31 says 'seventeen.'
③ See Aristot. Ath. Pol. 15.3.

their station and their ages, but the government was controlled by Hippias, who was the elder and was statesmanlike and wise by nature; whereas Hipparchus was fond of amusement and love-making, and had literary tastes: it was he who brought to Athens poets such as Anacreon and Simonides, and the others. Thettalus was much younger, and bold and insolent in his mode of life, which proved to be the source of all their misfortunes. For he fell in love with Harmodius, and when his advances were continually unsuccessful he could not restrain his anger, but displayed it bitterly in various ways, and finally when Harmodius's sister was going to be a Basket-carrier [①] in the procession at the Panathenaic Festival he prevented her by uttering some insult against Harmodius as being effeminate; and the consequent wrath of Harmodius let him and the Aristogeiton to enter on their plot with a number [②] of accomplices. At the Panathenaic Festival on the Acropolis they were already keeping a watch on Hippias (who happened to be receiving the procession, while Hipparchus was directing its start), when they saw one of their partners in the plot conversing in a friendly way with Hippias. They thought that he was giving information, and wishing to do something before their arrest they went down and took the initiative without waiting for their confederates, killing Hipparchus as he was arranging the procession by the Leocoreum. [③] This played havoc with the whole plot. Of the two of them Harmodius was at once dispatched by the spearmen, and Aristogeiton died later, having been taken into custody and tortured for a long time. Under the strain of the tortures he gave the names of a number of men that belonged by birth to families of distinction, and were friends of the tyrants, as confederates. For they were not able immediately to find any trace of the plot, but the current story that Hippias made the people in the procession fall out

---

[①] Baskets holding the requisites for the religious service were carried by maidens of high birth.

[②] Thuc. 6.56.3 says 'not many'.

[③] A monument to three daughters of Leon who in obedience to an oracle gave their lives for their country by running against the enemy's ranks in battle.

away from their arms and searched for those that retained their daggers is not true, for in those days they did not walk in the procession armed, but this custom was instituted later by the democracy. According to the account of people of popular sympathies, Aristogeiton accused the tyrants' friends for the purpose of making his captors commit an impiety and weaken themselves at the same time by making away with men who were innocent and their own friends, but others say that his accusations were not fictitious but that he disclosed his actual accomplices. Finally, as do what he would he was unable to die, he offered to give information against many more, and induced Hippias to give him his right hand as a pledge of good faith, and when he grasped it he taunted him with giving his hand to his brother's murderer, and so enraged Hippias that in his anger he could not control himself but drew his dagger and made away with him.

After this it began to come about that the tyranny was much harsher; for Hippias's numerous executions and sentences of exile in revenge for his brother led to his being suspicious of everybody and embittered. About four years after Hipparchus's death the state of affairs in the city was so bad that he set about fortifying Munychia, [1] with the intention of moving his establishment there. While engaged in this he was driven out by the king of Sparta, Cleomenes, as oracles were constantly being given to the Spartans to put down the tyranny, for the following reason. The exiles headed by the Alcmeonidae were not able to effect their return by their own unaided efforts, but were always meeting reverses; for besides the other plans that were complete failures, they built the fort of Leipsydrion [2] in the country, on the slopes of Parnes, where some of their friends in the city came out and joined them, but they were besieged and dislodged by the tyrants, owing to which afterwards they used to refer to this disaster in singing their catches:

"Faithless Dry Fountain! Lackaday,

---

① A hill above the sea S. of the city, commanding Peiraeus and the two other harbors.
② The name suggests 'water-failure.' Parnes is a mountain in N.E. Attica.

What good men's lives you threw away!

True patriots and fighters game,

They showed the stock from which they came!"

Anon.

So as they were failing in everything else, they contracted to build the temple at Delphi, [①] and so acquired a supply of money for the assistance of the Spartans. And the Pythian priestess constantly uttered a command to the Spartans, when they consulted the oracle, to liberate Athens, until she brought the Spartiates to the point, although the Peisistratidae were strangers to them; and an equally great amount of incitement was contributed to the Spartans by the friendship that subsisted between the Argives and the Peisistratidae. As a first step, therefore, they dispatched Anchimolus with a force by sea; but he was defeated and lost his life, because the Thessalian Cineas came to the defence with a thousand cavalry. Enraged at this occurrence, they dispatched their king Cleomenes by land with a larger army; he won a victory over the Thessalian cavalry who tried to prevent his reaching Attica, and so shut up Hippias in the fortress called the Pelargicum [②] and began to lay siege to it with the aid of the Athenians. While he was sitting down against it, it occurred that the sons of Peisistratidae were caught when trying secretly to get away; and these being taken they came to terms on the condition of the boys' safety, and conveyed away their belongings in five days, surrendering the Acropolis to the Athenians; this was in the archonship of Harpactides, and Peisistratus's sons had retained the tyranny for about seventeen years after their father's death making when added to the period of their father's power a total of forty-nine years.

When the tyranny had been put down, there was a period of faction-strife

---

① It had been burnt down in 548 B.C. Apparently they made a profit on the contract, but rebuilt it to the satisfaction of the priestess.

② The fortification surrounding the west end of the Acropolis.

between Isagoras son of Teisander, who was a friend of the tyrants, and Cleisthenes, who belonged to the family of the Alcmaeonidae. Cleisthenes having got the worst of it in the Comradeships [①] enlisted the people on his side, offering to hand over the government to the multitude. Isagoras began to lose power, so he again called in the aid of Cleomenes, who was a great friend of his, and jointly persuaded him to drive out the curse, [②] because the Alcmaeonidae were reputed to be a family that was under a curse. Cleisthenes secretly withdrew, and Cleomenes with a few troops proceeded to expel as accursed seven hundred Athenian households; and having accomplished this he tried to put down the Council and set up Isagoras and three hundred of his friends with him in sovereign power over the state. But the Council resisted, and the multitude banded together, so the forces of Cleomenes and Isagoras took refuge in the Acropolis, and the people invested it and laid siege to it for two days. On the third day they let Cleomenes and his comrades go away under a truce, and sent for Cleisthenes and the other exiles to come back. The people having taken control of affairs, Cleisthenes was their leader and was head of the people. For almost the chief initiative in the expulsion of the tyrants was taken by the Alcmaeonids, and they accomplished most of it by party faction. And even before the Alcmaeonids Cedon had attacked the tyrants, owing to which people also sang in his honor in their catches:

"Now fill to Cedon, boy! let's drink him too,

If duty bids us toast good men and true."

Anon.

These were the causes, therefore, that led the people to trust in Cleisthenes. And when this time he had become Chief of the multitude, in the fourth year after the deposition of the tyrants, in the archonship of Isagoras, he first divided the whole body into ten tribes instead of the existing four, wishing to mix them

① Political clubs with anti-democratic leanings.

② Cf. ch. i.

up, in order that more might take part in the government [1] ; from which arose the saying, 'Don't draw distinctions between tribes,' addressed to those who want to inquire into people's clans. Next he made the Council to consist of five hundred members instead of four hundred, fifty from each Tribe, whereas under the old system there had been a hundred. This was the reason why he did not arrange them in twelve tribes, in order that he might not have to use the existing division of the Thirds [2] (for the four Tribes contained twelve Thirds), with the result that the multitude would not have been mixed up. He also portioned out the land among the demes into thirty parts, ten belonging to the suburbs, ten to the coast, and ten to the inland district; and he gave these parts the name of Thirds, and assigned them among the Tribes by lot, three to each, in order that each Tribe might have a share in all the districts. And he made all the inhabitants in each of the demes fellow-demesmen of one another, [3] in order that they might not call attention to the newly enfranchised citizens by addressing people by their fathers' names, but designate people officially by their demes; owing to which Athenians in private life also use the names of their demes as surnames. [4] And he also appointed Demarchs, having the same duties as the former Ship-commissioners, [5] for he put the demes in the place of the Ship-comissions. He named some of the demes from their localities, but others from their founders, for the demes were no longer all corresponding to the places. The clans and brotherhoods [6] and priesthoods belonging to the various demes he allowed to remain on the ancestral plan. As eponymous deities of the Tribes he instituted ten tutelary heroes selected by an

---

[1] Less incompletely stated in Aristot. Pol. 275b 37ff. Members of the same class might now belong to different tribes; and a number of new citizens were enrolled (see Aristot. Ath. Pol. 4), free-born aliens and emancipated slaves, who were not members of clans.

[2] See Aristot. Ath. Pol. 8.3 n.

[3] i.e. he made the deme a social group, united by almost a family feeling.

[4] C.f., e.g., Aristot. Ath. Pol. 28.3 'Callicrates of the Paeanian deme, ' and subsequent designations of persons by their demes; up to that point the father's name is used.

[5] See Aristot. Ath. Pol. 8.3 n.

[6] In Aristot. Pol. 1319b 23 it is said that 'Cleisthenes increased the number of the brotherhoods, ' but that no doubt refers to the new citizens.

oracle of the Pythian priestess from a previously chosen list of a hundred.

These reforms made the constitution much more democratic than that of Solon; for it had come about that the tyranny had obliterated the laws of Solon by disuse, and Cleisthenes aiming at the multitude had instituted other new ones, including the enactment of the law about ostracism. First of all, in the fifth year ① after these enactments, in the archonship of Hermocreon, they instituted the oath of induction for the Council of Five Hundred that is still in use. Next they began to elect the Generals by tribes, one from each tribe, while the whole army was under the command of the War-lord. Eleven years afterwards came their victory in the battle of Marathon; and in the archonship of Phaenippus, two years after the victory, the people being now in high courage, they put in force for the first time the law about ostracism, which had been enacted owing to the suspicion felt against the men in the positions of power because Peisistratus when leader of the people and general set himself up as tyrant. The first person banished by ostracism was one of his relatives, Hipparchus son of Charmus of the deme of Collytus, the desire to banish whom had been Cleisthenes' principal motive in making the law. For the Athenians permitted all friends of the tyrants that had not taken part with them in their offences during the disorders to dwell in the city, —in this the customary mildness of the people was displayed; and Hipparchus was the leader and chief of these persons. But directly afterwards, in the next year, in the archonship of Telesinus, they elected the Nine Archons by lot, tribe by tribe, from a preliminary list of five hundred chosen by the demesmen: this was the date of the first election on these lines, after the tyranny, the previous Archons having all been elected by vote. And Megacles son of Hippocrates of the deme Alopeke was ostracized. For three years they went on ostracizing the friends of the tyrants, at whom the legislation had been aimed, but afterwards in the fourth year it was

---

① i.e. in 504 B.C.; but if Marathon (490 B.C.) was eleven years later (Aristot. Ath. Pol. 3), perhaps the Greek should be altered here to give 'in the eighth year after.'

also used to remove any other person who seemed to be too great; the first person unconnected with the tyranny to be ostracized was Xanthippus son of Ariphron. Two years later, in the archonship of Nicomedes, in consequence of the discovery of the mines at Maronea, ① the working of which had given the state a profit of a hundred talents, the advice was given by some persons that the money should be distributed among the people; but Themistocles prevented this, not saying what use he would make of the money, but recommending that it should be lent to the hundred richest Athenians, each receiving a talent, so that if they should spend it in a satisfactory manner, the state would have the advantage, but if they did not, the state should call in the money from the borrowers. On these terms the money was put at his disposal, and he used it to get a fleet of a hundred triremes built, each of the hundred borrowers having one ship built, and with these they fought the naval battle at Salamis against the barbarians. And it was during this period that Aresteides son of Lysimachus was ostracized. Three years later in the archonship of Hypsechides they allowed all the persons ostracized to return, because of the expedition of Xerxes; and they fixed a boundary thenceforward for persons ostracized, prohibiting them from living ② within a line drawn from Geraestus ③ to Scyllaeum ④ under penalty of absolute loss of citizenship.

一　文献出处

Aristotle, in 23 Volumes, Vol. 20, translated by H. Rackham, Cambridge, M.A.: Harvard University Press; London: William Heinemann Ltd., 1952.

---

① Possibly five miles north of Cape Sunium.
② The MS. gives 'enacting that they must live.'
③ The S. point of Euboea.
④ The S.E. point of Argolis.

二 文献导读

从公元前335年开始，亚里士多德（Aristotle，公元前384~前322年）在其众弟子的大力协助下，奔赴150多个城邦，开始了一项空前规模的对当时的城邦政体的调查和研究计划，经过仅十年的时间，公元前328~前325年，这项调研工作基本得以完成。正是以这150余篇珍贵的第一手资料为素材，亚里士多德写出了他的专门探讨城邦政体之优劣的名著《政治学》。

进入公元前4世纪以后，希腊城邦普遍出现了危机的迹象，土地兼并盛行，贫富分化，公民意识和城邦凝聚力削弱，政局动荡不安，所有这些都激发了当时的哲学家、诗人对希腊的城邦制度进行全面的反思，试图从中找到使城邦走出危机的出路。柏拉图的《理想国》和亚里士多德的《政治学》正是这一时期最有代表性的政治学著作。与他的老师试图用抽象的演绎方法从思维中推演出一个理想国家的政体形式不同，亚里士多德更加注重对现存政体的观察、分析和比较，从中辨析各种政体的优劣，然后走向新的综合。这项调研工作正是在这种指导思想下设计和进行的。这批关于政体的调查报告，在亚里士多德著作的古代书目中，据说共有158部，每部都包括了两部分内容，一是探究该城邦的政制发展的历史，二是描述该城邦现有的政体机构及其如何运作。可惜的是，除了留下个别篇目和后人零星的征引之外，原文全部遗失了，直到19世纪末叶《雅典政制》的残篇才被发现。

1880年，在埃及沙漠中发现了两小页残损颇多的纸草，经专家鉴定，这两页纸草正是从上述所有调研报告中最重要的一篇，也就是《雅典政制》中抄录的，这是该文残篇的第一次被发现，这两页纸草现在保存在德国的柏林博物馆，古文字专家鉴定它们是公元4世纪的抄本。十年之后的1890年，英国不列颠博物馆的工作人员刻泥嗡（F. G. Kenyon）在该馆收藏的埃及纸草中发现了四页纸草，经辨认和研究，上面抄录的正是《雅典政制》的全文，这个抄本的时间在公元100年前后，正反两面都写着字，正面是埃及赫尔摩波利斯城（Hermopolis）附近的一个庄园的管理人为他的主人保存的一些收支账目，背面就是这篇论文。论文基本完整，但没有开头部分，据推测它本身也是从一个已经缺损的本子抄过来的，最后一卷是十分破碎的断片，文中也有若干重要的缺文，不过，专家从后来的希腊作家的引文中发现了一些，并填补到文中。从字体上看，抄录者共有四人，这篇纸草后来成为其中一个人的随葬品。1891 年，刻泥嗡公布了纸草的影印本，1893 年，珊底斯（Sandys）发表了一部经过修正的原文，并附以完善的注释。此后，刻泥嗡对第四卷的断片进行了修复和整理，最后定本于 1920 年发表。从此，这篇珍贵的古代文献被翻译成各种文字，成为研究古希腊政制尤其是雅典政制的最为重要的历史文献。1959 年，由日知、力野翻译的《雅典政制》（商务印书馆）的中译本问世，它是根据劳埃伯古典丛书（The Loeb Classical Library）的拉克汉（H. Rachkam）的英译本并参考亚里士多德全集中刻泥嗡的英译本翻译过来的。此后，西方学者对《雅典政制》的新的翻译和专门研究不断问世，其中最有代表性的就是罗德斯（P. J. Rhodes）的《雅典政制》的注释本。

从这篇文献的内容来看，分为两个部分：前半部分叙述公元前 403 年以前的雅典政制史，从王政时代开始，包括传说中的提修斯改革、基伦暴动、德拉古立法、梭伦改革、皮西特拉图僭主政制、克力斯提尼改革、厄菲阿尔特民主改革、四百人政变、三十僭主等史事；后一部分则细述雅典当时的宪法。文中引用了很多原始材料，如梭伦的诗歌、民间歌词和谚语等，还征引了希罗多德和修昔底德的著作。《雅典政制》中所记述的最后事件发生在刻腓索丰（Cephisophon）担任执政官的那一年，即公元前 329 年，因此，该文写成年代应该在公元前 328 年到前 325 年之间。

《雅典政制》的发现极大地推动了雅典政制史，尤其是雅典直接民主制度史的研究，在一定程度上填补了前梭伦时代雅典政治史研究资料上的空白状态，为研究雅典民主政制的起源问题提供了重要的参考。但由于该文献并不完整，且存在一些抄录错误，加之很多有关雅典早期历史的记述也属于追述性质，又十分简略，所以在使用的时候也需要与其他古典著作对读和互证，尤其要关注古典学家对该文献所做的大量考释和注解。

以上原文选自《雅典政制》的英文译本，内容涉及雅典民主政制发展过程中最重要的三段史事，即梭伦改革、皮西特拉图僭主政制和克力斯提尼改革。

三　延伸阅读

Day, J., and M. Chambers, *Aristotle*'s *History of Athenian Democracy*, Berkeley, 1962.

Hignett, C., *A History of the Athenian Contitution to the End of the Fifth Century B.C.*, Oxford, 1952.

Keaney, J. J., *The Composition of Aristotle*'s *Athenaion Politeia*, Oxford, 1992.

Lavelle, Brian M., *Fame, Money and Power: The Rise of Peisistratos and "Democratic" Tyranny at Athens*, University of Michigan Press, 2005.

Raaflaub, Kurt A., ed., *Origins of Democracy in Ancient Greece*, University of California Press, 2007.

Rhodes, P. J., *A Commentary on Aristotelian Athenian Constitution*, Oxford, 1981.

Plutarch: Lycurgus [*]

The Lacedaemonians missed Lycurgus sorely, and sent for him many times. They felt that their kings were such in name and station merely, but in everything else were nothing better than their subjects, while in him there was a nature fitted to lead, and a power to make men follow him. However, not even the kings were averse to having him at home, but hoped that in his presence their subjects would treat them with less insolence. Returning, then, to a people thus disposed, he at once undertook to change the existing order of things and revolutionize the civil polity.

He was convinced that a partial change of the laws would be of no avail whatsoever, but that he must proceed as a physician would with a patient who was debilitated and full of all sorts of diseases; he must reduce and alter the existing temperament by means of drugs and purges, and introduce a new and different regimen.

Full of this determination, he first made a journey to Delphi, and after sacrificing to the god and consulting the oracle, he returned with that famous response in which the Pythian priestess addressed him as "beloved of the gods, and rather god than man," and said that the god had granted his prayer for good

---

[*] 普鲁塔克《莱库古传》节选，出自《希腊罗马名人传》。本文节选《莱库古传》的第 5~27 小节。以下皆为英文译本原书注释。

laws, and promised him a constitution which should be the best in the world.

Thus encouraged, he tried to bring the chief men of Sparta over to his side, and exhorted them to put their hands to the work with him, explaining his designs secretly to his friends at first, then little by little engaging more and uniting them to attempt the task. And when the time for action came, he ordered thirty of the chief men to go armed into the market-place at break of day, to strike consternation and terror into those of the opposite party. The names of twenty of the most eminent among them have been recorded by Hermippus; but the man who had the largest share in all the undertakings of Lycurgus and cooperated with him in the enactment of his laws, bore the name of Arthmiadas.

When the tumult began, King Charilaüs, fearing that the whole affair was a conspiracy against himself, fled for refuge to the Brazen House ① but he was soon convinced of his error, and having exacted oaths for his safety from the agitators, left his place of refuge, and even joined them in their enterprise, being of a gentle and yielding disposition, so much so, indeed, that Archelaüs, his royal colleague, is said to have remarked to those who were extolling the young king, "How can Charilaüs be a good man, when he has no severity even for the bad?"

Among the many innovations which Lycurgus made, the first and most important was his institution of a senate, or Council of Elders, which, as Plato says, ② by being blended with the "feverish" government of the kings, and by having an equal vote with them in matters of the highest importance, brought safety and due moderation into counsels of state. For before this the civil polity was veering and unsteady, inclining at one time to follow the kings towards tyranny, and at another to follow the multitude towards democracy; but now, by making the power of the senate a sort of ballast for the ship of state and putting her on a steady keel, it achieved the safest and the most orderly arrangement, since the twenty-eight senators always took the side of the kings when it was a

---

① A temple of Athena.
② Laws, p. 691 e.

question of curbing democracy, and, on the other hand, always strengthened the people to withstand the encroachments of tyranny. The number of the senators was fixed at twenty-eight because, according to Aristotle, two of the thirty original associates of Lycurgus abandoned the enterprise from lack of courage.

But Sphaerus says that this was originally the number of those who shared the confidence of Lycurgus Possibly there is some virtue in this number being made up of seven multiplied by four, apart from the fact that, being equal to the sum of its own factors, it is the next perfect number after six. But in my own opinion, Lycurgus made the senators of just that number in order that the total might be thirty when the two kings were added to the eight and twenty.

So eager was Lycurgus for the establishment of this form of government, that he obtained an oracle from Delphi about it, which they call a "rhetra." And this is the way it runs: "When thou hast built a temple to Zeus Syllanius and Athena Syllania, divided the people into 'phylai' and into 'obai,' and established a senate of thirty members, including the 'archagetai,' then from time to time 'appellazein' between Babyca and Cnacion [1] and there introduce and rescind measures; but the people must have the deciding voice and the power."

In these clauses, the "phylai" and the "obai" refer to divisions and distributions of the people into clans and phratries, or brotherhoods; by "archagetai" the kings are designated, and "apellazein" means to assemble the people, with a reference to Apollo, the Pythian god, who was the source and author of the polity. The Babyca is now called Cheimarrus, and the Cnacion Oenus; but Aristotle says that Cnacion is a river, and Babyca a bridge.

Between these they held their assemblies, having neither halls nor any other kind of building for the purpose. For by such things Lycurgus thought good counsel was not promoted, but rather discouraged, since the serious purposes

---

[1] Probably names of small tributaries of the river Eurotas.

of an assembly were rendered foolish and futile by vain thoughts, as they gazed upon statues and paintings, or scenic embellishments, or extravagantly decorated roofs of council halls. When the multitude was thus assembled, no one of them was permitted to make a motion, but the motion laid before them by the senators and kings could be accepted or rejected by the people.

Afterwards, however, when the people by additions and subtractions perverted and distorted the sense of motions laid before them, Kings Polydorus and Theopompus inserted this clause into the rhetra: "But if the people should adopt a distorted motion, the senators and kings shall have power of adjournment"; that is, should not ratify the vote, but dismiss outright and dissolve the session, on the ground that it was perverting and changing the motion contrary to the best interests of the state. And they were actually able to persuade the city that the god authorized this addition to the rhetra, as Tyrtaeus reminds us in these verses: — " Phoebus Apollo's the mandate was which they brought from Pytho, Voicing the will of the god, nor were his words unfulfilled: Sway in the council and honours divine belong to the princes.Under whose care has been set Sparta's city of charm;Second to them are the elders, and next come the men of the people.Duly confirming by vote unperverted decrees."

Although Lycurgus thus tempered his civil polity, nevertheless the oligarchical element in it was still unmixed and dominant, and his successors, seeing it "swelling and foaming," as Plato says, [1] "imposed as it were a curb upon it, namely, the power of the ephors." It was about a hundred and thirty years after Lycurgus that the first ephors, Elatus and his colleagues, were appointed, in the reign of Theopompus.

This king, they say, on being reviled by his wife because the royal power, when he handed it over to his sons, would be less than when he received it, said: "Nay, but greater, in that it will last longer." And in fact, by renouncing excessive

---

[1] Laws, p. 692 a.

claims and freeing itself from jealous hate, royalty at Sparta escaped its perils, so that the Spartan kings did not experience the fate which the Messenians and Argives inflicted upon their kings, who were unwilling to yield at all or remit their power in favour of the people. And this brings into the clearest light the wisdom and foresight of Lycurgus, when we contrast the factions and misgovernment of the peoples and kings of Messenia and Argos, who were kinsmen and neighbours of the Spartans.

They were on an equality with the Spartans in the beginning, and in the allotment of territory were thought to be even better off than they, and yet their prosperity did not last long, but what with the insolent temper of their kings and the unreasonableness of their peoples, their established institutions were confounded, and they made it clear that it was in very truth a divine blessing which the Spartans had enjoyed in the man who framed and tempered their civil polity for them. These events, however, were of later date.

A second, and a very bold political measure of Lycurgus, in his redistribution of the land. For there was a dreadful inequality in this regard, the city was heavily burdened with indigent and helpless people, and wealth was wholly concentrated in the hands of a few. Determined, therefore, to banish insolence and envy and crime and luxury, and those yet more deep-seated and afflictive diseases of the state, poverty and wealth, he persuaded his fellow-citizens to make one parcel of all their territory and divide it up anew, and to live with one another on a basis of entire uniformity and equality in the means of subsistence, seeking pre-eminence through virtue alone, assured that there was no other difference or inequality between man and man than that which was established by blame for base actions and praise for good ones.

Suiting the deed to the word, he distributed the rest of the Laconian land among the "perioeci," or free provincials, in thirty thousand lots, and that which belonged to the city of Sparta, in nine thousand lots, to as many genuine Spartans. But some say that Lycurgus distributed only six thousand lots among the Spartans, and that three thousand were afterwards added by Polydorus; others still, that Polydorus added half of the nine thousand to the half distributed by Lycurgus.

The lot of each was large enough to produce annually seventy bushels of barley for a man and twelve for his wife, with a proportionate amount of wine and oil. Lycurgus thought that a lot of this size would be sufficient for them, since they needed sustenance enough to promote vigour and health of body, and nothing else. And it is said that on returning from a journey some time afterwards, as he traversed the land just after the harvest, and saw the heaps of grain standing parallel and equal to one another, he smiled, and said to them that were by: "All Laconia looks like a family estate newly divided among many brothers."

Next, he undertook to divide up their movable property also, in order that every vestige of unevenness and inequality might be removed; and when he saw that they could not bear to have it taken from them directly, he took another course, and overcame their avarice by political devices. In the first place, he withdrew all gold and silver money from currency, and ordained the use of iron money only. Then to a great weight and mass of this he gave a trifling value, so that ten minas' worth ① required a large store-room in the house, and a yoke of cattle to transport it.

When this money obtained currency, many sorts of iniquity went into exile from Lacedaemon. For who would steal, or receive as a bribe, or rob, or plunder that which could neither be concealed, nor possessed with satisfaction, nay, nor even cut to pieces with any profit? For vinegar was used, as we are told, to quench the red-hot iron, robbing it of its temper and making it worthless for any other purpose, when once it had become brittle and hard to work.

In the next place, he banished the unnecessary and superfluous arts. And

① About £ 40, or $200.

even without such banishment most of them would have departed with the old coinage, since there was no sale for their products. For the iron money could not be carried into the rest of Greece, nor had it any value there, but was rather held in ridicule. It was not possible, therefore, to buy any foreign wares or bric-à-brac; no merchant-seamen brought freight into their harbours; no rhetoric teacher set foot on Laconian soil, no vagabond soothsayer, no keeper of harlots, no gold- or silver-smith, since there was no money there.

But luxury, thus gradually deprived of that which stimulated and supported it, died away of itself, and men of large possessions had no advantage over the poor, because their wealth found no public outlet, but had to be stored up at home in idleness. In this way it came about that such common and necessary utensils as bedsteads, chairs, and tables were most excellently made among them, and the Laconian "kothon," or drinking-cup, was in very high repute for usefulness among soldiers in active service, as Critias tells us.

For its colour concealed the disagreeable appearance of the water which they were often compelled to drink, and its curving lips caught the muddy sediment and held it inside, so that only the purer part reached the mouth of the drinker. For all this they had to thank their lawgiver; since their artisans were now freed from useless tasks, and displayed the beauty of their workmanship in objects of constant and necessary use.

With a view to attack luxury still more and remove the thirst for wealth, he introduced his third and most exquisite political device, namely, the institution of common messes, so that they might eat with one another in companies, of common and specified foods, and not take their meals at home, reclining on costly couches at costly tables, delivering themselves into the hands of servants and cooks to be fattened in the dark, like voracious animals, and ruining not only their characters but also their bodies, by surrendering them to every desire and all sorts of surfeit, which call for long sleeps, hot baths, abundant rest, and, as it were, daily nursing and tending. This was surely a great achievement, but it was a still greater one to make wealth "an object of no desire, "as Theophrastus says, and even "unwealth," [1] by this community of meals and simplicity of diet.

For the rich man could neither use nor enjoy nor even see or display his abundant means, when he went to the same meal as the poor man; so that it was in Sparta alone, of all the cities under the sun, that men could have that far-famed sight, a Plutus blind, and lying as lifeless and motionless as a picture. For the rich could not even dine beforehand at home and then go to the common mess with full stomachs, but the rest kept careful watch of him who did not eat and drink with them, and reviled him as a weakling, and one too effeminate for the common diet.

Lycurgus, however, was far from yielding in consequence of this calamity, but confronted his countrymen, and showed them his face besmeared with blood and his eye destroyed. Whereupon they were so filled with shame and sorrow at the sight, that they placed Alcander in his hands, and conducted him to his house with sympathetic indignation. Lycurgus commended them for their conduct, and dismissed them, but took Alcander into the house with him, where he did the youth no harm by word or deed, but after sending away his customary servants and attendants, ordered him to minister to his wants.

The youth, who was of a noble disposition, did as he was commanded, without any words, and abiding thus with Lycurgus, and sharing his daily life, he came to know the gentleness of the man, the calmness of his spirit, the rigid simplicity of his habits, and his unwearied industry. He thus became a devoted follower of Lycurgus, and used to tell his intimates and friends that the man was not harsh nor self-willed, as he had supposed, but the mildest and gentlest of them all.

Such, then, was the chastisement of this young man, and such the penalty laid upon him, namely, to become, instead of a wild and impetuous youth, a most decorous and discreet man. Lycurgus, moreover, in memory of his misfortune,

---

[1] Cf. Morals, p. 527 b.

built a temple to Athena Optilitis, so called from "optilus," which is the local Doric word for eye. Some writers, however, of whom one is Dioscorides, who wrote a treatise on the Spartan civil polity, say that although Lycurgus was struck in the eye, his eye was not blinded, but he built the temple to the goddess as a thank-offering for its healing. Be that as it may, the Spartan practice of carrying staves into their assemblies was abandoned after this unfortunate accident.

As for the public messes, the Cretans call them "andreia," but the Lacedaemonians, "phiditia," either because they are conducive to friendship and friendliness, "phiditia" being equivalent to "philitia"; or because they accustom men to simplicity and thrift, for which their word is "pheido." But it is quite possible, as some say, that the first letter of the word "phiditia" has been added to it, making "phiditia" out of "editia," which refers merely to meals and eating.

They met in companies of fifteen, a few more or less, and each one of the mess-mates contributed monthly a bushel of barley-meal, eight gallons of wine, five pounds of cheese, two and a half pounds of figs, and in addition to this, a very small sum of money for such relishes as flesh and fish. Besides this, whenever any one made a sacrifice of first fruits, or brought home game from the hunt, he sent a portion to his mess. For whenever any one was belated by a sacrifice or the chase, he was allowed to sup at home, but the rest had to be at the mess.

For a long time this custom of eating at common mess-tables was rigidly observed. For instance, when King Agis, on returning from an expedition in which he had been victorious over the Athenians, wished to sup at home with his wife, and sent for his rations, the polemarchs ① refused to send them to him; and when on the following day his anger led him to omit the customary sacrifice, they laid a fine upon him.

---

① At Sparta, military commanders under the kings.

Boys also used to come to these public messes, as if they were attending schools of sobriety; there they would listen to political discussions and see instructive models of liberal breeding. There they themselves also became accustomed to sport and jest without scurrility, and to endure jesting without displeasure. Indeed, it seems to have been especially characteristic of a Spartan to endure jesting; but if any one could not bear up under it, he had only to ask it, and the jester ceased.

As each one came in, the eldest of the company pointed to the door and said to him: "Through that door no word goes forth outside." And they say that a candidate for membership in one of these messes underwent the following ordeal. Each of the mess-mates took in his hand a bit of soft bread, and when a servant came along with a bowl upon his head, then they cast it into this without a word, like a ballot, leaving it just as it was if he approved of the candidate, but if he disapproved, squeezing it tight in his hand first.

For the flattened piece of bread had the force of a perforated, or negative, ballot. And if one such is found in the bowl, the candidate is not admitted to the mess, because they wish all its members to be congenial. The candidate thus rejected is said to have been "caddished," for "caddichus" ① is the name of the bowl into which they cast the pieces of bread. Of their dishes, the black broth is held in the highest esteem, so that the elderly men do not even ask for a bit of meat, but leave it for the young men, while they themselves have the broth poured out for their meals.

And it is said that one of the kings of Pontus actually bought a Spartan cook for the sake of having this broth, and then, when he tasted it, disliked it; whereupon the cook said: "O King, those who relish this broth must first have bathed in the river Eurotas." After drinking moderately, they go off home without a torch; for they are not allowed to walk with a light, either on this or

---

① Or "caddos," from which the verb in the Greek text is formed.

any other occasion, that they may accustom themselves to marching boldly and without fear in the darkness of night. Such, then, is the fashion of their common messes.

None of his laws were put into writing by Lycurgus, indeed, one of the so-called "rhetras" forbids it. For he thought that if the most important and binding principles which conduce to the prosperity and virtue of a city were implanted in the habits and training of its citizens, they would remain unchanged and secure, having a stronger bond than compulsion in the fixed purposes imparted to the young by education, which performs the office of a law-giver for every one of them.

And as for minor matters, such as business contracts, and cases where the needs vary from time to time, it was better, as he thought, not to hamper them by written constraints or fixed usages, but to suffer them, as occasion demanded, to receive such modifications as educated men should determine. Indeed, he assigned the function of law-making wholly and entirely to education.

One of his rhetras accordingly, as I have said, prohibited the use of written laws. Another was directed against extravagance, ordaining that every house should have its roof fashioned by the axe, and its doors by the saw only, and by no other tool. For, as in later times Epaminondas is reported to have said at his own table, that such a meal did not comport with treachery, so Lycurgus was the first to see clearly that such a house does not comport with luxury and extravagance.

Nor is any man so vulgar and senseless as to introduce into a simple and common house silver-footed couches, purple coverlets, gold drinking-cups, and all the extravagance which goes along with these, but one must of necessity adapt and proportion his couch to his house, his coverlets to his couch, and to this the rest of his supplies and equipment.

It was because he was used to this simplicity that Leotychides the Elder, as we are told, when he was dining in Corinth, and saw the roof of the house adorned with costly panellings, asked his host if trees grew square in that country.

A third rhetra of Lycurgus is mentioned, which forbids making frequent expeditions against the same enemies, in order not to accustom such enemies to frequent defence of themselves, which would make them warlike.

And this was the special grievance which they had against King Agesilaüs in later times, namely, that by his continual and frequent incursions and expeditions into Boeotia he rendered the Thebans a match for the Lacedaemonians. And therefore, when Antalcidas saw the king wounded, he said: "This is a fine tuition-fee which thou art getting from the Thebans, for teaching them how to fight, when they did not wish to do it, and did not know how." Such ordinances as these were called "rhetras" by Lycurgus, implying that they came from the god and were oracles.

In the matter of education, which he regarded as the greatest and noblest task of the law-giver, he began at the very source, by carefully regulating marriages and births. For it is not true that, as Aristotle says, [①] he tried to bring the women under proper restraint, but desisted, because he could not overcome the great licence and power which the women enjoyed on account of the many expeditions in which their husbands were engaged. During these the men were indeed obliged to leave their wives in sole control at home, and for this reason paid them greater deference than was their due, and gave them the title of Mistress. But even to the women Lycurgus paid all possible attention.

He made the maidens exercise their bodies in running, wrestling, casting the discus, and hurling the javelin, in order that the fruit of their wombs might have vigorous root in vigorous bodies and come to better maturity, and that they themselves might come with vigour to the fulness of their times, and struggle successfully and easily with the pangs of child-birth. He freed them from softness and delicacy and all effeminacy by accustoming the maidens no less

---

① Pol. ii. 6, 8.

than the youths to wear tunics only in processions, and at certain festivals to dance and sing when the young men were present as spectators.

There they sometimes even mocked and railed good-naturedly at any youth who had misbehaved himself; and again they would sing the praises of those who had shown themselves worthy, and so inspire the young men with great ambition and ardour. For he who was thus extolled for his valour and held in honour among the maidens, went away exalted by their praises; while the sting of their playful raillery was no less sharp than that of serious admonitions, especially as the kings and senators, together with the rest of the citizens, were all present at the spectacle.

Nor was there anything disgraceful in this scant clothing of the maidens, for modesty attended them, and wantonness was banished; nay, rather, it produced in them habits of simplicity and an ardent desire for health and beauty of body. It gave also to woman-kind a taste of lofty sentiment, for they felt that they too had a place in the arena of bravery and ambition. Wherefore they were led to think and speak as Gorgo, the wife of Leonidas, is said to have done. When some foreign woman, as it would seem, said to her: "You Spartan women are the only ones who rule their men," she answered: "Yes, we are the only ones that give birth to men."

Moreover, there were incentives to marriage in these things, —I mean such things as the appearance of the maidens without much clothing in processions and athletic contests where young men were looking on, for these were drawn on by necessity, "not geometrical, but the sort of necessity which lovers know," as Plato says. ① Nor was this all; Lycurgus also put a kind of public stigma upon confirmed bachelors. They were excluded from the sight of the young men and maidens at their exercises, and in winter the magistrates ordered them to march round the market-place in their tunics only, and as they marched, they

---

① Republic, p. 458 d.

sang a certain song about themselves, and its burden was that they were justly punished for disobeying the laws. Besides this, they were deprived of the honour and gracious attentions which the young men habitually paid to their elders. Therefore there was no one to find fault with what was said to Dercyllidas, reputable general though he was. As he entered a company, namely, one of the younger men would not offer him his seat, but said: "Indeed, thou hast begotten no son who will one day give his seat to me."

For their marriages the women were carried off by force, not when they were small and unfit for wedlock, but when they were in full bloom and wholly ripe. After the woman was thus carried off the bride's-maid, so called, took her in charge, cut her hair off close to the head, put a man's cloak and sandals on her, and laid her down on a pallet, on the floor, alone, in the dark. Then the bride-groom, not flown with wine nor enfeebled by excesses, but composed and sober, after supping at his public mess-table as usual, slipped stealthily into the room where the bride lay, loosed her virgin's zone, and bore her in his arms to the marriage-bed.

Then, after spending a short time with his bride, he went away composedly to his usual quarters, there to sleep with the other young men. And so he continued to do from that time on, spending his days with his comrades, and sleeping with them at night, but visiting his bride by stealth and with every precaution, full of dread and fear lest any of her household should be aware of his visits, his bride also contriving and conspiring with him that they might have stolen interviews as occasion offered.

And this they did not for a short time only, but long enough for some of them to become fathers before they had looked upon their own wives by daylight. Such interviews not only brought into exercise self-restraint and moderation, but united husbands and wives when their bodies were full of creative energy and their affections new and fresh, not when they were sated and dulled by unrestricted intercourse; and there was always left behind in their hearts some residual spark of mutual longing and delight.

After giving marriage such traits of reserve and decorum, he none the less freed men from the empty and womanish passion of jealous possession, by making it honourable for them, while keeping the marriage relation free from all wanton irregularities, to share with other worthy men in the begetting of children, laughing to scorn those who regard such common privileges as intolerable, and resort to murder and war rather than grant them.

For example, an elderly man with a young wife, if he looked with favour and esteem on some fair and noble young man, might introduce him to her, and adopt her offspring by such a noble father as his own. And again, a worthy man who admired some woman for the fine children that she bore her husband and the modesty of her behaviour as a wife, might enjoy her favours, if her husband would consent, thus planting, as it were, in a soil of beautiful fruitage, and begetting for himself noble sons, who would have the blood of noble men in their veins.

For in the first place, Lycurgus did not regard sons as the peculiar property of their fathers, but rather as the common property of the state, and therefore would not have his citizens spring from random parentage, but from the best there was. In the second place, he saw much folly and vanity in what other peoples enacted for the regulation of these matters; in the breeding of dogs and horses they insist on having the best sires which money or favour can secure, but they keep their wives under lock and key, demanding that they have children by none but themselves, even though they be foolish, or infirm, or diseased;as though children of bad stock did not show their badness to those first who possessed and reared them, and children of good stock, contrariwise, their goodness. The freedom which thus prevailed at that time in marriage relations was aimed at physical and political well-being, and was far removed from the licentiousness which was afterwards attributed to their women, so much so that adultery was wholly unknown among them.

And a saying is reported of one Geradas, [1] a Spartan of very ancient type, who, on being asked by a stranger what the punishment for adulterers was among them, answered: "Stranger, there is no adulterer among us." "Suppose, then," replied the stranger, "there should be one." "A bull," said Geradas, "would be his forfeit, a bull so large that it could stretch over Mount Taÿgetus and drink from the river Eurotas." Then the stranger was astonished and said: "But how could there be a bull so large?" To which Geradas replied, with a smile: "But how could there be an adulterer in Sparta?" Such, then, are the accounts we find of their marriages.

Offspring was not reared at the will of the father, but was taken and carried by him to a place called Lesche, where the elders of the tribes officially examined the infant, and if it was well-built and sturdy, they ordered the father to rear it, and assigned it one of the nine thousand lots of land; but if it was ill-born and deformed, they sent it to the so-called Apothetae, a chasm-like place at the foot of Mount Taÿgetus, in the conviction that the life of that which nature had not well equipped at the very beginning for health and strength, was of no advantage either to itself or the state. On the same principle, the women used to bathe their new-born babes not with water, but with wine, thus making a sort of test of their constitutions. For it is said that epileptic and sickly infants are thrown into convulsions by the strong wine and loose their senses, while the healthy ones are rather tempered by it, like steel, and given a firm habit of body.

Their nurses, too, exercised great care and skill; they reared infants without swaddling-bands, and thus left their limbs and figures free to develop; besides, they taught them to be contented and happy, not dainty about their food, nor fearful of the dark, nor afraid to be left alone, nor given to contemptible peevishness and whimpering. This is the reason why foreigners sometimes bought Spartan nurses for their children. Amycla, for instance, the nurse of the

---

[1] The name is Geradatas in Morals, p. 228 c (Apophtheg. Lacon, 20).

Athenian Alcibiades, is said to have been a Spartan. [1]

And yet Alcibiades, as Plato says, [2] had for a tutor, set over him by Pericles, one Zopyrus, who was just a common slave. But Lycurgus would not put the sons of Spartans in charge of purchased or hired tutors, nor was it lawful for every father to rear or train his son as he pleased, but as soon as they were seven years old, Lycurgus ordered them all to be taken by the state and enrolled in companies, where they were put under the same discipline and nurture, and so became accustomed to share one another's sports and studies.

The boy who excelled in judgement and was most courageous in fighting, was made captain of his company; on him the rest all kept their eyes, obeying his orders, and submitting to his punishments, so that their boyish training was a practice of obedience. Besides, the elderly men used to watch their sports, and by ever and anon egging them on to mimic battles and disputes, learned accurately how each one of them was naturally disposed when it was a question of boldness and aggressiveness in their struggles.

Of reading and writing, they learned only enough to serve their turn; all the rest of their training was calculated to make them obey commands well, endure hardships, and conquer in battle. Therefore, as they grew in age, their bodily exercise was increased; their heads were close-clipped, and they were accustomed to going bare-foot, and to playing for the most part without clothes. When they were twelve years old, they no longer had tunics to wear, received one cloak a year, had hard, dry flesh, and knew little of baths and ointments; only on certain days of the year, and few at that, did they indulge in such amenities.

They slept together, in troops and companies, on pallet-beds which they collected for themselves, breaking off with their hands—no knives allowed—the tops of the rushes which grew along the river Eurotas. In the winter-time, they added to the stuff of these pallets the so-called "lycophon," or thistle-down,

---

[1] Cf. Alcibiades, i. 2.

[2] Alcibiades I. p. 122 b.

which was thought to have warmth in it.

When the boys reached this age, they were favoured with the society of lovers from among the reputable young men. The elderly men also kept close watch of them, coming more frequently to their places of exercise, and observing their contests of strength and wit, not cursorily, but with the idea that they were all in a sense the fathers and tutors and governors of all the boys. In this way, at every fitting time and in every place, the boy who went wrong had someone to admonish and chastise him.

Nor was this all; one of the noblest and best men of the city was appointed paedonome, or inspector of the boys, and under his directions the boys, in their several companies, put themselves under the command of the most prudent and warlike of the so called Eirens. This was the name given to those who had been for two years out of the class of boys, and Melleirens, or Would-be Eirens, was the name for the oldest of the boys. This eiren, then, a youth of twenty years, commands his subordinates in their mimic battles, and in doors makes them serve him at his meals.

He commissions the larger ones to fetch wood, and the smaller ones potherbs. And they steal what they fetch, some of them entering the gardens, and others creeping right slyly and cautiously into the public messes of the men; but if a boy is caught stealing, he is soundly flogged, as a careless and unskilful thief. They steal, too, whatever food they can, and learn to be adept in setting upon people when asleep or off their guard.

But the boy who is caught gets a flogging and must go hungry. For the meals allowed them are scanty, in order that they may take into their own hands the fight against hunger, and so be forced into boldness and cunning.

This is the main object of their spare diet; a secondary one is to make them grow tall. For it contributes to height of stature when the vitality is not impeded and hindered by a mass of nourishment which forces it into thickness and width, but ascends of its own lightness, and when the body grows freely and easily.

The same tiling seems also to conduce to beauty of form; for lean and meagre habits yield more readily to the force of articulation, whereas the gross and over-fed are so heavy as to resist it. Just so, we may be sure, women who take physic while they are pregnant, bear children which are lean, it may be, but well-shaped and fine, because the lightness of the parent matter makes it more susceptible to moulding. However, the reason for this I must leave for others to investigate.

The boys make such a serious matter of their stealing, that one of them, as the story goes, who was carrying concealed under his cloak a young fox which he had stolen, suffered the animal to tear out his bowels with its teeth and claws, and died rather than have his theft detected. And even this story gains credence from what their youths now endure, many of whom I have seen expiring under the lash at the altar of Artemis Orthia.

The eiren, as he reclined after supper, would order one of the boys to sing a song, and to another would put a question requiring a careful and deliberate answer, as, for instance, "Who is the best man in the city?" or, "What thinkest thou of this man's conduct?" In this way the boys were accustomed to pass right judgements and interest themselves at the very outset in the conduct of the citizens. For if one of them was asked who was a good citizen, or who an infamous one, and had no answer to make, he was judged to have a torpid spirit, and one that would not aspire to excellence.

And the answer must not only have reasons and proof given for it, but also be couched in very brief and concise language, and the one who gave a faulty answer was punished with a bite in the thumb from the eiren. Often-times, too, the eiren punished the boys in the presence of the elders and magistrates, thus showing whether his punishments were reasonable and proper or not. While he was punishing them, he suffered no restraint, but after the boys were gone, he was brought to an account if his punishments were harsher than was necessary, or, on the other hand, too mild and gentle.

The boys' lovers also shared with them in their honour or disgrace; and it is said that one of them was once fined by the magistrates because his favourite boy had let an ungenerous cry escape him while he was fighting. Moreover, though this sort of love was so approved among them that even the maidens found lovers in good and noble women, still, there was no jealous rivalry in it, but those who fixed their affections on the same boys made this rather a foundation for friendship with one another, and persevered in common efforts to make their loved one as noble as possible.

The boys were also taught to use a discourse which combined pungency with grace, and condensed much observation into a few words. His iron money, indeed, Lycurgus made of large weight and small value, as I have observed, [①] but the current coin of discourse he adapted to the expression of deep and abundant meaning with simple and brief diction, by contriving that the general habit of silence should make the boys sententious and correct in their answers. For as sexual incontinence generally produces unfruitfulness and sterility, so intemperance in talking makes discourse empty and vapid.

King Agis, accordingly, when a certain Athenian decried the Spartan swords for being so short, and said that jugglers on the stage easily swallowed them, replied: "And yet we certainly reach our enemies with these daggers." And I observe that although the speech also of the Spartans seems short, yet it certainly reaches the point, and arrests the thought of the listener.

And indeed Lycurgus himself seems to have been short and sententious in his speech, if we may judge from his recorded sayings; that, for instance, on forms of government, to one who demanded the establishment of democracy in the city: "Go thou," said he, "and first establish democracy in thy household." That, again, to one who inquired why he ordained such small and inexpensive sacrifices: "That we may never omit," said he, "to honour the gods."

Again, in the matter of athletic contests, he allowed the citizens to engage only

---

① Chapter ix. 1.

in those where there was no stretching forth of hands. ① There are also handed down similar answers which he made by letter to his fellow-citizens. When they asked how they could ward off an invasion of enemies, he answered: "By remaining poor, and by not desiring to be greater the one than the other." And when they asked about fortifying their city, he answered: "A city will be well fortified which is surrounded by brave men and not by bricks." Now regarding these and similar letters, belief and scepticism are alike difficult.

Of their aversion to long speeches, the following apophthegms are proof. King Leonidas, when a certain one discoursed with him out of all season on matters of great concern, said: "My friend, the matter urges, but not the time." Charilaüs, the nephew of Lycurgus, when asked why his uncle had made so few laws, answered: "Men of few words need few laws."

Archidamidas, when certain ones found fault with Hecataeus the Sophist for saying nothing after being admitted to their public mess, answered: "He who knows how, knows also when to speak." Instances of the pungent sayings not devoid of grace, of which I spoke, ② are the following. Demaratus, when a troublesome fellow was pestering him with ill-timed questions, and especially with the oft repeated query who was the best of the Spartans, answered at last: "He who is least like thee."

And Agis, when certain ones were praising the Eleians for their just and honourable conduct of the Olympic games, said: "And what great matter is it for the Eleians to practise righteousness one day in five years?" And Theopompus, when a stranger kept saying, as he showed him kindness, that in his own city he was called a lover of Sparta, remarked: "My good Sir, it were better for thee to be called a lover of thine own city."

And Pleistoanax, the son of Pausanias, when an Athenian orator declared that the Lacedaemonians had no learning, said: "True, we are indeed the only

---

① After the manner of men begging their conquerors to spare their lives.
② Chapter xix. 1.

Hellenes who have learned no evil from you." And Archidamus, when some one asked him how many Spartans there were, replied: "Enough, good Sir, to keep evil men away."

And even from their jests it is possible to judge of their character. For it was their wont never to talk at random, and to Jet slip no speech which did not have some thought or other worth serious attention. For instance, when one of them was invited to hear a man imitate the nightingale, he said: "I have heard the bird herself." And another, on reading the epitaph: — " Tyranny's fires they were trying to quench when panoplied Ares.Slew them; Selinus looked down from her gates on their death,"said: "The men deserved to die; they should have let the fires burn out entirely."

And a youth, when some one promised to give him game-cocks that would die fighting, said, "Don't do that, but give me some of the kind that kill fighting." Another, seeing men seated on stools in a privy, said: "May I never sit where I cannot give place to an elder." The character of their apophthegms, then, was such as to justify the remark that love of wisdom rather than love of bodily exercise was the special characteristic of a Spartan.

Nor was their training in music and poetry any less serious a concern than the emulous purity of their speech, nay, their very songs had a stimulus that roused the spirit and awoke enthusiastic and effectual effort; the style of them was simple and unaffected, and their themes were serious and edifying. They were for the most part praises of men who had died for Sparta, calling them blessed and happy; censure of men who had played the coward, picturing their grievous and ill-starred life; and such promises and boasts of valour as befitted the different ages.

Of the last, it may not be amiss to cite one, by way of illustration. They had three choirs at their festivals, corresponding to the three ages, and the choir of old men would sing first: — " We once did deeds of prowess and were strong young men."Then the choir of young men would respond: — " We are so now, and if you wish, behold and see."And then the third choir, that of the boys, would sing: — " We shall be sometime mightier men by far than both.

In short, if one studies the poetry of Sparta, of which some specimens were still extant in my time, and makes himself familiar with the marching songs which they used, to the accompaniment of the flute, when charging upon their foes, he will conclude that Terpander and Pindar were right in associating valour with music. The former writes thus of the Lacedaemonians: — " Flourish there both the spear of the brave and the Muse's clear message,

Justice, too, walks the broad streets—."

And Pindar says: — [1]

" There are councils of Elders,

And young men's conquering spears,

And dances, the Muse, and joyousness."

The Spartans are thus shown to be at the same time most musical and most warlike; " In equal poise to match the sword hangs the sweet art of the harpist,"as their poet says. For just before their battles, the king sacrificed to the Muses, reminding his warriors, as it would seem, of their training, and of the firm decisions they had made, in order that they might be prompt to face the dread issue, and might perform such martial deeds as would be worthy of some record. [2]

In time of war, too, they relaxed the severity of the young men's discipline, and permitted them to beautify their hair and ornament their arms and clothing, rejoicing to see them, like horses, prance and neigh for the contest. Therefore they wore their hair long as soon as they ceased to be youths, and particularly in times of danger they took pains to have it glossy and well-combed, remembering a certain saying of Lycurgus, that a fine head of hair made the handsome more comely still, and the ugly more terrible.

---

[1] Fragment 199, Bergk, Poet. Lyr. Gr. i.4 p. 448.

[2] The Greek of this sentence is obscure, and the translation doubtful.

Their bodily exercises, too, were less rigorous during their campaigns, and in other ways their young warriors were allowed a regimen which was less curtailed and rigid, so that they were the only men in the world with whom war brought a respite in the training for war. And when at last they were drawn up in battle array and the enemy was at hand, the king sacrificed the customary she-goat, commanded all the warriors to set garlands upon their heads, and ordered the pipers to pipe the strains of the hymn to Castor;then he himself led off in a marching paean, and it was a sight equally grand and terrifying when they marched in step with the rhythm of the flute, without any gap in their line of battle, and with no confusion in their souls, but calmly and cheerfully moving with the strains of their hymn into the deadly fight. Neither fear nor excessive fury is likely to possess men so disposed, but rather a firm purpose full of hope and courage, believing as they do that Heaven is their ally.

The king marched against the enemy in close companionship with one who had been crowned victor in the great games. And they tell of a certain Spartan who refused to be bought off from a contest at Olympia by large sums of money, and after a long struggle outwrestled his antagonist. When some one said to him then: "What advantage, O Spartan, hast thou got from thy victory?" he answered, with a smile: "I shall stand in front of my king when I fight our enemies."

When they had conquered and routed an enemy, they pursued him far enough to make their victory secure by his flight, and then at once retired, thinking it ignoble and unworthy of a Hellene to hew men to pieces who had given up the fight and abandoned the field. And this was not only a noble and magnanimous policy, but it was also useful. For their antagonists, knowing that they slew those who resisted them, but showed mercy to those who yielded to them, were apt to think flight more advantageous than resistance.

Hippias the Sophist says that Lycurgus himself was very well versed in war and took part in many campaigns, and Philostephanus attributes to him the arrangement of the Spartan cavalry by "oulamoi," explaining that the "oulamos," as constituted by him, was a troop of fifty horsemen in a square formation. But Demetrius the Phalerean says he engaged in no warlike undertakings, and established his constitution in a time of peace.

And indeed the design of the Olympic truce would seem to bespeak a man of gentleness, and predisposed to peace. And yet there are some who say, as Hermippus reminds us, that at the outset Lycurgus had nothing whatever to do with Iphitus and his enterprise, but happened to come that way by chance, and be a spectator at the games; that he heard behind him, however, what seemed to be a human voice, chiding him and expressing amazement that he did not urge his fellow-citizens to take part in the great festival; and since, on turning round, he did not see the speaker anywhere, he concluded that the voice was from heaven, and therefore betook himself to Iphitus, and assisted him in giving the festival a more notable arrangement and a more enduring basis.

The training of the Spartans lasted into the years of full maturity. No man was allowed to live as he pleased, but in their city, as in a military encampment, they always had a prescribed regimen and employment in public service, considering that they belonged entirely to their country and not to themselves, watching over the boys, if no other duty was laid upon them, and either teaching them some useful thing, or learning it themselves from their elders.

For one of the noble and blessed privileges which Lycurgus provided for his fellow-citizens, was abundance of leisure, since he forbade their engaging in any mechanical art whatsoever, and as for money-making, with its laborious efforts to amass wealth, there was no need of it at all, since wealth awakened no envy and brought no honour.

Besides, the Helots tilled their ground for them, and paid them the produce mentioned above. [①] Therefore it was that one of them who was sojourning at Athens when the courts were in session, and learned that a certain Athenian

---

① Chapter viii. 4.

had been fined for idleness and was going home in great distress of mind and attended on his way by sympathetic and sorrowing friends, begged the bystanders to show him the man who had been fined for living like a freeman.

So servile a thing did they regard the devotion to the mechanical arts and to money-making. And law-suits, of course, vanished from among them with their gold and silver coinage, for they knew neither greed nor want, but equality in well-being was established there, and easy living based on simple wants. Choral dances and feasts and festivals and hunting and bodily exercise and social converse occupied their whole time, when they were not on a military expedition.

Those who were under thirty years of age did not go into the market-place at all, but had their household wants supplied at the hands of their kinsfolk and lovers. And it was disreputable for the elderly men to be continually seen loitering there, instead of spending the greater part of the day in the places of exercise that are called "leschai." [1] For if they gathered in these, they spent their time suitably with one another, making no allusions to the problems of money-making or of exchange, nay, they were chiefly occupied there in praising some noble action or censuring some base one, with jesting and laughter which made the path to instruction and correction easy and natural. For not even Lycurgus himself was immoderately severe; indeed, Sosibius tells us that he actually dedicated a little statue of Laughter, and introduced seasonable jesting into their drinking parties and like diversions, to sweeten, as it were, their hardships and meagre fare.

In a word, he trained his fellow-citizens to have neither the wish nor the ability to live for themselves; but like bees they were to make themselves always integral parts of the whole community, clustering together about their leader, almost beside themselves with enthusiasm and noble ambition, and to belong

---

① Places where men assembled for conversation.

wholly to their country. This idea can be traced also in some of their utterances.

For instance, Paedaretus, when he failed to be chosen among the three hundred best men, went away with a very glad countenance, as if rejoicing that the city had three hundred better men than himself. And again, Polycratidas, one of an embassy to the generals of the Persian king, on being asked by them whether the embassy was there in a private or a public capacity, replied: "If we succeed, in a public capacity; if we fail, in a private."

Again, Argileonis, the mother of Brasidas, when some Amphipolitans who had come to Sparta paid her a visit, asked them if Brasidas had died nobly and in a manner worthy of Sparta. Then they greatly extolled the man and said that Sparta had not such another, to which she answered: "Say not so, Strangers; Brasidas was noble and brave, but Sparta has many better men than he."

The senators were at first appointed by Lycurgus himself, as I have said, [1] from those who shared his counsels; but afterwards he arranged that any vacancy caused by death should be filled by the man elected as most deserving out of those above sixty years of age. And of all the contests in the world this would seem to have been the greatest and the most hotly disputed. For it was not the swiftest of the swift, nor the strongest of the strong, but the best and wisest of the good and wise who was to be elected, and have for the rest of his life, as a victor's prize for excellence, what I may call the supreme power in the state, lord as he was of life and death, honour and dishonour, and all the greatest issues of life.

The election was made in the following manner. An assembly of the people having been convened, chosen men were shut up in a room near by so that they could neither see nor be seen, but only hear the shouts of the assembly. For as in other matters, so here, the cries of the assembly decided between

---

[1] Chapter v. 7. f.

the competitors. These did not appear in a body, but each one was introduced separately, as the lot fell, and passed silently through the assembly.

Then the secluded judges, who had writing-tablets with them, recorded in each case the loudness of the shouting, not knowing for whom it was given, but only that he was introduced first, second, or third, and so on. Whoever was greeted with the most and loudest shouting, him they declared elected. The victor then set a wreath upon his head and visited in order the temples of the gods. He was followed by great numbers of young men, who praised and extolled him, as well as by many women, who celebrated his excellence in songs, and dwelt on the happiness of his life.

Each of his relations and friends set a repast before him, saying: "The city honours thee with this table." When he had finished his circuit, he went off to his mess-table. Here he fared in other ways as usual, but a second portion of food was set before him, which he took and put by. After the supper was over, the women who were related to him being now assembled at the door of the mess-hall, he called to him the one whom he most esteemed and gave her the portion he had saved, saying that he had received it as a meed of excellence, and as such gave it to her. Upon this, she too was lauded by the rest of the women and escorted by them to her home.

Furthermore, Lycurgus made most excellent regulations in the matter of their burials. To begin with, he did away with all superstitious terror by allowing them to bury their dead within the city, and to have memorials of them near the sacred places, thus making the youth familiar with such sights and accustomed to them, so that they were not confounded by them, and had no horror of death as polluting those who touched a corpse or walked among graves. In the second place, he permitted nothing to be buried with the dead; they simply covered the body with a scarlet robe and olive leaves when they laid it away.

To inscribe the name of the dead upon the tomb was not allowed, unless it were that of a man who had fallen in war, or that of a woman who had died in sacred office. He set apart only a short time for mourning, eleven days; on the twelfth, they were to sacrifice to Demeter and cease their sorrowing. Indeed, nothing was left untouched and neglected, but with all the necessary details of life he blended some commendation of virtue or rebuke of vice; and he filled the city full of good examples, whose continual presence and society must of necessity exercise a controlling and moulding influence upon those who were walking the path of honour.

This was the reason why he did not permit them to live abroad at their pleasure and wander in strange lands, assuming foreign habits and imitating the lives of peoples who were without training and lived under different forms of government. Nay more, he actually drove away from the city the multitudes which streamed in there for no useful purpose, not because he feared they might become imitators of his form of government and learn useful lessons in virtue, as Thucydides says, [①] but rather that they might not become in any wise teachers of evil. For along with strange people, strange doctrines must come in; and novel doctrines bring novel decisions, from which there must arise many feelings and resolutions which destroy the harmony of the existing political order. Therefore he thought it more necessary to keep bad manners and customs from invading and filling the city than it was to keep out infectious diseases.

一 文献出处

Plutarch, *Lives*, with an English translation by Bernadotte Perrin, Cambridge, M.A.: Harvard University Press; London: William Heinemann Ltd., 1914.

---

① In the Funeral Oration of Pericles, ii. 39, 1.

二 文献导读

《希腊罗马名人传》，通称《名人传》（*Lives*），原书名《希腊罗马人物平行列传》（*The Parallel Lives of Grecians and Romans*），是罗马帝国时代的希腊历史学家普鲁塔克的传记作品。其诞生以来，《名人传》以其丰富的史料、生动的叙述和渗透其间的伦理思想一直受到世人的推崇和喜爱。尽管它并不是严格意义上的历史专著，但因为作者详细地描述了很多古希腊、罗马重要的历史人物和事件，同时又汇集了很多已经散失的文献资料和轶闻传说，因此不失为一部研究希腊罗马史的重要史料。

关于普鲁塔克的生平，直接的记述十分有限。在与其同一时代或稍后的诸如塔西佗、小普林尼等罗马作家的作品中，从未引用过普鲁塔克的著作，可见，在用拉丁文写作的罗马，这位用希腊文写作的史家还没有受到足够的重视。因此，我们对普鲁塔克生平的了解主要是通过一些散见于其本人作品中的叙说推断而来。根据有关史料的推断，普鲁塔克约生于公元46年，卒于120年，此时正值罗马帝国的繁荣和稳定时期，历经克劳狄、尼禄、图密善等皇帝，终于图拉真、哈德良统治下的黄金时代。他出生于希腊中部彼奥提亚地区的一个名叫凯罗尼亚的小镇，家庭富有而颇有文化教养，据说他的父亲就是一位对哲学很有研究的历史学者。普鲁塔克有两个兄弟，膝下四儿一女，过着十分美满和睦的家庭生活。

普鲁塔克在少年时代就曾经游学于雅典，拜逍遥派哲学家阿摩尼乌斯为师，兼取柏拉图、亚里士多德以及毕达哥拉斯众学派学说之长，但他还是对伦理哲学情有独钟，坚信斯多噶学派提倡的"幸福来源于品德"的教义，这成为他后来的史著中弥漫的伦理说教的思想来源。后来，普鲁塔克遍游底比斯、科林斯等希腊名城，到过埃及的亚历山大里亚和小亚细亚，还到过罗马和意大利的其他地方，而且在罗马住过相当长的时间。普鲁塔克一生担任过很多公职，结识了罗马帝国时代的很多显要人物。他曾在罗马帝国驻希腊总督手下供职，担任过本镇的地方行政长官，其间被派往罗马履行公务并在那里讲授哲学，之后返回故乡凯罗尼亚，在潜心著述的同时仍未脱离公共生活。他笃信神祇，热心于公益事业，多次兼任德尔菲阿波罗神庙的祭司，乐于参加家乡的所有公共活动。他长期讲授道德哲学，听众中有不少名人和显贵。他为人谦和，淡泊名利，在勤奋好学的同时并没有选择离群索居的生活。

普鲁塔克是一位多产的作家，一生著述达到 277 种，除去 130 种已经散失，还有一部分断定为伪书之外，保存至今的尚有 100 多种，大体上可以分为两类：一类统称为《道德论集》，约 60 篇，主要是道德、宗教、哲学、政治、科学和文艺等方面的论述；另一类即《名人传》，包括希腊罗马名人传记 50 篇。虽然普鲁塔克的《名人传》更负盛名，但《道德论集》对于了解他的伦理思想和道德学说更为直接，实际上，这两个部分是互为表里、相辅相成的，因为作者之所以撰述这些名人传记，与其说是为了记述历史，不如说是为了通过这些人物的行为阐发他的道德学说，这也就成为《名人传》的一大特色。普鲁塔克信奉中庸之道，尊崇神性和天意，善与恶、美德与恶行的对立构成了这些论说文章和名人传记的一条主线。

普鲁塔克自幼熟读荷马史诗、希腊悲剧、抒情诗和民谣，通晓柏拉图、亚里士多德、伊壁鸠鲁和斯多噶派的哲学思想，博览群书，再加上后来游历各方，广交杰出人士，所以，其作品的取材十分广泛和丰富。就《名人传》而言，资料来源大概分成三类：一是前人的历史著作；二是当时存留的典籍文献；三是亲自搜集的传闻轶事。希罗多德的《历史》和修昔底德的《伯罗奔尼撒战争史》是普鲁塔克经常征引的重要史料，尤其对后者的文风推崇备至。但是，与修昔底德主要记述重大的历史事件，十分注重史料的翔实和分析的客观不同的是，普鲁塔克更加关注历史人物的命运，以引人入胜的人物性格描写和生动活泼的轶闻趣事的记述而见长。除了希腊作家，包括李维、传记作家涅波斯、西西里历史学家狄奥多洛斯等罗马时代的作家对普鲁塔克撰写《名人传》也产生过直接影响。

那么，普鲁塔克为什么要采用希腊罗马名人平行传记或合传的形式呢？他创作这部作品的动机又是什么呢？答案就在于普鲁塔克生活的特殊时代及其本人的双重身份。一方面，作为罗马时期的希腊语作家，普鲁塔克具有强烈的泛希腊主义的爱国情节，为古希腊过去的光荣感到骄傲和自豪；另一方面，作为一个罗马帝国的公民，亲身领略到罗马帝国的强大，对罗马建城以来的文治武功也充满了发自内心的赞美之情。因此，他写作此书的目的正是为了证明远古的希腊和晚近的罗马一样拥有自己杰出的立法者、军事家、政治家、演说家，在促进希腊人和罗马人相互尊重的同时，也为世人树立起道德行为的典范。正是基于这样的考虑，他才采取了合传的形式，即把一位希腊名人和一位属于同一领域的罗马名人放在一起，在分别叙述之后继之以一篇合论。例如，他把从波斯手中拯救了希腊的雅典将军泰米斯托克里与从高卢人手中挽救了罗马的卡米卢斯相匹配，把斯巴达立法者莱库古和罗马的立法者努马放在一起。在现存的 50 篇传记中，有 46 篇是名副其实的平行传记，在平行传记中，除了《阿吉斯传》是四传对比，其余各篇均是两相对比，并附以合论。书末的包括《薛西斯传》在内的 4 篇是单独的传记。当然，由于时代和认识上的局限，这些传记并没有涵盖希腊罗马时代所有重要的历史人物，而且选取的对象主要是政治家、军事家，没有一位思想家、诗人和科学家，因此，普鲁塔克仍然没有脱离古代社会以帝王将相和英雄豪杰为中心的历史观念。

在史学界，普鲁塔克一度被认为只以讲故事取胜，材料有欠翔实，因而评价度不高。其实这种看法是有失公允的。一方面，作为当事人和亲历者，普鲁塔克的这部作品记录了大量罗马帝国时代的轶闻史事，其中有一大部分是他亲自采访得来的，这些第一手资料无疑是罗马史研究的宝贵资料；另一方面，作者对已经过去了几百年的希腊历史虽然带有追述的性质，但他对希腊时代的文献资料极为熟悉，有着自己独到的研究和理解，更为可贵的是，书中引用了大量的希腊时代的历史、哲学和诗歌材料，其中包括很多早已散失，后人无法见到的文献，比如梭伦的残诗、欧里庇得斯已经失传的戏剧，等等。毕竟，普鲁塔克生活的时代距希腊的古典时代并不遥远，他还能见到很多古代的文献资料，从这个意义上说，普氏的这部作品对于希腊罗马史研究具有其他作品所不能替代的重要参考价值。当然，作为一部文学传记，这部作品与严格意义上的史著还是有一定的距离，比如书中对年代的记述、财产和货币数量的统计等具体问题还带有很大的随意性，在引用的时候需要十分谨慎。

普鲁塔克的《名人传》虽然在当时没有引起足够的关注，但在后来却对西方文化产生了十分深远的影响。晚期罗马帝国和东罗马的皇帝都十分喜爱普鲁塔克的作品。在文艺复兴时代，他的作品通过拜占庭的学者传入意大利，先后被翻译成拉丁文、意大利文、法文和英文，此后，在西欧各国的影响日益扩大，对法国的拉伯雷、蒙田，英国的莎士比亚、培根等文学家和思想家都产生过很大的影响，现在成为最为世人熟悉和喜爱的古典名著之一。

以上内容选自普鲁塔克的《莱库古传》。莱库古是斯巴达城邦传说中的一位古代的立法者，在这一段中记述了莱库古的立法活动，对斯巴达的贵族寡头政制、社会等级制度、黑劳士制度、公餐制度以及教育制度的创建过程和内容进行了十分详细的说明。这篇传记被认为是描述古代斯巴达社会制度和社会风尚的集大成之作。

三 延伸阅读

Cartledge, Paul, *Sparta and Lakonia : A Regional History, 1300-362 B.C.*, London : Routledge & Kegan Paul, 2002.

Cartledge, Paul, *Spartan Reflections*, London : Gerald Duckworth & Co., Ltd., 2001.

Cartledge, Paul, *The Spartans : The World of the Warrior-heroes of Ancient Greece, from Utopia to Crisis and Collapse* , Woodstock, N.Y. : Overlook Press, 2003.

Forrest, W. G., *A History of Sparta*, London : Gerald Duckworth, 1980.

Hodkinson, Stephen, *Property and Wealth in Classical Sparta*, London: Gerald Duckworth & Co., Ltd., 2000.

Hodkinson, Stephen, *Sparta and War*, The Calassical Press of Wales, 2006.

Powell, Anton, and Stephen Hodkinson, eds., *The Shadow of Sparta*, The Classical Press of Wales, 1994.

Rawson, E.D., *The Sparta Tradition in European Thought*, Oxford, 1969.

Herodotus: Histories [*]

When the Eretrians learned that the Persian expedition was sailing to attack them, they asked for help from the Athenians. The Athenians did not refuse the aid, but gave them for defenders the four thousand tenant farmers who held the land of the Chalcidian horse-breeders. [①] But it seems that all the plans of the Eretrians were unsound; they sent to the Athenians for aid, but their counsels were divided.

Some of them planned to leave the city and make for the heights of Euboea; others plotted treason in hope of winning advantages from the Persians.

When Aeschines son of Nothon, a leading man in Eretria, learned of both designs, he told the Athenians who had come how matters stood, and asked them to depart to their own country so they would not perish like the rest. The Athenians followed Aeschines' advice.

So they saved themselves by crossing over to Oropus; the Persians sailed holding their course for Temenos and Choereae and Aegilea, all in Eretrian territory. Landing at these places, they immediately unloaded their horses and made preparation to attack their enemies.

---

[*] 希罗多德《历史》节选。本文选自该书的第 6 卷第 100~117 小节，第 7 卷第 201~233 小节。以下皆为英文译本原书注释。

① Cp. Hdt. 5.77.

The Eretrians had no intention of coming out and fighting; all their care was to guard their walls if they could, since it was the prevailing counsel not to leave the city. The walls were strongly attacked, and for six days many fell on both sides; but on the seventh two Eretrians of repute, Euphorbus son of Alcimachus and Philagrus son of Cineas, betrayed the city to the Persians.

They entered the city and plundered and burnt the temples, in revenge for the temples that were burnt at Sardis; moreover, they enslaved the townspeople, according to Darius' command.

After subduing Eretria, the Persians waited a few days and then sailed away to the land of Attica, pressing ahead in expectation of doing to the Athenians exactly what they had done to the Eretrians. Marathon [1] was the place in Attica most suitable for riding horses and closest to Eretria, so Hippias son of Pisistratus led them there.

When the Athenians learned this, they too marched out to Marathon, with ten generals leading them. The tenth was Miltiades, and it had befallen his father Cimon son of Stesagoras to be banished from Athens by Pisistratus son of Hippocrates.

While in exile he happened to take the Olympic prize in the four-horse chariot, and by taking this victory he won the same prize as his half-brother Miltiades. At the next Olympic games he won with the same horses but permitted Pisistratus to be proclaimed victor, and by resigning the victory to him he came back from exile to his own property under truce.

After taking yet another Olympic prize with the same horses, he happened to be murdered by Pisistratus' sons, since Pisistratus was no longer living. They murdered him by placing men in ambush at night near the town-hall. Cimon was buried in front of the city, across the road called "Through the Hollow", and buried opposite him are the mares who won the three Olympic prizes.

---

[1] For a detailed discussion of various questions connected with the battle of Marathon, readers are referred to How and Wells, Appendix XVIII .

The mares of Evagoras the Laconian did the same as these, but none others. Stesagoras, the elder of Cimon's sons, was then being brought up with his uncle Miltiades in the Chersonese. The younger was with Cimon at Athens, and he took the name Miltiades from Miltiades the founder of the Chersonese.

It was this Miltiades who was now the Athenian general, after coming from the Chersonese and escaping a two-fold death. The Phoenicians pursued him as far as Imbros, considering it of great importance to catch him and bring him to the king.

He escaped from them, but when he reached his own country and thought he was safe, then his enemies met him. They brought him to court and prosecuted him for tyranny in the Chersonese, but he was acquitted and appointed Athenian general, chosen by the people.

While still in the city, the generals first sent to Sparta the herald Philippides, an Athenian and a long-distance runner who made that his calling. As Philippides himself said when he brought the message to the Athenians, when he was in the Parthenian mountain above Tegea he encountered Pan.

Pan called out Philippides' name and bade him ask the Athenians why they paid him no attention, though he was of goodwill to the Athenians, had often been of service to them, and would be in the future.

The Athenians believed that these things were true, and when they became prosperous they established a sacred precinct of Pan beneath the Acropolis. Ever since that message they propitiate him with annual sacrifices and a torch-race.

This Philippides was in Sparta on the day after leaving the city of Athens, [1] that time when he was sent by the generals and said that Pan had appeared to him. He came to the magistrates and said,

"Lacedaemonians, the Athenians ask you to come to their aid and not allow the most ancient city among the Hellenes to fall into slavery at the hands of the

---

[1] According to Isocrates the distance traversed was 150 miles.

foreigners. Even now Eretria has been enslaved, and Hellas has become weaker by an important city."

He told them what he had been ordered to say, and they resolved to send help to the Athenians, but they could not do this immediately, for they were unwilling to break the law. It was the ninth day of the rising month, and they said that on the ninth they could not go out to war until the moon's circle was full. [1]

So they waited for the full moon, while the foreigners were guided to Marathon by Hippias son of Pisistratus. The previous night Hippias had a dream in which he slept with his mother.

He supposed from the dream that he would return from exile to Athens, recover his rule, and end his days an old man in his own country. Thus he reckoned from the dream. Then as guide he unloaded the slaves from Eretria onto the island of the Styrians called Aegilia, and brought to anchor the ships that had put ashore at Marathon, then marshalled the foreigners who had disembarked onto land.

As he was tending to this, he happened to sneeze and cough more violently than usual. Since he was an elderly man, most of his teeth were loose, and he lost one of them by the force of his cough. It fell into the sand and he expended much effort in looking for it, but the tooth could not be found.

He groaned aloud and said to those standing by him: "This land is not ours and we will not be able to subdue it. My tooth holds whatever share of it was mine."

Hippias supposed that the dream had in this way come true. As the Athenians were marshalled in the precinct of Heracles, the Plataeans came to help them in full force. The Plataeans had put themselves under the protection of the Athenians, [2] and the Athenians had undergone many labors on their behalf.

---

[1] This statement probably applies only to the month Carneius (Attic Metageitnion), when the Carneia was celebrated at Sparta in honor of Apollo, from the 7th to the 15th of the month.

[2] In 519, according to Thucydides (Thuc. 3.68); Grote gives a later date.

This is how they did it:

when the Plataeans were pressed by the Thebans, they first tried to put themselves under the protection of Cleomenes son of Anaxandrides and the Lacedaemonians, who happened to be there. But they did not accept them, saying, "We live too far away, and our help would be cold comfort to you. You could be enslaved many times over before any of us heard about it.

We advise you to put yourselves under the protection of the Athenians, since they are your neighbors and not bad men at giving help." The Lacedaemonians gave this advice not so much out of goodwill toward the Plataeans as wishing to cause trouble for the Athenians with the Boeotians.

So the Lacedaemonians gave this advice to the Plataeans, who did not disobey it. When the Athenians were making sacrifices to the twelve gods, ① they sat at the altar as suppliants and put themselves under protection. When the Thebans heard this, they marched against the Plataeans, but the Athenians came to their aid.

As they were about to join battle, the Corinthians, who happened to be there, prevented them and brought about a reconciliation. Since both sides desired them to arbitrate, they fixed the boundaries of the country on condition that the Thebans leave alone those Boeotians who were unwilling to be enrolled as Boeotian. After rendering this decision, the Corinthians departed. The Boeotians attacked the Athenians as they were leaving but were defeated in battle.

The Athenians went beyond the boundaries the Corinthians had made for the Plataeans, fixing the Asopus river as the boundary for the Thebans in the direction of Plataea and Hysiae. So the Plataeans had put themselves under the protection of the Athenians in the aforesaid manner, and now came to help at Marathon.

---

① The twelve gods were Zeus, Hera, Poseidon, Demeter, Apollo, Artemis, Hephaestus, Athena, Ares, Aphrodite, Hermes, Hestia. The βωμòς was a central altar in the agora, from which distances were reckoned.

The Athenian generals were of divided opinion, some advocating not fighting because they were too few to attack the army of the Medes; others, including Miltiades, advocating fighting.

Thus they were at odds, and the inferior plan prevailed. An eleventh man had a vote, chosen by lot to be polemarch ① of Athens, and by ancient custom the Athenians had made his vote of equal weight with the generals. Callimachus of Aphidnae was polemarch at this time. Miltiades approached him and said,

"Callimachus, it is now in your hands to enslave Athens or make her free, and thereby leave behind for all posterity a memorial such as not even Harmodius and Aristogeiton left. Now the Athenians have come to their greatest danger since they first came into being, and, if we surrender, it is clear what we will suffer when handed over to Hippias. But if the city prevails, it will take first place among Hellenic cities.

I will tell you how this can happen, and how the deciding voice on these matters has devolved upon you. The ten generals are of divided opinion, some urging to attack, others urging not to.

If we do not attack now, I expect that great strife will fall upon and shake the spirit of the Athenians, leading them to medize. But if we attack now, before anything unsound corrupts the Athenians, we can win the battle, if the gods are fair.

All this concerns and depends on you in this way: if you vote with me, your country will be free and your city the first in Hellas. But if you side with those eager to avoid battle, you will have the opposite to all the good things I enumerated."

By saying this Miltiades won over Callimachus. The polemarch's vote was counted in, and the decision to attack was resolved upon. Thereafter the generals who had voted to fight turned the presidency over to Miltiades as each one's day

---

① One of the nine archons, all chosen by lot.

came in turn. ① He accepted the office but did not make an attack until it was his own day to preside.

When the presidency came round to him, he arrayed the Athenians for battle, with the polemarch Callimachus commanding the right wing, since it was then the Athenian custom for the polemarch to hold the right wing. He led, and the other tribes were numbered out in succession next to each other. ② The Plataeans were marshalled last, holding the left wing.

Ever since that battle, when the Athenians are conducting sacrifices at the festivals every fourth year, ③ the Athenian herald prays for good things for the Athenians and Plataeans together.

As the Athenians were marshalled at Marathon, it happened that their line of battle was as long as the line of the Medes. The center, where the line was weakest, was only a few ranks deep, but each wing was strong in numbers.

When they had been set in order and the sacrifices were favorable, the Athenians were sent forth and charged the foreigners at a run. The space between the armies was no less than eight stadia.

The Persians saw them running to attack and prepared to receive them, thinking the Athenians absolutely crazy, since they saw how few of them there were and that they ran up so fast without either cavalry or archers.

So the foreigners imagined, but when the Athenians all together fell upon the foreigners they fought in a way worthy of record. These are the first Hellenes whom we know of to use running against the enemy. They are also the first to endure looking at Median dress and men wearing it, for up until then just hearing the name of the Medes caused the Hellenes to panic.

They fought a long time at Marathon. In the center of the line the foreigners

---

① Each general seems to have been head commander in turn.

② There was a fixed official order; but Plutarch's account of the battle places certain tribes according to a different system. Perhaps the battle-order was determined by lot.

③ e.g. the great Panathenaea, and the festival of Poseidon.

prevailed, where the Persians and Sacae were arrayed. The foreigners prevailed there and broke through in pursuit inland, but on each wing the Athenians and Plataeans prevailed.

In victory they let the routed foreigners flee, and brought the wings together to fight those who had broken through the center. The Athenians prevailed, then followed the fleeing Persians and struck them down. When they reached the sea they demanded fire and laid hold of the Persian ships.

In this labor Callimachus the polemarch was slain, a brave man, and of the generals Stesilaus son of Thrasylaus died. Cynegirus [①] son of Euphorion fell there, his hand cut off with an ax as he grabbed a ship's figurehead. Many other famous Athenians also fell there.

In this way the Athenians overpowered seven ships. The foreigners pushed off with the rest, picked up the Eretrian slaves from the island where they had left them, and sailed around Sunium hoping to reach the city before the Athenians. There was an accusation at Athens that they devised this by a plan of the Alcmaeonidae, who were said to have arranged to hold up a shield as a signal once the Persians were in their ships.

They sailed around Sunium, but the Athenians marched back to defend the city as fast as their feet could carry them and got there ahead of the foreigners. Coming from the sacred precinct of Heracles in Marathon, they pitched camp in the sacred precinct of Heracles in Cynosarges. The foreigners lay at anchor off Phalerum, the Athenian naval port at that time. After riding anchor there, they sailed their ships back to Asia.

In the battle at Marathon about six thousand four hundred men of the foreigners were killed, and one hundred and ninety-two Athenians; that many fell on each side.

The following marvel happened there: an Athenian, Epizelus son of

---

① Brother of the poet Aeschylus.

Couphagoras, was fighting as a brave man in the battle when he was deprived of his sight, though struck or hit nowhere on his body, and from that time on he spent the rest of his life in blindness.

I have heard that he tells this story about his misfortune: he saw opposing him a tall armed man, whose beard overshadowed his shield, but the phantom passed him by and killed the man next to him. I learned by inquiry that this is the story Epizelus tells.

......

King Xerxes lay encamped in Trachis in Malis and the Hellenes in the pass. [1] This place is called Thermopylae by most of the Hellenes, but by the natives and their neighbors Pylae. [2] Each lay encamped in these places. Xerxes was master of everything to the north [3] from Trachis, and the Hellenes of all that lay toward the south on the mainland. [4]

The Hellenes who awaited the Persians in that place were these: three hundred Spartan armed men; one thousand from Tegea and Mantinea, half from each place; one hundred and twenty from Orchomenus in Arcadia and one thousand from the rest of Arcadia; that many Arcadians, four hundred from Corinth, two hundred from Phlius, and eighty Mycenaeans. These were the Peloponnesians present; from Boeotia there were seven hundred Thespians and four hundred Thebans.

In addition, the Opuntian Locrians in full force and one thousand Phocians came at the summons. The Hellenes had called upon them through messengers who told them that this was only the advance guard, that the rest of the allies were expected any day now, and that the sea was being watched, with the Athenians and Aeginetans and all those enrolled in the fleet on guard. There was

---

① In the space between the eastern and western narrow ἔσοδοι.

② "the Gates", since it served as the entrance into Greece from the north. Thermopylae means "the Hot Gates", from the warm springs there.

③ West, properly speaking; "southward" below should be "eastward."

④ That is, Greece.

nothing for them to be afraid of.

The invader of Hellas was not a god but a human being, and there was not, and never would be, any mortal on whom some amount of evil was not bestowed at birth, with the greatest men receiving the largest share. The one marching against them was certain to fall from pride, since he was a mortal. When they heard this, the Locrians and Phocians marched to Trachis to help.

Each city had its own general, but the one most admired and the leader of the whole army was a Lacedaemonian, Leonidas, son of Anaxandrides, son of Leon, son of Eurycratides, son of Anaxandrus, son of Eurycrates, son of Polydorus, son of Alcamenes, son of Teleclus, son of Archelaus, son of Hegesilaus, son of Doryssus, son of Leobotes, son of Echestratus, son of Agis, son of Eurysthenes, son of Aristodemus, son of Aristomachus, son of Cleodaeus, son of Hyllus, son of Heracles. Leonidas had gained the kingship at Sparta unexpectedly.

Since he had two older brothers, Cleomenes and Dorieus, he had renounced all thought of the kingship. Cleomenes, however, died without male offspring, and Dorieus, who had met his end in Sicily, was also no longer alive. The succession therefore fell to Leonidas since he was older than Anaxandrides' youngest son Cleombrotus and had married Cleomenes' daughter.

He now came to Thermopylae with the appointed three hundred he had selected, ① all of whom had sons. He also brought those Thebans whom I counted among the number and whose general was Leontiades son of Eurymachus.

Leonidas took pains to bring only the Thebans among the Hellenes, because they were accused of medizing; he summoned them to the war wishing to know

---

① The regular number of the royal body-guard, the so-called ἱππεῖς. No other translation of this sentence than what I have given is possible; but if "all of whom had sons" are added to the 300, this is inconsistent with the received tradition that there were only 300 Spartans at Thermopylae. There seems to be no explanation of the matter except Dr. Macan's theory that Herodotus made a mistake. Of course if ἐπιλεξάμενος could mean "selecting from," the difficulty might be removed; but I do not think it can.

whether they would send their men with him or openly refuse the Hellenic alliance. They sent the men but intended something quite different.

The Spartans sent the men with Leonidas on ahead so that the rest of the allies would see them and march, instead of medizing like the others if they learned that the Spartans were delaying. At present the Carneia ① was in their way, but once they had completed the festival, they intended to leave a garrison at Sparta and march out in full force with all speed.

The rest of the allies planned to do likewise, for the Olympiad coincided with these events. They accordingly sent their advance guard, not expecting the war at Thermopylae to be decided so quickly.

This is what they intended, but the Hellenes at Thermopylae, when the Persians drew near the pass, fearfully took counsel whether to depart. The rest of the Peloponnesians were for returning to the Peloponnese and guarding the isthmus, but the Phocians and Locrians were greatly angered by this counsel. Leonidas voted to remain where they were and send messengers to the cities bidding them to send help, since they were too few to ward off the army of the Medes.

While they debated in this way, Xerxes sent a mounted scout to see how many there were and what they were doing. While he was still in Thessaly, he had heard that a small army was gathered there and that its leaders were Lacedaemonians, including Leonidas, who was of the Heracleid clan.

Riding up to the camp, the horseman watched and spied out the place. He could, however, not see the whole camp, for it was impossible to see those posted inside the wall which they had rebuilt and were guarding. He did take note of those outside, whose arms lay in front of the wall, and it chanced that at that time the Lacedaemonians were posted there.

He saw some of the men exercising naked and others combing their hair. He

---

① The national festival in honor of Apollo, held in September.

marvelled at the sight and took note of their numbers. When he had observed it all carefully, he rode back in leisure, since no one pursued him or paid him any attention at all. So he returned and told Xerxes all that he had seen.

When Xerxes heard that, he could not comprehend the fact that the Lacedaemonians were actually, to the best of their ability, preparing to kill or be killed. What they did appeared laughable to him, so he sent for Demaratus the son of Ariston, who was in his camp.

When this man arrived, he asked him about each of these matters, wanting to understand what it was that the Lacedaemonians were doing. Demaratus said, "You have already heard about these men from me, when we were setting out for Hellas, but when you heard, you mocked me, although I told you how I expected things to turn out. It is my greatest aim, O King, to be truthful in your presence.

So hear me now. These men have come to fight us for the pass, and it for this that they are preparing. This is their custom: when they are about to risk their lives, they arrange their hair.

Rest assured that if you overcome these men and those remaining behind at Sparta, there is no one else on earth who will raise his hands to withstand you, my King. You are now attacking the fairest kingdom in Hellas and men who are the very best."

What he said seemed completely incredible to Xerxes, so he then asked how they, who were so few in number, would fight against his army. Demaratus answered, "My King, take me for a liar if this does not turn out as I say." So he spoke, but he did not persuade Xerxes.

He let four days go by, expecting them to run away at any minute. They did not leave, and it seemed to him that they stayed out of folly and lack of due respect. On the fifth day he became angry and sent the Medes and Cissians against them, bidding them take them prisoner and bring them into his presence.

The Medes bore down upon the Hellenes and attacked. Many fell, but others attacked in turn, and they made it clear to everyone, especially to the king himself, that among so many people there were few real men. The battle lasted all day.

When the Medes had been roughly handled, they retired, and the Persians whom the king called Immortals, led by Hydarnes, attacked in turn. It was thought that they would easily accomplish the task.

When they joined battle with the Hellenes, they fared neither better nor worse than the Median army, since they used shorter spears than the Hellenes and could not use their numbers fighting in a narrow space.

The Lacedaemonians fought memorably, showing themselves skilled fighters amidst unskilled on many occasions, as when they would turn their backs and feign flight. The barbarians would see them fleeing and give chase with shouting and noise, but when the Lacedaemonians were overtaken, they would turn to face the barbarians and overthrow innumerable Persians. A few of the Spartans themselves were also slain. When the Persians could gain no inch of the pass, attacking by companies and in every other fashion, they withdrew.

It is said that during these assaults in the battle the king, as he watched, jumped up three times from the throne in fear for his army. This, then, is how the fighting progressed, and on the next day the barbarians fought no better. They joined battle supposing that their enemies, being so few, were now disabled by wounds and could no longer resist.

The Hellenes, however, stood ordered in ranks by nation, and each of them fought in turn, except the Phocians, who were posted on the mountain to guard the path. [1] When the Persians found nothing different from what they saw the day before, they withdrew.

The king was at a loss as to how to deal with the present difficulty. Epialtes son of Eurydemus, a Malian, thinking he would get a great reward from the king, came to speak with him and told him of the path leading over the mountain

---

[1] For which see below, Hdt. 7.215, 216.

to Thermopylae. In so doing he caused the destruction of the Hellenes remaining there.

Later he fled into Thessaly in fear of the Lacedaemonians, and while he was in exile, a price was put on his head by the Pylagori ① when the Amphictyons assembled at Pylae. Still later he returned from exile to Anticyra and was killed by Athenades, a Trachinian.

Athenades slew Epialtes for a different reason, which I will tell later in my history, ② but he was given no less honor by the Lacedaemonians. It was in this way, then, that Epialtes was later killed.

There is another story told, namely that Onetes son of Phanagoras, a Carystian, and Corydallus of Anticyra are the ones who gave the king this information and guided the Persians around the mountain, but I find it totally incredible.

One must judge by the fact that the Pylagori set a price not on Onetes and Corydallus but on Epialtes the Trachinian, and I suppose they had exact knowledge; furthermore, we know that Epialtes was banished on this charge.

Onetes might have known the path, although he was not a Malian, if he had often come to that country, but Epialtes was the one who guided them along the path around the mountain. It is he whom I put on record as guilty.

Xerxes was pleased by what Epialtes promised to accomplish. He immediately became overjoyed and sent out Hydarnes and the men under Hydarnes command, who set forth from the camp at about lamp-lighting time. This path ③ had been discovered by the native Malians, who used it to guide the Thessalians into Phocis when the Phocians had fenced off the pass with a wall and were sheltered from the war. So long ago the Malians had discovered that

---

① Cp. Hdt. 7.200 (note).

② The expression suggests Herodotus' intention of continuing his history beyond 479, the year with which Book IX ends; but see How-Wells ad loc.

③ Plutarch in his life of Cato (13) describes the difficulty which troops under Cato's command encountered in trying to follow it.

the pass was in no way a good thing. [1]

The course of the path is as follows: it begins at the river Asopus as it flows through the ravine, and this mountain and the path have the same name, Anopaea. This Anopaea stretches along the ridge of the mountain and ends at Alpenus, the Locrian city nearest to Malis, near the rock called Blackbuttock and the seats of the Cercopes, where it is narrowest. [2]

This, then, was the nature of the pass. The Persians crossed the Asopus and travelled all night along this path, with the Oetaean mountains on their right and the Trachinian on their left. At dawn they came to the summit of the pass.

In this part of the mountain one thousand armed men of the Phocians were on watch, as I have already shown, defending their own country and guarding the path. The lower pass was held by those I have mentioned, but the Phocians had voluntarily promised Leonidas to guard the path over the mountain.

The Phocians learned in the following way that the Persians had climbed up: they had ascended without the Phocians' notice because the mountain was entirely covered with oak trees. Although there was no wind, a great noise arose like leaves being trodden underfoot. The Phocians jumped up and began to put on their weapons, and in a moment the barbarians were there.

When they saw the men arming themselves, they were amazed, for they had supposed that no opposition would appear, but they had now met with an army. Hydarnes feared that the Phocians might be Lacedaemonians and asked Epialtes what country the army was from. When he had established what he wanted to know with certainty, he arrayed the Persians for battle.

The Phocians, assailed by thick showers of arrows and supposing that the

---

[1] This is Steins interpretation; others make οὐδὲν χρηστὴ refer to the ἀτραπός, meaning there "pernicious."

[2] The Cercopes, mischievous dwarfs, had been warned against a "μελάμπυγος" enemy. Heracles, to rid the country of them, carried off two on his back, hanging head downwards, in which position they had every opportunity of observing his title to the above epithet; until their jests on the subject moved him to release them.

Persians had set out against them from the start, fled to the top of the mountain and prepared to meet their destruction. This is what they intended, but the Persians with Epialtes and Hydarnes paid no attention to the Phocians and went down the mountain as fast as possible.

The seer Megistias, examining the sacrifices, first told the Hellenes at Thermopylae that death was coming to them with the dawn. Then deserters came who announced the circuit made by the Persians. These gave their signals while it was still night; a third report came from the watchers running down from the heights at dawn.

The Hellenes then took counsel, but their opinions were divided. Some advised not to leave their post, but others spoke against them. They eventually parted, some departing and dispersing each to their own cities, others preparing to remain there with Leonidas.

It is said that Leonidas himself sent them away because he was concerned that they would be killed, but felt it not fitting for himself and the Spartans to desert that post which they had come to defend at the beginning.

I, however, tend to believe that when Leonidas perceived that the allies were dispirited and unwilling to run all risks with him, he told then to depart. For himself, however, it was not good to leave; if he remained, he would leave a name of great fame, and the prosperity of Sparta would not be blotted out.

When the Spartans asked the oracle about this war when it broke out, the Pythia had foretold that either Lacedaemon would be destroyed by the barbarians or their king would be killed. She gave them this answer in hexameter verses running as follows:

"For you, inhabitants of wide-wayed Sparta, Either your great and glorious city must be wasted by Persian men, Or if not that, then the bound of Lacedaemon must mourn a dead king, from Heracles' line. The might of bulls or lions will not restrain him with opposing strength; for he has the might of Zeus. I declare that he will not be restrained until he utterly tears apart one of these."

Considering this and wishing to win distinction for the Spartans alone, he sent away the allies rather than have them leave in disorder because of a difference of opinion.

Not the least proof I have of this is the fact that Leonidas publicly dismissed the seer who attended the expedition, for fear that he might die with them. This was Megistias the Acarnanian, said to be descended from Melampus, the one who told from the sacrifices what was going to happen to them. He was dismissed but did not leave; instead he sent away his only son who was also with the army.

Those allies who were dismissed went off in obedience to Leonidas, only the Thespians and Thebans remaining with the Lacedaemonians. The Thebans remained against their will and desire, for Leonidas kept them as hostages. The Thespians very gladly remained, saying they would not abandon Leonidas and those with him by leaving; instead they would stay and die with them. Their general was Demophilus son of Diadromes.

Xerxes made libations at sunrise and waiting till about mid-morning, made his assault. Epialtes had advised this, for the descent from the mountain is more direct, and the way is much shorter than the circuit and ascent.

Xerxes and his barbarians attacked, but Leonidas and his Hellenes, knowing they were going to their deaths, advanced now much farther than before into the wider part of the pass. In all the previous days they had sallied out into the narrow way and fought there, guarding the defensive wall.

Now, however, they joined battle outside the narrows and many of the barbarians fell, for the leaders of the companies beat everyone with whips from behind, urging them ever forward. Many of them were pushed into the sea and drowned; far more were trampled alive by each other, with no regard for who perished.

Since the Hellenes knew that they must die at the hands of those who had come around the mountain, they displayed the greatest strength they had against the barbarians, fighting recklessly and desperately.

By this time most of them had had their spears broken and were killing the Persians with swords. Leonidas, proving himself extremely valiant, fell in that struggle and with him other famous Spartans, whose names I have learned by inquiry since they were worthy men. Indeed, I have learned by inquiry the names of all three hundred. ①

Many famous Persians also fell there, including two sons of Darius, Abrocomes and Hyperanthes, born to Darius by Phratagune daughter of Artanes. Artanes was the brother of king Darius and son of Hystaspes son of Arsames. When he gave his daughter in marriage to Darius, he gave his whole house as dowry, since she was his only child.

Two brothers of Xerxes accordingly fought and fell there. There was a great struggle between the Persians and Lacedaemonians over Leonidas' body, until the Hellenes by their courageous prowess dragged it away and routed their enemies four times. The battle went on until the men with Epialtes arrived.

When the Hellenes saw that they had come, the contest turned, for they retired to the narrow part of the way, passed behind the wall, and took their position crowded together on the hill, all except the Thebans. This hill is at the mouth of the pass, where the stone lion in honor of Leonidas now stands.

In that place they defended themselves with swords, if they still had them, and with hands and teeth. The barbarians buried them with missiles, some attacking from the front and throwing down the defensive wall, others surrounding them on all sides.

This then is how the Lacedaemonians and Thespians conducted themselves, but the Spartan Dieneces is said to have exhibited the greatest courage of all. They say that he made the following speech before they joined battle with the Medes: he had learned from a Trachinian that there were so many of

---

① Leonidas' body was brought to Sparta and there buried in 440; a column was erected on his grave bearing the names of the three hundred, which Herodotus probably saw.

the barbarians that when they shot their missiles, the sun was hidden by the multitude of their arrows.

He was not at all disturbed by this and made light of the multitude of the Medes, saying that their Trachinian foreigner brought them good news. If the Medes hid the sun, they could fight them in the shade instead of in the sun. This saying and others like it, they claim, Dieneces the Lacedaemonian left behind as a memorial.

Next after him two Lacedaemonian brothers, Alpheus and Maron, sons of Orsiphantus, are said to have been most courageous. The Thespian who gained most renown was one whose name was Dithyrambus son of Harmatides.

There is an inscription written over these men, who were buried where they fell, and over those who died before the others went away, dismissed by Leonidas. It reads as follows: "Here four thousand from the Peloponnese once fought three million."

That inscription is for them all, but the Spartans have their own: "Foreigner, go tell the Spartans that we lie here obedient to their commands."

That one is to the Lacedaemonians, this one to the seer: "This is a monument to the renowned Megistias, Slain by the Medes who crossed the Spercheius river. The seer knew well his coming doom, But endured not to abandon the leaders of Sparta."

Except for the seer's inscription, the Amphictyons are the ones who honored them by erecting inscriptions and pillars. That of the seer Megistias was inscribed by Simonides son of Leoprepes because of his tie of guest-friendship with the man. [1]

It is said that two of these three hundred, Eurytus and Aristodemus, could have agreed with each other either to come home safely together to Sparta, since Leonidas had dismissed them from the camp and they were lying at Alpeni very

---

[1] As a matter of fact Simonides composed all three inscriptions; but the epitaph of Megistias was the only one which he made at his own cost.

sick of ophthalmia, or to die with the others, if they were unwilling to return home. They could have done either of these things, but they could not agree and had different intentions. When Eurytus learned of the Persians circuit, he demanded his armor and put it on, bidding his helot to lead him to the fighting. The helot led him there and fled, but he rushed into the fray and was killed. Aristodemus, however, lost his strength and stayed behind.

Now if Aristodemus alone had been sick and returned to Sparta, or if they had both made the trip, I think the Spartans would not have been angry with them. When, however, one of them died, and the other had the same excuse but was unwilling to die, the Spartans had no choice but to display great anger towards Aristodemus.

Some say that Aristodemus came home safely to Sparta in this way and by this excuse. Others say that he had been sent out of the camp as a messenger and could have gotten back in time for the battle but chose not to, staying behind on the road and so surviving, while his fellow-messenger arrived at the battle and was killed.

When Aristodemus returned to Lacedaemon, he was disgraced and without honor. He was deprived of his honor in this way: no Spartan would give him fire or speak with him, and they taunted him by calling him Aristodemus the Trembler. In the battle at Plataea, however, he made up for all the blame brought against him.

It is said that another of the three hundred survived because he was sent as a messenger to Thessaly. His name was Pantites. When he returned to Sparta, he was dishonored and hanged himself.

The Thebans, whose general was Leontiades, fought against the king's army as long as they were with the Hellenes and under compulsion. When, however, they saw the Persian side prevailing and the Hellenes with Leonidas hurrying toward the hill, they split off and approached the barbarians, holding out their hands. With the most truthful words ever spoken, they explained that they were

Medizers, had been among the first to give earth and water to the king, had come to Thermopylae under constraint, and were guiltless of the harm done to the king.

By this plea they saved their lives, and the Thessalians bore witness to their words. They were not, however, completely lucky. When the barbarians took hold of them as they approached, they killed some of them even as they drew near. Most of them were branded by Xerxes command with the kings marks, starting with the general Leontiades. His son Eurymachus long afterwards [1] was murdered by the Plataeans when, as general of four hundred Thebans, he seized the town of Plataea.

一　文献出处

Herodotus, *Histories*, with an English translation by A. D. Godley, Cambridge: Harvard University Press, 1920.

二　文献导读

希罗多德（Herodotus，约公元前 484~ 前 430/420 年），古希腊著名历史学家、文学家、地理学家和旅行家，其所撰写的《历史》被公认为是西方史学史上第一部叙事体历史著作，故而被尊为"历史之父"。

与古希腊许多著名人物相仿，关于希罗多德的生平，流传下来的资料极其稀少。据说希罗多德出生于波斯统治下的小亚细亚西岸的希腊城市哈利卡那苏斯［Halicarnassus，今土耳其的博德鲁姆（Bodrum）］。希罗多德系出名门，父亲吕克瑟斯是当地的富人，他的叔父（一说堂兄弟）帕尼亚西斯是一位著名的史诗作家，据说曾经撰写过伊奥尼亚诸邦建城的史诗。希罗多德从小受到良好的教育，天资聪颖，勤奋好学，对赫西俄德、贺卡

---

[1]　In 431; cp. Thuc. 2.2 ff.

泰乌斯、梭伦等人的作品耳熟能详。公元前 461 年，希罗多德家族参与了反对当地听命于波斯人的僭主吕戈达米斯的斗争，但遭到失败，帕尼亚西斯被杀害，希氏受到株连也被迫迁居萨摩斯岛，哈利卡那苏斯本属多利亚方言区，在萨摩斯岛他开始学习伊奥尼亚方言，后来的《历史》就是用伊奥尼亚方言撰写的。

大约从公元前 455 年起，希罗多德开始了多年外出游历的生活，足迹遍布波斯帝国的大部分地区。除了小亚的城市外，他曾经到过巴比伦、腓尼基、埃及、利比亚、意大利、拜占庭、色雷斯、马其顿，甚至向北渡过伊斯特河（Ister，今多瑙河）进入斯基台，沿黑海北岸直抵顿河及其腹地。在古代交通条件极为恶劣的情况下，他不畏艰险，完成了如此惊人的长途跋涉。这期间，他每到一地，都会遍访名胜古迹，考察风土人情，搜集民间传说和轶闻趣事，积累了极为丰富的第一手资料，为后来《历史》的创作打下了坚实的基础。

大约在公元前 447 年，希罗多德来到了雅典。是时的雅典已经成为希腊世界的经济、政治和文化中心，成为"希腊的学校"。在居留雅典期间，希罗多德与雅典的"第一公民"伯利克里和戏剧家索福克利斯等社会名流有着密切的交往，他积极参与城邦的文化教育活动，据说曾经当众朗诵过自己的作品，并且获得一笔丰厚的奖金。公元前 443 年，希罗多德移居到雅典在意大利的殖民城邦图里（Thurii，在今天意大利半岛南部），在那里他专心著述，直至去世。虽然希氏去世的时间还存在争议，但可以肯定的是，公元前 425 年前后，他的《历史》已经完成并且广为人知了。

在希罗多德之前，公元前 6 世纪小亚地区曾经出现过一些"散文纪事家"（Logographoi），以简洁的散文形式把关于城市、民族、神庙等起源的口头传说记录下来，这些作品虽然已具备历史著作的雏形，但还不是真正意义上的历史著作。同时，在希罗多德之前，记述认为过往的"历史"和探询世界本源的"哲学"并无严格区别，二者都以探求真理为特征，在希腊语中，"历史"的本意即"探究""调查"。希罗多德以"历史"为自己的著作命名，并赋予这个词新的含义，从而开创了历史编纂的传统。

《历史》的主要内容是记述希腊波斯战争的缘起和过程，探讨希腊人是如何战胜人数众多的异族人的。但纵观全书，除了记述希波战争外，还有另外一个主题，就是全面记述希腊人所知道的周边各个民族的地理环境、社会生活和风土人情。《历史》全书共有 9 卷，明显地分为前、后两个部分。第一部分从开始到第 5 卷第 27 节，主要记述波斯帝国的兴起和扩张经过，从居鲁士率领波斯各部揭竿而起，反抗米底人的统治，到冈比西斯不断对外扩张，大流士一世改组帝国统治机构并准备进攻希腊为止。当中，希氏用较大的篇幅基本上按照波斯征服这些地区的顺序记述了吕底亚、米底、巴比伦、埃及、波斯、斯基台等地的地理、物产、风土人情、历史和现状。第二部分从第 5 卷第 28 节开始到全书结束，希罗多德集中地记述了希波战争的经过。这一部分从叙述小亚的伊奥尼亚诸邦的暴动开始，大体按照时间顺序记述了大流士镇压暴动并出兵希腊，在马拉松遭到败绩，接着薛西斯倾其整个帝国之力对希腊发动空前规模的进攻，斯巴达国王里奥尼达及其三百勇士在温泉关誓死抵抗，希腊海上联军在撒拉米斯湾海上战役的胜利，直到公元前 479 年希腊人又连续取得了普拉提亚的陆战和米卡尔海角战役的海战胜利，波斯势力退出爱琴海地区为止。全书正叙和插叙相结合，线索明晰，重点突出，中心明确，结构完整。

《历史》是希腊乃至于西方史学史上一部划时代的巨著，希罗多德一方面承继了散文纪事家每闻必录的特点，又开创了客观记述、力求真实的历史批判精神，其史学成就表现在以下几个方面：第一，希罗多德既是西方史学史上第一位真正意义上的历史学家，也是第一个拥有总体史的视野和"世界眼光"的历史学家。虽然该书以政治和军事内容为主，但记述历史的范围远远超出了这两个领域，包括地理环境、经济生活、民族分布、宗教信仰、风俗习惯等都有十分详尽的记载。与此同时，他并没有把眼光仅仅局限在希腊人和波斯人的活动上，而是扩大到当时希腊人已经知道的几乎整个世界，堪称是一部古代世界的百科全书式的历史著作。第二，在记述所见所闻的基础上，展开充分的实地调查，并试图探究种种历史现象背后的原因，探讨地理环境对人类社会的影响，在方法和理论上为历史学、地理学、民俗学、人类学、考古学等多种学科的产生和发展奠定了基础。第三，虽然不可避免地带有诸如"每闻必录"这样的早期史学的缺陷，但总体上看，作者还是以探求真理和客观记述为宗旨。例如，希氏在著作中没有表现出所谓的"文明的希腊人"和"落后的蛮族人"这样的种族歧视观念，而是以平等的眼光看待各民族之间的差异，不论是希腊人的还是异族的东西，凡是值得赞叹的都予以肯定和颂扬。第四，希罗多德虽然生活在一个宗教观念和迷信思想仍然十分浓厚的时代，神谕和占卜十分盛行，但在历史事件的记述中，希罗多德还是坚持以记载"人事"为本位，强调人在历史发展进程中的决定作用。例如，他对希腊人战胜波斯人的原因的分析，始终从"天时""地利""人和"以及战略战术等方面入手，闪耀出人本主义和唯物主义思想的光辉。

不过，在充分肯定这部著作的历史价值和开创性的同时，我们也要看到作为古希腊第一部历史著作，它还是存在着种种缺陷和不足之处，这是十分正常和在所难免的。比如，他在记述某些见闻的时候缺乏认真和细致的考证和批判，再有就是在叙述史事的时候常常枝蔓横生，偏离主题，等等。我们既需要通过研究指出这些不足，又不能完全用现代的眼光去过分地苛求古人。

上文即节选自《历史》的第 6 卷和第 7 卷，内容是希波战争中的两次最重要也是最著名的战役，即马拉松战役和温泉关战役。

三 延伸阅读

Cartledge, Paul, *Thermopylae: The Battle that Changed the World*, New York, 2006.

Fornara, C.W., *Herodotus: An Interpretative Essay*, Oxford, 1971.

Godolphin, Francis R.B., ed., *The Greek Historians*, translated by George Rawlinson, New York, 1942.

Gould, J., *Herodotus*, London, 1989.

Myres, J.L., *Herodotus: Father of History*, Oxford, 1953.

How, W.W., and J. Wells, *A Commentary on Herodotus*, in two volumes, Oxford, 1979.

Thucydides: The History of the Peloponnesian War [*]

'Most of those who have spoken here before me have commended the lawgiver who [①] added this oration to our other funeral customs; it seemed to them a worthy thing that such an honour should be given at their burial to the dead who have fallen on the field of battle. But I should have preferred that, when men's deeds have been brave, they should be honoured in deed only, and with such an honour as this public funeral, which you are now witnessing. Then the reputation of many would not have been imperilled on the eloquence or want of eloquence of one, and their virtues believed or not as he spoke well or ill. For it is difficult to say neither too little nor too much; and even moderation is apt not to give the impression of truthfulness. The friend of the dead who knows the facts is likely to think that the words of the speaker fall short of his knowledge and of his wishes; another who is not so well informed, when he hears of anything which surpasses his own powers, will be envious and will suspect exaggeration. Mankind are tolerant of the praises of others so long as each hearer thinks that he can do as well or nearly as well

---

[*] 修昔底德《伯罗奔尼撒战争史》节选。本文选自该书的第 2 卷第 35~46 小节，内容为伯利克里在阵亡将士墓前的演说。以下皆为英译本原书注释。

[①] The law which enjoins this oration has been often praised. But I should prefer to praise the brave by deeds only, not to imperil their reputation on the skill of an orator. Still, our ancestors approved the practice, and I must obey.

himself, but, when the speaker rises above him, jealousy is aroused and he begins to be incredulous.However, since our ancestors have set the seal of their approval upon the practice, I must obey, and to the utmost of my power shall endeavour to satisfy the wishes and beliefs of all who hear me.

'I will speak first of our ancestors, for it is right and seemly that now, when we are lamenting [1] the dead, a tribute should be paid to their memory. There has never been a time when they did not inhabit this land, which by their valour they have handed down from generation to generation, and we have received from them a free state. But if they were worthy of praise, still more were our fathers, who added to their inheritance, and after many a struggle transmitted to us their sons this great empire. And we ourselves assembled here to-day, who are still most of us in the vigour of life, have carried the work of improvement further, and have richly endowed our city with all things, so that she is sufficient for herself both in peace and war. Of the military exploits by which our various possessions were acquired, or of the energy with which we or our fathers drove back the tide of war, Hellenic or Barbarian, I will not speak; for the tale would be long and is familiar to you. But before I praise the dead, I should like to point out by what principles of action we rose [2] to power, and under what institutions and through what manner of life our empire became great, For I conceive that such thoughts are not unsuited to the occasion, and that this numerous assembly of citizens and strangers may profitably listen to them.

'Our form of government does not enter into rivalry with the institutions of others. We [3] do not copy our neighbours, but are an example to them. It is true that we are called a democracy, for the administration is in the hands of the

---

[1] I will first common rate our predecessors, who gave us freedom and empire. And before praising the dead, I will describe how Athens has won her greatness.

[2] Reading ἤλθομεν.

[3] Our government is a democracy, but we honour men of merit, whether rich or poor. Our public life is free from exclusiveness, our private from suspicion; yet we revere alike the injunctions of law and custom.

many and not of the few. But while the law secures equal justice to all alike in their private disputes, the claim of excellence is also recognized; and when a citizen is in any way distinguished, he is preferred to the public service, not as a matter of privilege, but as the reward of merit. Neither is poverty a bar, but a man may benefit his country whatever be the obscurity of his condition. There is no exclusiveness in our public life, and in our private intercourse we are not suspicious of one another, nor angry with our neighbour if he does what he likes; we do not put on sour looks at him which, though harmless, are not pleasant. While we are thus unconstrained in our private intercourse, a spirit of reverence pervades our public acts; we are prevented from doing wrong by respect for the authorities and for the laws, having an especial regard to those which are ordained for the protection of the injured as well as to those unwritten laws which bring upon the transgressor of them the reprobation of the general sentiment.

'And we have not forgotten to provide for our weary spirits many relaxations from toil; we [①] have regular games and sacrifices throughout the year; our homes are beautiful and elegant; and the delight which we daily feel in all these things helps to banish melancholy. Because of the greatness of our city the fruits of the whole earth flow in upon us; so that we enjoy the goods of other countries as freely as of our own.

'Then, again, our military training is in many respects superior to that of our adversaries. [②] Our city is thrown open to the world, and we never expel a foreigner or prevent him from seeing or learning anything of which the secret if revealed to an enemy might profit him. We rely not upon management or trickery, but upon our own hearts and hands. And in the matter of education, whereas they from early youth are always undergoing laborious exercises which

---

[①] We find relaxation in our amusements, and in our homes; and the whole world contributes to our enjoyment.

[②] In war we singly are a match for the Peloponnesian united; through we have no secrets and undergo no laborious training.

are to make them brave, we live at ease, and yet are equally ready to face [①] the perils which they face. And here is the proof. The Lacedaemonians come into Attica not by themselves, but with their whole confederacy following; we go alone into a neighbour's country; and although our opponents are fighting for their homes and we on a foreign soil, we have seldom any difficulty in overcoming them. Our enemies have never yet felt our united strength; the care of a navy divides our attention, and on land we are obliged to send our own citizens everywhere. But they, if they meet and defeat a part of our army, are as proud as if they had routed us all, and when defeated they pretend to have been vanquished by us all.

'If then we prefer to meet danger with a light heart but without laborious training, and with [②] a courage which is gained by habit and not enforced by law, are we not greatly the gainers? Since we do not anticipate the pain, although, when the hour comes, we can be as brave as those who never allow themselves to rest; and thus too our city is equally admirable in peace and in war.

For we are lovers of the beautiful, yet simple in our tastes, and we cultivate the mind without loss of manliness. Wealth we employ, not for talk and ostentation, but when there is a real use for it. To avow poverty with us is no disgrace; the true disgrace is in doing nothing to avoid it. An Athenian citizen does not neglect the state because he takes care of his own household; and even those of us who are engaged in business have a very fair idea of politics. We alone regard a man who takes no interest in public affairs, not as a harmless, but as a useless character; and if few of us are originators, we are all sound judges of a policy. The great impediment to action is, in our opinion, not discussion, but the want of that knowledge which is gained by discussion preparatory to action. For we have a peculiar power of thinking before we act and of acting too, whereas other men are courageous from ignorance but hesitate upon reflection. And they are surely

---

① Or, 'perils such as our strength can bear;' or 'perils which are enough to daunt us.'

② We are not enervated by culture, or vulgarised by wealth. We are all interested in public affairs, believing that nothing is lost by frce discussion. Our goodness to others springs not from interest, but from the generous confidence of freedom.

to be esteemed the bravest spirits who, having the clearest sense both of the pains and pleasures of life, do not on that account shrink from danger. In doing good, again, we are unlike others; we make our friends by conferring, not by receiving favours. Now he who confers a favour is the firmer friend, because he would fain by kindness keep alive the memory of an obligation; but the recipient is colder in his feelings, because he knows that in requiting another's generosity he will not be winning gratitude but only paying a debt. We alone do good to our neighbours not upon a calculation of interest, but in the confidence of freedom and in a frank and fearless spirit.

To sum up: I say that Athens is the school of Hellas, [①] and that the individual Athenian in his own person seems to have the power of adapting himself to the most varied forms of action with the utmost versatility and grace. This is no passing and idle word, but truth and fact; and the assertion is verified by the position to which these qualities have raised the state. For in the hour of trial Athens alone among her contemporaries is superior to the report of her. No enemy who comes against her is indignant at the reverses which he sustains at the hands of such a city; no subject complains that his masters are unworthy of him. And we shall assuredly not be without witnesses; there are mighty monuments of our power which will make us the wonder of this and of succeeding ages; we shall not need the praises of Homer or of any other panegyrist whose poetry may please for the moment [②], although his representation of the facts will not bear the light of day. For we have compelled every land and every sea to open a path for our valour, and have everywhere planted eternal memorials of our friendship and of our enmity. Such is the city for whose sake these men nobly fought and died; they could not bear the thought that she might be taken from them; and every one of us who survive should gladly toil on her behalf.

---

① In fine, Athens is the school of Hellas. She alone in the hour of trial rises above her reputation. Her citizens need no poet to sing their praises: for every land bears witness to their valour.

② Cp. 1.10 med., and 21.

'I have dwelt upon the greatness of Athens because I want to show you that we are contending[①] for a higher prize than those who enjoy none of these privileges, and to establish by manifest proof the merit of these men whom I am now commemorating. Their loftiest praise has been already spoken. For in magnifying the city I have magnified them, and men like them whose virtues made her glorious. And of how few Hellenes can it be said as of them, that their deeds when weighed in the balance have been found equal to their fame! Methinks that a death such as theirs has been gives the true measure of a man's worth; it may be the first revelation of his virtues, but is at any rate their final seal. For even those who come short in other ways may justly plead the valour with which they have fought for their country; they have blotted out the evil with the good, and have benefited the state more by their public services than they have injured her by their private actions. None of these men were enervated by wealth or hesitated to resign the pleasures of life; none of them put off the evil day in the hope, natural to poverty, that a man, though poor, may one day become rich. But, deeming that the punishment of their enemies was sweeter than any of these things, and that they could fall in no nobler cause, they determined at the hazard of their lives to be honourably avenged, and to leave the rest. They resigned to hope their unknown chance of happiness; but in the face of death they resolved to rely upon themselves alone. And when the moment came they were minded to resist and suffer, rather than to fly and save their lives; they ran away from the word of dishonour, but on the battle-field their feet stood fast, and[②] in an instant, at the height of their fortune, they passed away from the scene, not of their fear, but of their glory[③].

---

① The praise of the city is the praise of these men, for they made her great. Good and bad, rich and poor alike, preferred death to dishonour.

② Or, taking τύχης with καιροῦ: "while for a moment they were in the hands of fortune, at the height, not of terror but of glory, they passed away."

③ Or, taking τύχης with καιροῦ: "while for a moment they were in the hands of fortune, at the height, not of terror but of glory, they passed away."

'such was the end of these men; they were worthy of Athens, and the living need not desire [①] to have a more heroic spirit, although they may pray for a less fatal issue. The value of such a spirit is not to be expressed in words. Any one can discourse to you for ever about the advantages of a brave defence, which you know already. But instead of listening to him I would have you day by day fix your eyes upon the greatness of Athens, until you become filled with the love of her; and when you are impressed by the spectacle of her glory, reflect that this empire has been acquired by men who knew their duty and had the courage to do it, who in the hour of conflict had the fear of dishonour always present to them, and who, if ever they failed in an enterprise, would not allow their virtues to be lost to their country, but freely gave their lives to her as the fairest offering which they could present at her feast. The sacrifice which they collectively made was individually repaid to them; for they received again each one for himself a praise which grows not old, and the noblest of all sepulchers—I speak not of that in which their remains are laid, but of that in which their glory survives, and is proclaimed always and on every fitting occasion both in word and deed. For the whole earth is the sepulchre of famous men; not only are they commemorated by columns and inscriptions in their own country, but in foreign lands there dwells also an unwritten memorial of them, graven not on stone but in the hearts of men. Make them your examples, and, esteeming courage to be freedom and freedom to be happiness, do not weigh too nicely the perils of war. The unfortunate who has no hope of a change for the better has less reason to throw away his life than the prosperous who, if he survive, is always liable to a change for the worse, and to whom any accidental fall makes the most serious difference. To a man of spirit, cowardice and disaster coming together are far more bitter than death striking him unperceived at a time when he is full of courage and animated by the general hope.

---

① Contemplate and love Athens, and you will know how to value them. They were united in their deaths, but their glory is separate and single. Their sepulchre is the remembrance of them in the hearts of men. Follow their example Without fear: it is the prosperous, not the unfortunate, who should be reckless.

'Wherefore I do not now commiserate the parents of the dead who stand here; I would rather^① comfort them. You know that your life has been passed amid manifold vicissitudes; and that they may be deemed fortunate who have gained most honour, whether an honourable death like theirs, or an honourable sorrow like yours, and whose days have been so ordered that the term of their happiness is likewise the term of their life. I know how hard it is to make you feel this, when the good fortune of others will too often remind you of the gladness which once lightened your hearts. And sorrow is felt at the want of those blessings, not which a man never knew, but which were a part of his life before they were taken from him. Some of you are of an age at which they may hope to have other children, and they ought to bear their sorrow better; not only will the children who may hereafter be born make them forget their own lost ones, but the city will be doubly a gainer. She will not be left desolate, and she will be safer. For a man's counsel cannot have equal weight or worth, when he alone has no children to risk in the general danger. To those of you who have passed their prime, I say: ' Congratulate yourselves that you have been happy during the greater part of your days; remember that your life of sorrow will not last long, and be comforted by the glory of those who are gone. For the love of honour alone is ever young, and not riches, as some say, but honour is the delight of men when they are old and useless. '

'To you who are the sons and brothers of the departed, I see that the struggle to emulate them^② will be an arduous one. For all men praise the dead, and, however preeminent your virtue may be, hardly will you be thought, I do not say to equal, but even to approach them. The living have their rivals and detractors, but when a man is out of the way, the honour and good-will which he receives

---

① The parents of the dead are to be comforted rather than pitied. Some of them may yet have children who will lighten their sorrow and serve the state; while others should remember how large their share of happiness has been, and be consoled by the glory of those who are gone.

② Sons and brothers will find their example hard to imitate, for men are jealous of the living, but envy follows not the dead. Let the widows restrain their natural weakness, and avoid both praise and blame.

is unalloyed. And, if I am to speak of womanly virtues to those of you who will
henceforth be widows, let me sum them up in one short admonition: To a woman
not to show more weakness than is natural to her sex is a great glory, and not to
be talked about for good or for evil among men.

'I have paid the required tribute, in obedience to the law, making use of such
fitting words ① as I had. The tribute of deeds has been paid in part; for the dead
have been honourably interred, and it remains only that their children should be
maintained at the public charge until they are grown up: this is the solid prize
with which, as with a garland, Athens crowns her sons living and dead, after
a struggle like theirs. For where the rewards of virtue are greatest, there the
noblest citizens are enlisted in the service of the state. And now, when you have
duly lamented, every one his own dead, you may depart.'

一　文献出处

Thucydides, *The Hsitory of the Peloponnesian War*, translated by Benjamin
Jowett, Oxford: Clarendon Press, 1881.

二　文献导读

伯利克里（Pericles，约公元前 495~ 前 429 年）在雅典阵亡将士墓前
的演说是古代世界演说辞中脍炙人口的名篇。该演说发表于希腊伯罗奔尼
撒战争刚刚爆发的公元前 431 年冬天，全文收录在修昔底德（Thucydides，
约公元前 460~ 前 400/ 前 396 年）的《伯罗奔尼撒战争史》的第 2 卷第六
章当中。

墓前演说是希腊演说辞中十分重要和普遍的一种类型，是城邦为那些
在战争中阵亡的公民兵组织的集体公葬仪式的一个组成部分，演说者通常

---

① So have I paid a due tribute of words to the dead. The city will pay them in deeds, as by this
funeral, so too by the maintenance of their children.

是城邦的军事首领或德高望重的人物。墓前演说辞在开篇、起承转合以及结尾也有一些固定的程式和规定。修昔底德在这篇演说辞的前面对雅典人墓前演说的传统和程序做了如下的介绍：

> 在同一个冬季，雅典人要对那些在这次战斗中首批阵亡的将士予以公葬。按照他们祖先的习惯，公葬的仪式是这样举行的：在葬礼的三天前，把死者的遗骨运回来，安置在一个事先做好的帐篷中，他们的朋友可以拿他们所愿意拿的任何祭品带给死者的家属。在举行葬礼游行时，用四轮马车载着柏木棺材，各部落死者的遗骨装在各部落的棺材里。……不论是公民还是异邦人，只要愿意，都可以参加这个游行，死者的女性亲属在墓前志哀。遗骨被安葬在公共墓地，这是市郊一块风景如画的地区。雅典人总是把阵亡将士安葬在这里。……当遗骨被埋葬以后，雅典城邦选择一名他们认为最有智慧和最有威望的人发表演说，以讴歌阵亡者。演说之后，大家就地解散。这就是葬礼的程序。在整个战争中，每当雅典人安葬其阵亡将士时，人们都能够看到这种早已确定下来的习俗。这些将士是首批阵亡的，桑西浦斯之子伯利克里被推举出来发表演说。

这篇演说发表于伯罗奔尼撒战争的初始阶段，作为修昔底德作品中唯一的一篇墓前演说，其用意是十分明确的，那就是鼓舞雅典人的士气，它的核心思想是向雅典人和全体希腊人说明，雅典人是强大的，是有资格统辖臣属诸邦的，而弱者屈从于强者是天经地义的。作为雅典民主政制"黄金时代"的代表人物和亲历者，伯利克里现身说法，热情讴歌了雅典直接民主制度的原创性和优越性，演说辞全篇充满激情，饱含着骄傲、自豪和战胜敌人的乐观情绪。

从内容上讲，演说辞大体可以分为三个部分：第一部分包括第 35 节和第 36 节，首先简要说明阵亡将士墓前演说习俗的价值和准则，提出对死者的颂扬既是必要的，又要恰如其分；然后，歌颂雅典人光荣的祖先，回顾自由的传统；最后，指出雅典今天的强大完全得益于一种优良的"政体"和"民族习惯",为接下来的全面阐发做好铺垫。第二部分从第37节到第41节,是演说最重要和最具原创性的部分,伯利克里从雅典的民主制度及其优越性、精神和物质文化的丰富性、军事政策、教育制度、中庸之道等诸方面全面阐发雅典城邦的伟大,最后得出结论,"一言以蔽之,我们的城邦是全希腊人的学校","只有雅典,入侵的敌人不以战败为耻"。第三部分从第42节到第46节,回到演说的正题,即对阵亡将士进行颂扬,细述死者的光荣和生者的责任,安慰死者的家人,这一部分与第一部分相似,大部分是墓前演说的例行话语,但在吊唁死者、告慰生者的过程中也透露出雅典人对生死和妇女等问题的看法。

演说辞和对话的大量运用是修昔底德的这部史著最突出的特色之一,据统计,演说辞大约占据了全书篇幅的1/4。对于这些演说辞的产生过程,修昔底德做了如下说明:

> 在这部历史著作中,我援引了一些演说辞……有些演说辞是我亲耳听到的,有些是通过各种渠道得到的。无论如何,单凭一个人的记忆是很难逐字逐句记载下来的。我的习惯是这样的:一方面使演说者说出我认为各种场合所要说的话,另一方面当然要尽可能保持实际所讲的话的大意。

修昔底德生于雅典,有证据表明,从公元前431年战争爆发,到公元前424年他担任将军为止的七年间,他一直生活在雅典,而且,据他自己讲,从战争之初他就开始搜集有关资料撰写这部历史著作了,因此,伯利克里的这篇演说无疑属于"亲耳聆听"的一类,其真实性自然大于后一类。但在那时,毕竟没有"实录"的条件,就连修昔底德本人也不否认这些演说辞中含有追忆和撰述的成分,演说不可能是逐字逐句的"实录",记录者的提炼、加工、润色在所难免。修昔底德生活在一个口头资料占据主导地位的时代,在记述这些演说的过程中,也就难免在这些演说中夹杂进自己的看法,或者记录者和演说者的思想兼而有之,或者是一种带有创造性的记录,但这篇演说作为时代精神的真实反映这一点来说还是可以肯定的。原因在于，修昔底德是伯罗奔尼撒战争的一位"有心的"亲历者，亲耳聆听了这篇演说，属于当代人记当代事，同时，作为希罗多德之后的新一代史家，其全书对史料的处理始终贯以十分严格的批判精神。因此，正是以这种真实性为前提，这篇演说才能成为我们今天学习和研究雅典民主政治最重要的文献资料之一。

与此同时，尽管这篇演说的真实性可以肯定，但它毕竟是阐发雅典民主政治的"一面之词"。在这里，我们充分地看到了民主政体为雅典带来的国家的强盛、思想和文化的繁荣以及相对自由和多元的社会环境，但却看不到这种政体的种种局限性和隐藏的危机。就在这篇演说发表之后不久，雅典爆发了史无前例的大瘟疫，战争之初的乐观情绪被一扫而空，同时，雅典激进民主制度的问题也开始在一次又一次重大决策失误中暴露无遗。因此，要了解雅典的民主制度，仅仅依靠这篇"全面肯定"的文献是远远不够的，实际上，在雅典民主政治的鼎盛时期，一股强劲的"反民主思潮"也正在悄然兴起，而且势头越来越大。就在这篇演说发表的时候，伯利克里本人也正在陷入种种个人的丑闻和危机当中。这些都是我们在阅读这篇饱含骄傲自豪和理想主义光辉的文献时所应该加以注意的。

三　延伸阅读

Bowra, C.M., *Periclean Athens*, Lodon, 1971.

Connor, W.R., *Thucydides*, Princedon, 1984.

Cornford, F.M., *Thucydides Mythistoricus*, New York, 1907.

Croix, G.E.M. de Ste., *The Origins of the Peloponnesian War*, London, 1972.

Dover, J.K., *Thucydides*, Oxford, 1973.

Gomme, A.W., and A.Andrews, K.J.Dove, *A Historical Commentary on Thucydides*, Vol. IV, Oxford, 1945-1981.

Hornblower, S., A *Commentary on Thucydides*, Oxford, 1991.

Loraux, Nicole, *The Invention of Athens: The Funeral Oration in the Classical City*, New York, 2006.

Xenophon: Economics *

CHAPTER 4

"But why must you display all of them, Socrates?" said Critoboulus. "It's not easy to get possession of the kinds of workers that are necessary in all the arts; nor is it possible to become experienced in them; but the kinds of knowledge that are reputed to be the noblest and would be especially suitable for my concern—these you must display for me, as well as those who practice them, and you yourself must do what you can to benefit me in these matters by teaching me."

"You speak nobly, Critoboulus, " he said. "For indeed those that are called mechanical are spoken against everywhere and have quite plausibly come by a very bad reputation in the cities. For they utterly ruin the bodies of those who work at them and those who are concerned with them, [1] compelling them to sit still and remain indoors, [2] or in some cases even to spend the whole day by a fire. And when the bodies are made effeminate, the souls too become much

---

* 色诺芬《经济论》节选。本文选自该书的第四章和第五章。

[1] A distinction seems intended here between the workers and those who are merely "concerned" with the work, i.e., overseers of some kind. Cf.4.10 and 5.4.

[2] Literally," to sit and nourish themselves with shadows."

more diseased. Lack of leisure to join in the concerns of friends and of the city is another condition of those that are called mechanical; those who practice them are reputed to be bad friends as well as bad defenders of their fatherlands. indeed in some of the cities, especially those reputed to be good at war, no citizen is allowed to work at the mechanical arts."

"Then as for us, Socrates, which do you advise we make use of？ "

"Should we be ashamed," said Socrates, "to imitate the king of Persia? For they say he believes farming and the art of war are among the noblest and most necessary concerns, and concerns himself emphatically with both of them."

After having heard this, Critoboulus spoke."Do you take this too on trust, Socrates," he said. "that the king of Persia concerns himself in some way with farming?"

"If we investigate the matter as follows, Critoboulus," said Socrates, "perhaps we may learn whether in some way he does concern himself with it. We agree he is emphatically concerned with the works of war, since it is he who gives orders to the rulers of however many nations send him tribute, regarding just how many horsemen and archers and slingers and targeteers each must maintain, that they may be sufficient both to control the ruled and to defend the country should enemies invade it. Apart from these he maintains guards in the citadels, and the rulers are ordered in addition to provide maintenance for these garrisons. Every year the king holds an inspection of the mercenaries and the others he has ordered to be in arms, bringing together at various points of assembly all except those in the citadels. Those near his own residence he surveys himself; those further away he sends trusted officers to examine; and whichever rulers of garrison and field troops [1] and the satraps look to have the full number as ordered and provide them equipped with splendid horses and arms, these rulers

---

[1] "Garrison commanders" (*phrourarchoi*) and "commanders of a thousand" (*chiliarchoi*); the latter term may also designate the rule of a(Persian)military district. Xenophon goes on to suggest that these are "rulers" (*archontes*) not only in name.

he increases with honors and enriches with great presents; but whichever rulers he finds have neglected the garrisons or looked to their own profit, these he punishes harshly and, removing them from rule, appoints others more diligent. In doing these things, then, it seems to us he is indisputably concerned with the works of war. Again, whatever part of the country he rides through he surveys himself, and scrutinizes, and what he doesn't survey himself he examines by sending out trusted officers. And whichever rulers he perceives have provided that the country is well inhabited and that the earth is productive and replete with crops and with every kind of tree that it bears, these he enlarges with new territory, adorns With presents, and rewards with seats of honor; but whichever he sees have an inactive ① Country and few human beings, whether through harshness or arrogance or neglect, these he punishes and, removing them from rule, appoints other rulers. In doing these things, then, does he seem any less concerned that the earth be made productive by its inhabitants than that it be well guarded by the garrisons? The rulers he has ordered to each thing are, furthermore, not the same, but certain ones rule the inhabitants and the workers and collect taxes from them, and certain others rule the armed garrisons. ②
And if the ruler of the garrison doesn't sufficiently defend the country, the one who rules the inhabitants and is concerned with the works brings an accusation against him on the ground that the people cannot work because of the lack of a guard; but if the ruler of the garrison provides peace for the works, while the ruler provides but few human beings and an inactive country, then the ruler of the garrison brings an accusation against him. For those who work the land badly will hardly be able either to maintain the garrisons or to pay taxes. But wherever a satrap is appointed, he concerns himself with both these things."

---

① *Argos*, "inactive" or "lazy" (as in I. 19, 16.4), is the opposite of *energos*, "productive" both are related to the word for "work", *ergon*.

② In the Oxford text this phrase is emended to read, in translation: "both the armed [troops]and the garrisons."

Thereupon Critoboulus spoke. "If the King indeed acts in this way, Socrates, it seems to me at least that he concerns himself no less with the works of farming than with those of war."

"But again, in addition to this," said Socrates, "in whatever countries the king resides, or wherever he travels, he is concerned that there be gardens, the so-called pleasure gardens, 18 [①] filled with all the noble and good things that the earth wishes to bring forth, and in these he himself spends most of his time, when the season of the year doesn't preclude it."

"By Zeus, Socrates," said Critoboulus, "but the king necessarily concerns himself that the pleasure—gardens, where he spends time, be as beautifully equipped as possible with trees and an the other beautiful things that the earth brings forth."

"And some assert, Critobouius," said Socrates, "that when the king gives presents, he first sends for those who have proved themselves good in war, on the ground that there would be no benefit in plowing very much if there were no defenders; and that secondly he sends for those who cultivate their lands in the best manner and make them productive, saying that not even the brave could live if there were no workers. It is also said that Cyrus, a king of the highest reputation, once told those who were called to receive presents that he himself should justly take the presents for both these things; for he was best, he said, both in cultivating the land and in protecting what was cultivated."

"Cyrus, at any rate," said Critoboulus, "took no less pride, Socrates, if he said these things, in making his lands productive and cultivating them than he did in being a skilled warrior."

"Yes, by Zeus," said Socrates, "and Cyrus, it seems, had he lived, would have become an excellent ruler; of this there were many proofs provided, but particularly the fact that during the march against his brother, in the fight for

---

① Xenophon uses the Persian word *paradeisoi*.

the kingdom, it is said that no one deserted Cyrus for the king, while tens of thousands came from the king to Cyrus. [1] I regard it also as a great proof of virtue in a ruler when others willingly obey him [2] and are willing to remain with him even in terrible dangers. Cyrus' friends fought with him while he lived, and when he was dead they all died fighting near his corpse, except Ariaios; for Ariaios happened to have been ordered to the leftwing. [3] It was this Cyrus who is said to have received Lysander [4] with many marks of friendship when he came bringing presents from the allies—as Lysander himself once said in relating the story to a certain host in Megara——and in particular, he said, he displayed to him the pleasure garden in Sardis. After Lysander had wondered at it——that the trees should be so beautiful, the plantings so regular, the rows of trees so straight, the angles so beautifully laid, and that so many pleasant scents should accompany them as they walked-wondering at these things, he spoke.'I, Cyrus, am full of wonder at the beauty of everything, [5] but much more do I admire the one who has measured out and ordered each kind of thing for you.'On hearing this, Cyrus was pleased and spoke. 'All these things, Lysander, I measured out and ordered myself and there are some of them,'he said that he said, 'that I even planted myself. 'And Lysander said that, looking at him and seeing the

---

[1] This sums to refer to the younger Cyrus, Xenophon's contemporary and friend and leader of the revolt against his brother, the Persian king Artaxerxes.

[2] Or, "when others are readily persuaded [*peithōntai*] by him."

[3] Compare *Anabasis* 1. 8. 5 and 1. 9. 31.The commander of all Cyrus' non-Greek troops and his chief lieutenant, Ariaios fled the baffle as soon as he learned of Cyrus' death. Later he exchanged oaths of fidelity with the Greeks who had fought under Cyrus, but soon afterward deserted them altogether.

[4] Lysander was a Spartan and commander of the Peloponnesian fleet during the last years of the Peloponnesian War. The occasion and circumstances of his meeting with Cyrus, which took place in 407, are described by Xenophon in the *Hellenica* (1. 5. iff); its main object was to secure Persian assistance in the prosecution of the war against Athens. Xenophon does not, however, make mention in the *Heltenica* of the incident related here.

[5] In the Oxford text this phrase is emended to read, in translation: "the beauty of everything here" or "of all these things" (*panta tauta*). The insertion of *tauta* is without manuscript authority.

beauty of the clothes he wore, perceiving their scent and also the beauty of the necklaces and bracelets and the other ornaments he was wearing, he had spoken and said: 'What do you mean, Cyrus? You planted some of these with your own hands?'And Cyrus had replied, 'Do you wonder at this, Lysander? I swear to you by Mithras: as long as I'm healthy, I never go to dinner until I have worked up a sweat either by practicing some work of war or farming, or at any rate by always devoting my ambition [1] to someone thing. 'And Lysander himself said that on hearing this he took Cyrus' right hand and spoke: 'You, Cyrus, seem to me to be justly happy, for you are happy while being a good man."

CHAPTER 5

"This, Critoboulus, I relate,"said Socrates, "because not even the altogether blessed can abstain from farming. For the pursuit of farming seems to be at the same time some soft pleasure, an increase of the household, and a training of the bodies so that they can do whatever befits a free man. First, the earth bears, to those who work it, what human beings live on, and it bears in addition what they take pleasure in experiencing; then, it provides that with which they adorn altars and statues and are adorned themselves, together with the most pleasant scents and sights; then, it either brings forth or nourishes all manner of sauces [2] ——for the art of sheep breeding is linked to farming—that they may have something with which, by sacrificing, to win over the gods, as well as something to use themselves. But though providing the good things most abundantly, it doesn't yield them up to softness but accustoms all to bear the cold of winter and the heat of summer. It exercises those who work with their own hands and adds to their strength, and it produces a kind of manliness even in those who are merely concerned with farming, causing them to rise early in

---

[1] Here and throughout, "ambition" could be translated as, "love of honor."

[2] The Greek word (opson) signifies whatever is eaten with bread, i.e, both meat and vegetables.

the morning and compelling them to move about vigorously. For in the country as in town, the most important actions have always their proper season. Then, if someone wants to defend the city as a horseman, farming is most sufficient for helping to maintain a horse, or if one is a foot soldier, it provides a vigorous body. The earth also in some degree helps encourage a love of the toil in the hunt, since it provides the dogs with an easy source of nourishment and at the same time supports wild animals. And not only are the horses and dogs benefited by farming, but they benefit the country in turn, the horse by carrying the caretaker ① to his concerns early in the morning and allowing him to return late, and the dogs by keeping wild animals from damaging the' crops or the sheep and by helping to give safety to solitude. Further, the earth stimulates in some degree the farmers to armed protection of the country by nourishing her crops in the open for the strongest to take. what art makes mart more fit for running, throwing, and jumping than does farming? What art brings more gratification to those who work at it? What affords a more pleasant welcome to the one concerned with it—inviting whoever comes along to take whatever he requires? What welcomes foreigners with more abundance? Where are there more facilities than in the country for passing the winter with an abundance of fire and warm baths? And where can one spend a summer more pleasantly than in the country, amid waters and breezes and shade? What else provides more suitable first offerings for the gods or shows ampler feasts? What is more beloved by servants, more pleasant for the wire, more sharply missed by children, or more gratifying to friends? It would seem wonderful to me if any free human being possessed anything more pleasant than this or found a concern at once more pleasant and of greater benefit in life. Furthermore, the earth, being a goddess, teaches justice to those who are able to learn, for she gives the most goods in return to those who attend to her best. Then if those engaged in

---

① Evidently, the master. Xenophon uses a poetic and somewhat strange expression (*ho Kēdomenos*), literally, "the one who is troubled "the one who is concerned [for]."

137

farming and educated to vigor and manliness should at some time be deprived of their works by a multitude of invaders, they would be able—if a god didn't prevent them—being well prepared both in soul and in body, to go into the country of the preventers and take what they needed to maintain themselves. For in war it is often safer to seek to maintain oneself with arms rather than with the instruments of farming. At the same time farming educates in helping others. For in fighting one's enemies, as well as in working the earth, it is necessary to have the assistance of other human beings. The one who is going to farm well, then, must provide himself with eager workers who are willing to obey him; and the one who leads against enemies must devise means to accomplish the same things, by giving presents to those who act as the good ought to act and by punishing those who are disorderly. The farmer must often exhort his workers no less than the general his soldiers; and slaves require good hopes no less than the free, but rather more so, that they may be willing to remain. Whoever said that farming is the mother and nurse of all the other arts spoke nobly indeed, For when farming goes well, all the other arts also flourish, but wherever the earth is compelled to lie barren, the other arts almost cease to exist, at sea as well as on the earth." After having heard this, Critoboulus said: "In regard to these things, Socrates, you seem to me, at least, to speak nobly; but in regard to most of the things of farming, ① it's impossible for a human being to exercise forethought: sometimes hail, frost, drought, violent rains, blights, and often indeed other things wreck what has been nobly conceived and done; sometimes a herd of sheep raised in the noblest manner is most miserably destroyed by disease."

After having heard this, Socrates said: "But I for my part supposed you knew, Critoboulus, that the gods are lords of the works of farming no less than of those of war, Those who are at war you see, I suppose, trying to win over the gods before undertaking warlike actions, and consulting them by means of sacrifices

---

① Literally, "the things of the farming[art]." The adjective is used, as is common in Greek, with a substantive absent but understood: probably either "knowledge" or "art" is intended.

and auguries as to what must or must not be done; but in regard to the actions of farming, do you suppose it any less necessary to propitiate the gods? Know well, "he said, "that moderate men attend to the gods out of regard for their crops—the wet and the dry alike—and their oxen and horses and sheep and indeed all their possessions."

一　文献出处

Xenophon, *The Short Socratic Writings, Apology of Socrates to the Jury, Oeconomicus, and Symposium*, translation, with interpretive essays and notes by Robert C. Bartlett, Cornell University Press, Ithaca and London, 1996.

二　文献导读

色诺芬（Xenophon，约公元前 444~ 前 354 年），雅典人，出生在雅典的一个富有的贵族之家。关于色诺芬的生平，主要来源于他本人著作中的记述。

色诺芬自幼受过多方面的良好教育，熟悉军事和骑术，兴趣广泛。早年跟随苏格拉底学习，曾经在雅典骑兵服役，后来由于各种原因奔走他乡，一生经历了希腊城邦晚期的很多重大事件，其间撰写了大量著作，内容涉及政治、经济、军事、思想等各个方面，是一位十分多产的作家。色诺芬在政治上倾向于贵族制，反对雅典的民主制度，赞赏斯巴达的贵族寡头制。

有材料记载，色诺芬参加过公元前 424 年雅典与邻国的一次战役。公元前 420 年，在泛雅典娜节日期间，曾随老师苏格拉底一起到雅典富豪卡里阿斯家做客。公元前 401 年，波斯发生内讧，国王薛西斯的弟弟小居鲁士在小亚细亚起兵，斯巴达人支持小居鲁士，为他提供了大量希腊雇佣军，色诺芬经人介绍，参加了这支军队。后来他撰写的《远征记》记载的就是这次征战的经历。不料，小居鲁士本人在巴比伦附近的库纳克萨战败身亡。失去雇主的 1 万多名希腊雇佣军只得在自己选出的首领的领导下向希腊撤退，色诺芬就是被选出的首领之一。他表现出优秀的领导才能和组织才能，带领这支军队克服重重困难，终于在公元前 400 年年底把几千名希腊雇佣军带回了欧洲。但是，由于在拜占庭期间与当地的斯巴达驻军首领发生冲突，为安全起见，色诺芬只得投靠了色雷斯国王塞于特斯。不久，色诺芬与塞于特斯再起矛盾，在希腊雇佣兵的请求下，色诺芬再次回到小亚细亚为斯巴达人效力，这时候，斯巴达人正在与波斯人打仗。

在色雷斯逗留期间，色诺芬本有回雅典的打算，但形势已经不允许他这样做了。公元前 399 年，雅典人判处他的老师苏格拉底死刑，随即也宣布了对色诺芬的放逐令，理由是色诺芬曾经投靠小居鲁士，而小居鲁士正是支持斯巴达人在伯罗奔尼撒战争中打败雅典的人。公元前 396 年，斯巴达国王阿格西劳斯奉命到小亚细亚领导斯巴达军队与波斯作战，色诺芬很快就成为他的幕僚和好友。在科林斯战争（公元前 395~ 前 386 年）期间，色诺芬跟随斯巴达军队参加了反对雅典的战役。色诺芬把妻子和两个儿子也接到斯巴达。由于他对斯巴达人的忠诚，斯巴达赏赐给他一块位于奥林匹亚附近的斯基洛斯的地产，色诺芬在这里生活了 20 多年，这一时期是色诺芬生平最平静的时期，终日以著述、狩猎和宴享朋友为务，《居鲁士的教育》《远征记》等书可能就是在这里撰写的。除了斯巴达人赠送的地产之外，色诺芬在斯基洛斯还购得一块土地，有很多奴隶为他耕作，他的著作《经济论》中表现出的经营大地产的经验无疑就在这个时期积累下来的。

公元前 371 年，斯巴达与底比斯之间爆发战争，斯巴达战败。斯基洛斯重新归入其原来的主人埃里斯的版图，色诺芬也因此失去了地产，举家迁居到科林斯。这期间希腊政局又起变化，由于底比斯的崛起，斯巴达和雅典联合起来共同向底比斯宣战，色诺芬就此将两个儿子送回雅典，他们都参加了反对底比斯的战争，其中一人阵亡，于是，雅典公民大会通过决议，废除了以前关于放逐色诺芬的决定。此后，色诺芬虽然有了回到祖国的机会，但只是偶尔回去看一看，大部分时间还是住在科林斯，全心投入写作，直至去世。他的大部分著作，包括《希腊史》《论骑兵司令的指责》《论骑术》《阿格西劳斯传》《雅典的收入》等都完成于这一时期。

色诺芬生活在希腊政局动荡的城邦末期，丰富的经历、广博的知识和勤奋的写作使他成为古希腊最为多产的作家之一，其主要作品至少包括：《希腊史》（可以看作是修昔底德《伯罗奔尼撒战争史》的续篇，记述了从公元前411年到前362年的希腊历史）、《远征记》、《回忆苏格拉底》、《居鲁士的教育》、《阿格西劳斯传》、《经济论》、《雅典的收入》、《斯巴达政制》、《论骑兵司令的指责》、《论骑术》等，虽然有学者主张其中的一些作品有可能出自其他人之手（例如《斯巴达政制》和《雅典的收入》），但大多数著作的真实性还是不容置疑的。色诺芬的作品文字简练，词汇丰富，记述翔实，描写生动，成为后人学习希腊语文的必读教材。更为重要的是，这些作品大多记述的是当时的人和事，因而成为研究古希腊历史，尤其是城邦晚期历史不可多得的珍贵史料。同时，色诺芬的著作也不可避免地带有种种时代和个人的局限性和偏见。例如，对斯巴达政体的过分推崇使他不能对雅典的民主制度做出客观的评价；再如，虽然色诺芬的作品内容广泛，记述翔实，但思想性相对贫乏，缺乏深刻而透彻的分析，这些都是我们在使用他的作品的时候要加以注意的。

"经济"一词源于古代希腊，本意是"家庭管理"或"家政学"，据考证，最早使用该词的就是色诺芬。在古希腊的文献中，政治、军事的记述居多，反映经济生活的材料十分有限。色诺芬撰写的《经济论》是古希腊少有的专门记述当时人的经济生活的文献之一。该书围绕地产的经营和管理，对奴隶主的家庭经济进行了全面的记述，其中既记录和反映了当时农业生产的技术水平，同时也对手工业和商业活动有所涉及，并把农业和工商业活动做了对比，高度赞扬了农耕生活对城邦的重要性和优越性。在"重农抑商"的同时，色诺芬并不否认商业和商人存在的必要性，其理论依据就是劳动分工的思想。这篇文献对于我们认识和研究古代希腊人的经济生活和经济思想都具有十分重要的参考价值。以上部分即节选自该书的第四章和第五章，内容是关于农业和工商业活动的优劣和重要性的比较。

三　延伸阅读

Anderson, J.K., *Xenophon*, London, 1974.

Austin, M.M., and Vidal-Naquet, *Economic and Social History of Ancient Greece: An Introduction*, London, 1977.

Finley, M.I., *The Ancient Economy*, London, 1973.

Glotz, G., *Ancient Greece at Work: An Economic History from the Homeric Period to the Roman Conquest*, Routledge, 1996.

Lacey, W.K., *The Family in Classical Greece*, London, 1968.

Pomeroy, S.B., *Xenophon: Oeconomicus, a Social and Historical Commentary*, London, 1990.

Aristophanes: Plutus [*]

SCENE: —The Orchestra represents a public square in Athens. In the background is the house of Chremylus. A ragged old blind man enters, followed by Chremylus and his slave Cario.

Cario

What an unhappy fate, great gods, to be the slave of a fool! A servant may give the best of advice, but if his master does not follow it, the poor slave must inevitably have his share in the disaster; for fortune does not allow him to dispose of his own body, it belongs to his master who has bought it. Alas! 'tis the way of the world. But the god, Apollo, in tragic style whose oracles the Pythian priestess on her golden tripod makes known to us, deserves my censure, for surely he is a physician and a cunning diviner; and yet my master is leaving his temple infected with mere madness and insists on following a blind man. Is this not opposed to all good sense? It is for us, who see clearly, to guide those who don't; whereas he clings to the trail of a blind fellow and compels me to do the same without answering my questions with ever a word.To Chremylus Aye, master, unless you tell me why we are following this unknown fellow, I will not be silent, but I will worry and torment you, for you cannot beat me because of

---

* 阿里斯托芬《财神》节选。

my sacred chaplet of laurel.

Chremylus

No, but if you worry me I will take off your chaplets, and then you will only get a sounder thrashing.

Cario

That's an old song! I am going to leave you no peace till you have told me who this man is; and if I ask it, it's entirely because of my interest in you.

Chremylus

Well, be it so. I will reveal it to you as being the most faithful and the most rascally of all my servants. I honored the gods and did what was right, and yet I was none the less poor and unfortunate.

Cario

I know it but too well.

Chremylus

Others amassed wealth —the sacrilegious, the demagogues, the informers, indeed every sort of rascal.

Cario

I believe you.

Chremylus

Therefore I came to consult the oracle of the god, not on my own account, for my unfortunate life is nearing its end, but for my only son; I wanted to ask Apollo if it was necessary for him to become a thorough knave and renounce his virtuous principles, since that seemed to me to be the only way to succeed in life.

Cario

with ironic gravity

And with what responding tones did the sacred tripod resound?

Chremylus

You shall know. The god ordered me in plain terms to follow the first man I should meet upon leaving the temple and to persuade him to accompany me home.

Cario

And who was the first one you met?

Chremylus

This blind man.

Cario

And you are stupid enough not to understand the meaning of such an answer? Why, the god was advising you thereby, and that in the clearest possible way, to bring up your son according to the fashion of your country.

Chremylus

What makes you think that?

Cario

Is it not evident to the blind, that nowadays to do nothing that is right is the best way to get on?

Chremylus

No, that is not the meaning of the oracle; there must be another that is nobler. If this blind man would tell us who he is and why and with what object he has led us here, we should no doubt understand what our oracle really does mean.

Cario To Plutus

Come, tell us at once who you are, or I shall give effect to my threat. He menaces him. And quick too, be quick, I say.

Plutus

I'll thrash you.

Cario

To Chremylus

Do you understand who he says he is?

Chremylus

It's to you and not to me that he replies thus: your mode of questioning him was ill-advised. To Plutus Come, friend, if you care to oblige an honest man,

145

answer me.

Plutus

I'll knock you down.

Cario

Sarcastically

Ah! what a pleasant fellow and what a delightful prophecy the god has given you!

Chremylus

To Plutus

By Demeter, you'll have no reason to laugh presently. If you don't speak—

Cario

I will surely do you an ill turn.

Chremylus

Friends—

Plutus

Take yourselves off and leave me.

Chremylus

No, we won't.

Cario

This, master, is the best thing to do. I'll undertake to secure him the most frightful death; I will lead him to the verge of a precipice and then leave him there, so that he'll break his neck when he pitches over.

Chremylus

Well then, seize him right away.

Cario does so.

Plutus

Oh, no! Have mercy!

Chremylus

Will thou speak then?

Plutus

But if you learn who I am, I know well that you will ill-use me and will not let me go again.

Chremylus

I call the gods to witness that you have naught to fear if you will only speak.

Plutus

Well then, first unhand me.

Chremylus

There! we set you free.

Plutus

Listen then, since I must reveal what I had intended to keep a secret. I am Plutus.

Chremylus

Oh! you wretched rascal! You Plutus all the while, and you never said so!

Cario

You, Plutus, and in this piteous guise! Oh, Phoebus Apollo! oh, ye gods of heaven and hell! Oh, Zeus! is it really and truly as you say?

Plutus

Yes.

Chremylus

Plutus' very own self?

Plutus

His own very self and none other.

Chremylus

But tell me, how come you're so squalid?

Plutus

I have just left Patrocles' house, who has not had a bath since his birth.

Chremylus

But your infirmity; how did that happen? Tell me.

Plutus

Zeus inflicted it on me, because of his jealousy of mankind. When I was young, I threatened him that I would only go to the just, the wise, the men of ordered life; to prevent my distinguishing these, he struck me with blindness! so much does he envy the good!

Chremylus

And yet, it's only the upright and just who honor him.

Plutus

Quite true.

Chremylus

Therefore, if ever you recovered your sight, you would shun the wicked?

Plutus

Undoubtedly.

Chremylus

You would visit the good?

Plutus

Assuredly. It is a very long time since I saw them.

Chremylus

To the audience

That's not astonishing. I, who see clearly, don't see a single one.

Plutus

Now let me leave you, for I have told you everything.

Chremylus

No, certainly not! we shall fasten ourselves on to you faster than ever.

Plutus

Did I not tell you, you were going to plague me?

Chremylus

Oh! I adjure you, believe what I say and don't leave me; for you will seek in vain for a more honest man than myself.

Cario

There is only one man more worthy; and that is I.

Plutus

All talk like this, but as soon as they secure my favours and grow rich, their wickedness knows no bounds.

Chremylus

And yet all men are not wicked.

Plutus

All. There's no exception.

Cario

You shall pay for that opinion.

Chremylus

Listen to what happiness there is in store for you, if you but stay with us. I have hope; aye, I have good hope with the god's help to deliver you from that blindness, in fact to restore your sight.

Plutus

Oh! do nothing of the kind, for I don't wish to recover it.

Chremylus

What's that you say?

Cario

This fellow hugs his own misery.

Plutus

If you were mad enough to cure me, and Zeus heard of it, he would overwhelm me with his anger.

Chremylus

And is he not doing this now by leaving you to grope your wandering way?

Plutus

I don't know; but I'm horribly afraid of him.

Chremylus

Indeed? Ah! you are the biggest poltroon of all the gods! Why, Zeus with his throne and his lightnings would not be worth an obolus if you recovered your sight, were it but for a few moments.

Plutus

Impious man, don't talk like that.

Chremylus

Fear nothing! I will prove to you that you are far more powerful and mightier than he.

Plutus

I mightier than he?

Chremylus

Aye, by heaven! To Cario For instance, what is the basis of the power that Zeus wields over the other gods?

Cario

Money; he has so much of it.

Chremylus

And who gives it to him?

Cario pointing to Plutus

This fellow.

Chremylus

If sacrifices are offered to him, is not Plutus their cause?

Cario

Undoubtedly, for it's wealth that all demand and clamor most loudly for.

Chremylus

Thus it's Plutus who is the fount of all the honors rendered to Zeus, whose worship he can wither up at the root, if it so pleases him.

Plutus

And how so?

Chremylus

Not an ox, nor a cake, nor indeed anything at all could be offered, if you did not wish it.

Plutus

Why?

Chremylus

Why? but what means are there to buy anything if you are not there to give the money? Hence if Zeus should cause you any trouble, you will destroy his power without other help.

Plutus

So it's because of me that sacrifices are offered to him?

Chremylus

Most assuredly. Whatever is dazzling, beautiful or charming in the eyes of mankind, comes from you. Does not everything depend on wealth?

Cario

I myself was bought for a few coins; if I'm a slave, it's only because I was not rich.

Chremylus

And what of the Corinthian whores? If a poor man offers them proposals, they do not listen; but if it be a rich one, instantly they turn their arses to him.

Cario

It's the same with the lads; they care not for love, to them money means everything.

Chremylus

You speak of male whores; yet some of them are honest, and it's not money they ask of their patrons.

Cario

What then?

Chremylus

A fine horse, a pack of hounds.

Cario

Yes, they would blush to ask for money and cleverly disguise their shame.

Chremylus

It is in you that every art, all human inventions, have had their origin; it is through you that one man sits cutting leather in his shop.

Cario

That another fashions iron or wood.

Chremylus

That yet another chases the gold he has received from you.

Cario

This one steals clothes, by Zeus, and that one is a housebreaker.

Chremylus

That one is a clothes-cleaner.

Cario

And the other washes bedding.

Chremylus

That this one is a tanner.

Cario

And that other sells onions.

Chremylus

And if the adulterer, caught red-handed, is depilated, it's on account of you.

Plutus

Oh! great gods! I knew naught of all this!

Cario（**To Chremylus**）

Is it not he who lends the Great King all his pride?

Chremylus

Is it not he who draws the citizens to the Assembly?

Cario

And tell me, is it not you who equip the triremes?

Chremylus

And who feed our mercenaries at Corinth?

Cario

Are not you the cause of Pamphilus' sufferings?

Chremylus

And of the needle-seller's with Pamphilus?

Cario

It is not because of you that Agyrrhius farts so loudly?

Chremylus

And that Philepsius rolls off his fables? That troops are sent to succour the Egyptians? And that Lais is kept by Philonides?

Cario

That the tower of Timotheus—

Chremylus

To Cario May it fall upon your head! To Plutus In short, Plutus, it is through you that everything is done; you must realize that you are the sole cause both of good and evil.

Cario

In war, it's the flag under which you serve that victory favours.

Plutus

What! I can do so many things by myself and unaided?

Chremylus

And many others besides; wherefore men are never tired of your gifts. They get weary of all else, — of love ...

Cario

Bread.

Chremylus

Music.

Cario

Sweetmeats.

Chremylus

Honors.

Cario

Cakes.

Chremylus

Battles.

Cario

Figs.

Chremylus

Ambition.

Cario

Gruel.

Chremylus

Military advancement.

Cario

Lentil soup.

Chremylus

But of you they never tire. If a man has thirteen talents, he has all the greater ardor to possess sixteen; if that wish is achieved, he will want forty or will complain that he knows not how to make both ends meet.

Plutus

All this, I suppose, is very true; there is but one point that makes me feel a bit uneasy.

Chremylus

And that is?

Plutus

How could I use this power, which you say I have?

Chremylus

Ah! they were quite right who said there's nothing more timorous than Plutus.

Plutus

No, no; it was a thief who calumniated me. Having broken into a house, he found everything locked up and could take nothing, so he dubbed my prudence fear.

Chremylus

Don't be disturbed; if you support me zealously, I'll make you more sharp-sighted than Lynceus.

Plutus

And how should you be able to do that, you, who are but a mortal?

Chremylus

I have great hope, after the answer Apollo gave me, shaking his sacred laurels the while.

Plutus

Is he in the plot then?

Chremylus

Surely.

Plutus

Take care what you say.

Chremylus

Never fear, friend; for, be well assured, that if it has to cost me my life, I will carry out what I have in my head.

Cario

And I will help you, if you permit it.

Chremylus

We shall have many other helpers as well —all the worthy folk who are wanting for bread.

Plutus

Ah! they'll prove sorry helpers.

Chremylus

No, not so, once they've grown rich. But you, Cario, run quick ...

Cario

Where?

Chremylus

... to call my comrades, the other husbandmen (you'll probably find the poor fellows toiling away in the fields), that each of them may come here to take his share of the gifts of Plutus.

Cario

I'm off. But let someone come from the house to take this morsel of meat.

Chremylus

I'll see to that; you run your hardest. As for you, Plutus, the most excellent of all the gods, come in here with me; this is the house you must fill with riches to-day, by fair means or foul.

Plutus

I don't at all like going into other folks' houses in this manner; I have never got any good from it. If I got inside a miser's house, straightway he would bury me deep underground; if some honest fellow among his friends came to ask him for the smallest coin, he would deny ever having seen me. Then if I went to a fool's house, he would sacrifice in dicing and wenching, and very soon I should be completely stripped and pitched out of doors.

Chremylus

That's because you have never met a man who knew how to avoid the two extremes; moderation is the strong point in my character. I love saving as much as anybody, and I know how to spend, when it's needed. But let us go in; I want to make you known to my wife and to my only son, whom I love most of all after yourself.

Plutus

I'm quite sure of that.

Chremylus

Why should I hide the truth from you?

......

Poverty

Unwise, perverse, unholy men! What are you daring to do, you pitiful, wretched mortals? Whither are you flying? Stop! I command it!

Blepsidemus

Oh! great gods!

Poverty

My arm shall destroy you, you infamous beings! Such an attempt is not to be borne; neither man nor god has ever dared the like. You shall die!

Chremylus

And who are you? Oh! what a ghastly pallor!

Blepsidemus

Perhaps it's some Erinys, some Fury, from the theater; there's a kind of wild tragic look in her eyes.

Chremylus

But she has no torch.

Blepsidemus

Let's knock her down!

Poverty

Who do you think I am?

Chremylus

Some wine-shop keeper or egg-woman. Otherwise you would not have shrieked so loud at us, who have done nothing to you.

Poverty

Indeed? And have you not done me the most deadly injury by seeking to banish me from every country?

Chremylus

Why, have you not got the Barathrum left? But who are you? Answer me quickly!

Poverty

I am one that will punish you this very day for having wanted to make me disappear from here.

Blepsidemus

Might it be the tavern-keeper in my neighborhood, who is always cheating me in measure?

Poverty

I am Poverty, who have lived with you for so many years.

Blepsidemus

Oh! great Apollo! oh, ye gods! whither shall I fly?

He starts to run away.

Chremylus

Here! what are you doing! You coward! Are you going to leave me here?

Blepsidemus

still running

Not I.

Chremylus

Stop then! Are two men to run away from one woman?

Blepsidemus

But, you wretch, it's Poverty, the most fearful monster that ever drew breath.

Chremylus

Stay where you are, I beg of you.

Blepsidemus

No! no! a thousand times, no!

Chremylus

Could we do anything worse than leave the god in the lurch and fly before this woman without so much as ever offering to fight?

Blepsidemus

But what weapons have we? Are we in a condition to show fight? Where is the breastplate, the buckler, that this wretch has not pawned?

Chremylus

Be at ease. Plutus will readily triumph over her threats unaided.

Poverty

Dare you reply, you scoundrels, you who are caught red-handed at the most horrible crime?

Chremylus

As for you, you cursed jade, you pursue me with your abuse, though I have never done you the slightest harm.

Poverty

Do you think it is doing me no harm to restore Plutus to the use of his eyes?

Chremylus

Is this doing you harm, that we shower blessings on all men?

Poverty

And what do you think will ensure their happiness?

Chremylus

Ah! first of all we shall drive you out of Greece.

Poverty

Drive me out? Could you do mankind a greater harm?

Chremylus

Yes —if I gave up my intention to deliver them from you.

Poverty

Well, let us discuss this point first. I propose to show that I am the sole cause of all your blessings, and that your safety depends on me alone. If I don't succeed, then do what you like to me.

Chremylus

How dare you talk like this, you impudent hussy?

Poverty

Agree to hear me and I think it will be very easy for me to prove that you are entirely on the wrong road, when you want to make the just men wealthy.

Blepsidemus

Oh! cudgel and rope's end, come to my help!

Poverty

Why such wrath and these shouts, before you hear my arguments?

Blepsidemus

But who could listen to such words without exclaiming?

Poverty

Any man of sense.

Chremylus

But if you lose your case, what punishment will you submit to?

Poverty

Choose what you will.

Chremylus

That's all right.

Poverty

You shall suffer the same if you are beaten!

Chremylus

Do you think twenty deaths a sufficiently large stake?

Blepsidemus

Good enough for her, but for us two would suffice.

Poverty

You won't escape, for is there indeed a single valid argument to oppose me with?

Leader of the Chorus

To beat her in this debate, you must call upon all your wits. Make no allowances and show no weakness!

Chremylus

It is right that the good should be happy, that the wicked and the impious, on the other hand, should be miserable; that is a truth, I believe, which no one will gainsay. To realize this condition of things is a proposal as great as it is noble and useful in every respect, and we have found a means of attaining the object of our wishes. If Plutus recovers his sight and ceases from wandering about unseeing and at random, he will go to seek the just men and never leave them again; he will shun the perverse and ungodly; so, thanks to him, all men will become honest, rich and pious. Can anything better be conceived for the public weal?

Blepsidemus

Of a certainty, no! I bear witness to that. It is not even necessary she should reply.

Chremylus

Does it not seem that everything is extravagance in the world, or rather madness, when you watch the way things go? A crowd of rogues enjoy blessings they have won by sheer injustice, while more honest folks are miserable, die of hunger, and spend their whole lives with you. Now, if Plutus became clear-sighted again and drove out Poverty, it would be the greatest blessing possible for the human race.

Poverty

Here are two old men, whose brains are easy to confuse, who assist each other to talk rubbish and drivel to their hearts' content. But if your wishes were realized, your profit would be great! Let Plutus recover his sight and divide his favours out equally to all, and none will ply either trade or art any longer; all toil would be done away with. Who would wish to hammer iron, build ships, sew, turn, cut up leather, bake bricks, bleach linen, tan hides, or break up the soil of the earth with the plough and garner the gifts of Demeter, if he could live in idleness and free from all this work?

Chremylus

What nonsense all this is! All these trades which you just mention will be plied by our slaves.

Poverty

Your slaves! And by what means will these slaves be got?

Chremylus

We will buy them.

Poverty

But first say, who will sell them, if everyone is rich?

Chremylus

Some greedy dealer from Thessaly —the land which supplies so many.

Poverty

But if your system is applied, there won't be a single slave-dealer left. What rich man would risk his life to devote himself to this traffic? You will have to toil, to dig and submit yourself to all kinds of hard labour; so that your life would be more wretched even than it is now.

Chremylus

May this prediction fall upon yourself!

Poverty

You will not be able to sleep in a bed, for no more will ever be manufactured; nor no carpets, for who would weave them, if he had gold? When you bring a young bride to your dwelling, you will have no essences wherewith to perfume her, nor rich embroidered cloaks dyed with dazzling colors in which to clothe her. And yet what is the use of being rich, if you are to be deprived of all these enjoyments? On the other hand, you have all that you need in abundance, thanks to me; to the artisan I am like a severe mistress, who forces him by need and poverty to seek the means of earning his livelihood.

Chremylus

And what good thing can you give us, unless it be burns in the bath, and swarms of brats and old women who cry with hunger, and clouds uncountable of lice, gnats and flies, which hover about the wretch's head, trouble him, awake him and say, "You will be hungry, but get up!" Besides, to possess a rag in place of a mantle, a pallet of rushes swarming with bugs, that do not let you close your eyes, for a bed; a rotten piece of matting for a coverlet; a big stone for a pillow, on which to lay your head; to eat mallow roots instead of bread, and leaves of withered radish instead of cake; to have nothing but the cover of a broken jug for a stool, the stave of a cask, and broken at that, for a kneading-trough, that is the life you make for us! Are these the mighty benefits with which you pretend to load mankind?

Poverty

It's not my life that you describe; you are attacking the existence beggars lead.

Chremylus

Is Beggary not Poverty's sister?

Poverty

Thrasybulus and Dionysius are one and the same according to you. No, my life is not like that and never will be. The beggar, whom you have depicted to us, never possesses anything. The poor man lives thriftily and attentive to his work; he has not got too much, but he does not lack what he really needs.

Chremylus

Oh! what a happy life, by Demeter! to live sparingly, to toil incessantly and not to leave enough to pay for a tomb!

Poverty

That's it! Jest, jeer, and never talk seriously! But what you don't know is this, that men with me are worth more, both in mind and body, than with Plutus. With him they are gouty, big-bellied, heavy of limb and scandalously stout; with me they are thin, wasp-waisted, and terrible to the foe.

Chremylus

No doubt it's by starving them that you give them that waspish waist.

Poverty

As for behavior, I will prove to you that modesty dwells with me and insolence with Plutus.

Chremylus

Oh! the sweet modesty of stealing and burglary.

Blepsidemus

By Zeus, how is it not modesty if you have to go unnoticed?

Poverty

Look at the orators in our republics; as long as they are poor, both state and people can only praise their uprightness; but once they are fattened on the public funds, they conceive a hatred for justice, plan intrigues against the people and attack the democracy.

Chremylus

That is absolutely true, although your tongue is very vile. But it matters not, so don't put on those triumphant airs; you shall not be punished any the less for having tried to persuade me that poverty is worth more than wealth.

Poverty

Not being able to refute my arguments, you chatter at random and exert yourself to no purpose.

Chremylus

Then tell me this, why does all mankind flee from you?

Poverty

Because I make them better. Children do the very same; they flee from the wise counsels of their fathers. So difficult is it to see one's true interest.

Chremylus

Will you say that Zeus cannot discern what is best? Well, he takes Plutus to himself ...

Blepsidemus

... and banishes Poverty to the earth.

Poverty

Ah me! how purblind you are, you old fellows of the days of Cronus! Why, Zeus is poor, and I will clearly prove it to you. In the Olympic games, which he founded, and to which he convokes the whole of Greece every four years, why does he only crown the victorious athletes with wild olive? If he were rich he would give them gold.

Chremylus

That's the way he shows that he clings to his wealth; he is sparing with it, won't part with any portion of it, only bestows baubles on the victors and keeps his money for himself.

Poverty

But wealth coupled to such sordid greed is yet more shameful than poverty.

Chremylus

May Zeus destroy you, both you and your chaplet of wild olive!

Poverty

Thus you dare to maintain that Poverty is not the fount of all blessings!

Chremylus

Ask Hecate whether it is better to be rich or starving; she will tell you that the rich send her a meal every month and that the poor make it disappear before it is even served.

Chremylus

But go and hang yourself and don't breathe another syllable. I will not be convinced against my will.

Poverty

"Oh! citizens of Argos! do you hear what he says?"

Chremylus

Invoke Pauson, your boon companion, rather.

Poverty

Alas! what is to become of me?

Chremylus

Get you gone, be off quick and a pleasant journey to you.

Poverty

But where shall I go?

Chremylus

To gaol; but hurry up, let us put an end to this.

Poverty (as she departs)

One day you will recall me.

Chremylus

Then you can return; but disappear for the present. I prefer to be rich; you are free to knock your head against the walls in your rage.

Blepsidemus

And I too welcome wealth. I want, when I leave the bath all perfumed with essences, to feast bravely with my wife and children and to fart in the faces of toilers and Poverty.

Chremylus

So that hussy has gone at last! But let us make haste to put Plutus to bed in the Temple of Asclepius.

Blepsidemus

Let us make haste; else some bothering fellow may again come to interrupt us.

Chremylus（loudly）

Cario, bring the coverlets and all that I have got ready from the house; let us conduct the god to the temple, taking care to observe all the proper rites.

一　文献出处

Aristophanes, *Wealth*: *The Complete Greek Drama*, Vol. 2, Jr. O' Neill, ed., New York: Random House, 1938.

二　文献导读

阿里斯托芬（Aristophanes，公元前 446~ 约前 385 年）是古希腊最著名的喜剧作家。他生活的时代正值伯罗奔尼撒战争期间，当时的雅典正逐渐失去霸主的地位，开始由盛转衰，各种社会矛盾显露出来，城邦的危机日益加深，阿里斯托芬的喜剧作品正是产生在这样一个大的历史背景下，是全面反映希腊城邦晚期，尤其是雅典出现的各种社会问题的珍贵史料。

关于阿里斯托芬的生平，我们差不多一无所知，只能根据他的作品当中关于自己的只言片语进行一些推测。阿里斯托芬出生在雅典城内的库达忒奈翁区，族名潘狄俄尼斯。父亲名叫菲利波斯，母亲名叫仄诺多拉。他们有三个儿子，后来都成为喜剧作家。阿里斯托芬的少年时代大概生活在农村，后来才移居雅典，因而在作品中表现出他对农业生产的熟悉和对乡村生活的热爱和怀恋，这成为他的作品大多从普通人尤其是普通农民的角度看待社会问题的根源。阿里斯托芬虽然出生在农村，但在雅典受过良好的教育，对希腊的文学艺术作品十分熟悉，他生活的时代正值雅典民主政治的黄金时代，即所谓"伯利克里时代"，言论自由，思想活跃，民主制度为阿里斯托芬的喜剧创作提供了难得的外部条件，同时，阿里斯托芬对民主制度也给予了充分的肯定。

从公元前 427 年阿里斯托芬的第一部喜剧《宴会》（仅存残篇）上演，

到公元前 388 年写出最后一部喜剧《财神》，在长达近四十年的创作生涯中，阿里斯托芬写出了 44 部剧本（其中有 4 部仍然存在疑问），但其中的大部分已经散失，流传至今的完整作品只有 11 部，它们是：《阿卡奈人》（公元前 425 年，得头奖）、《骑士》（公元前 424 年，得头奖）、《云》（公元前 423 年，得三等奖，比赛失败）、《马蜂》（公元前 422 年，得次奖）、《和平》（公元前 421 年，得次奖）、《鸟》（公元前 414 年，得次奖）、《吕西斯特剌忒》（公元前 411 年）、《地母节妇女》（公元前 410 年）、《蛙》（公元前 405 年，得头奖）、《公民大会妇女》（公元前 392 年）、《财神》（公元前 388 年）。

如果说古希腊的悲剧作品主要取材于神话和史诗故事，更多地反映了古希腊人对人神关系和人之命运的思考的话，那么喜剧作品则主要取材于普通人的现实生活，背景均为诸如市场和庭院这样的日常生活场所，因而色诺芬称之为“现实生活的戏剧”。为体现真实性，作家常常会把真人真事搬上舞台，包括苏格拉底、克里昂在内的当时很多在世的人物都曾经成为阿里斯托芬嘲讽的对象。因此，阿里斯托芬的喜剧自然也就成为直接反映雅典社会的“万花筒”和“风俗画”，成为一种历史研究者可以直接加以使用的文献资料。

就喜剧的历史而言，雅典的喜剧创作经历了三个时期：“旧喜剧”时期，从公元前 488 年喜剧被正式创造出来到公元前 5 世纪末，内容以政治讽刺剧为主；“中期喜剧”时期，从公元前 4 世纪初到公元前 4 世纪末，是一个过渡时期，由于言论不自由，政治喜剧受到限制，这一时期的喜剧主要涉及哲学、文学和社会问题；“新喜剧”时期，从公元前 4 世纪末叶到公元前 3 世纪中叶，主要是世态喜剧，描写日常生活和恋爱故事。阿里斯托芬的喜剧主要属于“旧喜剧”类型，晚期作品表现出向“中期喜剧”过渡的特征。

可以说，作为希腊城邦尤其是雅典城邦由盛转衰时代的见证者，阿里斯托芬的喜剧全面而真实地反映了伯罗奔尼撒战争期间和战后在希腊出现的极具普遍性的各种社会问题，更重要的是，通过这些略带夸张和变形的舞台形象，利用打诨骂俏的方式表达了诗人对这些社会问题的深入和严肃的思考，并试图开出一副医治社会的良方。希波战争之后，雅典依靠提洛同盟的海上优势，取代斯巴达一跃而成为希腊头号强国，但随着提洛同盟逐渐蜕变为雅典推行霸权的工具，作为盟主的雅典与同盟各国之间的矛盾也日益加深。同时，以雅典为首的提洛同盟和以斯巴达为首的伯罗奔尼撒同盟之间的冲突也愈演愈烈，最终演变为一场旷日持久的大规模战争。在雅典内部，在工商业快速发展和城市日渐繁荣的同时，农业经济则渐趋衰败，再加上奴隶人数的大量增加，商人的各种投机活动和土地兼并越发猖獗，小农纷纷破产，城市贫民激增，贫富矛盾越来越严重。作为经济状况的反映和后果，就是在政治上出现党派之争，民主制度受到威胁，思想上盛行个人主义和怀疑主义，传统的伦理和道德观念从根本上受到动摇，诡辩学派的出现正是这一思潮的集中体现。面对这些矛盾和问题，雅典应该何去何从？这正是阿里斯托芬的喜剧试图揭示和回答的问题。

阿里斯托芬的喜剧始终是站在人民的立场上，以一种批判现实主义的态度，大胆无畏地提出自己的看法。一方面，他猛烈地抨击希腊民族的自相残杀、雅典对盟邦的高压、政治煽动家的愚弄人民、告密者的敲诈、官吏的贪腐、城市生活的堕落、教育的危机、财产的不平等以及一切危害城邦和人民的不良现象；另一方面，他十分向往已经成为过去的雅典民主政治的黄金时代，缅怀希波战争中希腊人所表现出的勇敢、正直、爱国主义精神。在他传世的喜剧中，大多数的主人公是单纯和质朴的乡下农民，出现在舞台上的有各色各样的人，包括官吏、商贩、告密者、讼师、诡辩家、奴隶、妓女等，虽然农民的愚昧、轻信和迷信经常成为笑料，但对他们的讽刺应该说是充满善意的，而对那些欺骗人民的政客、颠倒是非的告密者和弄虚作假的商人的挖苦和鞭挞却是无情和深刻的。这就使他的作品充满了思想性和斗争性，正是在这个意义上，恩格斯称阿里斯托芬为"强烈的倾向诗人"。

这里选编的是阿里斯托芬传世作品中的最后一部喜剧《财神》的片断。在这部戏当中，作者不仅通过"瞎眼的财神"揭示出当时社会上出现的好人受穷、坏人反而致富的不公平的社会现实，而且通过财神和穷神的对比对财富和道德的关系问题做出了深刻的哲学思考。

这部戏的主要情节是：一个名叫克瑞密罗斯（Chremylus）的阿提卡农民一生穷苦，看到好人受穷、坏人致富的社会现象，便到德尔菲去请求阿波罗的神谕，询问一下究竟是把他唯一的儿子教养成坏人还是好人更有利。结果，阿波罗叫他走出神庙的门以后，碰见谁就跟谁走。没承想克瑞密罗斯一出来就碰见一个衣衫褴褛的瞎子，这个人竟然就是财神（Plutus）。经过一番考虑，他下定决心找人医好财神的眼睛，这样的话他就会专找那些好人，不再登坏人的门。于是，他就打发自己的奴仆卡里翁（Cario）去召集他的邻居们，也就是那些贫苦的农民。克瑞密罗斯的老朋友布勒西得摩斯（Blepsidemus）赶到后开始以为克瑞密罗斯偷了神庙的钱，想偷着分给大家，后来才知道是怎么回事。正当他们准备把财神送到天医那里医治的时候，穷神（Poverty）出现了，对他们的行为大加责备，她说，贫穷对人类有莫大的贡献，人正是因为贫穷才肯劳动，一旦人人富有，还有谁去劳动呢？克瑞密罗斯回答说，奴隶会替主人劳动，可穷神又说，人人都有了钱，谁还肯去贩卖奴隶呢？克瑞密罗斯辩不过她，就把她赶走了。接着，他和布勒西得摩斯把财神送到了天医庙，第二天，财神终于复明了。克瑞密罗斯终于如愿以偿，家里富足了，所有从前受穷的正直的人现在都变得富有了，包括告密者在内的坏人现在都沦落为乞丐，就连小偷的主神赫尔墨斯也饿得没有办法，不得不向卡里翁讨一点东西吃。在欢乐的气氛中，全剧以心满意足的农人们护送复明的财神到存放国库的雅典娜神庙的后殿里去而结束。以上的内容选自该剧的开场和第二场。

三 延伸阅读

Bowie, A. M., *Aristophanes : Myth, Ritual, and Comedy*, Cambridge; New York : Cambridge University Press, 1996.

Lord, Louis Eleazer, *Aristophanes : His plays and His Influence*, New York: Cooper Square Pub., 1963.

Murray, Gilbert, *Aristophanes : A Study*, New York : Oxford University

Press, 1933.

Sidwell, Keith C., *Aristophanes the Democrat : The Politics of Satirical Comedy during the Peloponnesian War*, Cambridge ; New York : Cambridge University Press, 2009.

Wilson, Nigel Guy, *Aristophanea : Studies on the Text of Aristophanes*, Oxford ; New York : Oxford University Press, 2007.

Demosthenes: Third Philippic [*]

Many speeches are delivered, men of Athens, at almost every meeting of the Assembly, about the wrongs that Philip has been committing, ever since the conclusion of peace, not only against you but also against the other states, and all the speakers would, I am sure, admit in theory, though they do not put it in practice, that the object both of our words and deeds must be to check and chastise his arrogance; yet I perceive that all our interests have been so completely betrayed and sacrificed, that—I am afraid it is an ominous thing to say, but yet the truth—even if all who address you had wanted to propose, and all of you had wanted to pass, measures that were bound to bring our affairs into the worst possible plight, I do not think they could have been in a worse condition than they are today.

Perhaps, indeed, this condition of our affairs may be attributed to many causes and not just to one or two, but a careful examination will convince you that it is above all due to those who study to win your favour rather than to give you the best advice. Some of them, Athenians, interested in maintaining a system which brings them credit and influence, have no thought for the future [and therefore think you should have none either]; while others, by blaming and traducing those

---

in authority, make it their sole aim that our city shall concentrate her attention on punishing her own citizens, while Philip shall be free to say and do whatever he pleases.

But such methods of dealing with public affairs, familiar though they are to you, are the cause of your calamities. I claim for myself, Athenians, that if I utter some home-truths with freedom, I shall not thereby incur your displeasure. For look at it this way. In other matters you think it is so necessary to grant general freedom of speech to everyone in Athens that you even allow aliens and slaves to share in the privilege, and many more menials may be observed among you speaking their minds with more liberty than citizens enjoy in other states; but from your deliberations you have banished it utterly.

Hence the result is that in the Assembly your self-complacency is flattered by hearing none but pleasant speeches, but your policy and your practice are already involving you in the gravest peril. Therefore, if such is your temper now, I have nothing to say; but if, apart from flattery, you are willing to hear something to your advantage, I am ready to speak. For though the state of our affairs is in every way deplorable, and though much has been sacrificed, nevertheless it is possible, if you choose to do your duty, that all may yet be repaired.

And what I am going to say may perhaps seem a paradox, but it is true. The worst feature of the past is our best hope for the future. What, then, is that feature? It is that your affairs go wrong because you neglect every duty, great or small; since surely, if they were in this plight in spite of your doing all that was required, there would not be even a hope of improvement. But in fact it is your indifference and carelessness that Philip has conquered; your city he has not conquered. Nor have you been defeated—no! you have not even made a move.

[If, then, we were all agreed that Philip is at war with Athens and is violating the peace, the only task of a speaker would be to come forward and recommend the safest and easiest method of defence; but since some of you are in such a strange mood that, though Philip is seizing cities, and retaining many of your possessions, and inflicting injury on everybody, you tolerate some speakers who repeatedly assert in the Assembly that the real aggressors are certain of ourselves, we must be on our guard and set this matter right.

For there is grave danger that anyone who proposes and urges that we shall defend ourselves may incur the charge of having provoked the war. I therefore first of all state and define this question—whether it is in our power to discuss the alternative of peace or war.] [①]

If indeed Athens can remain at peace and if the choice rests with us— to take that point first—I personally feel that we are bound to do so; and if anyone says that we can, I call upon him to move a resolution and to do something and to play us no tricks; but if there is another person concerned, with sword in hand and a mighty force at his back, who imposes on you with the name of peace but himself indulges in acts of war, what is left but to defend ourselves? If you choose to follow his example and profess that you are at peace, I raise no objection.

But if anyone mistakes for peace an arrangement which will enable Philip, when he has seized everything else, to march upon us, he has taken leave of his senses, and the peace that he talks of is one that you observe towards Philip, but not Philip towards you. That is the advantage which he is purchasing by all his expenditure of money—that he should be at war with you, but that you should not be at war with him.

If we are going to wait for him to acknowledge a state of war with us, we are indeed the simplest of mortals; for even if he marches straight against Attica and the Piraeus, he will not admit it, if we may judge from his treatment of the other states.

For take the case of the Olynthians; when he was five miles from their city,

---

① Probably the second clause has no connection with the first, but is an alternative form of the beginning of the next sentence.

he told them there must be one of two things, either they must cease to reside in Olynthus, or he in Macedonia, though on all previous occasions, when accused of hostile intentions, he indignantly sent ambassadors to justify his conduct. Again, when he was marching against the Phocians, he still pretended that they were his allies, and Phocian ambassadors accompanied him on his march, and most people here at Athens contended that his passage through Thermopylae [1] would be anything but a gain to the Thebans.

And then again quite lately, after entering Thessaly as a friend and ally, he seized Pherae and still retains it; and lastly, he informed those poor wretches, the people of Oreus, that he had sent his soldiers to pay them a visit of sympathy in all goodwill, for he understood that they were suffering from acute internal trouble, and it was the duty of true friends and allies to be at their side on such occasions.

And do you imagine that, while in the case of those who could have inflicted no harm, though they might perhaps have protected themselves against it, he preferred to deceive them rather than to crush them after due warning, in your case he will give warning of hostilities, especially when you are so eager to be deceived?

Impossible! For indeed he would be the most fatuous man on earth if, when you, his victims, charge him with no crime, but throw the blame on some of your own fellow-citizens, he should compose your mutual differences and jealousies, and invite you to turn them against himself, and should deprive his own hirelings of the excuses with which they put you off, saying that at any rate it is not Philip who is making war on Athens.

But, in heaven's name, is there any intelligent man who would let words rather than deeds decide the question who is at peace and who is at war with him?

---

[1] In July 346, when the Phocians were holding Thermopylae against Philip, the Athenians refused to help them, being misled by Aeschines and Philocrates, who represented that Philip's real hostility was directed against the Thebans. See Dem. 18.35 and Dem. 5.10.

Surely no one. Now it was Philip who at the very start, as soon as peace was concluded, before Diopithes was appointed general, before the force now in the Chersonese had been dispatched, proceeded to occupy Serrium and Doriscus and expelled from the Fort Serreum and the Sacred Mount the garrison which your own general had posted there.

Yet what did that move of his mean? For it was peace that he had sworn[①] to observe; and let no one say, "What of all this? How do any of these things concern Athens?" For whether they were small things, or whether they were no concern of yours, may be another question. But religion and justice, whether a man violates them in a small matter or in a great, have the same importance. Tell me now: when he sends mercenaries to the Chersonese, your claim to which has been recognized by the king of Persia and by all the Greeks, when he admits that he is helping the Cardians and writes to tell you so, what does he mean? For he says that he is not at war,

but for my part, so far from admitting that in acting thus he is not observing the peace with you, I assert that when he lays hands on Megara, sets up tyrannies in Euboea, makes his way, as now, into Thrace, hatches plots in the Peloponnese, and carries out all operations with his armed force, he is breaking the peace and making war upon you—unless you are prepared to say that men who bring up the siege-engines are keeping the peace until they actually bring them to bear on the walls. But you will not admit that; for he who makes and devises the means by which I may be captured is at war with me, even though he has not yet hurled a javelin or shot a bolt.

In what then consists your danger, if anything should happen? In the alienation of the Hellespont, in the control of Megara and Euboea by one who is at war with you, and in the defection of the Peloponnesians to his side. Am I still to say that the man who brings this siege-engine to bear on your city is at peace

---

① Not strictly true; for Philip had not yet taken the oath, though the Athenians had. Hence Blass wished to read εἰρήνη...ὡμώμοτο.

with you?

So far from saying that, I date his hostility from the very day when he wiped out the Phocians. I say that you will be wise if you defend yourselves now, but if you let the opportunity pass, you will not be able to act even when you desire to. I so far dissent, Athenians, from all you counsellors that I do not think you ought to trouble yourselves now about the Chersonese or Byzantium.

Help them, if you will, guard them from harm [supply the troops already there with all that they require], but let your deliberations embrace all the Greek states and the great danger that besets them. But I wish to tell you the grounds for my alarm about our condition, so that if my reasoning is sound, you may adopt it as your own and take forethought for yourselves, even if you refuse to take it for the others also; but if I seem to you a driveler and a dotard, neither now nor at any other time pay any heed to me as if I were in my senses.

As for the fact, then, that Philip rose to greatness from small and humble beginnings, that the Greek states are mutually disloyal and factious, and that the increase of Philip's power in the past was a far greater miracle than the completion of his conquests now that he has already gained so much, these and all such topics on which I might expatiate, I will pass over in silence.

I observe, however, that all men, and you first of all, have conceded to him something which has been the occasion of every war that the Greeks have ever waged. And what is that? The power of doing what he likes, of calmly plundering and stripping the Greeks one by one, and of attacking their cities and reducing them to slavery.

Yet your hegemony in Greece lasted seventy-five years, that of Sparta twenty-nine, and in these later times Thebes too gained some sort of authority after the battle of Leuctra. But neither to you nor to the Thebans nor to the Lacedaemonians did the Greeks ever yet, men of Athens, concede the right of unrestricted action, or anything like it.

On the contrary, when you, or rather the Athenians of that day, were thought to be showing a want of consideration in dealing with others, all felt it their duty, even those who had no grievance against them, to go to war in support of those who had been injured; and again, when the Lacedaemonians had risen to power and succeeded to your position of supremacy, and when they set to work to encroach on others and interfered unduly with the established order of things, all the Greeks were up in arms, even those who had no grievance of their own.

Why need I refer to the other states? Nay, we ourselves and the Lacedaemonians, though at the outset we could not have specified any wrong at each other's hands, thought it our duty to fight on account of wrongs which we saw the other states suffering. Yet all the faults committed by the Lacedaemonians in those thirty years, and by our ancestors in their seventy years of supremacy, are fewer, men of Athens, than the wrongs which Philip has done to the Greeks in the thirteen incomplete years in which he has been coming to the top—or rather, they are not a fraction of them.

[And this is easily proved by a short calculation.] I pass over Olynthus and Methone and Apollonia and the two and thirty cities in or near Thrace, all of which Philip has destroyed so ruthlessly that a traveler would find it hard to say whether they had ever been inhabited. I say nothing of the destruction of the important nation of the Phocians. But how stands the case of the Thessalians? Has he not robbed them of their free constitutions and of their very cities, setting up tetrarchies in order to enslave them, not city by city, but tribe by tribe?

Are not tyrannies already established in Euboea, an island, remember, not far from Thebes and Athens? Does he not write explicitly in his letters, "I am at peace with those who are willing to obey me"? And he does not merely write this without putting it into practice; but he is off to the Hellespont, just as before he hurried to Ambracia; in the Peloponnese he occupies the important city of Elis; only the other day he intrigued against the Megarians. Neither the Greek nor the barbarian world is big enough for the fellow's ambition.

And we Greeks see and hear all this, and yet we do not send embassies to one another and express our indignation. We are in such a miserable position, we have so entrenched ourselves in our different cities, that to this very day we can do nothing that our interest or our duty demands; we cannot combine, we cannot take any common pledge of help or friendship;

But we idly watch the growing power of this man, each bent (or so it seems to me) on profiting by the interval afforded by another's ruin, taking not a thought, making not an effort for the salvation of Greece. For that Philip, like the recurrence or attack of a fever or some other disease, is threatening even those who think themselves out of reach, of that not one of you is ignorant.

Ay, and you know this also, that the wrongs which the Greeks suffered from the Lacedaemonians or from us, they suffered at all events at the hands of true-born sons of Greece, and they might have been regarded as the acts of a legitimate son, born to great possessions, who should be guilty of some fault or error in the management of his estate: so far he would deserve blame and reproach, yet it could not be said that it was not one of the blood, not the lawful heir who was acting thus.

But if some slave or superstitious bastard had wasted and squandered what he had no right to, heavens! how much more monstrous and exasperating all would have called it! Yet they have no such qualms about Philip and his present conduct, though he is not only no Greek, nor related to the Greeks, but not even a barbarian from any place that can be named with honor, but a pestilent knave from Macedonia, whence it was never yet possible to buy a decent slave.

Yet what is wanting to crown his insolence? Not content with the destruction of cities, is he not organizing the Pythian games, the common festival of the Greeks, and if he cannot be present in person, sending his menials to act as stewards? [Is he not master of Thermopylae and the passes into Greece, holding those places with his garrisons and his mercenaries? Has he not the right of precedence at the Oracle, ousting us and the Thessalians and the Dorians and the rest of the Amphictyons from a privilege which not even all Greek states can claim?]

Does he not dictate to the Thessalians their form of government? Does he not send mercenaries, some to Porthmus to expel the Eretrian democracy, others to Oreus to set up the tyranny of Philistides? Yet the Greeks see all this and suffer it. They seem to watch him just as they would watch a hailstorm, each praying that it may not come their way, but none making any effort to stay its course.

And it is not only his outrages on Greece that go unavenged, but even the wrongs which each suffers separately. For nothing can go beyond that. Are not the Corinthians hit by his invasion of Ambracia and Leucas? The Achaeans by his vow to transfer Naupactus to the Aetolians? The Thebans by his theft of Echinus? And is he not marching even now against his [1] allies the Byzantines?

Of our own possessions, not to mention other places, is he not holding Cardia, the greatest city in the Chersonese? In spite of such treatment, we hesitate one and all, we play the coward, we keep an eye on our neighbors, distrusting one another rather than our common foe. Yet if he treats us all with such brutality, what do you think he will do when he has got each of us separately into his clutches?

What then is the cause of this? For not without reason, not without just cause, the Greeks of old were as eager for freedom as their descendants today are for slavery. There was something, men of Athens, something which animated the mass of the Greeks but which is lacking now, something which triumphed over the wealth of Persia, which upheld the liberties of Hellas, which never lost a single battle by sea or land, something the decay of which has ruined everything and brought our affairs to a state of chaos. And what was that?

[It was nothing recondite or subtle, but simply that] men who took bribes from those who wished to rule Greece or ruin her, were hated by all, and it was

---

[1]　This translation is justified by Dem. 18.87. Others "their allies," since the Byzantines are known to have helped the Thebans with money in the Sacred War. (Cauer, Del. Inscr. Gr. 353.)

the greatest calamity to be convicted of receiving a bribe, and such a man was punished with the utmost severity [and no intercession, no pardon was allowed].

At each crisis, therefore, the opportunity for action, with which fortune often equips the careless against the vigilant [and those who shrink from deeds against those who fulfil their duties], could not be bought at a price from our politicians or our generals; no, nor our mutual concord, nor our distrust of tyrants and barbarians, nor, in a word, any such advantage.

Now, however, all these things have been sold in open market, and in place of them we have imported vices which have infected Greece with a mortal sickness. And what are those vices? Envy of the man who has secured his gains; contempt for him who confesses; [pardon for those who are convicted;] hatred for him who censures such dealings; and every other vice that goes hand in hand with corruption.

For war-galleys, men in abundance, money and material without stint, everything by which one might gauge the strength of our cities, these we as a body possess today in number and quantity far beyond the Greeks of former times. But all our resources are rendered useless, powerless, worthless by these traffickers.

That this is so, you surely see for yourselves with regard to the present, and you need no evidence of mine, but that it was the opposite in the days of old I will prove, not in my own words, but by the written record of your ancestors, which they engraved on a bronze pillar and set up in the Acropolis. [It was not for their own use, for without these documents their instinct was right; but it was that you might have these examples to remind you that such cases ought to be regarded seriously.]

"Arthmius of Zelea," it says, "son of Pythonax, outlaw and enemy of the people of Athens and of their allies, himself and his family." Then is recorded the reason for this punishment: "because he conveyed the gold of the Medes to the Peloponnese." So runs the inscription.

I earnestly implore you to consider what was the intention of the Athenians who did this thing, or what was their proud claim. They proscribed as their enemy and the enemy of their allies, disfranchising him and his family, a man of Zelea, one Arthmius, a slave of the Great King (for Zelea is in Asia) , because in the service of his master he conveyed gold, not to Athens but to the Peloponnese. [①]

This was not outlawry as commonly understood; for what mattered it to a native of Zelea if he was to be debarred from a share in the common rights of Athenian citizens? But the statutes relating to murder provide for cases where prosecution for murder is not allowed [but where it is a righteous act to slay the murderer]; "and he shall die an outlaw," says the legislator. This simply means that anyone slaying a member of Arthmius's family would be free from blood-guilt.

So our ancestors thought that they were bound to consider the welfare of all Greeks, for except on that assumption bribery and corruption in the Peloponnese would be no concern of theirs; and in chastising and punishing all whom they detected, they went so far as to set the offenders' names on a pillar. The natural result was that the Greek power was dreaded by the barbarian, not the barbarian by the Greeks. But that is no longer so. For that is not your attitude towards these and other offences. What then is your attitude?

[You know it yourselves. For why should you bear the whole blame, when all the other Greeks are just as bad as you? That is why I assert that the present crisis calls for earnest zeal and wise counsel. What counsel?] [②] Do you want

---

[①] The occasion of this decree, to which Demosthenes refers in Dem. 19.271, is not known. According to Plut. Them. 6 it was Themistocles who proposed it; but a schol. on Aristides names Cimon. The date in the former case would be before 471; in the latter it would be after 457, and may be connected with the mission of Megabazus to Sparta in 455, mentioned by Thuc. 1.109.

[②] The last two words seem pointless. Perhaps τίνος; is the attempt of a scribe to join the longer to the shorter version.

me to tell you, and will you promise not to be angry?"[He reads from an official record]" [1]

Now there is a foolish argument advanced by those who want to reassure the citizens. Philip, they say, after all is not yet what the Lacedaemonians were; they were masters of every sea and land; they enjoyed the alliance of the king of Persia; nothing could stand against them: and yet our city defended itself even against them and was not overwhelmed. But for my own part, while practically all the arts have made a great advance and we are living today in a very different world from the old one, I consider that nothing has been more revolutionized and improved than the art of war.

For in the first place I am informed that in those days the Lacedaemonians, like everyone else, would spend the four or five months of the summer "season" in invading and laying waste the enemy's territory with heavy infantry and levies of citizens, and would then retire home again; and they were so old-fashioned, or rather such good citizens, [2] that they never used money to buy an advantage from anyone, but their fighting was of the fair and open kind.

But now you must surely see that most disasters are due to traitors, and none are the result of a regular pitched battle. On the other hand you hear of Philip marching unchecked, not because he leads a phalanx of heavy infantry, but because he is accompanied by skirmishers, cavalry, archers, mercenaries, and similar troops.

When, relying on this force, he attacks some people that is at variance with itself, and when through distrust no one goes forth to fight for his country, then he brings up his artillery and lays siege. I need hardly tell you that he

---

[1] A frank description of the Athenian attitude, which should follow here, has dropped out, and the lemma, which is found in S and other good MSS., seems to be a poor attempt to fill the gap. It is difficult to imagine any official document that would be of use to the orator here.

[2] The Greek means true to the spirit of a free, constitutional state. Aristotle describes the πολιτικὸν πλῆθοςas one which is "naturally warlike and qualified to rule or be ruled according to laws which distribute offices by merit" (Aristot. Pol. 3.17.4)

makes no difference between summer and winter and has no season set apart for inaction.

Since, however, you all know this, you must take it into account and not let the war pass into your own country; you must not invite catastrophe through keeping your eyes fixed on the simple strategy of your old war with the Lacedaemonians, but arrange your political affairs and your military preparations so that your line of defence may be as far away from Athens as possible, give him no chance of stirring from his base, and never come to close grips with him.

For so far as a campaign is concerned, provided, men of Athens, we are willing to do what is necessary, we have many natural advantages, such as the nature of his territory, much of which may be harried and devastated, and countless others; but for a pitched battle he is in better training than we are.

But it is not enough to adopt these suggestions, nor even to oppose him with active military measures, but both from calculation and on principle you must show your hatred of those who speak publicly on his behalf; and you must reflect that it is impossible to defeat the enemies of our city until you have chastised those who within our very walls make themselves their servants.

And that, as all Heaven is my witness, you will never be able to do; but you have reached such a height of folly or of madness or—I know not what to call it, for this fear too has often haunted me, that some demon is driving you to your doom, that from love of calumny or envy or ribaldry, or whatever your motive may be, you clamor for a speech from these hirelings, some of whom would not even disclaim that title, and you derive amusement from their vituperations.

This is serious enough, but there is worse to follow; for you have granted to these men more security for the pursuance of their policy than to your own defenders. Yet mark what troubles are in store for those who lend an ear to such counsellors. I will mention some facts which will be familiar to you all.

At Olynthus there were two parties in the state: Philip's men, entirely subservient to him, and the patriots, striving to preserve the freedom of their countrymen. Which, pray, ruined their country? Which betrayed the cavalry, whose betrayal sealed the doom of Olynthus? The partisans of Philip; the men who, when the city was still standing, tried to defame and slander the patriotic statesmen, until the Olynthian democracy was actually induced to expel Apollonides. [1]

Now it was not at Olynthus only that this habit produced every kind of evil result; but at Eretria, when the democrats, ridding themselves of Plutarchus and his mercenaries, held the city together with Porthmus, some of them were for handing the government over to you, others to Philip. The latter on most points, or rather on all, gained the ear of the sorely tried and ill-starred Eretrians, and at last persuaded them to expel their real champions.

For of course Philip, whom they fancied their ally, sent Hipponicus with a thousand mercenaries, razed the walls of Porthmus, and set up three tyrants, Hipparchus, Automedon, and Clitarchus. Twice since then they have tried to deliver themselves, and twice he has driven them from their homes [on the first occasion sending Eurylochus with his mercenaries, on the second Parmenio].

And what need is there to mention most of the cases? But at Oreus Philistides, Menippus, Socrates, Thoas, and Agapaeus, the very men who now control the city, were, as everyone knew, Philip's agents, but Euphraeus, a man who once resided here at Athens, was working for the freedom and emancipation of his countrymen.

It would be a long story to tell you how this man was repeatedly outraged and insulted by the people; but a year before the capture of Eretria, detecting the machinations of Philistides and his party, he denounced him as a traitor. Then a number of fellows banded together, with Philip for their paymaster and managing director, and dragged Euphraeus off to prison for setting the city in an

---

[1] The democratic leader, afterwards honored with the citizenship of Athens.

uproar.

When the democrats of Oreus saw this, instead of rescuing him and knocking the others on the head, they showed no resentment against them and gloated over Euphraeus, saying that he deserved all he had got. Then having all the liberty of action they desired, they intrigued for the capture of the city and prepared to carry out their plot, while any of the common folk who saw what they were at were terrorized into silence, having the fate of Euphraeus before their eyes. And so abject was their condition that, with this danger looming ahead, no one dared to breathe a syllable until the enemy, having completed their preparations, were approaching the gates; and then some were for defence, the others for surrender.

But since that base and shameful capture of the city, the latter have been its rulers and tyrants; those who sheltered them before, and had been ready to take any measures against Euphraeus, were rewarded with banishment or death; and the noble Euphraeus slew himself, giving thus a practical proof of the honesty and disinterested patriotism of his opposition to Philip.

Perhaps you wonder why the people of Olynthus and Eretria and Oreus were more favorably inclined to Philip's advocates than to their own. The explanation is the same as at Athens, that the patriots, however much they desire it, cannot sometimes say anything agreeable, for they are obliged to consider the safety of the state; but the others by their very efforts to be agreeable are playing into Philip's hands. The patriots demanded a war-subsidy, the others denied its necessity; the patriots bade them fight on and mistrust Philip, the others bade them keep the peace, until they fell into the snare.

Not to go into particulars, it is the same tale everywhere, one party speaking to please their audience, the other giving advice that would have ensured their safety. But at the last there were many things that the people were induced to concede, not as before for their own gratification nor through ignorance, but gradually yielding because they thought that their discomfiture was inevitable and complete.

And, by Heaven, that is what I certainly fear will be your experience, when you count your chances and discover that there is nothing left for you to do. And yet I pray, Athenians, that such may not be the issue of events. Better to die a thousand times than pay court to Philip [and abandon any of your loyal counsellors.] A fine return the people of Oreus have gained for handing themselves over to Philip's friends and rejecting Euphraeus!

A fine return the democrats of Eretria have gained for spurning your embassy and capitulating to Clitarchus! They are slaves, doomed to the whipping-post and the scaffold. A fine clemency he showed to the Olynthians, who voted Lasthenes their master of the horse and banished Apollonides!

It is folly and cowardice to cherish such hopes, to follow ill counsel and refuse to perform any fraction of your duties, to lend an ear to the advocates of your enemies and imagine that your city is so great that no conceivable danger can befall it.

Ay, and a disgrace too it is to have to say, when all is over, "Why! who would have thought it? For of course we ought to have done this or that, and not so and so." Many things could be named by the Olynthians today, which would have saved them from destruction if only they had then foreseen them. Many could be named by the Orites, many by the Phocians, many by every ruined city.

But of what use to them is that? While the vessel is safe, whether it be a large or a small one, then is the time for sailor and helmsman arid everyone in his turn to show his zeal and to take care that it is not capsized by anyone's malice or inadvertence; but when the sea has overwhelmed it, zeal is useless.

So we too, Athenians, as long as we are safe, blessed with a very great city, ample advantages, and the fairest repute—what are we to do? Perhaps some of my hearers have long been eager to ask that question. I solemnly promise that I will answer it and will also move a resolution, for which you can vote if so disposed. To begin with ourselves, we must make provision for our defence, I mean with war-galleys, funds, and men; for even if all other states succumb to slavery, we surely must fight the battle of liberty.

Then having completed all these preparations and made our purpose clear, we must lose no time in calling upon the other Greeks, and we must inform them by sending ambassadors [in every direction, to the Peloponnese, to Rhodes, to Chios, to the Great King—for even his interests are not unaffected if we prevent Philip from subduing the whole country—] so that if you win them over, you may have someone to share your dangers and your expenses when the time comes, or if not, that you may at least delay the course of events.

For since the war is against an individual and not against the might of an organized community, even delay is not without its use; nor were those embassies useless which you sent round the Peloponnese last year to denounce Philip, when I and our good friend Polyeuctus here and Hegesippus and the rest went from city to city and succeeded in checking him, so that he never invaded Ambracia nor even started against the Peloponnese.

一　文献出处

Demosthenes, with an English translation by J. H. Vince, Cambridge, M.A.: Harvard University Press; London : William Heinemann Ltd., 1930.

二　文献导读

德摩斯提尼（Demosthenes，公元前 384~前 322 年）是古希腊著名的演说家和政治家。他生活的时代正值希腊城邦普遍地陷入危机。在城邦内部，贫富分化日益加剧，公民团体受到严重的破坏，个人主义思潮冲击和瓦解着传统的伦理道德；在城邦外部，在城邦之间的混战不断的同时，希腊北部边陲的落后部族马其顿人正在迅速崛起，随时准备南下入主希腊。对于马其顿人的威胁，希腊城邦内部意见不一，分成"亲马其顿派"和

"反马其顿派"。作为"反马其顿派"的主要代表人物，德摩斯提尼强烈呼吁希腊各邦团结一致，全力以赴阻止马其顿人的扩张，只有这样才能维护城邦的独立，保住传统的城邦民主制度。德摩斯提尼传世的一系列演说辞正是在这样的一个时代背景下产生的，作为希腊城邦危机时代的亲历者和见证者，德摩斯提尼的演说无疑是我们了解和研究公元前4世纪希腊的政治和社会状况的宝贵的第一手资料。

德摩斯提尼出生在一个富裕的雅典公民家庭。7岁的时候父亲去世，留下了价值约14塔兰特的遗产，包括一个武器作坊、一个家居作坊等其他财产。由于德摩斯提尼年纪尚幼，老德摩斯提尼临终前指定侄儿阿福布斯、外甥德摩芬和朋友特里皮德斯作为他的监护人共同监管这笔财产。没想到这些财产大部分被这些监护人侵吞了，到德摩斯提尼成年的时候，仅仅得到了一所房子、14名奴隶和半塔兰特现金，总值仅占父亲留下的遗产的1/12。公元前364年，年仅20岁的德摩斯提尼把阿福布斯告上雅典法庭，虽然胜诉，但由于阿福布斯使用各种手段拒不还钱，德摩斯提尼还是一无所得。根据雅典的法律，诉讼的当事人，无论是原告还是被告，都需要亲自在法庭上陈述自己的意见。为了从监护人那里索回应该属于他的遗产，德摩斯提尼决定拜师学艺，跟随当时雅典著名的演说家伊赛学习演说术，在这桩延续了长达五年的财产纠纷案中，德摩斯提尼前后共发表了五篇演说，德摩斯提尼最终胜诉。更为重要的是，经过这个人生的曲折，德摩斯提尼找到了自己发展的方向，此后，他成为雅典的一位著名的律师，专门代人撰写法庭辩护词，演说术的技艺也日益精湛。不过，替人辩护仅仅是一个谋生的手段，德摩斯提尼还有着更高的人生目标，就是成为一名政治家。从公元前354年起，德摩斯提尼开始积极地投身于雅典的政治活动，直到去世，在长达30年的演说家和政治家的生涯中，德摩斯提尼经历了雅典历史上很多重要的历史事件，尤其在与马其顿人的斗争中，德摩斯提尼以其坚毅的品格、雄辩的口才和卓越的组织才能成为雅典政坛上一位极其活跃的领军人物。

其实，这一切来之不易。据普鲁塔克的记载，德摩斯提尼最初的政治演说并不成功，由于发音不清，论证无力，听众把他轰下了讲坛。于是他向著名的演员请教朗诵的方法，为了练习发音，他把小石子含在嘴里，迎着大风和波涛大声说话；为了使声音洪亮，增加屏气量，他一面爬山，一面不停地吟诗；为了改进演说的姿态，他买了一面大镜子，对镜练习，头上还悬挂了一柄剑，迫使自己去掉多余的动作。作为一名政治演说家，不仅要有洪亮和清晰的发音，还要具备政治、外交、军事等各方面的知识，为此，德摩斯提尼博览群书，刻苦钻研，据说他曾经把修昔底德的《伯罗奔尼撒战争史》抄录过八遍，从中学会了如何运用简洁有力的语言表达丰富和深刻的思想。可以说，德摩斯提尼后来的每篇演说辞都是经过细心雕琢和反复修改而完成的，其中的很多篇成了希腊演说辞中的经典之作和传世名篇。

在当时的雅典不存在常设的负责内政和外交的专门机构，城邦的财政、军事、外交等大事都是由公民大会投票决定的，与此同时，也不存在现在所谓的"新闻媒体"，口头交流在社会生活中占据了主导地位，而投票的结果完全取决于代表不同政治派别的演说家在公民大会上的劝说技巧。正是在这样的历史环境下，演说术和修辞学得以繁荣，政治演说家也应运而生，成为可以左右政坛的风云人物，德摩斯提尼就是其中的佼佼者。

面对马其顿对希腊的巨大威胁，德摩斯提尼发表了一系列演说，号召全体希腊人停止内战，团结起来一致对外，殊死抵抗妄图奴役希腊人的马其顿。在德摩斯提尼传世的 61 篇演说辞中，有 19 篇政治演说，其中以 8 篇反对马其顿王腓力的演说最为著名，这些演说通称"腓力皮卡"，对腓力的野心进行了无情的揭露和猛烈的抨击。后来，"腓力皮卡"甚至成为一个专有名词，用来指称那些抨击政敌的演说。西赛罗就曾经把自己的反安东尼的演说称为"腓力皮卡"。

德摩斯提尼不仅在口头上大声疾呼，而且还身体力行地积极投身于反马其顿人的实际行动中。他有一句名言是："辞令的灵魂是行动，行动，再行动。"公元前 357~前 356 年，腓力利用雅典的困境，占领了色雷斯的很多希腊城邦。在这之后不久，德摩斯提尼发表了他的第一篇反腓力演说。公元前 349 年，腓力对卡尔基斯半岛的重要城市奥林托斯发动进攻，为了援助奥林托斯，德摩斯提尼连续三次在公民大会上发表演说，公民大会最终通过了出兵援助奥林托斯的建议，但由于行动迟缓，奥林托斯还是没有摆脱被夷为平地的命运。腓力在不要赎金的情况下释放了部分在奥林托斯被俘的雅典人，以此向雅典人示好。雅典随即派出由十个人组成的代表团到马其顿议和，德摩斯提尼就是其中之一。在谈判桌上，德摩斯提尼极力反对雅典试图自保而不顾色雷斯沿海地区利益的和约，但很多人对腓力仍抱有幻想，他的建议没有被接受。

腓力利用希腊各邦之间的矛盾，竭力煽动他们对斯巴达和雅典的敌视。为了挫败腓力的阴谋，德摩斯提尼亲赴伯罗奔尼撒进行游说，力陈利害关系，号召各邦放弃前嫌，共抵外辱。回来后发表了第二篇和第三篇反腓力演说。这些演说终于发生了作用，公民大会决定派出使者联络各邦。德摩斯提尼本人被派往拜占庭。公元前 340 年春天，雅典、麦加拉、科林斯等城邦结成了"反马其顿同盟"。同年，腓力对拜占庭发动了进攻，但是在希腊各邦的大力援助下，腓力只得放弃。这一胜利极大地鼓舞了希腊人的士气，德摩斯提尼被任命为海军总监，在他的倡导下，雅典进行了造舰捐助制度的改革，并把戏剧津贴的费用用于军费，全力备战。但是，德摩斯提尼的所有努力并没有能够阻止马其顿人在希腊不断推进。公元前338 年，在喀罗尼亚的决战中，腓力的军队打败了缺乏团结的希腊联军，德摩斯提尼以重装步兵的身份参加了这场战役。战役结束后，德摩斯提尼受托在喀罗尼亚战役的阵亡将士墓前致悼词。公元前 337 年，在德摩斯提尼的建议下，雅典决定全面修缮雅典城和比雷埃弗斯港的防御工事，他自己也当选为所在地区部落的修缮城墙的负责人，除了从国库领取的 10 塔兰特资金外，他自己又捐献了 3 塔兰特，作为建筑费用。

公元前 336 年春，腓力遇刺身亡。得知这个消息之后，德摩斯提尼欣喜若狂，尽管他的独生女儿刚刚在六天以前病逝，但他还是忍住悲伤，穿着节日的盛装出现在公民大会的会场上。此后，他一如既往地参加各种公共事务。公元前 324 年，德摩斯提尼因为亚历山大的财务官在雅典的行贿案而受到牵连，被罚款 50 塔兰特，因无力偿还而被捕入狱，随即逃亡。几个月后，亚历山大的去世再次点燃了希腊人摆脱马其顿统治的希望，德摩斯提尼被隆重地接回雅典，参与反马其顿的起义。公元前 322 年 8 月，起义被镇压，亚历山大的部将安提帕特尔要求雅典交出德摩斯提尼及其他起义首领。德摩斯提尼逃到阿尔哥斯附近的一个小岛，躲在波赛东神庙里。追赶而来的敌人包围了这座神庙，再三命他出来投降，德摩斯提尼走投无路，服毒自杀。德摩斯提尼的死标志着希腊城邦时代的最终结束。

上文即德摩斯提尼的《第三篇反腓力演说》的全文，当中在全面揭露腓力妄图分化和瓦解希腊人最终达到奴役和掠夺希腊的目标的同时，盛赞雅典民主制度辉煌的过去，号召雅典人重新燃起为国捐躯、抵御外敌的热情，为希腊的独立和自由而投入战斗。

三　延伸阅读

Goldhill, Simon, and Robin Osborne, eds., *Performance Culture and Athenian Democracy*, Cambridge University Press, 1999.

Hansen, Mogens Herman, *The Athenian Democracy in the Age of Demosthenes : Structure, Principles, and Ideology*, translated by J.A. Crook, Oxford, UK : Basil Blackwell Ltd., 1991.

Wooten, Cecil W., *A Commentary on Demosthenes's Philippic I : with Rhetorical Analyses of Philippics II and III*, Oxford University Press, 2008.

Worthington, Ian, ed., *Demosthenes : Statesman and Orator*, London ; New York : Routledge, 2000.

古罗马史文献选读

Polybius: The Histories[*]

I. On the Roman Constitution at its Prime

From the crossing of Xerxes to Greece...and for thirty years after this period, it was always one of those polities which was an object of special study, and it was at its best and nearest to perfection at the time of the Hannibalic war, the period at which I interrupted my narrative to deal with it. Therefore now that I have described its growth, I will explain what were the conditions at the time when by their defeat at Cannae the Romans were brought face to face with disaster.

I am quite aware that to those who have been born and bred under the Roman Republic my account of it will seem somewhat imperfect owing to the omission of certain details. For as they have complete knowledge of it and practical acquaintance with all its parts, having been familiar with these customs and institutions from childhood, they will not be struck by the extent of the information I give but will demand in addition all I have omitted: they will not think that the author has purposely omitted small peculiarities, but owing to ignorance he has been silent regarding the origins of many things and some points of capital importance. Had I mentioned them, they would not have been

---

[*] 波利比乌斯《世界通史》第 6 卷节选。

impressed by my doing so, regarding them as small and trivial points, but as they are omitted they will demand their inclusion as if they were vital matters, through a desire themselves to appear better informed than the author. Now a good critic should not judge authors by what they omit, but by what they relate, and if he finds any falsehood in this, he may conclude that the omissions are due to ignorance; but if all the writer says is true, he should admit that he has been silent about these matters deliberately and not from ignorance.

These remarks are meant for those who find fault with authors in cavilling rather than just spirit....

In so far as any view of matter we form applies to the right occasion, so far expressions of approval or blame are sound. When circumstances change, and when applied to these changed conditions, the most excellent and true reflections of authors seem often not only not acceptable, but utterly offensive....

The three kinds of government that I spoke of above all shared in the control of the Roman state. And such fairness and propriety in all respects was shown in the use of these three elements for drawing up the constitution and in its subsequent administration that it was impossible even for a native to pronounce with certainty whether the whole system was aristocratic, democratic, or monarchical. This was indeed only natural. For if one fixed one's eyes on the power of the consuls, the constitution seemed completely monarchical and royal; if on that of the senate it seemed again to be aristocratic; and when one looked at the power of the masses, it seemed clearly to be a democracy. The parts of the state falling under the control of each element were and with a few modifications still are as follows.

The consuls, previous to leading out their legions, exercise authority in Rome over all public affairs, since all the other magistrates except the tribunes are under them and bound to obey them, and it is they who introduce embassies to the senate. Besides this it is they who consult the senate on matters of urgency, they who carry out in detail the provisions of its decrees. Again as concerns all affairs of state administered by the people it is their duty to take these under their charge, to summon assemblies, to introduce measures, and to preside over the execution of the popular decrees. As for preparation for war and the general conduct of operations in the field, here their power is almost uncontrolled; for they are empowered to make what demands they choose on the allies, to appoint military tribunes, to levy soldiers and select those who are fittest for service. They also have the right of inflicting, when on active service, punishment on anyone under their command; 8 and they are authorized to spend any sum they decide upon from the public funds, being accompanied by a quaestor who faithfully executes their instructions. So that if one looks at this part of the administration alone, one may reasonably pronounce the constitution to be a pure monarchy or kingship. I may remark that any changes in these matters or in others of which I am about to speak that may be made in present or future times do not in any way affect the truth of the views I here state.

To pass to the senate. In the first place it has the control of the treasury, all revenue and expenditure being regulated by it. For with the exception of payments made to the consuls, the quaestors are not allowed to disburse for any particular object without a decree of the senate. And even the item of expenditure which is far heavier and more important than any other — the outlay every five years by the censors on public works, whether constructions or repairs — is under the control of the senate, which makes a grant to the censors for the purpose. Similarly crimes committed in Italy which require a public investigation, such as treason, conspiracy, poisoning, and assassination, are under the jurisdiction of the senate. Also if any private person or community in Italy is in need of arbitration or indeed claims damages or requires succour or protection, the senate attends to all such matters. It also occupies itself with the dispatch of all embassies sent to countries outside of Italy for the purpose either of settling differences, or of offering friendly advice, or indeed of imposing demands, or of receiving submission, or of declaring war; and in like manner with respect to embassies arriving in Rome it decides what reception and what answer lshould be given to them. All these matters are in the hands of the senate, nor have the people anything whatever to do with them. So that again to one residing in Rome during the absence of the consuls the constitution appears to be entirely aristocratic; and this is the conviction of many Greek states and many of the kings, as the senate manages all business connected with them.

After this we are naturally inclined to ask what part in the constitution is left for the people, considering that the senate controls all the particular matters I mentioned, and, what is most important, manages all matters of revenue and expenditure, and considering that the consuls again have uncontrolled authority as regards armaments and operations in the field. But nevertheless there is a part and a very important part left for the people. For it is the people which alone has the right to confer honours and inflict punishment, the only bonds by which kingdoms and states and in a word human society in general are held together. For where the distinction between these is overlooked or is observed but ill applied, no affairs can be properly administered. How indeed is this possible when good and evil men are held in equal estimation? It is by the people, then, in many cases the offences punishable by a fine are tried when the accused have held the highest office; and they are the only court which may try on capital charges. As regards the latter they have a practice which is praiseworthy and should be mentioned. Their usage allows those on trial for their lives when found guilty liberty to depart openly, thus inflicting voluntary exile on themselves, if even only one of the tribes that pronounce the verdict has not yet voted. Such exiles enjoy safety in the territories of Naples, Praeneste, Tibur, and other civitates foederatae. Again it is the people who bestow office on the deserving, the noblest regard of virtue in a state; the people have the power of approving or rejecting laws, and what is most important of all, they deliberate on the question of war and peace. Further in the case of alliances, terms of peace, and treaties, it is the people who ratify all these or the reverse. Thus here again one might plausibly say that the people's share in the government is the greatest, and that the constitution is a democratic one.

Having stated how political power is distributed among the different parts of the state, I will now explain how each of the three parts is enabled, if they wish, the counteract or co-operate with the others. The consul, when he leaves with his army invested with the powers I mentioned, appears indeed to have absolute authority in all matters necessary for carrying out his purpose; but in fact he requires the support of the people and the senate, and is not able to bring his operations to a conclusion without them. For it is obvious that the legions require constant supplies, and without the consent of the senate, neither corn, clothing, nor pay can be provided; so that the commander's plans come to nothing, if the senate chooses to be deliberately negligent and obstructive. It also depends on the senate whether or not a general can carry out completely his conceptions and designs, since it has the right of either superseding him when his year's term of office has expired or of retaining him in command. Again it is in its power to celebrate with pomp and to magnify the successes of a general or on the other hand to obscure and belittle them. For the processions they call triumphs, in which the generals bring the actual spectacle of their achievements before the eyes of their fellow-citizens, cannot be properly organized and sometimes even cannot be held at all, unless the senate consents and provides the requisite funds. As for the people it is most indispensable for the consuls to conciliate them, however far away from home they may be; for, as I said, it is the people which ratifies or annuls terms of peace and treaties, and what is most important, on laying down office the consuls are obliged to account for their actions to the people. So that in no respect is it safe for the consuls to neglect keeping in favour with both the senate and the people.

The senate again, which possesses such great power, is obliged in the first place to pay attention to the commons in public affairs and respect the wishes of the people, and it cannot carry out inquiries into the most grave and important offences against the state, punishable with death, and their correction, unless the senatus consultum is confirmed by the people. The same is the case in matters which directly affect the senate itself. For if anyone introduces a law meant to deprive the senate of some of its traditional authority, or to abolish the precedence and other distinctions of the senators or even to curtail them of their private fortunes, it is the people alone which has the power of passing or rejecting any such measure. And what is most important is that if a single one of the tribunes interposes, the senate is unable to decide finally about any matter, and cannot even meet and hold sittings; and here it is to be observed that the tribunes are always obliged to act as the people decree and to pay every attention to their wishes. Therefore for all these reasons the senate is afraid of the masses and must pay due attention to the popular will.

Similarly, again, the people must be submissive to the senate and respect its members both in public and in private. Through the whole of Italy a vast number of contracts, which it would not be easy to enumerate, are given out by the censors for the construction and repair of public buildings, and besides this there are many things which are farmed, such as navigable rivers, harbours, gardens, mines, lands, in fact everything that forms part of the Roman dominion. Now all these matters are undertaken by the people, and one may almost say that everyone is interested in these contracts and the work they involved. For certain people are the actual purchasers from the censors of the contracts, others are the partners of these first, others stand surety for them, others pledge their own fortunes to the state for this purpose. Now in all these matters the senate is supreme. It can grant extension of time; it can relieve the contractor if any accident occurs; and if the work proves to be absolutely impossible to carry out it can liberate him from his contract. There are in fact many ways in which the senate can either benefit or indicate those who manage public property, as all these matters are referred to it. What is even most important is that the judges in most civil trials, whether public or private, are appointed from its members, where the action involves large interests. So that all citizens being at the mercy of the senate, and looking forward with alarm to the uncertainty of litigation, are very shy of obstructing or resisting its decisions. Similarly everyone is reluctant to oppose the projects of the consuls as all are generally and individually under their authority when in the field.

Such being the power that each part has of hampering the others or co-operating with them, their union is adequate to all emergencies, so that it is impossible to find a better political system than this. For whenever the menace of some common danger from abroad compels them to act in concord and support each other, so great does the strength of the state become, that nothing which is requisite can be neglected, as all are zealously competing in devising means of meeting the need of the hour, nor can any decision arrived at fail to be executed promptly, as all are co-operating both in public and in private to the accomplishment of the task which they have set themselves; and consequently this peculiar form of constitution possesses an irresistible power of attaining every object upon which it is resolved. When again they are freed from external menace, and reap the harvest of good fortune and affluence which is the result of their success, and in the enjoyment of this prosperity are corrupted by flattery and idleness and wax insolent and overbearing, as indeed happens often enough, it is then especially that we see the state providing itself a remedy for the evil from which it suffers. For when one part having grown out of proportion to the others aims at supremacy and tends to become too predominant, it is evident that, as for the reasons above given none of the three is absolute, but the purpose of the one can be counterworked and thwarted by the others, none of them will excessively outgrow the others or treat them with contempt. All in fact remains in statu quo, on the one hand, because any aggressive impulse is sure to be checked and from the outset each estate stands in dread of being interfered with by the others....

VII. The Roman Republic compared with others

One may say that nearly all authors have handed down to us the reputation for excellence enjoyed by the constitutions of Sparta, Crete, Mantinea, and Carthage. Some make mention also of those of Athens and Thebes. I leave these last two aside; for I am myself convinced that the constitutions of Athens and Thebes need not be dealt with at length, considering that these states neither grew by a normal process, nor did they remain for long in their most flourishing state, nor were the changes they underwent immaterial; but after a sudden effulgence so to speak, the work of chance and circumstance, while still apparently prosperous and with every prospect of a bright future, they experienced a complete reverse of fortune. For the Thebans, striking at the Lacedaemonians through their mistaken policy and the hatred their allies bore them, owing to the admirable qualities of one or at most two men, who had detected these weaknesses, gained in Greece a reputation for superiority. Indeed, that the successes of the Thebans at that time were due not to the form of their constitution, but to the high qualities of their leading men, was made manifest to all by Fortune immediately afterwards. For the success of Thebes grew, attained its height, and ceased with the lives of Epaminondas and Pelopidas; and therefore we must regard the temporary splendour of that state as due not to its constitution, but to its men. We must hold very much the same opinion about the Athenian constitution. For Athens also, though she perhaps enjoyed more frequent periods of success, after her most glorious one of all which was coeval with the excellent administration of Themistocles, rapidly experienced a complete reverse of fortune owing to the inconstancy of her nature. For the Athenian populace always more or less resembles a ship without a commander. In such a ship when fear of the billows or the danger of a storm induces the mariners to be sensible and attend to the orders of the skipper, they do their duty admirably. But when they grow over-confident and begin to entertain contempt for their superiors and to quarrel with each other, as they are no longer all of the same way of thinking, then with some of them determined to continue the voyage, and others putting pressure on the skipper to anchor, with some letting out the sheets and others preventing them and ordering the sails to be taken it, not only does the spectacle strike anyone who watches it as disgraceful owing to their disagreement and contention, but the position of affairs is a source of actual danger to the rest of those on board; so that often after escaping from the perils of the widest seas and fiercest storms they are shipwrecked in harbour and when close to the shore. This is what has more than once befallen the Athenian state. After having averted the greatest and most terrible dangers owing to the high qualities of the people and their leaders, it has come to grief at times by sheer heedlessness and unreasonableness in seasons of unclouded tranquillity. Therefore I need say no more about this constitution or that of Thebes, states in which everything is managed by the uncurbed impulse of a mob in the one case exceptionally headstrong and ill-tempered and in the other brought up in an atmosphere of violence and passion.

To pass to the constitution of Crete, two points here demand our attention. How was it that the most learned of the ancient writers — Ephorus, Xenophon, Callisthenes, and Plato — state in the first place that it is one and the same with that of Lacedaemon and in the second place pronounce it worthy of commendation? In my own opinion neither of these assertions is true. Whether or not I am right the following observations will show. And first as to its dissimilarity with the constitution of Sparta. The peculiar features of the Spartan state are said to be first the land laws by which no citizen may own more than another, but all must possess an equal share of the public land; secondly their view of money-making; for, money being esteemed of no value at all among them, the jealous contention due to the possession of more or less is utterly done away with; and thirdly the fact that of the magistrates by whom or by whose co-operation the whole administration is conducted, the kings hold a hereditary office and the members of the Gerousia are elected for life. In all these respects the Cretan practice is exactly the opposite. Their laws go as far as possible in letting them acquire land to the extent of their power, as the saying is, and money is held in such high honour among them that its acquisition is not only regarded as necessary, but as most honourable. So much in fact do sordid love of gain and lust for wealth prevail among them, that the Cretans are the only people in the world in whose eyes no gain is disgraceful. Again their magistracies are annual and elected on a democratic system. So that it often causes surprise how these authors proclaim to us, that two political systems the nature of which is so opposed, are allied and akin to each other. Besides overlooking such differences, these writers go out of their way to give us their general views, saying that Lycurgus was the only man who ever saw the points of vital importance for good government. For, there being two things to which a state owes its preservation, bravery against the enemy and concord among the citizens, Lycurgus by doing away with the lust for wealth did away also with all civil discord and broils. In consequence of which the Lacedaemonians, being free from these evils, excel all the Greeks in the conduct of their internal affairs and in their spirit of union. After asserting this, although they witness that the Cretans, on the other hand, owing to their ingrained lust of wealth are involved in constant broils both public and private, and in murders and civil wars, they regard this as immaterial, and have the audacity to say that the two political systems are similar. Ephorus actually, apart from the names, uses the same phrases in explaining the nature of the two states; so that if one did not attend to the proper names it would be impossible to tell of which he is speaking.

Such are the points in which I consider these two political systems to differ, and I will now give my reasons for not regarding that of Crete as worthy of praise or imitation. In my opinion there are two fundamental things in every state, by virtue of which its principle and constitution is either desirable or the reverse. I mean customs and laws. What is desirable in these makes men's private lives righteous and well ordered and the general character of the state gentle and just, while what is to be avoided has the opposite effect. So just as when we observe the laws and customs of a people to be good, we have no hesitation in pronouncing that the citizens and the state will consequently be good also, thus when we notice that men are covetous in their private lives and that their public actions are unjust, we are plainly justified in saying that their laws, their particular customs, and the state as a whole are bad. Now it would be impossible to find except in some rare instances personal conduct more treacherous or a public policy more unjust than in Crete. Holding then the Cretan constitution to be neither similar to that of Sparta nor in any way deserving of praise and imitation, I dismiss it from the comparison which I have proposed to make.

Nor again is it fair to introduce Plato's republic which also is much belauded by some philosophers. For just as we do not admit to athletic contests artists or athletes who are not duly entered and have not been in training, so we have no right to admit this constitution to the competition for the prize of merit, unless it first give an exhibition of its actual working. Up to the present it would be just the same thing to discuss it with a view to comparison with the constitutions of Sparta, Rome, and Carthage, as to take some statue and compare it with living and breathing men. For even if the workmanship of the statue were altogether praiseworthy, the comparison of a lifeless thing with a living being would strike spectators as entirely imperfect and incongruous.

Dismissing, therefore, these constitutions, we will return to that of Sparta. To me it seems as far as regards the maintenance of concord among the citizens, the security of the Laconian territory and the preservation of the freedom of Sparta, the legislation of Lycurgus and the foresight he exhibited were so admirable that one is forced to regard his institutions as of divine rather than human origin. For the equal division of landed property and the simple and common diet were calculated to produce temperance in the private lives of the citizens and to secure the commonwealth as a whole from civil strife, as was the training in the endurance of hardships and dangers to form brave and valorous men. Now when both these virtues, fortitude and temperance, are combined in one soul or in one city, evil will not readily originate within such men or such peoples, nor will they be easily overmastered by their neighbours. By constructing, therefore, his constitution in this manner and out of these elements, Lycurgus secured the absolute safety of the whole territory of Laconia, and left to the Spartans themselves a lasting heritage of freedom. But as regards the annexation of neighbouring territories, supremacy in Greece, and, generally speaking, an ambitious policy, he seems to me to have made absolutely no provision for such contingencies, either in particular enactments or in the general constitution of the state. What he left undone, therefore, was to bring to bear on the citizens some force or principle, by which, just as he had made them simple and contented in their private lives, he might make the spirit of the city as a whole likewise contented and moderate. But now, while he made them most unambitious and sensible people as regards their private lives and the institutions of their city, he left them most ambitious, domineering, and aggressive towards the rest of the Greeks.

For who is not aware that they were almost the first of the Greeks to cast longing eyes on the territory of their neighbours, making war on the Messenians out of covetousness and for the purpose of enslaving them? And is it not narrated by all historians how out of sheer obstinacy they bound themselves by an oath not to desist from the siege before they had taken Messene? It is no less universally known that owing to their desire of domination in Greece they were obliged to execute the behests of the very people they had conquered in battle. For they conquered the Persians when they invaded Greece, fighting for her freedom; but when the invaders had withdrawn and fled they betrayed the Greek cities to them by the peace of Antalcidas, in order to procure money for establishing their sovereignty over the Greeks; and here a conspicuous defect in their constitution revealed itself. For as long as they aspired to rule over their neighbours or over the Peloponnesians alone, they found the supplies and resources furnished by Laconia itself adequate, as they had all they required ready to hand, and quickly returned home whether by land or sea. But once they began to undertake naval expeditions and to make military campaigns outside the Peloponnese, it was evident that neither their iron currency nor the exchange of their crops for commodities which they lacked, as permitted by the legislation of Lycurgus, would suffice for their needs, since these enterprises demanded a currency in universal circulation and supplies drawn from abroad; and so they were compelled to be beggars from the Persians, to impose tribute on the islanders, and exact contributions from all the Greeks, as they recognized that under the legislation of Lycurgus it was impossible to aspire, I will not say to supremacy in Greece, but to any position of influence.

But what is the purpose of this digression? It is to show from the actual evidence of facts, that for the purpose of remaining in secure possession of their own territory and maintaining their freedom the legislation of Lycurgus is amply sufficient, and to those who maintain this to be the object of political constitutions we must admit that there is not and never was any system or constitution superior to that of Lycurgus. But if anyone is ambitious of greater things, and esteems it finer and more glorious than that to be the leader of many men and to rule and lord it over many and have the eyes of all the world turned to him, it must be admitted that from this point of view the Laconian constitution is defective, while that of Rome is superior and better framed for the attainment of power, as is indeed evident from the actual course of events. For when the Lacedaemonians endeavoured to obtain supremacy in Greece, they very soon ran the risk of losing their own liberty; whereas the Romans, who had aimed merely at the subjection of Italy, in a short time brought the whole world under their sway, the abundant of supplies they had at their command conducing in no small measure to this result.

The constitution of Carthage seems to me to have been originally well contrived as regards its most distinctive points. For there were kings, and the house of Elders was an aristocratical force, and the people were supreme in matters proper to them, the entire frame of the state much resembling that of Rome and Sparta. But at the time when they entered on the Hannibalic War, the Carthaginian constitution had degenerated, and that of Rome was better. For as every body or state or action has its natural periods first of growth, then of prime, and finally of decay, and as everything in them is at its best when they are in their prime, it was for this reason that the difference between the two states manifested itself at this time. For by as much as the power and prosperity of Carthage had been earlier than that of Rome, by so much had Carthage already begun to decline; while Rome was exactly at her prime, as far as at least as her system of government was concerned. Consequently the multitude at Carthage had already acquired the chief voice in deliberations; while at Rome the senate still retained this; and hence, as in one case the masses deliberated and in the other the most eminent men, the Roman decisions on public affairs were superior, so that although they met with complete disaster, they were finally by the wisdom of their counsels victorious over the Carthaginians in the war.

But to pass to differences of detail, such as, to begin with, the conduct of war, the Carthaginians naturally are superior at sea both in efficiency and equipment, because seamanship has long been their national craft, and they busy themselves with the sea more than any other people; but as regards military service on land the Romans are much more efficient. They indeed devote their whole energies to this matter, whereas the Carthaginians entirely neglect their infantry, though they do pay some slight attention to their cavalry. The reason of this is that the troops they employ are foreign and mercenary, whereas those of the Romans are natives of the soil and citizens. So that in this respect also we must pronounce the political system of Rome to be superior to that of Carthage, the Carthaginians continuing to depend for the maintenance of their freedom on the courage of a mercenary force but the Romans on their own valour and on the aid of their allies. Consequently even if they happen to be worsted at the outset, the Romans redeem defeat by final success, while it is the contrary with the Carthaginians. For the Romans, fighting as they are for their country and their children, never can abate their fury but continue to throw their whole hearts into the struggle until they get the better of their enemies. It follows that though the Romans are, as I said, much less skilled in naval matters, they are on the whole successful at sea owing to the gallantry of their men; for although skill in seamanship is of no small importance in naval battles, it is chiefly the courage of the marines that turns the scale in favour of victory. Now not only do Italians in general naturally excel Phoenicians and Africans in bodily strength and personal courage, but by their institutions also they do much to foster a spirit of bravery in the young men. A single instance will suffice to indicate the pains taken by the state to turn out men who will be ready to endure everything in order to gain a reputation in their country for valour.

Whenever any illustrious man dies, he is carried at his funeral into the forum to the so-called rostra, sometimes conspicuous in an upright posture and more rarely reclined. Here with all the people standing round, a grown-up son, if he has left one who happens to be present, or if not some other relative mounts the rostra and discourses on the virtues and successful achievements of the dead. As a consequence the multitude and not only those who had a part in these achievements, but those also who had none, when the facts are recalled to their minds and brought before their eyes, are moved to such sympathy that the loss seems to be not confined to the mourners, but a public one affecting the whole people. Next after the interment and the performance of the usual ceremonies, they place the image of the departed in the most conspicuous position in the house, enclosed in a wooden shrine. This image is a mask reproducing with remarkable fidelity both the features and complexion of the deceased. On the occasion of public sacrifices they display these images, and decorate them with much care, and when any distinguished member of the family dies they take them to the funeral, putting them on men who seem to them to bear the closest resemblance to the original in stature and carriage. These representatives wear togas, with a purple border if the deceased was a consul or praetor, whole purple if he was a censor, and embroidered with gold if he had celebrated a triumph or achieved anything similar. They all ride in chariots preceded by the fasces, axes, and other insignia by which the different magistrates are wont to be accompanied according to the respective dignity of the offices of state held by each during his life; and when they arrive at the rostra they all seat themselves in a row on ivory chairs. There could not easily be a more ennobling spectacle for a young man who aspires to fame and virtue. For who would not be inspired by the sight of the images of men renowned for their excellence, all together and as if alive and breathing? What spectacle could be more glorious than this? Besides, he who makes the oration over the man about to be buried, when he has finished speaking of him recounts the successes and exploits of the rest whose images are present, beginning with the most ancient. By this means, by this constant renewal of the good report of brave men, the celebrity of those who performed noble deeds is rendered immortal, while at the same time the fame of those who did good service to their country becomes known to the people and a heritage for future generations. But the most important result is that young men are thus inspired to endure every suffering for public welfare in the hope of winning the glory that attends on brave men. What I say is confirmed by the facts. For many Romans have voluntarily engaged in single combat in order to decide a battle, not a few have faced certain death, some in war to save the lives of the rest, and others in peace to save the republic. Some even when in office have put their own sons to death contrary to every law or custom, setting a higher value on the interest of their country than on the ties of nature that bound them to their nearest and dearest.

Many such stories about many men are related in Roman history, but one told of a certain person will suffice for the present as an example and as a confirmation of what I say. It is narrated that when Horatius Cocles was engaged in combat with two of the enemy at the far end of the bridge over the Tiber that lies in the front of the town, he saw large reinforcements coming up to help the enemy, and fearing lest they should force the passage and get into town, he turned round and called to those behind him to retire and cut the bridge with all speed. His order was obeyed, and while they were cutting the bridge, he stood to his ground receiving many wounds, and arrested the attack of the enemy who were less astonished at his physical strength than at his endurance and courage. The bridge once cut, the enemy were prevented from attacking; and Cocles, plunging into the river in full armour as he was, deliberately sacrificed his life, regarding the safety of his country and the glory which in future would attach to his name as of more importance than his present existence and the years of life which remained to him. Such, if I am not wrong, is the eager emulation of achieving noble deeds engendered in the Roman youth by their institutions.

Again, the laws and customs relating to the acquisition of wealth are better in Rome than at Carthage. At Carthage nothing which results in profit is regarded as disgraceful; at Rome nothing is considered more so than to accept bribes and seek gain from improper channels. For no less strong than their approval of money-making is their condemnation of unscrupulous gain from forbidden sources. A proof of this is that at Carthage candidates for office practise open bribery, whereas at Rome death is the penalty for it. Therefore as the rewards offered to merit are the opposite in the two cases, it is natural that the steps taken to gain them should also be dissimilar.

But the quality in which the Roman commonwealth is most distinctly superior is in my opinion the nature of their religious convictions. I believe that it is the very thing which among other peoples is an object of reproach, I mean superstition, which maintains the cohesion of the Roman State. These matters are clothed in such pomp and introduced to such an extent into their public and private life that nothing could exceed it, a fact which will surprise many. My own opinion at least is that they have adopted this course for the sake of the common people. It is a course which perhaps would not have been necessary had it been possible to form a state composed of wise men, but as every multitude is fickle, full of lawless desires, unreasoned passion, and violent anger, the multitude must be held in by invisible terrors and suchlike pageantry. For this reason I think, not that the ancients acted rashly and at haphazard in introducing among the people notions concerning the gods and beliefs in the terrors of hell, but that the moderns are most rash and foolish in banishing such beliefs. The consequence is that among the Greeks, apart from other things, members of the government, if they are entrusted with no more than a talent, though they have ten copyists and as many seals and twice as many witnesses, cannot keep their faith; whereas among the Romans those who as magistrates and legates are dealing with large sums of money maintain correct conduct just because they have pledged their faith by oath. Whereas elsewhere it is a rare thing to find a man who keeps his hands off public money, and whose record is clean in this respect, among the Romans one rarely comes across a man who has been detected in such conduct....

VIII. Conclusion of the Treatise on the Roman Republic

That all existing things are subject to decay and change is a truth that scarcely needs proof; for the course of nature is sufficient to force this conviction on us. There being two agencies by which every kind of state is liable to decay, the one external and the other a growth of the state itself, we can lay down no fixed rule about the former, but the latter is a regular process. I have already stated what kind of state is the first to come into being, and what the next, and how the one is transformed into the other; so that those who are capable of connecting the opening propositions of this inquiry with its conclusion will now be able to foretell the future unaided. And what will happen is, I think, evident. When a state has weathered many great perils and subsequently attains to supremacy and uncontested sovereignty, it is evident that under influence of long established prosperity, life will become more extravagant and the citizens more fierce in their rivalry regarding office and other objects than they ought to be. As these defects go on increasing, the beginning of the change for the worse will be due to love of office and the disgrace entailed by obscurity, as well as to extravagance and purse-proud display; and for this change the populace will be responsible when on the one hand they think they have a grievance against certain people who have shown themselves grasping, and when, on the other hand, they are puffed up by the flattery of others who aspire to office. For now, stirred to fury and swayed by passion in all their counsels, they will no longer consent to obey or even to be the equals of the ruling caste, but will demand the lion's share for themselves. When this happens, the state will change its name to the finest sounding of all, freedom and democracy, but will change its nature to the worst thing of all, mob-rule.

Having dealt with the origin and growth of the Roman republic, and with its prime and its present condition, and also with the differences for better or worse between it and others, I may now close this discourse more or less so.

But, drawing now upon the period immediately subsequent to the date at which I abandoned my narrative to enter on this digression, I will make brief and summary mention of one occurrence; so that, as if exhibiting a single specimen of a good artist's work, I may make manifest not by words only but by actual fact the perfection and strength of principle of the Republic such as it then was. Hannibal, when, after his victory over the Romans at Cannae, the eight thousand who garrisoned the camp fell into his hands, after making them all prisoners, allowed them to send a deputation to those at home on the subject of their ransom and release. Upon their naming ten of their most distinguished members, he sent them off after making them swear that they would return to him. One of those nominated just as he was going out of the camp said he had forgotten something and went back, and after recovering the thing he had left behind again took his departure, thinking that by his return he had kept his faith and absolved himself of his oath. Upon their arrival in Rome they begged and entreated the senate not to grudge the prisoners their release, but to allow each of them to pay three minae and return to his people; for Hannibal, they said, had made this concession. The men deserved to be released, for they had neither been guilty of cowardice in the battle nor had they done anything unworthy of Rome; but having been left behind to guard the camp, they had, when all the rest had perished in the battle, been forced to yield to circumstances and surrender to the enemy. But the Romans, though they had met with severe reverses in the war, and had now, roughly speaking, lost all their allies and were in momentary expectation of Rome itself being placed in peril, after listening to this plea, neither disregarded their dignity under the pressure of calamity, nor neglected to take into consideration every proper step; but seeing that Hannibal's object in acting thus was both to obtain funds and to deprive the troops opposed to him of their high spirit, by showing that, even if defeated, they might hope for safety, they were so far from acceding to this request, that they did not allow their pity for their kinsmen, or the consideration of the service the men would render them, to prevail, but defeated Hannibal's calculation and the hopes he had based on them by refusing to ransom the men, and at the same time imposed by law on their own troops the duty of either conquering or dying in the field, as there was no hope of safety for them if defeated. Therefore after coming to this decision they dismissed the nine delegates who returned of their own free will, as bound by their oath, while as for the man who had thought to free himself from the oath by a ruse they put him in irons and returned him to the enemy; so that Hannibal's joy at his victory in the battle was not so great as his dejection, when he saw with amazement how steadfast and high-spirited were the Romans in their deliberations.

一 文献出处

Polybius, *The Histories*, Ⅲ, The Loeb Classical Library, W. R. Paton (trans.), Cambridge, Massachusetts: Harvard University Press, 1989.

二 文献导读

公元前 2 世纪，罗马出现了古代欧洲见识最广的历史学家波利比乌斯（Polybius，约公元前 200~ 前 118 年）。他是希腊人，出生在伯罗奔尼撒半岛的麦加洛波利斯（Megalopolis）。公元前 169 年任阿卡亚同盟骑兵长官。第三次马其顿战争（公元前 171~ 前 168 年）后，作为阿卡亚同盟的 1000 个贵族人质之一被押送至罗马。在罗马深得西庇奥家族宠信，跟随小西庇奥（Scipio Aemilianus）远征东方，先后目睹了迦太基、科林斯和努曼提亚被毁。他竭力利用与罗马军阀的人情关系保护了许多希腊城市免于东征兵燹，因此口碑颇佳。波利比乌斯运用游历地中海沿岸各国查访的史料，兼容并蓄地参考了观点对立的罗马史家法比乌斯和亲近迦太基的希腊史家菲利努斯，以及索西鲁斯、西勒努斯等人的著作，撰写了《世界通史》。该书共 40 卷 / 章，不仅记述了公元前 264~ 前 146 年罗马统一地中海世界的扩张原因和详细经过，而且附带反映了当时已知世界各国的历史。该书十分推崇罗马政制。他的远见卓识主要表现在首倡联系各地综合考察"全世界"的历史因果关系。现存前 5 章主记布匿战争，其余 35 章是残篇。由于他所述大多基于亲身经历，加之善于精选前人史料，长于宏观分析，因此该书是西方第一本世界通史杰作。

波利比乌斯的《世界通史》卷 1~2 写公元前 264~ 前 220 年，卷 3 从公元前 220 年写到公元前 216 年的坎奈（Cannae）之战，卷 4~5 描述当时的希腊和亚细亚，卷 6 述评罗马政制，对比了雅典、底比斯、克里特、斯巴达和迦太基的政制。他认为罗马的政制平衡地融合了君主制、贵族制和民主制的因素，是罗马成功的基础，也是罗马的伟大所在。卷 7 从公元前 215 年开始，根据奥林匹亚运动会（Olympiads）的历法纪年，即每一届奥林匹亚运动会间隔 4 年。他的每一年叙述从西部向东部，先后叙述西西里、西班牙、北非、意大利，然后叙述希腊、马其顿、亚细亚和埃及。卷 30~39 描述公元前 167 年～前 144 年的事，其中卷 34 对整个有人居住的世界地理给予了概括性描绘。

三　延伸阅读

Momigliano, Arnaldo M., *Sesto Contributo alla Storia degli Studi Classici e del Mondo Antico*, Rome, 1980.

Moore, John M., *The Manuscript Tradition of Polybius*, Cambridge University Press, 1965.

T. Livy: The History of Rome[*]

1.40

When Tarquin had been about thirty-eight years on the throne, Servius Tullius

was held in by far the highest esteem of any one, not only with the king but also

with the patricians and the commons. The two sons of Ancus had always felt

most keenly their being deprived of their father's throne through the treachery of

their guardian; its occupation by a foreigner who was not even of Italian, much

less Roman descent, increased their indignation, when they saw that not even

after the death of Tarquin would the crown revert to them, but would suddenly

descend to a slave-that crown which Romulus, the offspring of a god, and

himself a god, had worn whilst he was on earth, now to be the possession of a

slave-born slave a hundred years later! They felt that it would be a disgrace to

the whole Roman nation, and especially to their house, if, while the male issue

of Ancus was still alive, the sovereignty of Rome should be open not only to

foreigners but even to slaves. They determined, therefore, to repel that insult

by the sword. But it was on Tarquin rather than on Servius that they sought to

avenge their wrongs; if the king were left alive he would be able to deal more

summary vengeance than an ordinary citizen, and in the event of Servius being

---

[*] 李维《罗马通史》第 1 卷节选。

killed, the king would certainly make any one else whom he chose for a son-in-law heir to the crown. These considerations decided them to form a plot against the king's life. Two shepherds, perfect desperadoes, were selected for the deed. They appeared in the vestibule of the palace, each with his usual implement, and by pretending to have a violent and outrageous quarrel, they attracted the attention of all the royal guards. Then, as they both began to appeal to the king, and their clamour had penetrated within the palace, they were summoned before the king. At first they tried, by shouting each against the other, to see who could make the most noise, until, after being repressed by the lictor and ordered to speak in turn, they became quiet, and one of the two began to state his case. Whilst the king's attention was absorbed in listening to him, the other swung aloft his axe and drove it into the king's head, and leaving the weapon in the wound both dashed out of the palace.

1.41

Whilst the bystanders were supporting the dying Tarquin in their arms, the lictors caught the fugitives. The shouting drew a crowd together, wondering what had happened. In the midst of the confusion, Tanaquil ordered the palace to be cleared and the doors closed; she then carefully prepared medicaments for dressing the wound, should there be hopes of life; at the same time she decided on other precautions, should the case prove hopeless, and hastily summoned Servius. She showed him her husband at the point of death, and taking his hand, implored him not to leave his father-in-law's death unavenged, nor to allow his mother-in-law to become the sport of her enemies. "The throne is yours, Servius," she said, "if you are a man; it does not belong to those who have, through the hands of others, wrought this worst of crimes. Up! follow the guidance of the gods who presaged the exaltation of that head round which divine fire once played! Let that heaven-sent flame now inspire you. Rouse yourself in earnest! We, too, though foreigners, have reigned. Bethink yourself not whence you sprang, but who you are. If in this sudden emergency you are slow to resolve, then follow my counsels." As the clamour and impatience of the populace could hardly be restrained, Tanaquil went to a window in the upper part of the palace looking out on the Via Nova-the king used to live by the temple of Jupiter Stator-and addressed the people. She bade them hope for the best; the king had been stunned by a sudden blow, but the weapon had not penetrated to any depth, he had already recovered consciousness, the blood had been washed off and the wound examined, all the symptoms were favourable, she was sure they would soon see him again, meantime it was his order that the people should recognise the authority of Servius Tullius, who would administer justice and discharge the other functions of royalty. Servius appeared in his trabea attended by the lictors, and after taking his seat in the royal chair decided some cases and adjourned others under presence of consulting the king. So for several days after Tarquin's death Servius continued to strengthen his position by giving out that he was exercising a delegated authority. At length the sounds of mourning arose in the palace and divulged the fact of the king's death. Protected by a strong bodyguard Servius was the first who ascended the throne without being elected by the people, though without opposition from the senate. When the sons of Ancus heard that the instruments of their crime had been arrested, that the king was still alive, and that Servius was so powerful, they went into exile at Suessa Pometia.

1.42

Servius consolidated his power quite as much by his private as by his public measures. To guard against the children of Tarquin treating him as those of Ancus had treated Tarquin, he married his two daughters to the scions of the royal house, Lucius and Arruns Tarquin. Human counsels could not arrest the inevitable course of destiny, nor could Servius prevent the jealousy aroused by his ascending the throne from making his family the scene of disloyalty and hatred. The truce with the Veientines had now expired, and the resumption of war with them and other Etruscan cities came most opportunely to help in maintaining tranquillity at home. In this war the courage and good fortune of Tullius were conspicuous, and he returned to Rome, after defeating an immense force of the enemy, feeling quite secure on the throne, and assured of the goodwill of both patricians and commons. Then he set himself to by far the greatest of all works in times of peace. Just as Numa had been the author of religious laws and institutions, so posterity extols Servius as the founder of those divisions and classes in the State by which a clear distinction is drawn between the various grades of dignity and fortune. He instituted the census, a most beneficial institution in what was to be a great empire, in order that by its means the various duties of peace and war might be assigned, not as heretofore, indiscriminately, but in proportion to the amount of property each man possessed. From it he drew up the classes and centuries and the following distribution of them, adapted for either peace or war.

1.43

Those whose property amounted to, or exceeded 100, 000 lbs. weight of copper were formed into eighty centuries, forty of juniors and forty of seniors. These were called the First Class. The seniors were to defend the City, the juniors to serve in the field. The armour which they were to provide themselves with comprised helmet, round shield, greaves, and coat of mail, all of brass; these were to protect the person. Their offensive weapons were spear and sword. To this class were joined two centuries of carpenters whose duty it was to work the engines of war; they were without arms. The Second Class consisted of those whose property amounted to between 75, 000 and 100, 000 lbs. weight of copper; they were formed, seniors and juniors together, into twenty centuries. Their regulation arms were the same as those of the First Class, except that they had an oblong wooden shield instead of the round brazen one and no coat of mail. The Third Class he formed of those whose property fell as low as 50, 000 lbs.; these also consisted of twenty centuries, similarly divided into seniors and juniors. The only difference in the armour was that they did not wear greaves. In the Fourth Class were those whose property did not fall below 25, 000 lbs. They also formed twenty centuries; their only arms were a spear and a javelin. The Fifth Class was larger it formed thirty centuries. They carried slings and stones, and they included the supernumeraries, the horn-blowers, and the trumpeters, who formed three centuries. This Fifth Class was assessed at 11, 000 lbs. The rest of the population whose property fell below this were formed into one century and were exempt from military service.

After thus regulating the equipment and distribution of the infantry, he re-arranged the cavalry. He enrolled from amongst the principal men of the State twelve centuries. In the same way he made six other centuries (though only three had been formed by Romulus) under the same names under which the first had been inaugurated. For the purchase of the horse, 10, 000 lbs. were assigned them from the public treasury; whilst for its keep certain widows were assessed to pay 2000 lbs. each, annually. The burden of all these expenses was shifted from the poor on to the rich. Then additional privileges were conferred. The former kings had maintained the constitution as handed down by Romulus, viz., manhood suffrage in which all alike possessed the same weight and enjoyed the same rights. Servius introduced a graduation; so that whilst no one was ostensibly deprived of his vote, all the voting power was in the hands of the principal men of the State. The knights were first summoned to record their vote, then the eighty centuries of the infantry of the First Class; if their votes were divided, which seldom happened, it was arranged for the Second Class to be summoned; very seldom did the voting extend to the lowest Class. Nor need it occasion any surprise, that the arrangement which now exists since the completion of the thirty-five tribes, their number being doubled by the centuries of juniors and seniors, does not agree with the total as instituted by Servius Tullius. For, after dividing the City with its districts and the hills which were inhabited into four parts, he called these divisions "tribes," I think from the tribute they paid, for he also introduced the practice of collecting it at an equal rate according to the assessment. These tribes had nothing to do with the distribution and number of the centuries.

1.44

The work of the census was accelerated by an enactment in which Servius denounced imprisonment and even capital punishment against those who evaded assessment. On its completion he issued an order that all the citizens of Rome, knights and infantry alike, should appear in the Campus Martius, each in their centuries. After the whole army had been drawn up there, he purified it by the triple sacrifice of a swine, a sheep, and an ox. This was called "a closed lustrum," because with it the census was completed. Eighty thousand citizens are said to have been included in that census. Fabius Pictor, the oldest of our historians, states that this was the number of those who could bear arms. To contain that population it was obvious that the City would have to be enlarged. He added to it the two hills-the Quirinal and the Viminal-and then made a further addition by including the Esquiline, and to give it more importance he lived there himself. He surrounded the City with a mound and moats and wall; in this way he extended the "pomoerium." Looking only to the etymology of the word, they explain "pomoerium" as "postmoerium"; but it is rather a "circamoerium." For the space which the Etruscans of old, when founding their cities, consecrated in accordance with auguries and marked off by boundary stones at intervals on each side, as the part where the wall was to be carried, was to be kept vacant so that no buildings might connect with the wall on the inside (whilst now they generally touch), and on the outside some ground might remain virgin soil untouched by cultivation. This space, which it was forbidden either to build upon or to plough, and which could not be said to be behind the wall any more than the wall could be said to be behind it, the Romans called the "pomoerium." As the City grew, these sacred boundary stones were always moved forward as far as the walls were advanced.

1.45

After the State was augmented by the expansion of the City and all domestic arrangements adapted to the requirements of both peace and war, Servius endeavoured to extend his dominion by state-craft, instead of aggrandising it by arms, and at the same time made an addition to the adornment of the City. The temple of the Ephesian Diana was famous at that time, and it was reported to have been built by the co-operation of the states of Asia. Servius had been careful to form ties of hospitality and friendship with the chiefs of the Latin nation, and he used to speak in the highest praise of that co-operation and the common recognition of the same deity. By constantly dwelling on this theme he at length induced the Latin tribes to join with the people of Rome in building a temple to Diana in Rome. Their doing so was an admission of the predominance of Rome; a question which had so often been disputed by arms. Though the Latins, after their many unfortunate experiences in war, had as a nation laid aside all thoughts of success, there was amongst the Sabines one man who believed that an opportunity presented itself of recovering the supremacy through his own individual cunning. The story runs that a man of substance belonging to that nation had a heifer of marvellous size and beauty. The marvel was attested in after ages by the horns which were fastened up in the vestibule of the temple of Diana. The creature was looked upon as-what it really was-a prodigy, and the soothsayers predicted that, whoever sacrificed it to Diana, the state of which he was a citizen should be the seat of empire. This prophecy had reached the ears of the official in charge of the temple of Diana. When the first day on which the sacrifice could properly be offered arrived, the Sabine drove the heifer to Rome, took it to the temple, and placed it in front of the altar. The official in charge was a Roman, and, struck by the size of the victim, which was well known by report, he recalled the prophecy and addressing the Sabine, said, "Why, pray, are you, stranger, preparing to offer a polluted sacrifice to Diana? Go and bathe yourself first in running water. The Tiber is flowing down there at the bottom of the valley." Filled with misgivings, and anxious for everything to be done properly that the prediction might be fulfilled, the stranger promptly went down to the Tiber. Meanwhile the Roman sacrificed the heifer to Diana. This was a cause of intense gratification to the king and to his people.

1.46

Servius was now confirmed on the throne by long possession. It had, however, come to his ears that the young Tarquin was giving out that he was reigning without the assent of the people. He first secured the goodwill of the plebs by assigning to each householder a slice of the land which had been taken from the enemy. Then he was emboldened to put to them the question whether it was their will and resolve that he should reign. He was acclaimed as king by a unanimous vote such as no king before him had obtained. This action in no degree damped Tarquin's hopes of making his way to the throne, rather the reverse. He was a bold and aspiring youth, and his wife Tullia stimulated his restless ambition. He had seen that the granting of land to the commons was in defiance of the opinion of the senate, and he seized the opportunity it afforded him of traducing Servius and strengthening his own faction in that assembly. So it came about that the Roman palace afforded an instance of the crime which tragic poets have depicted, with the result that the loathing felt for kings hastened the advent of liberty, and the crown won by villainy was the last that was worn.

This Lucius Tarquinius-whether he was the son or the grandson of King Priscus Tarquinius is not clear; if I should give him as the son I should have the preponderance of authorities-had a brother, Arruns Tarquinius, a youth of gentle character. The two Tullias, the king's daughters, had, as I have already stated, married these two brothers; and they themselves were of utterly unlike dispositions. It was, I believe, the good fortune of Rome which intervened to prevent two violent natures from being joined in marriage, in order that the reign of Servius Tullius might last long enough to allow the State to settle into its new constitution. The high-spirited one of the two Tullias was annoyed that there was nothing in her husband for her to work on in the direction of either greed or ambition. All her affections were transferred to the other Tarquin; he was her admiration, he, she said, was a man, he was really of royal blood. She despised her sister, because having a man for her husband she was not animated by the spirit of a woman. Likeness of character soon drew them together, as evil usually consorts best with evil. But it was the woman who was the originator of all the mischief. She constantly held clandestine interviews with her sister's husband, to whom she unsparingly vilified alike her husband and her sister, asserting that it would have been better for her to have remained unmarried and he a bachelor, rather than for them each to be thus unequally mated, and fret in idleness through the poltroonery of others. Had heaven given her the husband she deserved, she would soon have seen the sovereignty which her father wielded established in her own house. She rapidly infected the young man with her own recklessness. Lucius Tarquin and the younger Tullia, by a double murder, cleared from their houses the obstacles to a fresh marriage; their nuptials were solemnised with the tacit acquiescence rather than the approbation of Servius.

1.47

From that time the old age of Tullius became more embittered, his reign more unhappy. The woman began to look forward from one crime to another; she allowed her husband no rest day or night, for fear lest the past murders should prove fruitless. What she wanted, she said, was not a man who was only her husband in name, or with whom she was to live in uncomplaining servitude; the man she needed was one who deemed himself worthy of a throne, who remembered that he was the son of Priscus Tarquinius, who preferred to wear a crown rather than live in hopes of it. "If you are the man to whom I thought I was married, then I call you my husband and my king; but if not, I have changed my condition for the worse, since you are not only a coward but a criminal to boot. Why do you not prepare yourself for action? You are not, like your father, a native of Corinth or Tarquinii, nor is it a foreign crown you have to

225

win. Your father's household gods, your father's image, the royal palace, the kingly throne within it, the very name of Tarquin, all declare you king. If you have not courage enough for this, why do you excite vain hopes in the State? Why do you allow yourself to be looked up to as a youth of kingly stock? Make your way back to Tarquinii or Corinth, sink back to the position whence you sprung; you have your brother's nature rather than your father's ." With taunts like these she egged him on. She, too, was perpetually haunted by the thought that whilst Tanaquil, a woman of alien descent, had shown such spirit as to give the crown to her husband and her son-in-law in succession, she herself, though of royal descent, had no power either in giving it or taking it away. Infected by the woman's madness Tarquin began to go about and interview the nobles, mainly those of the Lesser Houses; he reminded them of the favour his father had shown them, and asked them to prove their gratitude; he won over the younger men with presents. By making magnificent promises as to what he would do, and by bringing charges against the king, his cause became stronger amongst all ranks.

At last, when he thought the time for action had arrived, he appeared suddenly in the Forum with a body of armed men. A general panic ensued, during which he seated himself in the royal chair in the senate-house and ordered the Fathers to be summoned by the crier "into the presence of King Tarquin." They hastily assembled, some already prepared for what was coming; others, apprehensive lest their absence should arouse suspicion, and dismayed by the extraordinary nature of the incident, were convinced that the fate of Servius was sealed. Tarquin went back to the king's birth, protested that he was a slave and the son of a slave, and after his (the speaker's) father had been foully murdered, seized the throne, as a woman's gift, without any interrex being appointed as heretofore, without any assembly being convened, without any vote of the people being taken or any confirmation of it by the Fathers. Such was his origin, such was his right to the crown. His sympathies were with the dregs of society from which he had sprung, and through jealousy of the ranks to which he did not belong, he had taken the land from the foremost men in the State and divided it amongst the vilest; he had shifted on to them the whole of the burdens which had formerly been borne in common by all; he had instituted the census that the fortunes of the wealthy might be held up to envy, and be an easily available source from which to shower doles, whenever he pleased, upon the neediest.

1.48

Servius had been summoned by a breathless messenger, and arrived on the scene while Tarquin was speaking. As soon as he reached the vestibule, he exclaimed in loud tones, "What is the meaning of this, Tarquin? How dared you, with such insolence, convene the senate or sit in that chair whilst I am alive?" Tarquin replied fiercely that he was occupying his father's seat, that a king's son was a much more legitimate heir to the throne than a slave, and that he, Servius, in playing his reckless game, had insulted his masters long enough. Shouts arose from their respective partisans, the people made a rush to the senate-house, and it was evident that he who won the fight would reign. Then Tarquin, forced by sheer necessity into proceeding to the last extremity, seized Servius round the waist, and being a much younger and stronger man, carried him out of the senate-house and flung him down the steps into the Forum below. He then returned to call the senate to order. The officers and attendants of the king fled. The king himself, half dead from the violence, was put to death by those whom Tarquin had sent in pursuit of him. It is the current belief that this was done at Tullia's suggestion, for it is quite in keeping with the rest of her wickedness. At all events, it is generally agreed that she drove down to the Forum in a two-wheeled car, and, unabashed by the presence of the crowd, called her husband out of the senate-house and was the first to salute him as king. He told her to make her way out of the tumult, and when on her return she had got as far as the top of the Cyprius Vicus, where the temple of Diana lately stood, and was turning to the right on the Urbius Clivus, to get to the Esquiline, the driver stopped horror-struck and pulled up, and pointed out to his mistress the corpse of the murdered Servius. Then, the tradition runs, a foul and unnatural crime was committed, the memory of which the place still bears, for they call it the Vicus Sceleratus. It is said that Tullia, goaded to madness by the avenging spirits of her sister and her husband, drove right over her father's body, and carried back some of her father's blood with which the car and she herself were defiled to her own and her husband's household gods, through whose anger a reign which began in wickedness was soon brought to a close by a like cause. Servius Tullius reigned forty-four years, and even a wise and good successor would have found it difficult to fill the throne as he had done. The glory of his reign was all the greater because with him perished all just and lawful kingship in Rome. Gentle and moderate as his sway had been, he had nevertheless, according to some authorities, formed the intention of laying it down, because it was vested in a single person, but this purpose of giving freedom to the State was cut short by that domestic crime.

1.49

Lucius Tarquinius now began his reign. His conduct procured for him the nickname of "Superbus, " for he deprived his father-in-law of burial, on the plea that Romulus was not buried, and he slew the leading nobles whom he suspected of being partisans of Servius. Conscious that the precedent which he had set, of winning a throne by violence, might be used against himself, he surrounded himself with a guard. For he had nothing whatever by which to make good his claim to the crown except actual violence; he was reigning without either being elected by the people, or confirmed by the senate. As, moreover, he had no hope of winning the affections of the citizens, he had to maintain his dominion by fear. To make himself more dreaded, he conducted the trials in capital cases without any assessors, and under this presence he was able to put to death, banish, or fine not only those whom he suspected or disliked, but also those from whom his only object was to extort money. His main object was so to reduce the number of senators, by refusing to fill up any vacancies, that the dignity of the order itself might be lowered through the smallness of its numbers, and less indignation felt at all public business being taken out of its hands. He was the first of the kings to break through the traditional custom of consulting the senate on all questions, the first to conduct the government on the advice of his palace favourites. War, peace, treaties, alliances were made or broken off by him, just as he thought good, without any authority from either people or senate. He made a special point of securing the Latin nation, that through his power and influence abroad he might be safer amongst his subjects at home; he not only formed ties of hospitality with their chief men, but established family connections. He gave his daughter in marriage to Octavius Mamilius of Tusculum, who was quite the foremost man of the Latin race, descended, if we are to believe traditions, from Ulysses and the goddess Circe; through that connection he gained many of his son-in-law's relations and friends. he historian, and I have no intention of establishing either their truth or their falsehood. This much licence is conceded to the ancients, that by intermingling human actions with divine they may confer a more august dignity on the origins of states. Now, if any nation ought to be allowed to claim a sacred origin and point back to a divine paternity that nation is Rome. For such is her renown in war that when she chooses to represent Mars as her own and her founder's father, the nation.

1.50

Tarquin had now gained considerable influence amongst the Latin nobility, and he sent word for them to meet on a fixed date at the Grove of Ferentina, as there were matters of mutual interest about which he wished to consult them. They assembled in considerable numbers at daybreak; Tarquin kept his appointment, it is true, but did not arrive till shortly before sunset. The council spent the whole day in discussing many topics. Turnus Herdonius, from Aricia, had made a fierce attack on the absent Tarquin. It was no wonder, he said, that the epithet "Tyrant" had been bestowed upon him at Rome-for this was what people commonly called him, though only in whispers-could anything show the tyrant more than his thus trifling with the whole Latin nation? After summoning the chiefs from distant homes, the man who had called the council was not present. He was in fact trying how far he could go, so that if they submitted to the yoke he might crush them. Who could not see that he was making his way to sovereignty over the Latins? Even supposing that his own countrymen did well to entrust him with supreme power, or rather that it was entrusted and not seized by an act of parricide, the Latins ought not, even in that case, to place it in the hands of an alien. But if his own people bitterly rue his sway, seeing how they are being butchered, sent into exile, stripped of all their property, what better fate can the Latins hope for? If they followed the speaker's advice they would go home and take as little notice of the day fixed for the council as he who had fixed it was taking. Just while these and similar sentiments were being uttered by the man who had gained his influence in Aricia by treasonable and criminal practice, Tarquin appeared on the scene. That put a stop to his speech, for all turned from the speaker to salute the king. When silence was restored, Tarquin was advised by those near to explain why he had come so late. He said that having been chosen as arbitrator between a father and a son, he had been detained by his endeavours to reconcile them, and as that matter had taken up the whole day, he would bring forward the measures he had decided upon the next day. It is said that even this explanation was not received by Turnus without his commenting on it; no case, he argued, could take up less time than one between a father and a son, it could be settled in a few words; if the son did not comply with the father's wishes he would get into trouble.

1.51

With these censures on the Roman king he left the council. Tarquin took the matter more seriously than he appeared to do and at once began to plan Turnus' death, in order that he might inspire the Latins with the same terror through which he had crushed the spirits of his subjects at home. As he had not the power to get him openly put to death, he compassed his destruction by bringing a false charge against him. Through the agency of some of the Aricians who were opposed to Turnus, he bribed a slave of his to allow a large quantity of swords to be carried secretly into his quarters. This plan was executed in one night. Shortly before daybreak Tarquin summoned the Latin chiefs into his presence, as though something had happened to give him great alarm. He told them that his delay on the previous day had been brought about by some divine providence, for it had proved the salvation both of them and himself. He was informed that Turnus was planning his murder and that of the leading men in the different cities, in order that he might hold sole rule over the Latins. He would have attempted it the previous day in the council; but the attempt was deferred owing to the absence of the convener of the council, the chief object of attack. Hence the abuse levelled against him in his absence, because his delay had frustrated the hopes of success. If the reports which reached him were true, he had no doubt that, on the assembling of the council at daybreak, Turnus would come armed and with a strong body of conspirators. It was asserted that a vast number of swords had been conveyed to him. Whether this was an idle rumour or not could very soon be ascertained, he asked them to go with him to Turnus. The restless, ambitious character of Turnus, his speech of the previous day, and Tarquin's delay, which easily accounted for the postponement of the murder, all lent colour to their suspicions. They went, inclined to accept Tarquin's statement, but quite prepared to regard the whole story as baseless, if the swords were not discovered. When they arrived, Turnus was roused from sleep and placed under guard, and the slaves who from affection to their master were preparing to defend him were seized. Then, when the concealed swords were produced from every corner of his lodgings, the matter appeared only too certain and Turnus was thrown into chains. Amidst great excitement a council of the Latins was at once summoned. The sight of the swords, placed in the midst, aroused such furious resentment that he was condemned, without being heard in his defence, to an unprecedented mode of death. He was thrown into the fountain of Ferentina and drowned by a hurdle weighted with stones being placed over him.

1.52

After the Latins had reassembled in council and had been commended by Tarquin for having inflicted on Turnus a punishment befitting his revolutionary and murderous designs, Tarquin addressed them as follows: It was in his power to exercise a long-established right, since, as all the Latins traced their origin to Alba, they were included in the treaty made by Tullus under which the whole of the Alban State with its colonies passed under the suzerainty of Rome. He thought, however, that it would be more advantageous for all parties if that treaty were renewed, so that the Latins could enjoy a share in the prosperity of the Roman people, instead of always looking out for, or actually suffering, the demolition of their towns and the devastation of their fields, as happened in the reign of Ancus and afterwards whilst his own father was on the throne. The Latins were persuaded without much difficulty, although by that treaty Rome was the predominant State, for they saw that the heads of the Latin League were giving their adhesion to the king, and Turnus afforded a present example of the danger incurred by any one who opposed the king's wishes. So the treaty was renewed, and orders were issued for the "juniors" amongst the Latins to muster under arms, in accordance with the treaty, on a given day, at the Grove of Ferentina. In compliance with the order contingents assembled from all the thirty towns, and with a view to depriving them of their own general or a separate command, or distinctive standards, he formed one Latin and one Roman century into a maniple, thereby making one unit out of the two, whilst he doubled the strength of the maniples, and placed a centurion over each half.

1.53

However tyrannical the king was in his domestic administration he was by no means a despicable general; in military skill he would have rivalled any of his predecessors had not the degeneration of his character in other directions prevented him from attaining distinction here also. He was the first to stir up war with the Volscians-a war which was to last for more than two hundred years after his time-and took from them the city of Pomptine Suessa. The booty was sold and he realised out of the proceeds forty talents of silver. He then sketched out the design of a temple to Jupiter, which in its extent should be worthy of the king of gods and men, worthy of the Roman empire, worthy of the majesty of the City itself. He set apart the above-mentioned sum for its construction. The next war occupied him longer than he expected. Failing to capture the neighbouring city of Gabii by assault and finding it useless to attempt an investment, after being defeated under its walls, he employed methods against it which were anything but Roman, namely, fraud and deceit. He pretended to have given up all thoughts of war and to be devoting himself to laying the foundations of his temple and other undertakings in the City. Meantime, it was arranged that Sextus, the youngest of his three sons, should go as a refugee to Gabii, complaining loudly of his father's insupportable cruelty, and declaring that he had shifted his tyranny from others on to his own family, and even regarded the presence of his children as a burden and was preparing to devastate his own family as he had devastated the senate, so that not a single descendant, not a single heir to the crown might be left. He had, he said, himself escaped from the murderous violence of his father, and felt that no place was safe for him except amongst Lucius Tarquin's enemies. Let them not deceive themselves, the war which apparently was abandoned was hanging over them, and at the first chance he would attack them when they least expected it. If amongst them there was no place for suppliants, he would wander through Latium, he would petition the Volsci, the Aequi, the Hernici, until he came to men who know how to protect children against the cruel and unnatural persecutions of parents. Perhaps he would find people with sufficient spirit to take up arms against a remorseless tyrant backed by a warlike people. As it seemed probable that if they paid no attention to him he would, in his angry mood, take his departure, the people of Gabii gave him a kind reception. They told him not to be surprised if his father treated his children as he had treated his own subjects and his allies; failing others he would end by murdering himself. They showed pleasure at his arrival and expressed their belief that with his assistance the war would be transferred from the gates of Gabii to the walls of Rome.

1.54

He was admitted to the meetings of the national council. Whilst expressing his agreement with the elders of Gabii on other subjects, on which they were better informed, he was continually urging them to war, and claimed to speak with special authority, because he was acquainted with the strength of each nation, and knew that the king's tyranny, which even his own children had found insupportable, was certainly detested by his subjects. So after gradually working up the leaders of the Gabinians to revolt, he went in person with some of the most eager of the young men on foraging and plundering expeditions. By playing the hypocrite both in speech and action, he gained their mistaken confidence more and more; at last he was chosen as commander in the war. Whilst the mass of the population were unaware of what was intended, skirmishes took place between Rome and Gabii in which the advantage generally rested with the latter, until the Gabinians from the highest to the lowest firmly believed that Sextus Tarquin had been sent by heaven to be their leader. As for the soldiers, he became so endeared to them by sharing all their toils and dangers, and by a lavish distribution of the plunder, that the elder Tarquin was not more powerful in Rome than his son was in Gabii.

When he thought himself strong enough to succeed in anything that he might attempt, he sent one of his friends to his father at Rome to ask what he wished him to do now that the gods had given him sole and absolute power in Gabii. To this messenger no verbal reply was given, because, I believe, he mistrusted him. The king went into the palace-garden, deep in thought, his son's messenger following him. As he walked along in silence it is said that he struck off the tallest poppy-heads with his stick. Tired of asking and waiting for an answer, and feeling his mission to be a failure, the messenger returned to Gabii, and reported what he had said and seen, adding that the king, whether through temper or personal aversion or the arrogance which was natural to him, had not uttered a single word. When it had become clear to Sextus what his father meant him to understand by his mysterious silent action, he proceeded to get rid of the foremost men of the State by traducing some of them to the people, whilst others fell victims to their own unpopularity. Many were publicly executed, some against whom no plausible charges could be brought were secretly assassinated. Some were allowed to seek safety in flight, or were driven into exile; the property of these as well as of those who had been put to death was distributed in grants and bribes. The gratification felt by each who received a share blunted the sense of the public mischief that was being wrought, until, deprived of all counsel and help, the State of Gabii was surrendered to the Roman king without a single battle.

1.55

After the acquisition of Gabii, Tarquin made peace with the Aequi and renewed the treaty with the Etruscans. Then he turned his attention to the business of the City. The first thing was the temple of Jupiter on the Tarpeian Mount, which he was anxious to leave behind as a memorial of his reign and name; both the Tarquins were concerned in it, the father had vowed it, the son completed it. That the whole of the area which the temple of Jupiter was to occupy might be wholly devoted to that deity, he decided to deconsecrate the fanes and chapels, some of which had been originally vowed by King Tatius at the crisis of his battle with Romulus, and subsequently consecrated and inaugurated. Tradition records that at the commencement of this work the gods sent a divine intimation of the future vastness of the empire, for whilst the omens were favourable for the deconsecration of all the other shrines, they were unfavourable for that of the fane of Terminus. This was interpreted to mean that as the abode of Terminus was not moved and he alone of all the deities was not called forth from his consecrated borders, so all would be firm and immovable in the future empire. This augury of lasting dominion was followed by a prodigy which portended the greatness of the empire. It is said that whilst they were digging the foundations of the temple, a human head came to light with the face perfect; this appearance unmistakably portended that the spot would be the stronghold of empire and the head of all the world. This was the interpretation given by the soothsayers in the City, as well as by those who had been called into council from Etruria. The king's designs were now much more extensive; so much so that his share of the spoils of Pometia, which had been set apart to complete the work, now hardly met the cost of the foundations. This makes me inclined to trust Fabius -who, moreover is the older authority-when he says that the amount was only forty talents, rather than Piso, who states that forty thousand pounds of silver were set apart for that object. For not only is such a sum more than could be expected from the spoils of any single city at that time, but it would more than suffice for the foundations of the most magnificent building of the present day.

1.56

Determined to finish his temple, he sent for workmen from all parts of Etruria, and not only used the public treasury to defray the cost, but also compelled the plebeians to take their share of the work. This was in addition to their military service, and was anything but a light burden. Still they felt it less of a hardship to build the temples of the gods with their own hands, than they did afterwards when they were transferred to other tasks less imposing, but involving greater toil-the construction of the "ford" in the Circus and that of the Cloaca Maxima, a subterranean tunnel to receive all the sewage of the City. The magnificence of these two works could hardly be equalled by anything in the present day. When the plebeians were no longer required for these works, he considered that such a multitude of unemployed would prove a burden to the State, and as he wished the frontiers of the empire to be more widely colonised, he sent colonists to Signia and Circeii to serve as a protection to the City by land and sea. While he was carrying out these undertakings a frightful portent appeared; a snake gliding out of a wooden column created confusion and panic in the palace. The king himself was not so much terrified as filled with anxious forebodings. The Etruscan soothsayers were only employed to interpret prodigies which affected the State; but this one concerned him and his house personally, so he decided to send to the world-famed oracle of Delphi. Fearing to entrust the oracular response to any one else, he sent two of his sons to Greece, through lands at that time unknown and over seas still less known. Titus and Arruns started on their journey. They had as a travelling companion L. Junius Brutus, the son of the king's sister, Tarquinia, a young man of a very different character from that which he had assumed. When he heard of the massacre of the chiefs of the State, amongst them his own brother, by his uncle's orders, he determined that his intelligence should give the king no cause for alarm nor his fortune any provocation to his avarice, and that as the laws afforded no protection, he would seek safety in obscurity and neglect. Accordingly he carefully kept up the appearance and conduct of an idiot, leaving the king to do what he liked with his person and property, and did not even protest against his nickname of "Brutus"; for under the protection of that nickname the soul which was one day to liberate Rome was awaiting its destined hour. The story runs that when brought to Delphi by the Tarquins, more as a butt for their sport than as a companion, he had with him a golden staff enclosed in a hollow one of corner wood, which he offered to Apollo as a mystical emblem of his own character. After executing their father's commission the young men were desirous of ascertaining to which of them the kingdom of Rome would come. A voice came from the lowest depths of the cavern: "Whichever of you, young men, shall be the first to kiss his mother, he shall hold supreme sway in Rome." Sextus had remained behind in Rome, and to keep him in ignorance of this oracle and so deprive him of any chance of coming to the throne, the two Tarquins insisted upon absolute silence being kept on the subject. They drew lots to decide which of them should be the first to kiss his mother on their return to Rome. Brutus, thinking that the oracular utterance had another meaning, pretended to stumble, and as he fell kissed the ground, for the earth is of course the common mother of us all. Then they returned to Rome, where preparations were being energetically pushed forward for a war with the Rutulians.

1.57

This people, who were at that time in possession of Ardea, were, considering the nature of their country and the age in which they lived, exceptionally wealthy. This circumstance really originated the war, for the Roman king was anxious to repair his own fortune, which had been exhausted by the magnificent scale of his public works, and also to conciliate his subjects by a distribution of the spoils of war. His tyranny had already produced disaffection, but what moved their special resentment was the way they had been so long kept by the king at manual and even servile labour. An attempt was made to take Ardea by assault; when that failed recourse was had to a regular investment to starve the enemy out. When troops are stationary, as is the case in a protracted more than in an active campaign, furloughs are easily granted, more so to the men of rank, however, than to the common soldiers. The royal princes sometimes spent their leisure hours in feasting and entertainments, and at a wine party given by Sextus Tarquinius at which Collatinus, the son of Egerius, was present, the conversation happened to turn upon their wives, and each began to speak of his own in terms of extraordinarily high praise. As the dispute became warm, Collatinus said that there was no need of words, it could in a few hours be ascertained how far his Lucretia was superior to all the rest. "Why do we not," he exclaimed, "if we have any youthful vigour about us, mount our horses and pay our wives a visit and find out their characters on the spot? What we see of the behaviour of each on the unexpected arrival of her husband, let that be the surest test." They were heated with wine, and all shouted: "Good! Come on!" Setting spur to their horses they galloped off to Rome, where they arrived as darkness was beginning to close in. Thence they proceeded to Collatia, where they found Lucretia very differently employed from the king's daughters-in-law, whom they had seen passing their time in feasting and luxury with their acquaintances. She was sitting at her wool work in the hall, late at night, with her maids busy round her. The palm in this competition of wifely virtue was awarded to Lucretia. She welcomed the arrival of her husband and the Tarquins, whilst her victorious spouse courteously invited the royal princes to remain as his guests. Sextus Tarquin, inflamed by the beauty and exemplary purity of Lucretia, formed the vile project of effecting her dishonour. After their youthful frolic they returned for the time to camp.

1.58

A few days afterwards Sextus Tarquin went, unknown to Collatinus, with one companion to Collatia. He was hospitably received by the household, who suspected nothing, and after supper was conducted to the bedroom set apart for guests. When all around seemed safe and everybody fast asleep, he went in the frenzy of his passion with a naked sword to the sleeping Lucretia, and placing his left hand on her breast, said, "Silence, Lucretia! I am Sextus Tarquin, and I have a sword in my hand; if you utter a word, you shall die." When the woman, terrified out of her sleep, saw that no help was near, and instant death threatening her, Tarquin began to confess his passion, pleaded, used threats as well as entreaties, and employed every argument likely to influence a female heart. When he saw that she was inflexible and not moved even by the fear of death, he threatened to disgrace her, declaring that he would lay the naked corpse of the slave by her dead body, so that it might be said that she had been slain in foul adultery. By this awful threat, his lust triumphed over her inflexible chastity, and Tarquin went off exulting in having successfully attacked her honour. Lucretia, overwhelmed with grief at such a frightful outrage, sent a messenger to her father at Rome and to her husband at Ardea, asking them to come to her, each accompanied by one faithful friend; it was necessary to act, and to act promptly; a horrible thing had happened. Spurius Lucretius came with Publius Valerius, the son of Volesus; Collatinus with Lucius Junius Brutus, with whom he happened to be returning to Rome when he was met by his wife's messenger. They found Lucretia sitting in her room prostrate with grief. As they entered, she burst into tears, and to her husband's inquiry whether all was well, replied, "No! what can be well with a woman when her honour is lost? The marks of a stranger, Collatinus, are in your bed. But it is only the body that has been violated, the soul is pure; death shall bear witness to that. But pledge me your solemn word that the adulterer shall not go unpunished. It is Sextus Tarquin, who, coming as an enemy instead of a guest, forced from me last night by brutal violence a pleasure fatal to me, and, if you are men, fatal to him." They all successively pledged their word, and tried to console the distracted woman by turning the guilt from the victim of the outrage to the perpetrator, and urging that it is the mind that sins, not the body, and where there has been no consent there is no guilt. "It is for you," she said, "to see that he gets his deserts; although I acquit myself of the sin, I do not free myself from the penalty; no unchaste woman shall henceforth live and plead Lucretia's example." She had a knife concealed in her dress which she plunged into her heart, and fell dying on the floor. Her father and husband raised the death-cry.

1.59

Whilst they were absorbed in grief, Brutus drew the knife from Lucretia's wound, and holding it, dripping with blood, in front of him, said, "By this blood-most pure before the outrage wrought by the king's son-I swear, and you, O gods, I call to witness that I will drive hence Lucius Tarquinius Superbus, together with his cursed wife and his whole brood, with fire and sword and every means in my power, and I will not suffer them or any one else to reign in Rome." Then he handed the knife to Collatinus and then to Lucretius and Valerius, who were all astounded at the marvel of the thing, wondering whence Brutus had acquired this new character. They swore as they were directed; all their grief changed to wrath, and they followed the lead of Brutus, who summoned them to abolish the monarchy forthwith. They carried the body of Lucretia from her home down to the Forum, where, owing to the unheard-of atrocity of the crime, they at once collected a crowd. Each had his own complaint to make of the wickedness and violence of the royal house. Whilst all were moved by the father's deep distress, Brutus bade them stop their tears and idle laments, and urged them to act as men and Romans and take up arms against their insolent foes. All the high-spirited amongst the younger men came forward as armed volunteers, the rest followed their example. A portion of this body was left to hold Collatia, and guards were stationed at the gates to prevent any news of the movement from reaching the king; the rest marched in arms to Rome with Brutus in command. On their arrival, the sight of so many men in arms spread panic and confusion wherever they marched, but when again the people saw that the foremost men of the State were leading the way, they realised that whatever the movement was it was a serious one. The terrible occurrence created no less excitement in Rome than it had done in Collatia; there was a rush from all quarters of the City to the Forum. When they had gathered there, the herald summoned them to attend the "Tribune of the Celeres"; this was the office which Brutus happened at the time to be holding. He made a speech quite out of keeping with the character and temper he had up to that day assumed. He dwelt upon the brutality and licentiousness of Sextus Tarquin, the infamous outrage on Lucretia and her pitiful death, the bereavement sustained by her father, Tricipitinus, to whom the cause of his daughter's death was more shameful and distressing than the actual death itself. Then he dwelt on the tyranny of the king, the toils and sufferings of the plebeians kept underground clearing out ditches and sewers-Roman men, conquerors of all the surrounding nations, turned from warriors into artisans and stonemasons! He reminded them of the shameful murder of Servius Tullius and his daughter driving in her accursed chariot over her father's body, and solemnly invoked the gods as the avengers of murdered parents. By enumerating these and, I believe, other still more atrocious incidents which his keen sense of the present injustice suggested, but which it is not easy to give in detail, he goaded on the incensed multitude to strip the king of his sovereignty and pronounce a sentence of banishment against Tarquin with his wife and children. With a picked body of the "Juniors," who volunteered to follow him, he went off to the camp at Ardea to incite the army against the king, leaving the command in the City to Lucretius, who had previously been made Prefect of the City by the king. During the commotion Tullia fled from the palace amidst the execrations of all whom she met, men and women alike invoking against her her father's avenging spirit.

1.60

When the news of these proceedings reached the camp, the king, alarmed at the turn affairs were taking, hurried to Rome to quell the outbreak. Brutus, who was on the same road had become aware of his approach, and to avoid meeting him took another route, so that he reached Ardea and Tarquin Rome almost at the same time, though by different ways. Tarquin found the gates shut, and a decree of banishment passed against him; the Liberator of the City received a joyous welcome in the camp, and the king's sons were expelled from it. Two of them followed their father into exile amongst the Etruscans in Caere. Sextus Tarquin proceeded to Gabii, which he looked upon as his kingdom, but was killed in revenge for the old feuds he had kindled by his rapine and murders. Lucius Tarquinius Superbus reigned twenty-five years. The whole duration of the regal government from the foundation of the City to its liberation was two hundred and forty-four years. Two consuls were then elected in the assembly of centuries by the prefect of the City, in accordance with the regulations of Servius Tullius. They were Lucius Junius Brutus and Lucius Tarquinius Collatinus.

一 文献出处

T. Livy, *The History of Rome*, Vol. I , Ernest Rhys, ed., translated. by Canon Roberts, New York, 1912.

二 文献导读

李维（T. Livy，公元前 59 年~公元 17 年），是第一位用拉丁语写作的重要历史作家。生于意大利北部的帕塔维乌姆（今帕多瓦），家教良好。移居罗马后与奥古斯都过从甚密。李维著述丰富，但流传下来的只有他用母语拉丁文写成的《建城以来史》（AB URBE CONDITA，英译为 *From the Founding of the City,* 或者 *The History of Rome*），也译《罗马通史》，共有 142 卷。其中第 11~20 卷和第 46~142 卷散佚。现仅存 35 卷，包括第 1~10 卷、第 21~45 卷。作者从内战后着手编写，至公元前 27 年写完第 1 卷；以后每年写 3~4 卷，直到他去世为止。

第 1~10 卷描写传说中的埃涅阿斯到达意大利，公元前 753 年罗马建城直到第三次萨姆尼姆战争末期的历史（公元前 753~前 293 年）；第 21~45 卷描写第二次布匿战争开始到第三次马其顿战争结束的历史（公元前 219~前 167 年）。李维不懂古代罗马典章制度和军事，在使用前人史料时无力加以有效的甄别，并且很少指明出处，例如，他曾大量引用波利比乌斯的著作却没有说明出处。最令人遗憾的是，他总是为了崇高的宗教、爱国和道德说教随意篡改曲解历史，这在一定程度上减损了《罗马通史》的史学价值。但是，因为它不仅是至今唯一一部出自古罗马人之手、详尽记载王政时代以及共和早期历史的著作，而且是第一部出自没有当官履历的平民书生之手的史书，加之文笔生动，细节富于戏剧性，所以它在众多的罗马史著作中地位特殊。

上文节选自该书的第 1 卷。该卷叙述了罗马的建城经过。公元前 753 年罗穆鲁斯建立罗马，通过抢劫萨宾妇女促进繁衍人口。继位诸王都有神话色彩，其中努玛（公元前 715~ 前 673 年在位）创建了宗教礼仪。第三王图鲁斯（公元前 672~ 前 641 年在位）打败了维伊和萨宾部落，摧毁了阿尔巴隆加，创建了元老院以及公民大会会场。第四王安库斯（公元前 640~ 前 617 年在位）创建了奥斯提亚港口，开采盐矿，建立高桥水渠，开始在阿芬丁山建立平民区并被称为"义王"。第五王老塔克文（公元前 616~ 前 579 年在位）是埃特鲁里亚人，其父因逃避暴君而移民罗马。他把元老院人数从 100 名扩充至 300 名。第六王塞尔维乌斯（公元前 578~ 前 535 年在位）实行了系列改革，比如创建百人队组织、部落行政区，基于财产普查划分社会等级等。他的女儿和女婿高傲者塔克文（公元前 534~ 前 510 年）合谋弑父篡位。高傲者塔克文创建了拉丁同盟，后因儿子惹祸被布鲁图斯率众驱逐，罗马从此建立共和国（公元前 509~ 前 31 年）。

三　延伸阅读

Dorey, T.A., ed., *Livy*, London & Toronto: Routledge & K. Paul, 1971.

Fotheringham, John Knight, *The Bodleian Manuscript of Jerome's Version of the Chronicles of Eusebius*, Oxford: The Clarendon Press, 1905.

Kraus, C. S., and A. J.Woodman, *Latin Historians*, Oxford University Press, 2006.

M. T. Cicero: On the Republic [*]

BOOK I.

Withoutthe virtue of Patriotism, neither Duelius, Regulus, nor Metellus, had delivered Rome by their courage, from the terror of Carthage—nor had the two Scipios, when the fire of the second Punic War was kindled, quenched it in their blood—nor when it revived in greater force, would Fabius have enervated it—nor would Marcellus have reduced it—nor when it was repulsed from the gates of our own city, would Scipio have confined it within the walls of our enemies.

Cato, at first a new and unknown man, whom all we who aspire to the same honours consider as our exemplar in the practice of virtue, was undoubtedly free to enjoy his repose at Tusculum, a most salubrious, and convenient retreat. But this great hero, (whom some, forsooth, suspect of madness) though no necessity compelled him, preferred casting himself into the tempestuous waves of politics, even in extreme old age, to living so luxuriously in that tranquillity and relaxation. I omit innumerable men who have devoted themselves to the protection of our Commonwealth; and those whose lives are within the memory

---

* 西塞罗《论共和国》第 1 卷节选。

of the present generation, I will not mention them, lest any one should complain that I had invidiously forgotten himself or his family. This only I insist on—so great is the necessity of this patriotism which nature has implanted in man, so great is the ambition to defend the safety of our country, that its energy has continually overcome all the blandishments of pleasure and repose.

Nor is it sufficient to possess this virtue as an art, unless we reduce it to practice. An art, indeed, though not exercised, may still be retained in knowledge; but all virtue consists in its proper use and action. Now the noblest use of virtue is the government of the Commonwealth, and the realization of all those patriotic theories which are discussed in the schools. For nothing is spoken by philosophers, so far as they speak wisely, which has not been discovered and confirmed by those who established the laws of states. For whence comes piety, or whence religion, or whence the law of nations, and the civil law?—whence comes justice, faith, equity?—whence modesty, continence, the horror of baseness, the emulation of praise and renown?—whence fortitude in labours and perils? doubtless, from those, who instilled some of these moral principles by education, and confirmed others by manners, and sanctioned others by laws.

It is reported of Xenocrates, one of the sublimest philosophers, when some one asked him what his disciples learned, that he replied, "they do that of their own accord, which they might be compelled to do by law." That citizen, therefore, who obliges all to those virtuous actions, by the authority of laws and penalties, to which the philosophers can scarcely persuade a few by the force of their eloquence, is certainly to be preferred to the sagest of the doctors, who spend their lives in discussions. Which of their exquisite orations is so admirable, as a well constituted government, public justice, and popular good manners? Without question, so far as magnificent and imperious cities (to quote Ennius) excel castles and villages; so, I imagine, those who regulate their cities by their counsel and authority, those who are expert in all public business, surpass other men in useful knowledge. And since we are so strongly urged to augment the prosperity of the human race, let us endeavour by our counsels and exertions to render man's life safer and wealthier. And since we are incited to this blessing, by the spur of nature herself, let us prosecute this glorious enterprize, always so dear to the best men, nor listen for a moment to the seductions of those who sound a retreat so loudly, that they sometimes call back the aspirants who have made considerable advancement.

These reasons, so certain and so evident, are opposed by those, who, on the other side object, —the labours that must necessarily be sustained in maintaining the Commonwealth. These form but a slight impediment to the vigilant and industrious, and a contemptible obstacle not only in these grand affairs, but also in common studies, offices, and employments. They add, the peril of life, that base fear of death, which has ever been opposed by brave men, to whom it appears far more miserable to waste away in inglorious old age, than to embrace an occasion of gallantly sacrificing their lives to their country, which must otherwise be sacrificed to natural decay.

On this point, however, our antagonists esteem themselves copious and eloquent, when they collect all the calamities of heroic men, and the injuries inflicted on them by ungrateful states. Here they bring forward examples borrowed from the Greeks. They tell us that Miltiades, the vanquisher and exterminator of the Persians, with those unrecovered wounds which he had received in his renowned victory, only preserved his life from the weapons of his enemies to be cast into chains by the Athenian citizens. They cite Themistocles, expelled and proscribed by the country he had rescued, who could not find shelter in the Grecian ports he had defended; and was obliged to fly to the bosom of the barbarous power he had defeated. There is, indeed, no deficiency of examples to illustrate the levity and cruelty of the Athenians to their noblest citizens, — examples which originating and multiplying among them, are said at different times to have abounded in our own august empire. Such were the exile of Camillus, the disgrace of Ahala, the unpopularity of Nasica, the expulsion of Lænas, the condemnation of Opimius, the flight of Metellus, the cruel destruction of Marius, the massacre of our chieftains, and the many atrocious crimes which followed. — My own history is by no means free from such calamities, and I imagine, that when they recollect, that by my counsel and perils they were preserved in life and liberty, they will more deeply and tenderly bewail my misfortunes. But I cannot tell why those who sail over the seas for the sake of knowledge and experience, should wonder at seeing still greater hazards braved in the service of the Commonwealth.

Since, on my quitting the consulship, I affirmed in the assembly of the Roman people, who reechoed my words, that I had saved the Commonwealth, I console myself with this remembrance, for all my cares, troubles, and injuries. Indeed, my dismission had more of honour than misfortune, and more of glory than disaster; and I derive greater pleasure from the regrets of good men than sorrow from the exultation of the reprobate. But if it had happened otherwise, why should I complain? Nothing befel me unforseen, or more painful than I expected, as a return for my illustrious actions. I was one, who on occasion, could derive more profit from leisure than most men, on account of the diversified sweetness of my studies, in which I have lived from boyhood. And if any public calamity had happened, I might have borne no more than an equal share in the misfortune. Yet I hesitated not to oppose myself almost alone to the tempests and torrents of sedition, for the sake of preserving the state; and by my own danger, to secure the safety of my fellow-countrymen. For our country did not beget and educate us gratuitously, or without the expectation of receiving our support. She does not afford us so many blessings for nothing, and supply us with a secure refuge for useless idleness and self-indulgence; but rather that she may turn to her own advantage the nobler portion of our genius, heart, and counsel; and give us back for our private service, only what she can spare from her public interests.

Those apologies, therefore, which undertake to furnish us with an easy excuse for living in selfish inactivity, are certainly not worth hearing. They tell us that to meddle with public affairs and popular demagogues, incapable of all goodness, with whom it is disgraceful to mix; and to struggle with the passions of the insensate multitude, is a most miserable and hazardous life. On which account, no wise man will take the reins, since he cannot restrain the insane and unregulated movements of the lower orders. Nor is it acting like a gentleman (say they) thus to contend with antagonists so unwashed and so unrefined (impuris atque immanibus adversariis) or subject yourself to the lashings of contumely, of which the wisest will always have most to bear. As if to virtuous, brave, and magnanimous men, there could be a juster reason for seeking the government than this, that we should not be subjected to scoundrels, nor suffer the commonwealth to be distracted by them, lest we should discover, too late, when we desire to save her, that we are without the power.

But this restriction who can approve, which would interdict the wise man from taking any share in the government, at least if the necessity of circumstances does not compel him to it? Surely no greater necessity can happen to any man than happened to me. In this, how could I have acted if I had not been a Consul? And how could I have been a Consul, unless I had maintained that course of life, even from childhood, which raised me from the order of knights, in which I was born, to the very highest station. You cannot produce extempore, and just when you please, the power of corroborating a commonwealth, whatever be its dangers, unless you have attained the position which enables you to act effectively. And what most surprises me in the discourses of our philosophers, is to hear the same men who confess themselves incapable of steering the vessel of the state in smooth seas, (which indeed they never learnt, and never cared to know,) profess themselves ready to assume the helm amid the fiercest tempests. It is a subject on which they like to talk in an elevated style, and to indulge in a large share of boasting, but they never inquired, nor can they explain the means which conduce to the establishment and the stability of states; and they look on this practical science as foreign to the meditations of sages and philosophers, and leave it to those men, who have made it their especial study. Is it reasonable for men who are so totally devoid of experience, to promise their assistance to the state, when they shall be compelled to it by necessity, while unequal to a much easier task, they know not how to govern, when the state is free from all such perils. Indeed, admitting that the wise man loves not to thrust himself as a matter of choice into the administration of public affairs, but that, if circumstances oblige him to it, he will not refuse the office; yet I think this science of civil legislation should in nowise be neglected by the philosopher, that all those resources may be ready to his hand, which he knows not how soon he may be called on to use.

I have spoken thus at large, for this reason, because this work is a discussion which I have prosecuted on the government of the state; and in order to render it useful, I had first of all to refute this pusillanimous hesitation to negociate public affairs. If there be any, therefore, who are too much influenced by the authority of the philosophers, let them principally attend to those whose glory and wisdom are greatest among learned men. These, I affirm, though they have not personally governed the state, are worthy of our consideration, because by their investigations and writings, they exercised a kind of political magistracy. As to those whom the Greeks entitle "the seven sages," I find them almost all conversant with public business. Nor indeed is there anything in which human virtue can more closely resemble the divine powers, than by establishing new states, or in preserving those already established.

In these affairs, since it has been our good fortune to achieve something worthy of memorial in the government of our country, and to acquire some facility of explaining the powers and resources of politics, we can treat of this subject with the weight of personal experience, and the habit of instruction and illustration. Whereas before us many skilful in the theory, have not been able to illustrate it by practice; and many practical statesmen have been unfamiliar with the arts of literary exposition. It is not at all our intention to establish a new and self-invented system of government. I wish only to revive the discussion of the most illustrious men of their age in our commonwealth, which you and I, in our youth, when at Smyrna, heard mentioned by Rutilius, who reported to us a conference of many days, in which in my opinion, there was nothing omitted that could throw light on political affairs.

In the year of the consulship of Tuditanus and Aquilius, Scipio Africanus, the son of Paulus Æmilius, formed the project of spending the Latin holidays in his gardens, where his most intimate friends had promised him frequent visits during this season of relaxation. In the morning of the first holiday, his nephew, Quintus Tubero, made his appearance. When Scipio had greeted him heartily, and embraced him, —"How is it my dear Tubero (said he) that I see you so early? These holidays must afford you a capital opportunity of pursuing your favourite studies." "Ah! (replied Tubero) I can study my books at any time, for they are always disengaged; but it is a great privilege, my Scipio, to find you at leisure, especially in this restless period of public affairs." "To speak truth (replied Scipio) I am rather relaxing from business than from study." "Nay, (said Tubero) you must try to relax from your studies too; here are several of us, as we have appointed, all ready, if it suits your convenience, to spend our vacation as sociably as possible." I am very willing to consent (answered Scipio), and we may be able to compare notes respecting the several topics that interest us."

"Be it so (said Tubero); and since you invite me to discussion, and present the opportunity, let us first examine, before our friends arrive, what can be the nature of the parhelion, or double sun, which was mentioned in the senate. Those that affirm they witnessed this prodigy, are neither few nor unrespectable, so that there is more reason for investigation than incredulity."

"Ah! (said Scipio) I wish we had our friend Panaetius with us, who, in the researches of his speculative genius, is beyond measure delighted with these celestial miracles. As for my opinion, Tubero, for I always tell you just what I think, I hardly agree in these subjects with our friend aforesaid, since respecting things of which we can scarcely form a conjecture, he is as positive as if he had seen them with his own eyes, and felt them with his own hands. And I cannot but the more admire the wisdom of Socrates, who disposed of all anxiety respecting things of this kind, and who affirmed that these inquiries concerning the secrets of nature, were either above the efforts of human reason, or of little consequence to human life."

"But, my Africanus, (replied Tubero) of what credit is this tradition which states that Socrates rejected all these physical investigations, and confined his whole attention to men and manners? In this respect, what better authority can we cite than Plato's? And in many passages of his works, Socrates speaks in a very different manner, and even in his discussions respecting morals, and virtues, and politics, he endeavours to interweave, after the fashion of Pythagoras, the doctrines of arithmetic, geometry, and harmonic proportions."

"That is true, replied Scipio; but you are aware, I believe, that Plato, after the death of Socrates, was induced to visit Egypt, by his love of science, and next Italy and Sicily, by his desire of understanding the Pythagorean dogmas; that he conversed much with Archytas of Tarentum, and Timæus of Locris; that he collected the works of Philolaus; and that finding in these places the renown of Pythagoras flourishing, he addicted himself exceedingly to these Pythagoreans and their studies; yet as he loved Socrates with his whole heart, and wished to attribute all great discoveries to him, he interwove the Socratic elegance and subtlety of eloquence, with somewhat of the obscurity of Pythagoras, and the gravity of his diversified arts."

When Scipio had spoken thus, he saw Furius approaching, and saluting him, and embracing him most affectionately, he gave him a seat at his side. He then observed Rutilius, the worthy reporter of the conference to us, and when he had saluted him, he placed him by the side of Tubero. "Pray do not let us disturb you (said Furius), I am afraid our entrance has interrupted your conversation." "By no means (said Scipio), for you are yourself a studious truth-searcher in the subjects on which Tubero was making some inquiries; and our friend Rutilius, at the siege of Numantia, used to converse with me on the same questions." "What then was the subject of your discussion (said Philus)." "We were talking (said Scipio) of the double suns that recently appeared, and I wish, my Philus, to hear what you think of them."

Just as he was speaking, a boy announced that Lælius was coming to call on him, and that he had already left his house. Scipio, putting on his sandals and robes, immediately quitted his seat, and had hardly passed the portico, when he met Lælius, and welcomed him and those that accompanied him. They were Spurius, Mummius, an intimate friend of Scipio; C. Fannius, and Quintus Scavola, sons-in-law of Lælius, two very intelligent young men, twenty–five years of age.

When he had saluted them all, he returned through the portico, placing Lælius in the middle, for there was in their friendship a law of reciprocal courtesy. In the camp, Lælius paid Scipio almost divine honours, on account of his African conquests; and in private life, Scipio reverenced Lælius, even as a father, in regard of his advanced age.

After they had exchanged a few words, as they walked up and down, Scipio, to whom their visit was extremely agreeable, wished to assemble them in a sunny corner of the gardens, for the weather was still rather wintry. When they had agreed to this, there came in another friend, a learned and gentlemanly man, beloved by all of them, M. Manilius. After being most warmly welcomed by Scipio and the rest, he seated himself next to Laelius.

Then Philus commencing the conversation, —"It does not appear to me (said he) that the presence of our new guests, need alter the subject of our discussion, but should only induce us to treat it more philosophically, and in a manner more worthy of our increased audience." "What do you allude to?" said Laelius. "What was the discussion we broke in upon?" "Scipio was asking me (replied Philus), what I thought of the parhelion, or mock sun, whose recent apparition was so strongly attested."

一　文献出处

M. T. Cicero, *On the Republic*, trans. by Francis Barham, London, 1841-42.

二　文献导读

西塞罗（M. Tullius Cicero, 公元前 106 年～前 43 年），是罗马政治家、法学家、雄辩家。因为文笔典雅，西塞罗著作常被选为古典拉丁文教材。西塞罗出生在拉丁姆地区阿皮努姆的一个富裕骑士家庭，27~29 岁时先后在希腊的雅典和罗德斯学习哲学和修辞学，结识了好友阿提库斯。回罗马后在抨击苏拉的演讲中展示了非凡的口才和学识，一鸣惊人。公元前 76 年在西西里担任财务官，公元前 63 年任执政官，操纵元老院镇压卡提林纳阴谋的参与者，遭到平民党凯撒等人的反对。公元前 60 年，因拒绝凯撒要他参加"前三雄"同盟（公元前 60 年，凯撒与庞培、克拉苏的秘密结盟）的邀请，于公元前 58 年被放逐，次年被召回。公元前 51 年任齐里齐亚行省总督。公元前 49 年内战爆发后追随庞培。凯撒被刺后热衷于恢复共和，连续发表 14 篇演说抨击安东尼。公元前 43 年 12 月 7 日被安东尼部下擒杀。

西塞罗著述丰富，代表作是他模仿柏拉图写的 6 卷本《论共和国》和 5 卷本《论法律》，现存演讲辞 58 篇，有关政法、哲学、修辞的著论 19 种以及大量书信。特别是他与阿提库斯和布鲁图斯的信件，保留了公元前 60 年～前 40 年的珍贵史料。上文节选自《论共和国》第 1 卷。

三　延伸阅读

Smith, R.E. , *Cicero the Statesman*, Cambridge University Press, 1966.

Stockton, David, *Cicero: A Political Biography*, Oxford University Press, 1971.

Strachan-Davidson, James Leigh, *Cicero and the Fall of the Roman Republic*, Oxford: Oxford University Press, 1936.

Julius Caesar: The Gallic War[*]

BOOK I.

All Gaul is divided into three parts, one of which the Belgae inhabit, the Aquitani another, those who in their own language are called Celts, in our Gauls, the third. All these differ from each other in language, customs and laws. The river Garonne separates the Gauls from the Aquitani; the Marne and the Seine separate them from the Belgae. Of all these, the Belgae are the bravest, because they are furthest from the civilization and refinement of [our] Province, and merchants least frequently resort to them, and import those things which tend to effeminate the mind; and they are the nearest to the Germans, who dwell beyond the Rhine, with whom they are continually waging war; for which reason the Helvetii also surpass the rest of the Gauls in valor, as they contend with the Germans in almost daily battles, when they either repel them from their own territories, or themselves wage war on their frontiers. One part of these, which it has been said that the Gauls occupy, takes its beginning at the river Rhone; it is bounded by the river Garonne, the ocean, and the territories of the Belgae; it borders, too, on the side of the Sequani and the Helvetii, upon the river Rhine,

---

[*] 凯撒《高卢战记》第 1 卷节选。

and stretches toward the north. The Belgae rises from the extreme frontier of Gaul, extend to the lower part of the river Rhine; and look toward the north and the rising sun. Aquitania extends from the river Garonne to the Pyrenaean mountains and to that part of the ocean which is near Spain: it looks between the setting of the sun, and the north star.

Among the Helvetii, Orgetorix was by far the most distinguished and wealthy. He, when Marcus Messala and Marcus Piso were consuls, incited by lust of sovereignty, formed a conspiracy among the nobility, and persuaded the people to go forth from their territories with all their possessions, [saying] that it would be very easy, since they excelled all in valor, to acquire the supremacy of the whole of Gaul. To this he the more easily persuaded them, because the Helvetii, are confined on every side by the nature of their situation; on one side by the Rhine, a very broad and deep river, which separates the Helvetian territory from the Germans; on a second side by the Jura, a very high mountain, which is [situated] between the Sequani and the Helvetii; on a third by the Lake of Geneva, and by the river Rhone, which separates our Province from the Helvetii. From these circumstances it resulted, that they could range less widely, and could less easily make war upon their neighbors; for which reason men fond of war [as they were] were affected with great regret. They thought, that considering the extent of their population, and their renown for warfare and bravery, they had but narrow limits, although they extended in length 240, and in breadth 180 [Roman] miles.

Induced by these considerations, and influenced by the authority of Orgetorix, they determined to provide such things as were necessary for their expedition-to buy up as great a number as possible of beasts of burden and wagons-to make their sowings as large as possible, so that on their march plenty of corn might be in store-and to establish peace and friendship with the neighboring states. They reckoned that a term of two years would be sufficient for them to execute their designs; they fix by decree their departure for the third year. Orgetorix is chosen to complete these arrangements. He took upon himself the office of embassador to the states: on this journey he persuades Casticus, the son of Catamantaledes (one of the Sequani, whose father had possessed the sovereignty among the people for many years, and had been styled "friend" by the senate of the Roman people), to seize upon the sovereignty in his own state, which his father had held before him, and he likewise persuades Dumnorix, an Aeduan, the brother of Divitiacus, who at that time possessed the chief authority in the state, and was exceedingly beloved by the people, to attempt the same, and gives him his daughter in marriage. He proves to them that to accomplish their attempts was a thing very easy to be done, because he himself would obtain the government of his own state; that there was no doubt that the Helvetii were the most powerful of the whole of Gaul; he assures them that he will, with his own forces and his own army, acquire the sovereignty for them. Incited by this speech, they give a pledge and oath to one another, and hope that, when they have seized the sovereignty, they will, by means of the three most powerful and valiant nations, be enabled to obtain possession of the whole of Gaul.

When this scheme was disclosed to the Helvetii by informers, they, according to their custom, compelled Orgetorix to plead his cause in chains; it was the law that the penalty of being burned by fire should await him if condemned. On the day appointed for the pleading of his cause, Orgetorix drew together from all quarters to the court, all his vassals to the number of ten thousand persons; and led together to the same place all his dependents and debtor-bondsmen, of whom he had a great number; by means of those he rescued himself from [the necessity of] pleading his cause. While the state, incensed at this act, was endeavoring to assert its right by arms, and the magistrates were mustering a large body of men from the country, Orgetorix died; and there is not wanting a suspicion, as the Helvetii think, of his having committed suicide.

After his death, the Helvetii nevertheless attempt to do that which they had resolved on, namely, to go forth from their territories. When they thought that they were at length prepared for this undertaking, they set fire to all their towns, in number about twelve-to their villages about four hundred-and to the private dwellings that remained; they burn up all the corn, except what they intend to carry with them; that after destroying the hope of a return home, they might be the more ready for undergoing all dangers. They order every one to carry forth from home for himself provisions for three months, ready ground. They persuade the Rauraci, and the Tulingi, and the Latobrigi, their neighbors, to adopt the same plan, and after burning down their towns and villages, to set out with them: and they admit to their party and unite to themselves as confederates the Boii, who had dwelt on the other side of the Rhine, and had crossed over into the Norican territory, and assaulted Noreia.

There were in all two routes, by which they could go forth from their country one through the Sequani narrow and difficult, between Mount Jura and the river Rhone (by which scarcely one wagon at a time could be led; there was, moreover, a very high mountain overhanging, so that a very few might easily intercept them; the other, through our Province, much easier and freer from obstacles, because the Rhone flows between the boundaries of the Helvetii and those of the Allobroges, who had lately been subdued, and is in some places crossed by a ford. The furthest town of the Allobroges, and the nearest to the territories of the Helvetii, is Geneva. From this town a bridge extends to the Helvetii. They thought that they should either persuade the Allobroges, because they did not seem as yet well-affected toward the Roman people, or compel them by force to allow them to pass through their territories. Having provided every thing for the expedition, they appoint a day, on which they should all meet on the bank of the Rhone. This day was the fifth before the kalends of April [i.e. the 28th of March], in the consulship of Lucius Piso and Aulus Gabinius [B.C. 58.]

When it was reported to Caesar that they were attempting to make their route through our Province he hastens to set out from the city, and, by as great marches as he can, proceeds to Further Gaul, and arrives at Geneva. He orders the whole Province [to furnish] as great a number of soldiers as possible, as there was in all only one legion in Further Gaul: he orders the bridge at Geneva to be broken down. When the Helvetii are apprized of his arrival they send to him, as embassadors, the most illustrious men of their state (in which embassy Numeius and Verudoctius held the chief place), to say "that it was their intention to march through the Province without doing any harm, because they had" [according to their own representations,] "no other route: that they requested, they might be allowed to do so with his consent." Caesar, inasmuch as he kept in remembrance that Lucius Cassius, the consul, had been slain, and his army routed and made to pass under the yoke by the Helvetii, did not think that [their request] ought to be granted: nor was he of opinion that men of hostile disposition, if an opportunity of marching through the Province were given them, would abstain from outrage and mischief. Yet, in order that a period might intervene, until the soldiers whom he had ordered [to be furnished] should assemble, he replied to the ambassadors, that he would take time to deliberate; if they wanted any thing, they might return on the day before the ides of April [on April 12th].

Meanwhile, with the legion which he had with him and the soldiers which had assembled from the Province, he carries along for nineteen [Roman, not quite eighteen English] miles a wall, to the height of sixteen feet, and a trench, from the Lake of Geneva, which flows into the river Rhone, to Mount Jura, which separates the territories of the Sequani from those of the Helvetii. When that work was finished, he distributes garrisons, and closely fortifies redoubts, in order that he may the more easily intercept them, if they should attempt to cross over against his will. When the day which he had appointed with the embassadors came, and they returned to him; he says, that he can not, consistently with the custom and precedent of the Roman people, grant any one a passage through the Province; and he gives them to understand, that, if they should attempt to use violence he would oppose them. The Helvetii, disappointed in this hope, tried if they could force a passage (some by means of a bridge of boats and numerous rafts constructed for the purpose; others, by the fords of the Rhone, where the depth of the river was least, sometimes by day, but more frequently by night), but being kept at bay by the strength of our works, and by the concourse of the soldiers, and by the missiles, they desisted from this attempt.

There was left one way, [namely] through the Sequani, by which, on account of its narrowness, they could not pass without the consent of the Sequani. As they could not of themselves prevail on them, they send embassadors to Dumnorix the Aeduan, that through his intercession, they might obtain their request from the Sequani. Dumnorix, by his popularity and liberality, had great influence among the Sequani, and was friendly to the Helvetii, because out of that state he had married the daughter of Orgetorix; and, incited by lust of sovereignty, was anxious for a revolution, and wished to have as many states as possible attached to him by his kindness toward them. He, therefore, undertakes the affair, and prevails upon the Sequani to allow the Helvetii to march through their territories, and arranges that they should give hostages to each other-the Sequani not to obstruct the Helvetii in their march-the Helvetii, to pass without mischief and outrage.

It is again told Caesar, that the Helvetii intended to march through the country of the Sequani and the Aedui into the territories of the Santones, which are not far distant from those boundaries of the Tolosates, which [viz. Tolosa, Toulouse] is a state in the Province. If this took place, he saw that it would be attended with great danger to the Province to have warlike men, enemies of the Roman people, bordering upon an open and very fertile tract of country. For these reasons he appointed Titus Labienus, his lieutenant, to the command of the fortification which he had made. He himself proceeds to Italy by forced marches, and there levies two legions, and leads out from winter-quarters three which were wintering around Aquileia, and with these five legions marches rapidly by the nearest route across the Alps into Further Gaul. Here the Centrones and the

Graioceli and the Caturiges, having taken possession of the higher parts, attempt to obstruct the army in their march. After having routed these in several battles, he arrives in the territories of the Vocontii in the Further Province on the seventh day from Ocelum, which is the most remote town of the Hither Province; thence he leads his army into the country of the Allobroges, and from the Allobroges to the Segusiani. These people are the first beyond the Province on the opposite side of the Rhone.

The Helvetii had by this time led their forces over through the narrow defile and the territories of the Sequani, and had arrived at the territories of the Aedui, and were ravaging their lands. The Aedui, as they could not defend themselves and their possessions against them, send embassadors to Caesar to ask assistance, [pleading] that they had at all times so well deserved of the Roman people, that their fields ought not to have been laid waste-their children carried off into slavery-their towns stormed, almost within sight of our army. At the same time the Ambarri, the friends and kinsmen of the Aedui, apprize Caesar, that it was not easy for them, now that their fields had been devastated, to ward off the violence of the enemy from their towns: the Allobroges likewise, who had villages and possessions on the other side of the Rhone, betake themselves in flight to Caesar, and assure him that they had nothing remaining, except the soil of their land. Caesar, induced by these circumstances, decides, that he ought not to wait until the Helvetii, after destroying all the property of his allies, should arrive among the Santones.

There is a river [called] the Saone, which flows through the territories of the Aedui and Sequani into the Rhone with such incredible slowness, that it can not be determined by the eye in which direction it flows. This the Helvetii were crossing by rafts and boats joined together. When Caesar was informed by spies that the Helvetii had already conveyed three parts of their forces across that river, but that the fourth part was left behind on this side of the Saone, he set out from the camp with three legions during the third watch, and came up with that division which had not yet crossed the river. Attacking them encumbered with baggage, and not expecting him, he cut to pieces a great part of them; the rest betook themselves to flight, and concealed themselves in the nearest woods. That canton [which was cut down] was called the Tigurine; for the whole Helvetian state is divided into four cantons. This single canton having left their country, within the recollection of our fathers, had slain Lucius Cassius the consul, and had made his army pass under the yoke. Thus, whether by chance, or by the design of the immortal gods, that part of the Helvetian state which had brought a signal calamity upon the Roman people, was the first to pay the penalty. In this Caesar avenged not only the public but also his own personal wrongs, because the Tigurini had slain Lucius Piso the lieutenant [of Cassius], the grandfather of Lucius Calpurnius Piso, his [Caesar's] father-in-law, in the same battle as Cassius himself.

This battle ended, that he might be able to come up with the remaining forces of the Helvetii, he procures a bridge to be made across the Saone, and thus leads his army over. The Helvetii, confused by his sudden arrival, when they found that he had effected in one day, what they, themselves had with the utmost difficulty accomplished in twenty namely, the crossing of the river, send embassadors to him; at the head of which embassy was Divico, who had been commander of the Helvetii, in the war against Cassius. He thus treats with Caesar: -that, "if the Roman people would make peace with the Helvetii they would go to that part and there remain, where Caesar might appoint and desire them to be; but if he should persist in persecuting them with war that he ought to remember both the ancient disgrace of the Roman people and the characteristic valor of the Helvetii. As to his having attacked one canton by surprise, [at a time] when those who had crossed the river could not bring assistance to their friends, that he ought not on that account to ascribe very much to his own valor, or despise them; that they had so learned from their sires and ancestors, as to rely more on valor than on artifice and stratagem. Wherefore let him not bring it to pass that the place, where they were standing, should acquire a name, from the disaster of the Roman people and the destruction of their army or transmit the remembrance [of such an event to posterity]."

To these words Caesar thus replied: -that "on that very account he felt less hesitation, because he kept in remembrance those circumstances which the Helvetian embassadors had mentioned, and that he felt the more indignant at them, in proportion as they had happened undeservedly to the Roman people: for if they had been conscious of having done any wrong, it would not have been difficult to be on their guard, but for that very reason had they been deceived, because neither were they aware that any offense had been given by them, on account of which they should be afraid, nor did they think that they ought to be afraid without cause. But even if he were willing to forget their former outrage, could he also lay aside the remembrance of the late wrongs, in that they had against his will attempted a route through the Province by force, in that they had molested the Aedui, the Ambarri, and the Allobroges? That as to their so insolently boasting of their victory, and as to their being astonished that they had so long committed their outrages with impunity, [both these things] tended to the same point; for the immortal gods are wont to allow those persons whom they wish to punish for their guilt sometimes a greater prosperity and longer impunity, in order that they may suffer the more severely from a reverse of circumstances. Although these things are so, yet, if hostages were to be given him by them in order that he may be assured these will do what they promise, and provided they will give satisfaction to the Aedui for the outrages which they had committed against them and their allies, and likewise to the Allobroges, he [Caesar] will make peace with them." Divico replied, that "the Helvetii had been so trained by their ancestors, that they were accustomed to receive, not to give hostages; of that fact the Roman people were witness." Having given this reply, he withdrew.

On the following day they move their camp from that place; Caesar does the same, and sends forward all his cavalry, to the number of four thousand (which he had drawn together from all parts of the Province and from the Aedui and their allies), to observe toward what parts the enemy are directing their march. These, having too eagerly pursued the enemy's rear, come to a battle with the cavalry of the Helvetii in a disadvantageous place, and a few of our men fall. The Helvetii, elated with this battle, because they had with five hundred horse repulsed so large a body of horse, began to face us more boldly, sometimes too from their rear to provoke our men by an attack. Caesar [however] restrained his men from battle, deeming it sufficient for the present to prevent the enemy from rapine, forage, and depredation. They marched for about fifteen days in such a manner that there was not more than five or six miles between the enemy's rear and our van.

Meanwhile, Caesar kept daily importuning the Aedui for the corn which they had promised in the name of their state; for, in consequence of the coldness (Gaul, being as before said, situated toward the north), not only was the corn in the fields not ripe, but there was not in store a sufficiently large quantity even of fodder: besides he was unable to use the corn which he had conveyed in ships up the river Saone, because the Helvetii, from whom he was unwilling to retire had diverted their march from the Saone. The Aedui kept deferring from day to day, and saying that it was being collected-brought in-on the road." When he saw that he was put off too long, and that the day was close at hand on which he ought to serve out the corn to his soldiers;-having called together their chiefs, of whom he had a great number in his camp, among them Divitiacus and Liscus who was invested with the chief magistracy (whom the Aedui style the Vergobretus, and who is elected annually and has power of life or death over his countrymen), he severely reprimands them, because he is not assisted by them on so urgent an occasion, when the enemy were so close at hand, and when [corn] could neither be bought nor taken from the fields, particularly as, in a great measure urged by their prayers, he had undertaken the war; much more bitterly, therefore does he complain of his being forsaken.

Then at length Liscus, moved by Caesar's speech, discloses what he had hitherto kept secret: -that there are some whose influences with the people is very great, who, though private men, have more power than the magistrates themselves: that these by seditions and violent language are deterring the populace from contributing the corn which they ought to supply; [by telling them] that, if they can not any longer retain the supremacy of Gaul, it were better to submit to the government of Gauls than of Romans, nor ought they to doubt that, if the Romans should overpower the Helvetii, they would wrest their freedom from the Aedui together with the remainder of Gaul. By these very men, [said he], are our plans and whatever is done in the camp, disclosed to the enemy; that they could not be restrained by him: nay more, he was well aware, that though compelled by necessity, he had disclosed the matter to Caesar, at how great a risk he had done it; and for that reason, he had been silent as long as he could."

Caesar perceived that by this speech of Liscus, Dumnorix, the brother of Divitiacus, was indicated; but, as he was unwilling that these matters should be discussed while so many were present, he speedily dismisses: the council, but detains Liscus: he inquires from him when alone, about those things which he had said in the meeting. He [Liscus] speaks more unreservedly and boldly. He [Caesar] makes inquiries on the same points privately of others, and discovered that it is all true; that "Dumnorix is the person, a man of the highest daring, in great favor with the people on account of his liberality, a man eager for a revolution: that for a great many years he has been in the habit of contracting for the customs and all the other taxes of the Aedui at a small cost, because when he bids, no one dares to bid against him. By these means he has both increased his own private property, and amassed great means for giving largesses; that he maintains constantly at his own expense and keeps about his own person a great number of cavalry, and that not only at home, but even among the neighboring states, he has great influence, and for the sake of strengthening this influence has

265

given his mother in marriage among the Bituriges to a man the most noble and most influential there; that he has himself taken a wife from among the Helvetii, and has given his sister by the mother's side and his female relations in marriage into other states; that he favors and wishes well to the Helvetii on account of this connection; and that he hates Caesar and the Romans, on his own account, because by their arrival his power was weakened, and his brother, Divitiacus, restored to his former position of influence and dignity: that, if any thing should happen to the Romans, he entertains the highest hope of gaining the sovereignty by means of the Helvetii, but that under the government of the Roman people he despairs not only of royalty, but even of that influence which he already has." Caesar discovered too, on inquiring into the unsuccessful cavalry engagement which had taken place a few days before, that the commencement of that flight had been made by Dumnorix and his cavalry (for Dumnorix was in command of the cavalry which the Aedui had sent for aid to Caesar); that by their flight the rest of the cavalry were dismayed.

After learning these circumstances, since to these suspicions the most unequivocal facts were added, viz., that he had led the Helvetii through the territories of the Sequani; that he had provided that hostages should be mutually given; that he had done all these things, not only without any orders of his [Caesar's] and of his own state's, but even without their [the Aedui] knowing any thing of it themselves; that he [Dumnorix] was reprimanded: by the [chief] magistrate of the Aedui; he [Caesar] considered that there was sufficient reason, why he should either punish him himself, or order the state to do so. One thing [however] stood in the way of all this-that he had learned by experience his brother Divitiacus's very high regard for the Roman people, his great affection toward him, his distinguished faithfulness, justice, and moderation; for he was afraid lest by the punishment of this man, he should hurt the feelings of Divitiacus. Therefore, before he attempted any thing, he orders Divitiacus to be summoned to him, and, when the ordinary interpreters had been withdrawn, converses with him through Caius Valerius Procillus, chief of the province of Gaul, an intimate friend of his, in whom he reposed the highest confidence in every thing; at the same time he reminds him of what was said about Dumnorix in the council of the Gauls, when he himself was present, and shows what each had said of him privately in his [Caesar's] own presence; he begs and exhorts him, that, without offense to his feelings, he may either himself pass judgment on him [Dumnorix] after trying the case, or else order the [Aeduan] state to do so.

一 文献出处

Julius Caesar, *The Gallic War*, trans. by W. A. McDevitte & W. S. Bohn, Harper & Brothers, New York, 1869.

二 文献导读

凯撒（C. Julius Caesar, 约公元前 100 年~前 44 年）是古罗马知名度最高、对后世西方的政治影响最大的政治家、文学家。他出身贵族，是马略的妻侄，秦纳的女婿，因慷慨好施而负债。他因积极参加反苏拉斗争而出名，后因苏拉迫害背井离乡。公元前 75 年到罗德斯学习修辞学，公元前 63 年当选总司祭，公元前 62 年任政法官、西班牙总督，公元前 60 年与庞培、克拉苏秘密结盟，史称"前三雄"。为了结盟，他把年仅 14 岁的女儿嫁给年过半百的庞培。翌年任执政官、山内高卢总督。公元前 58~前 51 年，通过多次征战山外高卢将罗马的西北边疆拓展到莱茵河畔，赢得了雄厚财力和唯己是从的大军。公元前 55 年先后侵入日耳曼、不列颠。公元前 53 年克拉苏毙于安息作战后，凯撒与庞培及元老院的矛盾不断激化导致内战。公元前 49 年 1 月，凯撒率军渡过鲁比孔河，速占意大利。随后又在西班牙击溃庞培。公元前 48 年法萨罗一战全歼庞军，接着挥师埃及追杀残敌。公元前 45 年庞培被杀，内战暂告一段。

凯撒曾获得终身独裁官、执政官等职，兼领大将军总祭司。其任内实行一系列改革，开帝政先河，如改善行省管理，授予高卢行省和西班牙某些自治市以公民权，建立老兵殖民地，颁布自治法，增加职官人数，整顿元老院，颁行"儒略历"等。虽然他为政宽容，兼顾不同阶层利益，但其独裁仍然不能消弭共和派的强烈不满。公元前 44 年 3 月 15 日，被布鲁图斯和喀西约等阴谋分子刺杀于元老院。凯撒不仅善于治军，足智多谋，而且很有文采。公元前 52~前 51 年写成 8 卷《高卢战记》(*Commentarii de bello Gallico /The Gallic War*)。该书前 7 卷由凯撒执笔，涵盖公元前 58~前 52 年历史，第 8 卷由部将奥鲁斯·赫提鲁斯续写公元前 51~前 50 年历史。该书详述了凯撒征战高卢、日耳曼以及公元前 55~前 54 年两次入侵不列颠的经过，以及沿途所见的地理物产、民族风情。西塞罗称赞此书"文笔典雅、直率"。该书长期被西方作为古典拉丁文教材。另外还有 3 卷《内战记》(*Commentarii de bello Civili /The Civil Wars*)，涵盖公元前 49~前 48 年历史，可能撰写于公元前 45 年，记述了凯撒战胜庞培及其党羽的经过。

凯撒能在戎马倥偬间抽闲去写两部回忆录，主要是为了在罗马上层为自己表功，为他的过错辩护，难免文过饰非、夸张其词。但这两部著作毕竟是难得的当事人亲笔撰写，因而具有很高的史料价值。

上文节选自《高卢战记》第 1 卷。

三　延伸阅读

Freeman, Philip, *Julius Caesar*, Simon and Schuster, 2008.

Goldsworthy, Adrian, *Caesar: Life of a Colossus*, Yale University Press, 2006.

Holland, Tom, *Rubicon: The Last Years of the Roman Republic*, Anchor Books, 2003.

Virgil: Aeneid [*]

BOOK I

Arms, and the man I sing, who, forc'd by fate,

And haughty Juno's unrelenting hate,

Expell'd and exil'd, left the Trojan shore.

Long labors, both by sea and land, he bore,

And in the doubtful war, before he won

The Latian realm, and built the destin'd town;

His banish'd gods restor'd to rites divine,

And settled sure succession in his line,

From whence the race of Alban fathers come,

And the long glories of majestic Rome.

O Muse! the causes and the crimes relate;

What goddess was provok'd, and whence her hate;

For what offense the Queen of Heav'n began

To persecute so brave, so just a man;

---

* 维吉尔《埃涅阿斯纪》第 1 卷节选。

Involv'd his anxious life in endless cares,

Expos'd to wants, and hurried into wars!

Can heav'nly minds such high resentment show,

Or exercise their spite in human woe?

Against the Tiber's mouth, but far away,

An ancient town was seated on the sea;

A Tyrian colony; the people made

Stout for the war, and studious of their trade:

Carthage the name; belov'd by Juno more

Than her own Argos, or the Samian shore.

Here stood her chariot; here, if Heav'n were kind,

The seat of awful empire she design'd.

Yet she had heard an ancient rumor fly,

(Long cited by the people of the sky,)

That times to come should see the Trojan race

Her Carthage ruin, and her tow'rs deface;

Nor thus confin'd, the yoke of sov'reign sway

Should on the necks of all the nations lay.

She ponder'd this, and fear'd it was in fate;

Nor could forget the war she wag'd of late

For conqu'ring Greece against the Trojan state.

Besides, long causes working in her mind,

And secret seeds of envy, lay behind;

Deep graven in her heart the doom remain'd

Of partial Paris, and her form disdain'd;

The grace bestow'd on ravish'd Ganymed,

Electra's glories, and her injur'd bed.

Each was a cause alone; and all combin'd

To kindle vengeance in her haughty mind.

For this, far distant from the Latian coast

She drove the remnants of the Trojan host;

And sev'n long years th' unhappy wand'ring train

Were toss'd by storms, and scatter'd thro' the main.

Such time, such toil, requir'd the Roman name,

Such length of labor for so vast a frame.

Now scarce the Trojan fleet, with sails and oars,

Had left behind the fair Sicilian shores,

Ent'ring with cheerful shouts the wat'ry reign,

And plowing frothy furrows in the main;

When, lab'ring still with endless discontent,

The Queen of Heav'n did thus her fury vent:

"Then am I vanquish'd? must I yield?" said she,

"And must the Trojans reign in Italy?

So Fate will have it, and Jove adds his force;

Nor can my pow'r divert their happy course.

Could angry Pallas, with revengeful spleen,

The Grecian navy burn, and drown the men?

She, for the fault of one offending foe,

The bolts of Jove himself presum'd to throw:

With whirlwinds from beneath she toss'd the ship,

And bare expos'd the bosom of the deep;

Then, as an eagle gripes the trembling game,

The wretch, yet hissing with her father's flame,

She strongly seiz'd, and with a burning wound

Transfix'd, and naked, on a rock she bound.

But I, who walk in awful state above,

The majesty of heav'n, the sister wife of Jove,

For length of years my fruitless force employ

Against the thin remains of ruin'd Troy!

What nations now to Juno's pow'r will pray,

Or off'rings on my slighted altars lay?"

Thus rag'd the goddess; and, with fury fraught.

The restless regions of the storms she sought,

Where, in a spacious cave of living stone,

The tyrant Aeolus, from his airy throne,

With pow'r imperial curbs the struggling winds,

And sounding tempests in dark prisons binds.

This way and that th' impatient captives tend,

And, pressing for release, the mountains rend.

High in his hall th' undaunted monarch stands,

And shakes his scepter, and their rage commands;

Which did he not, their unresisted sway

Would sweep the world before them in their way;

Earth, air, and seas thro' empty space would roll,

And heav'n would fly before the driving soul.

In fear of this, the Father of the Gods

Confin'd their fury to those dark abodes,

And lock'd 'em safe within, oppress'd with mountain loads;

Impos'd a king, with arbitrary sway,

To loose their fetters, or their force allay.

To whom the suppliant queen her pray'rs address'd,

And thus the tenor of her suit express'd:

"O Aeolus! for to thee the King of Heav'n

The pow'r of tempests and of winds has giv'n;

Thy force alone their fury can restrain,

And smooth the waves, or swell the troubled main-

A race of wand'ring slaves, abhorr'd by me,

With prosp'rous passage cut the Tuscan sea;

To fruitful Italy their course they steer,

And for their vanquish'd gods design new temples there.

Raise all thy winds; with night involve the skies;

Sink or disperse my fatal enemies.

Twice sev'n, the charming daughters of the main,

Around my person wait, and bear my train:

Succeed my wish, and second my design;

The fairest, Deiopeia, shall be thine,

And make thee father of a happy line."

To this the god: "'T is yours, O queen, to will

The work which duty binds me to fulfil.

These airy kingdoms, and this wide command,

Are all the presents of your bounteous hand:

Yours is my sov'reign's grace; and, as your guest,

I sit with gods at their celestial feast;

Raise tempests at your pleasure, or subdue;

Dispose of empire, which I hold from you."

He said, and hurl'd against the mountain side

His quiv'ring spear, and all the god applied.

The raging winds rush thro' the hollow wound,

And dance aloft in air, and skim along the ground;

Then, settling on the sea, the surges sweep,
Raise liquid mountains, and disclose the deep.
South, East, and West with mix'd confusion roar,
And roll the foaming billows to the shore.
The cables crack; the sailors' fearful cries
Ascend; and sable night involves the skies;
And heav'n itself is ravish'd from their eyes.
Loud peals of thunder from the poles ensue;
Then flashing fires the transient light renew;
The face of things a frightful image bears,
And present death in various forms appears.
Struck with unusual fright, the Trojan chief,
With lifted hands and eyes, invokes relief;
And, "Thrice and four times happy those, " he cried,
"That under Ilian walls before their parents died!
Tydides, bravest of the Grecian train!
Why could not I by that strong arm be slain,
And lie by noble Hector on the plain,
Or great Sarpedon, in those bloody fields
Where Simois rolls the bodies and the shields
Of heroes, whose dismember'd hands yet bear
The dart aloft, and clench the pointed spear!"

Thus while the pious prince his fate bewails,
Fierce Boreas drove against his flying sails,
And rent the sheets; the raging billows rise,
And mount the tossing vessels to the skies:
Nor can the shiv'ring oars sustain the blow;
The galley gives her side, and turns her prow;

While those astern, descending down the steep,

Thro' gaping waves behold the boiling deep.

Three ships were hurried by the southern blast,

And on the secret shelves with fury cast.

Those hidden rocks th' Ausonian sailors knew:

They call'd them Altars, when they rose in view,

And show'd their spacious backs above the flood.

Three more fierce Eurus, in his angry mood,

Dash'd on the shallows of the moving sand,

And in mid ocean left them moor'd aland.

Orontes' bark, that bore the Lycian crew,

(A horrid sight!) ev'n in the hero's view,

From stem to stern by waves was overborne:

The trembling pilot, from his rudder torn,

Was headlong hurl'd; thrice round the ship was toss'd,

Then bulg'd at once, and in the deep was lost;

And here and there above the waves were seen

Arms, pictures, precious goods, and floating men.

The stoutest vessel to the storm gave way,

And suck'd thro' loosen'd planks the rushing sea.

Ilioneus was her chief: Alethes old,

Achates faithful, Abas young and bold,

Endur'd not less; their ships, with gaping seams,

Admit the deluge of the briny streams.

Meantime imperial Neptune heard the sound

Of raging billows breaking on the ground.

Displeas'd, and fearing for his wat'ry reign,

He rear'd his awful head above the main,

Serene in majesty; then roll'd his eyes

Around the space of earth, and seas, and skies.

He saw the Trojan fleet dispers'd, distress'd,

By stormy winds and wintry heav'n oppress'd.

Full well the god his sister's envy knew,

And what her aims and what her arts pursue.

He summon'd Eurus and the western blast,

And first an angry glance on both he cast;

Then thus rebuk'd: "Audacious winds! from whence

This bold attempt, this rebel insolence?

Is it for you to ravage seas and land,

Unauthoriz'd by my supreme command?

To raise such mountains on the troubled main?

Whom I- but first 't is fit the billows to restrain;

And then you shall be taught obedience to my reign.

Hence! to your lord my royal mandate bear-

The realms of ocean and the fields of air

Are mine, not his. By fatal lot to me

The liquid empire fell, and trident of the sea.

His pow'r to hollow caverns is confin'd:

There let him reign, the jailer of the wind,

With hoarse commands his breathing subjects call,

And boast and bluster in his empty hall."

He spoke; and, while he spoke, he smooth'd the sea,

Dispell'd the darkness, and restor'd the day.

Cymothoe, Triton, and the sea-green train

Of beauteous nymphs, the daughters of the main,

Clear from the rocks the vessels with their hands:

The god himself with ready trident stands,

And opes the deep, and spreads the moving sands;

Then heaves them off the shoals. Where'er he guides

His finny coursers and in triumph rides,

The waves unruffle and the sea subsides.

As, when in tumults rise th' ignoble crowd,

Mad are their motions, and their tongues are loud;

And stones and brands in rattling volleys fly,

And all the rustic arms that fury can supply:

If then some grave and pious man appear,

They hush their noise, and lend a list'ning ear;

He soothes with sober words their angry mood,

And quenches their innate desire of blood:

So, when the Father of the Flood appears,

And o'er the seas his sov'reign trident rears,

Their fury falls: he skims the liquid plains,

High on his chariot, and, with loosen'd reins,

Majestic moves along, and awful peace maintains.

The weary Trojans ply their shatter'd oars

To nearest land, and make the Libyan shores.

Within a long recess there lies a bay:

An island shades it from the rolling sea,

And forms a port secure for ships to ride;

Broke by the jutting land, on either side,

In double streams the briny waters glide.

Betwixt two rows of rocks a sylvan scene

Appears above, and groves for ever green:

A grot is form'd beneath, with mossy seats,

To rest the Nereids, and exclude the heats.

Down thro' the crannies of the living walls

The crystal streams descend in murm'ring falls:

No haulsers need to bind the vessels here,

Nor bearded anchors; for no storms they fear.

Sev'n ships within this happy harbor meet,

The thin remainders of the scatter'd fleet.

The Trojans, worn with toils, and spent with woes,

Leap on the welcome land, and seek their wish'd repose.

First, good Achates, with repeated strokes

Of clashing flints, their hidden fire provokes:

Short flame succeeds; a bed of wither'd leaves

The dying sparkles in their fall receives:

Caught into life, in fiery fumes they rise,

And, fed with stronger food, invade the skies.

The Trojans, dropping wet, or stand around

The cheerful blaze, or lie along the ground:

Some dry their corn, infected with the brine,

Then grind with marbles, and prepare to dine.

Aeneas climbs the mountain's airy brow,

And takes a prospect of the seas below,

If Capys thence, or Antheus he could spy,

Or see the streamers of Caicus fly.

No vessels were in view; but, on the plain,

Three beamy stags command a lordly train

Of branching heads: the more ignoble throng

Attend their stately steps, and slowly graze along.

He stood; and, while secure they fed below,

He took the quiver and the trusty bow

Achates us'd to bear: the leaders first

He laid along, and then the vulgar pierc'd;

Nor ceas'd his arrows, till the shady plain

Sev'n mighty bodies with their blood distain.

For the sev'n ships he made an equal share,

And to the port return'd, triumphant from the war.

The jars of gen'rous wine (Acestes' gift,

When his Trinacrian shores the navy left)

He set abroach, and for the feast prepar'd,

In equal portions with the ven'son shar'd.

Thus while he dealt it round, the pious chief

With cheerful words allay'd the common grief:

"Endure, and conquer! Jove will soon dispose

To future good our past and present woes.

With me, the rocks of Scylla you have tried;

Th' inhuman Cyclops and his den defied.

What greater ills hereafter can you bear?

Resume your courage and dismiss your care,

An hour will come, with pleasure to relate

Your sorrows past, as benefits of Fate.

Thro' various hazards and events, we move

To Latium and the realms foredoom'd by Jove.

Call'd to the seat (the promise of the skies)

Where Trojan kingdoms once again may rise,

Endure the hardships of your present state;

Live, and reserve yourselves for better fate."

These words he spoke, but spoke not from his heart;

His outward smiles conceal'd his inward smart.

The jolly crew, unmindful of the past,

The quarry share, their plenteous dinner haste.

Some strip the skin; some portion out the spoil;

The limbs, yet trembling, in the caldrons boil;

Some on the fire the reeking entrails broil.

Stretch'd on the grassy turf, at ease they dine,

Restore their strength with meat, and cheer their souls with

wine.

Their hunger thus appeas'd, their care attends

The doubtful fortune of their absent friends:

Alternate hopes and fears their minds possess,

Whether to deem 'em dead, or in distress.

Above the rest, Aeneas mourns the fate

Of brave Orontes, and th' uncertain state

Of Gyas, Lycus, and of Amycus.

The day, but not their sorrows, ended thus.

When, from aloft, almighty Jove surveys

Earth, air, and shores, and navigable seas,

At length on Libyan realms he fix'd his eyes-

Whom, pond'ring thus on human miseries,

When Venus saw, she with a lowly look,

Not free from tears, her heav'nly sire bespoke:

"O King of Gods and Men! whose awful hand

Disperses thunder on the seas and land,

Disposing all with absolute command;

How could my pious son thy pow'r incense?

Or what, alas! is vanish'd Troy's offense?

Our hope of Italy not only lost,

On various seas by various tempests toss'd,

But shut from ev'ry shore, and barr'd from ev'ry coast.

You promis'd once, a progeny divine

Of Romans, rising from the Trojan line,

In after times should hold the world in awe,

And to the land and ocean give the law.

How is your doom revers'd, which eas'd my care

When Troy was ruin'd in that cruel war?

Then fates to fates I could oppose; but now,

When Fortune still pursues her former blow,

What can I hope? What worse can still succeed?

What end of labors has your will decreed?

Antenor, from the midst of Grecian hosts,

Could pass secure, and pierce th' Illyrian coasts,

Where, rolling down the steep, Timavus raves

And thro' nine channels disembogues his waves.

At length he founded Padua's happy seat,

And gave his Trojans a secure retreat;

There fix'd their arms, and there renew'd their name,

And there in quiet rules, and crown'd with fame.

But we, descended from your sacred line,

Entitled to your heav'n and rites divine,

Are banish'd earth; and, for the wrath of one,

Remov'd from Latium and the promis'd throne.

Are these our scepters? these our due rewards?

And is it thus that Jove his plighted faith regards?"

To whom the Father of th' immortal race,

Smiling with that serene indulgent face,

With which he drives the clouds and clears the skies,

First gave a holy kiss; then thus replies:

"Daughter, dismiss thy fears; to thy desire

The fates of thine are fix'd, and stand entire.

Thou shalt behold thy wish'd Lavinian walls;

And, ripe for heav'n, when fate Aeneas calls,

Then shalt thou bear him up, sublime, to me:

No councils have revers'd my firm decree.

And, lest new fears disturb thy happy state,

Know, I have search'd the mystic rolls of Fate:

Thy son (nor is th' appointed season far)

In Italy shall wage successful war,

Shall tame fierce nations in the bloody field,

And sov'reign laws impose, and cities build,

Till, after ev'ry foe subdued, the sun

Thrice thro' the signs his annual race shall run:

This is his time prefix'd. Ascanius then,

Now call'd Iulus, shall begin his reign.

He thirty rolling years the crown shall wear,

Then from Lavinium shall the seat transfer,

And, with hard labor, Alba Longa build.

The throne with his succession shall be fill'd

Three hundred circuits more: then shall be seen

Ilia the fair, a priestess and a queen,

Who, full of Mars, in time, with kindly throes,

Shall at a birth two goodly boys disclose.

The royal babes a tawny wolf shall drain:

Then Romulus his grandsire's throne shall gain,

Of martial tow'rs the founder shall become,

The people Romans call, the city Rome.

To them no bounds of empire I assign,

Nor term of years to their immortal line.

Ev'n haughty Juno, who, with endless broils,

Earth, seas, and heav'n, and Jove himself turmoils;

At length aton'd, her friendly pow'r shall join,

To cherish and advance the Trojan line.

The subject world shall Rome's dominion own,

And, prostrate, shall adore the nation of the gown.

An age is ripening in revolving fate

When Troy shall overturn the Grecian state,

And sweet revenge her conqu'ring sons shall call,

To crush the people that conspir'd her fall.

Then Caesar from the Julian stock shall rise,

Whose empire ocean, and whose fame the skies

Alone shall bound; whom, fraught with eastern spoils,

Our heav'n, the just reward of human toils,

Securely shall repay with rites divine;

And incense shall ascend before his sacred shrine.

Then dire debate and impious war shall cease,

And the stern age be soften'd into peace:

Then banish'd Faith shall once again return,

And Vestal fires in hallow'd temples burn;

And Remus with Quirinus shall sustain

The righteous laws, and fraud and force restrain.

Janus himself before his fane shall wait,

And keep the dreadful issues of his gate,

With bolts and iron bars: within remains

Imprison'd Fury, bound in brazen chains;

High on a trophy rais'd, of useless arms,

He sits, and threats the world with vain alarms."

He said, and sent Cyllenius with command

To free the ports, and ope the Punic land

To Trojan guests; lest, ignorant of fate,

The queen might force them from her town and state.

Down from the steep of heav'n Cyllenius flies,

And cleaves with all his wings the yielding skies.

Soon on the Libyan shore descends the god,

Performs his message, and displays his rod:

The surly murmurs of the people cease;

And, as the fates requir'd, they give the peace:

The queen herself suspends the rigid laws,

The Trojans pities, and protects their cause.

Meantime, in shades of night Aeneas lies:

Care seiz'd his soul, and sleep forsook his eyes.

But, when the sun restor'd the cheerful day,

He rose, the coast and country to survey,

Anxious and eager to discover more.

It look'd a wild uncultivated shore;

But, whether humankind, or beasts alone

Possess'd the new-found region, was unknown.

Beneath a ledge of rocks his fleet he hides:

Tall trees surround the mountain's shady sides;

The bending brow above a safe retreat provides.

Arm'd with two pointed darts, he leaves his friends,

And true Achates on his steps attends.

Lo! in the deep recesses of the wood,

Before his eyes his goddess mother stood:

A huntress in her habit and her mien;

Her dress a maid, her air confess'd a queen.

Bare were her knees, and knots her garments bind;

Loose was her hair, and wanton'd in the wind;

Her hand sustain'd a bow; her quiver hung behind.

She seem'd a virgin of the Spartan blood:

With such array Harpalyce bestrode

Her Thracian courser and outstripp'd the rapid flood.

"Ho, strangers! have you lately seen, " she said,

"One of my sisters, like myself array'd,

Who cross'd the lawn, or in the forest stray'd?

A painted quiver at her back she bore;

Varied with spots, a lynx's hide she wore;

And at full cry pursued the tusky boar."

Thus Venus: thus her son replied again:

"None of your sisters have we heard or seen,

O virgin! or what other name you bear

Above that style- O more than mortal fair!

Your voice and mien celestial birth betray!

If, as you seem, the sister of the day,

Or one at least of chaste Diana's train,

Let not an humble suppliant sue in vain;

But tell a stranger, long in tempests toss'd,

What earth we tread, and who commands the coast?

Then on your name shall wretched mortals call,

And offer'd victims at your altars fall."

"I dare not, " she replied, "assume the name

Of goddess, or celestial honors claim:

For Tyrian virgins bows and quivers bear,

And purple buskins o'er their ankles wear.

Know, gentle youth, in Libyan lands you are-

A people rude in peace, and rough in war.

The rising city, which from far you see,

Is Carthage, and a Tyrian colony.

Phoenician Dido rules the growing state,

Who fled from Tyre, to shun her brother's hate.

Great were her wrongs, her story full of fate;

Which I will sum in short. Sichaeus, known

For wealth, and brother to the Punic throne,

Possess'd fair Dido's bed; and either heart

At once was wounded with an equal dart.

Her father gave her, yet a spotless maid;

Pygmalion then the Tyrian scepter sway'd:

One who condemn'd divine and human laws.

Then strife ensued, and cursed gold the cause.

The monarch, blinded with desire of wealth,

With steel invades his brother's life by stealth;

Before the sacred altar made him bleed,

And long from her conceal'd the cruel deed.

Some tale, some new pretense, he daily coin'd,

To soothe his sister, and delude her mind.

At length, in dead of night, the ghost appears

Of her unhappy lord: the specter stares,

And, with erected eyes, his bloody bosom bares.

The cruel altars and his fate he tells,

And the dire secret of his house reveals,

Then warns the widow, with her household gods,

To seek a refuge in remote abodes.

Last, to support her in so long a way,

He shows her where his hidden treasure lay.

Admonish'd thus, and seiz'd with mortal fright,

The queen provides companions of her flight:

They meet, and all combine to leave the state,

Who hate the tyrant, or who fear his hate.

They seize a fleet, which ready rigg'd they find;

Nor is Pygmalion's treasure left behind.

The vessels, heavy laden, put to sea

With prosp'rous winds; a woman leads the way.

I know not, if by stress of weather driv'n,

Or was their fatal course dispos'd by Heav'n;

At last they landed, where from far your eyes

May view the turrets of new Carthage rise;

There bought a space of ground, which (Byrsa call'd,

From the bull's hide) they first inclos'd, and wall'd.

But whence are you? what country claims your birth?

What seek you, strangers, on our Libyan earth?"

To whom, with sorrow streaming from his eyes,

And deeply sighing, thus her son replies:

"Could you with patience hear, or I relate,

O nymph, the tedious annals of our fate!

Thro' such a train of woes if I should run,

287

The day would sooner than the tale be done!

From ancient Troy, by force expell'd, we came-

If you by chance have heard the Trojan name.

On various seas by various tempests toss'd,

At length we landed on your Libyan coast.

The good Aeneas am I call'd- a name,

While Fortune favor'd, not unknown to fame.

My household gods, companions of my woes,

With pious care I rescued from our foes.

To fruitful Italy my course was bent;

And from the King of Heav'n is my descent.

With twice ten sail I cross'd the Phrygian sea;

Fate and my mother goddess led my way.

Scarce sev'n, the thin remainders of my fleet,

From storms preserv'd, within your harbor meet.

Myself distress'd, an exile, and unknown,

Debarr'd from Europe, and from Asia thrown,

In Libyan desarts wander thus alone."

His tender parent could no longer bear;

But, interposing, sought to soothe his care.

"Whoe'er you are- not unbelov'd by Heav'n,

Since on our friendly shore your ships are driv'n-

Have courage: to the gods permit the rest,

And to the queen expose your just request.

Now take this earnest of success, for more:

Your scatter'd fleet is join'd upon the shore;

The winds are chang'd, your friends from danger free;

Or I renounce my skill in augury.

Twelve swans behold in beauteous order move,

And stoop with closing pinions from above;

Whom late the bird of Jove had driv'n along,

And thro' the clouds pursued the scatt'ring throng:

Now, all united in a goodly team,

They skim the ground, and seek the quiet stream.

As they, with joy returning, clap their wings,

And ride the circuit of the skies in rings;

Not otherwise your ships, and ev'ry friend,

Already hold the port, or with swift sails descend.

No more advice is needful; but pursue

The path before you, and the town in view."

Thus having said, she turn'd, and made appear

Her neck refulgent, and dishevel'd hair,

Which, flowing from her shoulders, reach'd the ground.

And widely spread ambrosial scents around:

In length of train descends her sweeping gown;

And, by her graceful walk, the Queen of Love is known.

The prince pursued the parting deity

With words like these: "Ah! whither do you fly?

Unkind and cruel! to deceive your son

In borrow'd shapes, and his embrace to shun;

Never to bless my sight, but thus unknown;

And still to speak in accents not your own."

Against the goddess these complaints he made,

But took the path, and her commands obey'd.

They march, obscure; for Venus kindly shrouds

With mists their persons, and involves in clouds,

That, thus unseen, their passage none might stay,

Or force to tell the causes of their way.

This part perform'd, the goddess flies sublime

To visit Paphos and her native clime;

Where garlands, ever green and ever fair,

With vows are offer'd, and with solemn pray'r:

A hundred altars in her temple smoke;

A thousand bleeding hearts her pow'r invoke.

They climb the next ascent, and, looking down,

Now at a nearer distance view the town.

The prince with wonder sees the stately tow'rs,

Which late were huts and shepherds' homely bow'rs,

The gates and streets; and hears, from ev'ry part,

The noise and busy concourse of the mart.

The toiling Tyrians on each other call

To ply their labor: some extend the wall;

Some build the citadel; the brawny throng

Or dig, or push unwieldly stones along.

Some for their dwellings choose a spot of ground,

Which, first design'd, with ditches they surround.

Some laws ordain; and some attend the choice

Of holy senates, and elect by voice.

Here some design a mole, while others there

Lay deep foundations for a theater;

From marble quarries mighty columns hew,

For ornaments of scenes, and future view.

Such is their toil, and such their busy pains,

As exercise the bees in flow'ry plains,

When winter past, and summer scarce begun,

Invites them forth to labor in the sun;

Some lead their youth abroad, while some condense

Their liquid store, and some in cells dispense;

Some at the gate stand ready to receive

The golden burthen, and their friends relieve;

All with united force, combine to drive

The lazy drones from the laborious hive:

With envy stung, they view each other's deeds;

The fragrant work with diligence proceeds.

"Thrice happy you, whose walls already rise!"

Aeneas said, and view'd, with lifted eyes,

Their lofty tow'rs; then, entiring at the gate,

Conceal'd in clouds (prodigious to relate)

He mix'd, unmark'd, among the busy throng,

Borne by the tide, and pass'd unseen along.

一 文献出处

Virgil, *Aeneid*, trans. by H. Rushton Fairclough, revised by G. P. Goold, Harvard University Press, 1916.

二 文献导读

诗人维吉尔（Vergilius Maro，公元前 70 年～前 19 年）生于山南高卢曼图亚地区的农村；这一带农业兴旺，文化发达，出现过卡图卢斯和科涅利乌斯、奈波斯等文人名流。维吉尔家境富裕。17 岁赴罗马和意大利南部学习修辞学和哲学，受到良好教育。因体弱多病，内战期间未服兵役，专心写作。公元前 42 年，屋大维（奥古斯都）为给复员老兵分配土地，曾没收维吉尔父亲的家园，迫使他们迁居意大利南部；不久屋大维又把土地还给他家，以后维吉尔便投靠屋大维，不断吟诗为屋大维歌功颂德。公元前39年因发表《牧歌》而得以加入贵族梅塞纳斯赞助的文学协会，公元前29年把他写的《农事诗》献给梅塞纳斯。屋大维建立罗马帝国，加封奥古斯都称号之后，维吉尔一直是宫廷红人。

维吉尔最早的重要作品是《牧歌》十章，大概写于公元前42~前37年之间。这些诗歌的写法模仿亚历山大城著名诗人忒奥克里托斯的风格，通过对话或对唱，抒发田园爱情之乐，有时也涉及一些社会政治问题。例如在第1章和第9章里，诗人就描写了被迫背井离乡的哀怨和重归故里的感激心情。牧歌第4章通过歌颂一个婴儿的诞生宣告黄金时代的到来，后人对此争议较多。从公元4世纪起，不少基督徒认为这个诞生婴儿是指耶稣基督，是对未来天国的预言。实际上，这个初生婴儿可能是指生于公元前42年的马尔切鲁斯，是奥古斯都的妹妹屋大维娅的儿子，深为奥古斯都所宠爱，曾被认为是潜在的王位继承人。公元前25年马尔切鲁斯尽管迎娶了奥古斯都的女儿尤莉娅为妻，却在公元前23年病死，只活到20岁，未能如愿继承帝位。维吉尔在他后来的史诗《埃涅阿斯纪》里，曾特别增加了哀悼马尔切鲁斯早夭的一段（第6卷第860~886行）。把这个婴儿附会为耶稣显然难以成立，因为基督教在当时的影响还很小。

维吉尔第二部重要作品是他在公元前29年发表的四卷《农事诗》，全诗共2188行，用了7年写成。这首长诗与赫西俄德的《工作与时日》很类似，第1卷谈种庄稼，第2卷谈种植葡萄树和橄榄树，第3卷谈放牧牛马，第4卷谈养蜂。

维吉尔死于公元前19年，只活了51岁。他用最后十年写的12卷1万多行史诗《埃涅阿斯纪》在他死前只完成初稿，还没有定稿，因此一向态度严谨的维吉尔在遗嘱里要求把这部初稿烧掉，幸亏得到奥古斯都的重视才保存下来。史诗借用神话传说歌颂罗马传统的神圣非凡，暗示奥古斯都统治的历史必然性。其情节结构虽然模仿《荷马史诗》（第1~6卷模仿《奥德赛》，第7~12卷模仿《伊里亚特》），但又增加了自己的特色。全诗情节曲折，故事性强，语言凝练。一般认为《荷马史诗》是集体创作的民间文学作品，而《埃涅阿斯纪》则是欧洲文学史上第一部个人创作的史诗，因此备受重视。

维吉尔在生前就已被公认为是罗马的大诗人，死后声名经久不衰。由于教会从公元 4 世纪起就误认为他是未来基督世界的预言家和圣人，他在中古时代也一直享有尊荣。但丁在他虚构的神话故事《神曲》中说维吉尔是其导师和带路人，解救了迷路的他，并邀请他去游览了地狱和天国。文艺复兴后，许多用史诗体裁写作的欧洲著名诗人，如塔索、卡蒙斯、弥尔顿等都把维吉尔的作品奉为圭臬。文学界一般认为维吉尔是荷马以后最重要的史诗诗人。

以上内容节选自《埃涅阿斯纪》第 1 卷。

三　延伸阅读

Heinze, R., *Virgils Epische Technik*, Berlin, 1928.

Jackson, Knight W. F. , *Roman Vergil*, London, 1944.

Ziolkowski, Jan M., and Michael C. J. Putnam, eds., *The Virgilian Tradition: The First Fifteen Hundred Years*, New Haven: Yale University Press, 2008.

Ovid: Metamorphoses[*]

The Creation of the World

Of bodies chang'd to various forms, I sing:
Ye Gods, from whom these miracles did spring,
Inspire my numbers with coelestial heat;
'Till I my long laborious work compleat:
And add perpetual tenour to my rhimes,
Deduc'd from Nature's birth, to Caesar's times.
Before the seas, and this terrestrial ball,
And Heav'n's high canopy, that covers all,
One was the face of Nature; if a face:
Rather a rude and indigested mass:
A lifeless lump, unfashion'd, and unfram'd,
Of jarring seeds; and justly Chaos nam'd.
No sun was lighted up, the world to view;
No moon did yet her blunted horns renew:

---
* 奥维德《变形记》第 1 卷节选。

Nor yet was Earth suspended in the sky,

Nor pois'd, did on her own foundations lye:

Nor seas about the shores their arms had thrown;

But earth, and air, and water, were in one.

Thus air was void of light, and earth unstable,

And water's dark abyss unnavigable.

No certain form on any was imprest;

All were confus'd, and each disturb'd the rest.

For hot and cold were in one body fixt;

And soft with hard, and light with heavy mixt.

But God, or Nature, while they thus contend,

To these intestine discords put an end:

Then earth from air, and seas from earth were driv'n,

And grosser air sunk from aetherial Heav'n.

Thus disembroil'd, they take their proper place;

The next of kin, contiguously embrace;

And foes are sunder'd, by a larger space.

The force of fire ascended first on high,

And took its dwelling in the vaulted sky:

Then air succeeds, in lightness next to fire;

Whose atoms from unactive earth retire.

Earth sinks beneath, and draws a num'rous throng

Of pondrous, thick, unwieldy seeds along.

About her coasts, unruly waters roar;

And rising, on a ridge, insult the shore.

Thus when the God, whatever God was he,

Had form'd the whole, and made the parts agree,

That no unequal portions might be found,

He moulded Earth into a spacious round:

Then with a breath, he gave the winds to blow;

And bad the congregated waters flow.

He adds the running springs, and standing lakes;

And bounding banks for winding rivers makes.

Some part, in Earth are swallow'd up, the most

In ample oceans, disembogu'd, are lost.

He shades the woods, the vallies he restrains

With rocky mountains, and extends the plains.

And as five zones th' aetherial regions bind,

Five, correspondent, are to Earth assign'd:

The sun with rays, directly darting down,

Fires all beneath, and fries the middle zone:

The two beneath the distant poles, complain

Of endless winter, and perpetual rain.

Betwixt th' extreams, two happier climates hold

The temper that partakes of hot, and cold.

The fields of liquid air, inclosing all,

Surround the compass of this earthly ball:

The lighter parts lye next the fires above;

The grosser near the watry surface move:

Thick clouds are spread, and storms engender there,

And thunder's voice, which wretched mortals fear,

And winds that on their wings cold winter bear.

Nor were those blustring brethren left at large,

On seas, and shores, their fury to discharge:

Bound as they are, and circumscrib'd in place,

They rend the world, resistless, where they pass;

And mighty marks of mischief leave behind;

Such is the rage of their tempestuous kind.

First Eurus to the rising morn is sent

(The regions of the balmy continent);

And Eastern realms, where early Persians run,

To greet the blest appearance of the sun.

Westward, the wanton Zephyr wings his flight;

Pleas'd with the remnants of departing light:

Fierce Boreas, with his off-spring, issues forth

T' invade the frozen waggon of the North.

While frowning Auster seeks the Southern sphere;

And rots, with endless rain, th' unwholsom year.

High o'er the clouds, and empty realms of wind,

The God a clearer space for Heav'n design'd;

Where fields of light, and liquid aether flow;

Purg'd from the pondrous dregs of Earth below.

Scarce had the Pow'r distinguish'd these, when streight

The stars, no longer overlaid with weight,

Exert their heads, from underneath the mass;

And upward shoot, and kindle as they pass,

And with diffusive light adorn their heav'nly place.

Then, every void of Nature to supply,

With forms of Gods he fills the vacant sky:

New herds of beasts he sends, the plains to share:

New colonies of birds, to people air:

And to their oozy beds, the finny fish repair.

A creature of a more exalted kind

Was wanting yet, and then was Man design'd:

Conscious of thought, of more capacious breast,

For empire form'd, and fit to rule the rest:

Whether with particles of heav'nly fire

The God of Nature did his soul inspire,

Or Earth, but new divided from the sky,

And, pliant, still retain'd th' aetherial energy:

Which wise Prometheus temper'd into paste,

And, mixt with living streams, the godlike image cast.

Thus, while the mute creation downward bend

Their sight, and to their earthly mother tend,

Man looks aloft; and with erected eyes

Beholds his own hereditary skies.

From such rude principles our form began;

And earth was metamorphos'd into Man.

The Golden Age

The golden age was first; when Man yet new,

No rule but uncorrupted reason knew:

And, with a native bent, did good pursue.

Unforc'd by punishment, un-aw'd by fear,

His words were simple, and his soul sincere;

Needless was written law, where none opprest:

The law of Man was written in his breast:

No suppliant crowds before the judge appear'd,

No court erected yet, nor cause was heard:

But all was safe, for conscience was their guard.

The mountain-trees in distant prospect please,

E're yet the pine descended to the seas:

E're sails were spread, new oceans to explore:

And happy mortals, unconcern'd for more,

Confin'd their wishes to their native shore.

No walls were yet; nor fence, nor mote, nor mound,

Nor drum was heard, nor trumpet's angry sound:

Nor swords were forg'd; but void of care and crime,

The soft creation slept away their time.

The teeming Earth, yet guiltless of the plough,

And unprovok'd, did fruitful stores allow:

Content with food, which Nature freely bred,

On wildings and on strawberries they fed;

Cornels and bramble-berries gave the rest,

And falling acorns furnish'd out a feast.

The flow'rs unsown, in fields and meadows reign'd:

And Western winds immortal spring maintain'd.

In following years, the bearded corn ensu'd

From Earth unask'd, nor was that Earth renew'd.

From veins of vallies, milk and nectar broke;

And honey sweating through the pores of oak.

The Silver Age

But when good Saturn, banish'd from above,

Was driv'n to Hell, the world was under Jove.

Succeeding times a silver age behold,

Excelling brass, but more excell'd by gold.

Then summer, autumn, winter did appear:

And spring was but a season of the year.

The sun his annual course obliquely made,

Good days contracted, and enlarg'd the bad.

Then air with sultry heats began to glow;

The wings of winds were clogg'd with ice and snow;

And shivering mortals, into houses driv'n,

Sought shelter from th' inclemency of Heav'n.

Those houses, then, were caves, or homely sheds;

With twining oziers fenc'd; and moss their beds.

Then ploughs, for seed, the fruitful furrows broke,

And oxen labour'd first beneath the yoke.

The Brazen Age

To this came next in course, the brazen age:

A warlike offspring, prompt to bloody rage,

Not impious yet...

The Iron Age

Hard steel succeeded then:

And stubborn as the metal, were the men.

Truth, modesty, and shame, the world forsook:

Fraud, avarice, and force, their places took.

Then sails were spread, to every wind that blew.

Raw were the sailors, and the depths were new:

Trees, rudely hollow'd, did the waves sustain;

E're ships in triumph plough'd the watry plain.

Then land-marks limited to each his right:
For all before was common as the light.
Nor was the ground alone requir'd to bear
Her annual income to the crooked share,
But greedy mortals, rummaging her store,
Digg'd from her entrails first the precious oar;
Which next to Hell, the prudent Gods had laid;
And that alluring ill, to sight display'd.
Thus cursed steel, and more accursed gold,
Gave mischief birth, and made that mischief bold:
And double death did wretched Man invade,
By steel assaulted, and by gold betray'd,
Now (brandish'd weapons glittering in their hands)
Mankind is broken loose from moral bands;
No rights of hospitality remain:
The guest, by him who harbour'd him, is slain,
The son-in-law pursues the father's life;
The wife her husband murders, he the wife.
The step-dame poyson for the son prepares;
The son inquires into his father's years.
Faith flies, and piety in exile mourns;
And justice, here opprest, to Heav'n returns.

The Giants' War

Nor were the Gods themselves more safe above;
Against beleaguer'd Heav'n the giants move.
Hills pil'd on hills, on mountains mountains lie,
To make their mad approaches to the skie.

'Till Jove, no longer patient, took his time

T' avenge with thunder their audacious crime:

Red light'ning plaid along the firmament,

And their demolish'd works to pieces rent.

Sing'd with the flames, and with the bolts transfixt,

With native Earth, their blood the monsters mixt;

The blood, indu'd with animating heat,

Did in th' impregnant Earth new sons beget:

They, like the seed from which they sprung, accurst,

Against the Gods immortal hatred nurst,

An impious, arrogant, and cruel brood;

Expressing their original from blood.

Which when the king of Gods beheld from high

(Withal revolving in his memory,

What he himself had found on Earth of late,

Lycaon's guilt, and his inhumane treat),

He sigh'd; nor longer with his pity strove;

But kindled to a wrath becoming Jove:

Then call'd a general council of the Gods;

Who summon'd, issue from their blest abodes,

And fill th' assembly with a shining train.

A way there is, in Heav'n's expanded plain,

Which, when the skies are clear, is seen below,

And mortals, by the name of Milky, know.

The ground-work is of stars; through which the road

Lyes open to the Thunderer's abode:

The Gods of greater nations dwell around,

And, on the right and left, the palace bound;

The commons where they can: the nobler sort

With winding-doors wide open, front the court.

This place, as far as Earth with Heav'n may vie,

I dare to call the Louvre of the skie.

When all were plac'd, in seats distinctly known,

And he, their father, had assum'd the throne,

Upon his iv'ry sceptre first he leant,

Then shook his head, that shook the firmament:

Air, Earth, and seas, obey'd th' almighty nod;

And, with a gen'ral fear, confess'd the God.

At length, with indignation, thus he broke

His awful silence, and the Pow'rs bespoke.

I was not more concern'd in that debate

Of empire, when our universal state

Was put to hazard, and the giant race

Our captive skies were ready to imbrace:

For tho' the foe was fierce, the seeds of all

Rebellion, sprung from one original;

Now, wheresoever ambient waters glide,

All are corrupt, and all must be destroy'd.

Let me this holy protestation make,

By Hell, and Hell's inviolable lake,

I try'd whatever in the godhead lay:

But gangren'd members must be lopt away,

Before the nobler parts are tainted to decay.

There dwells below, a race of demi-gods,

Of nymphs in waters, and of fawns in woods:

Who, tho' not worthy yet, in Heav'n to live,

Let 'em, at least, enjoy that Earth we give.

Can these be thought securely lodg'd below,

When I my self, who no superior know,

I, who have Heav'n and Earth at my command,

Have been attempted by Lycaon's hand?

At this a murmur through the synod went,

And with one voice they vote his punishment.

Thus, when conspiring traytors dar'd to doom

The fall of Caesar, and in him of Rome,

The nations trembled with a pious fear;

All anxious for their earthly Thunderer:

Nor was their care, o Caesar, less esteem'd

By thee, than that of Heav'n for Jove was deem'd:

Who with his hand, and voice, did first restrain

Their murmurs, then resum'd his speech again.

The Gods to silence were compos'd, and sate

With reverence, due to his superior state.

Cancel your pious cares; already he

Has paid his debt to justice, and to me.

Yet what his crimes, and what my judgments were,

Remains for me thus briefly to declare.

The clamours of this vile degenerate age,

The cries of orphans, and th' oppressor's rage,

Had reach'd the stars: I will descend, said I,

In hope to prove this loud complaint a lye.

Disguis'd in humane shape, I travell'd round

The world, and more than what I heard, I found.

O'er Maenalus I took my steepy way,

By caverns infamous for beasts of prey:

Then cross'd Cyllene, and the piny shade

More infamous, by curst Lycaon made:

Dark night had cover'd Heaven, and Earth, before

I enter'd his unhospitable door.

Just at my entrance, I display'd the sign

That somewhat was approaching of divine.

The prostrate people pray; the tyrant grins;

And, adding prophanation to his sins,

I'll try, said he, and if a God appear,

To prove his deity shall cost him dear.

'Twas late; the graceless wretch my death prepares,

When I shou'd soundly sleep, opprest with cares:

This dire experiment he chose, to prove

If I were mortal, or undoubted Jove:

But first he had resolv'd to taste my pow'r;

Not long before, but in a luckless hour,

Some legates, sent from the Molossian state,

Were on a peaceful errand come to treat:

Of these he murders one, he boils the flesh;

And lays the mangled morsels in a dish:

Some part he roasts; then serves it up, so drest,

And bids me welcome to this humane feast.

Mov'd with disdain, the table I o'er-turn'd;

And with avenging flames, the palace burn'd.

The tyrant in a fright, for shelter gains

The neighb'ring fields, and scours along the plains.

Howling he fled, and fain he wou'd have spoke;

But humane voice his brutal tongue forsook.

About his lips the gather'd foam he churns,

And, breathing slaughters, still with rage he burns,

But on the bleating flock his fury turns.

His mantle, now his hide, with rugged hairs

Cleaves to his back; a famish'd face he bears;

His arms descend, his shoulders sink away

To multiply his legs for chase of prey.

He grows a wolf, his hoariness remains,

And the same rage in other members reigns.

His eyes still sparkle in a narr'wer space:

His jaws retain the grin, and violence of his face

This was a single ruin, but not one

Deserves so just a punishment alone.

Mankind's a monster, and th' ungodly times

Confed'rate into guilt, are sworn to crimes.

All are alike involv'd in ill, and all

Must by the same relentless fury fall.

Thus ended he; the greater Gods assent;

By clamours urging his severe intent;

The less fill up the cry for punishment.

Yet still with pity they remember Man;

And mourn as much as heav'nly spirits can.

They ask, when those were lost of humane birth,

What he wou'd do with all this waste of Earth:

If his dispeopl'd world he would resign

To beasts, a mute, and more ignoble line;

Neglected altars must no longer smoke,

If none were left to worship, and invoke.

To whom the Father of the Gods reply'd,

Lay that unnecessary fear aside:

Mine be the care, new people to provide.

I will from wondrous principles ordain

A race unlike the first, and try my skill again.

Already had he toss'd the flaming brand;

And roll'd the thunder in his spacious hand;

Preparing to discharge on seas and land:

But stopt, for fear, thus violently driv'n,

The sparks should catch his axle-tree of Heav'n.

Remembring in the fates, a time when fire

Shou'd to the battlements of Heaven aspire,

And all his blazing worlds above shou'd burn;

And all th' inferior globe to cinders turn.

His dire artill'ry thus dismist, he bent

His thoughts to some securer punishment:

Concludes to pour a watry deluge down;

And what he durst not burn, resolves to drown.

The northern breath, that freezes floods, he binds;

With all the race of cloud-dispelling winds:

The south he loos'd, who night and horror brings;

And foggs are shaken from his flaggy wings.

From his divided beard two streams he pours,

His head, and rheumy eyes distill in show'rs,

With rain his robe, and heavy mantle flow:

And lazy mists are lowring on his brow;

Still as he swept along, with his clench'd fist

He squeez'd the clouds, th' imprison'd clouds resist:

The skies, from pole to pole, with peals resound;

And show'rs inlarg'd, come pouring on the ground.

Then, clad in colours of a various dye,

Junonian Iris breeds a new supply

To feed the clouds: impetuous rain descends;

The bearded corn beneath the burden bends:

Defrauded clowns deplore their perish'd grain;

And the long labours of the year are vain.

Nor from his patrimonial Heaven alone

Is Jove content to pour his vengeance down;

Aid from his brother of the seas he craves,

To help him with auxiliary waves.

The watry tyrant calls his brooks and floods,

Who rowl from mossie caves (their moist abodes);

And with perpetual urns his palace fill:

To whom in brief, he thus imparts his will.

Small exhortation needs; your pow'rs employ:

And this bad world, so Jove requires, destroy.

Let loose the reins to all your watry store:

Bear down the damms, and open ev'ry door.

The floods, by Nature enemies to land,

And proudly swelling with their new command,

Remove the living stones, that stopt their way,

And gushing from their source, augment the sea.

Then, with his mace, their monarch struck the ground;

With inward trembling Earth receiv'd the wound;

And rising streams a ready passage found.

Th' expanded waters gather on the plain:

They float the fields, and over-top the grain;

Then rushing onwards, with a sweepy sway,

Bear flocks, and folds, and lab'ring hinds away.

Nor safe their dwellings were, for, sap'd by floods,

Their houses fell upon their houshold Gods.

The solid piles, too strongly built to fall,

High o'er their heads, behold a watry wall:

Now seas and Earth were in confusion lost;

A world of waters, and without a coast.

One climbs a cliff; one in his boat is born:

And ploughs above, where late he sow'd his corn.

Others o'er chimney-tops and turrets row,

And drop their anchors on the meads below:

Or downward driv'n, they bruise the tender vine,

Or tost aloft, are knock'd against a pine.

And where of late the kids had cropt the grass,

The monsters of the deep now take their place.

Insulting Nereids on the cities ride,

And wond'ring dolphins o'er the palace glide.

On leaves, and masts of mighty oaks they brouze;

And their broad fins entangle in the boughs.

The frighted wolf now swims amongst the sheep;

The yellow lion wanders in the deep:

His rapid force no longer helps the boar:

The stag swims faster, than he ran before.

The fowls, long beating on their wings in vain,

Despair of land, and drop into the main.

Now hills, and vales no more distinction know;

And levell'd Nature lies oppress'd below.

The most of mortals perish in the flood:

The small remainder dies for want of food.

A mountain of stupendous height there stands

Betwixt th' Athenian and Boeotian lands,

The bound of fruitful fields, while fields they were,

But then a field of waters did appear:

Parnassus is its name; whose forky rise

Mounts thro' the clouds, and mates the lofty skies.

High on the summit of this dubious cliff,

Deucalion wafting, moor'd his little skiff.

He with his wife were only left behind

Of perish'd Man; they two were human kind.

The mountain nymphs, and Themis they adore,

And from her oracles relief implore.

The most upright of mortal men was he;

The most sincere, and holy woman, she.

When Jupiter, surveying Earth from high,

Beheld it in a lake of water lie,

That where so many millions lately liv'd,

But two, the best of either sex, surviv'd;

He loos'd the northern wind; fierce Boreas flies

To puff away the clouds, and purge the skies:

Serenely, while he blows, the vapours driv'n,

Discover Heav'n to Earth, and Earth to Heav'n.

The billows fall, while Neptune lays his mace

On the rough sea, and smooths its furrow'd face.

Already Triton, at his call, appears

Above the waves; a Tyrian robe he wears;

And in his hand a crooked trumpet bears.

The soveraign bids him peaceful sounds inspire,

And give the waves the signal to retire.

His writhen shell he takes; whose narrow vent

Grows by degrees into a large extent,

Then gives it breath; the blast with doubling sound,

Runs the wide circuit of the world around:

The sun first heard it, in his early east,

And met the rattling ecchos in the west.

The waters, listning to the trumpet's roar,

Obey the summons, and forsake the shore.

A thin circumference of land appears;

And Earth, but not at once, her visage rears,

And peeps upon the seas from upper grounds;

The streams, but just contain'd within their bounds,

By slow degrees into their channels crawl;

And Earth increases, as the waters fall.

In longer time the tops of trees appear,

Which mud on their dishonour'd branches bear.

At length the world was all restor'd to view;

But desolate, and of a sickly hue:

Nature beheld her self, and stood aghast,

A dismal desart, and a silent waste.

Which when Deucalion, with a piteous look

Beheld, he wept, and thus to Pyrrha spoke:

Oh wife, oh sister, oh of all thy kind

The best, and only creature left behind,

By kindred, love, and now by dangers joyn'd;

Of multitudes, who breath'd the common air,

We two remain; a species in a pair:

The rest the seas have swallow'd; nor have we

Ev'n of this wretched life a certainty.

The clouds are still above; and, while I speak,

A second deluge o'er our heads may break.

Shou'd I be snatcht from hence, and thou remain,

Without relief, or partner of thy pain,

How cou'dst thou such a wretched life sustain?

Shou'd I be left, and thou be lost, the sea

That bury'd her I lov'd, shou'd bury me.

Oh cou'd our father his old arts inspire,

And make me heir of his informing fire,

That so I might abolisht Man retrieve,

And perisht people in new souls might live.

But Heav'n is pleas'd, nor ought we to complain,

That we, th' examples of mankind, remain.

He said; the careful couple joyn their tears:

And then invoke the Gods, with pious prayers.

Thus, in devotion having eas'd their grief,

From sacred oracles they seek relief;

And to Cephysus' brook their way pursue:

The stream was troubled, but the ford they knew;

With living waters, in the fountain bred,

They sprinkle first their garments, and their head,

Then took the way, which to the temple led.

The roofs were all defil'd with moss, and mire,

The desart altars void of solemn fire.

Before the gradual, prostrate they ador'd;

The pavement kiss'd; and thus the saint implor'd.

O righteous Themis, if the Pow'rs above

By pray'rs are bent to pity, and to love;

If humane miseries can move their mind;

If yet they can forgive, and yet be kind;

Tell how we may restore, by second birth,

Mankind, and people desolated Earth.

Then thus the gracious Goddess, nodding, said;

Depart, and with your vestments veil your head:

And stooping lowly down, with losen'd zones,

Throw each behind your backs, your mighty mother's bones.

Amaz'd the pair, and mute with wonder stand,

'Till Pyrrha first refus'd the dire command.

Forbid it Heav'n, said she, that I shou'd tear

Those holy reliques from the sepulcher.

They ponder'd the mysterious words again,

For some new sense; and long they sought in vain:

At length Deucalion clear'd his cloudy brow,

And said, the dark Aenigma will allow

A meaning, which, if well I understand,

From sacrilege will free the God's command:

This Earth our mighty mother is, the stones

In her capacious body, are her bones:

These we must cast behind. With hope, and fear,

The woman did the new solution hear:

The man diffides in his own augury,

And doubts the Gods; yet both resolve to try.

Descending from the mount, they first unbind

Their vests, and veil'd, they cast the stones behind:

The stones (a miracle to mortal view,

But long tradition makes it pass for true)

Did first the rigour of their kind expel,

And suppled into softness, as they fell;

Then swell'd, and swelling, by degrees grew warm;

And took the rudiments of human form.

Imperfect shapes: in marble such are seen,

When the rude chizzel does the man begin;

While yet the roughness of the stone remains,

Without the rising muscles, and the veins.

The sappy parts, and next resembling juice,

Were turn'd to moisture, for the body's use:

Supplying humours, blood, and nourishment;

The rest, too solid to receive a bent,

Converts to bones; and what was once a vein,

Its former name and Nature did retain.

By help of pow'r divine, in little space,

What the man threw, assum'd a manly face;

And what the wife, renew'd the female race.

Hence we derive our nature; born to bear

Laborious life; and harden'd into care.

The rest of animals, from teeming Earth

Produc'd, in various forms receiv'd their birth.

The native moisture, in its close retreat,

Digested by the sun's aetherial heat,

As in a kindly womb, began to breed:

Then swell'd, and quicken'd by the vital seed.

And some in less, and some in longer space,

Were ripen'd into form, and took a sev'ral face.

Thus when the Nile from Pharian fields is fled,

And seeks, with ebbing tides, his ancient bed,

The fat manure with heav'nly fire is warm'd;

And crusted creatures, as in wombs, are form'd;

These, when they turn the glebe, the peasants find;

Some rude, and yet unfinish'd in their kind:

Short of their limbs, a lame imperfect birth:

One half alive; and one of lifeless earth.

For heat, and moisture, when in bodies join'd,

The temper that results from either kind

Conception makes; and fighting 'till they mix,

Their mingled atoms in each other fix.

Thus Nature's hand the genial bed prepares

With friendly discord, and with fruitful wars.

From hence the surface of the ground, with mud

And slime besmear'd (the faeces of the flood),

Receiv'd the rays of Heav'n: and sucking in

The seeds of heat, new creatures did begin:

Some were of sev'ral sorts produc'd before,

But of new monsters, Earth created more.

Unwillingly, but yet she brought to light

Thee, Python too, the wondring world to fright,

And the new nations, with so dire a sight:

So monstrous was his bulk, so large a space

Did his vast body, and long train embrace.

Whom Phoebus basking on a bank espy'd;

E're now the God his arrows had not try'd

But on the trembling deer, or mountain goat;

At this new quarry he prepares to shoot.

Though ev'ry shaft took place, he spent the store

Of his full quiver; and 'twas long before

Th' expiring serpent wallow'd in his gore.

Then, to preserve the fame of such a deed,

For Python slain, he Pythian games decred.

Where noble youths for mastership shou'd strive,

To quoit, to run, and steeds, and chariots drive.

The prize was fame: in witness of renown

An oaken garland did the victor crown.

The laurel was not yet for triumphs born;

But every green alike by Phoebus worn,

Did, with promiscuous grace, his flowing locks adorn.

一　文献出处

Ovid, *Metamorphoses*, translated by Sir Samuel Garth, John Dryden, Wordsworth Editions Ltd., 1999.

二　文献导读

诗人奥维德（P. Ovidius Naso，公元前 43 年～公元 18 年）出生于罗马附近的小城苏尔莫的一个富裕的骑士家庭。青年时受到良好教育，学习演说修辞，后在雅典深造，游历西西里和小亚细亚一带，最后回到罗马。虽然担任过一些低级官职，但不爱政治，酷爱诗歌，18 岁蜚声文坛。他的妻子出身名门，同元首奥古斯都家庭关系密切，这使他能在罗马上层社会出入 30 多年。他在 50 多岁时，即公元 8 年，因为奥古斯都认为他写的《爱的艺术》有伤风化，被流放到黑海东岸的托弥（今罗马尼亚的康斯坦察）。他在流放期间曾多次给奥古斯都写信，希望得到宽恕，但始终未能如愿返回罗马，流放 10 年后病死异乡。

奥维德的主要著作是《爱情诗》《爱的艺术》《蓬图斯诗笺》《岁时记》《女英雄》《论仪容》《变形记》《爱的医疗》《哀怨集》。

长诗《变形记》和《岁时记》是奥维德创作成熟时期的作品。《变形记》是他的代表作，全诗共 15 卷，取材于古希腊罗马神话。根据古希腊哲学家毕达哥拉斯的"灵魂轮回"理论，即人由于某种原因和需要可以随机应变为动物、植物、星星、石头等，共串联了大小"变形"故事 250 多个（其中以爱情故事为主），是古希腊罗马神话的汇编。故事按照时间顺序叙述，由开天辟地、人类起源，一直写到罗马建立、凯撒遇刺变为星辰和奥古斯都奉神谕建立统治为止。诗人运用丰富的想象力，根据神话传说的某些外在联系，把它们串联起来。为了使情节生动，作者采用了不同的叙述手法，使许多著名的古代神话得到精彩描述。作者着力于人物心理描写。《变形记》原稿在奥维德被流放前已基本完成，但未及最后加工。《岁时记》原计划为 12 卷，按时间顺序叙述罗马宗教节日及其有关的传说、历史事件和祭祀仪式、民间习俗等，作者只写了前6卷，即因流放而中断。残稿在作者死后由友人发表。《变形记》和《岁时记》共同的思想倾向是宣扬罗马的伟大及其光荣的历史，赞扬奥古斯都的统治，这表明作者这一时期已有意识地把自己的创作纳入官方意识轨道。

奥维德的诗在当时和中世纪都受到欢迎。从文艺复兴开始，他的《变形记》因向欧洲人展示了丰富多彩的古代神话而受到特别推崇，许多作家、艺术家从中吸取创作材料。他的诗对但丁、莎士比亚、歌德的影响尤其大。

上文节选自《变形记》第1卷。

三　延伸阅读

Liveley, G., *Ovid's Metamorphoses,* London, 2011.

Rand, E.K., *Ovid and his Influence*, Boston, 1925.

Appian of Alexandria: Histories of Rome [*]

Book I

Introduction

The plebeians and Senate of Rome were often at strife with each other concerning the enactment of laws, the cancelling of debts, the division of lands, or the election of magistrates. Internal discord did not, however, bring them to blows; there were dissensions merely and contests within the limits of the law, which they composed by making mutual concessions, and with much respect for each other. Once when the plebeians were entering on a campaign they fell into a controversy of the sort, but they did not use the weapons in their hands, but withdrew to the hill, which from that time on was called the Sacred Mount. Even then no violence was done, but they created a magistrate for their protection and called him the Tribune of the Plebs, to serve especially as a check upon the consuls, who were chosen by the Senate, so that political power should not be exclusively in their hands. From this arose still greater bitterness, and the magistrates were arrayed in stronger animosity to each other from this time on, and the Senate and plebeians

---

  * 阿庇安《罗马史》第 6 卷节选。

took sides with them, each believing that it would prevail over the other by augmenting the power of its own magistrates. It was in the midst of contests of this kind that Marcius Coriolanus, having been banished contrary to justice, took refuge with the Volsci and levied war against his country.

This is the only case of armed strife that can be found in the ancient seditions, and this was caused by an exile. The sword was never carried into the assembly, and there was no civil butchery until Tiberius Gracchus, while serving as a tribune and bringing forward new laws, was the first to fall a victim to internal commotion; and with him many others, who were crowded together at the Capitol round the temple, were also slain. Sedition did not end with this abominable deed. Repeatedly the parties came into open conflict, often carrying daggers; and from time to time in the temples, or the assemblies, or the forum, some tribune, or praetor, or consul, or candidate for these offices, or some person otherwise distinguished, would be slain. Unseemly violence prevailed almost constantly, together with shameful contempt for law and justice. As the evil gained in magnitude open insurrections against the government and large warlike expeditions against their country were undertaken by exiles, or criminals, or persons contending against each other for some office or military command. There arose chiefs of factions quite frequently, aspiring to supreme power, some of them refusing to disband the troops entrusted to them by the people, others even hiring forces against each other on their own account, without public authority. Whenever either side first got possession of the city, the opposition party made war nominally against their own adversaries, but actually against their country. They assailed it like an enemy's capital, and ruthless and indiscriminate massacres of citizens were perpetrated. Some were proscribed, others banished, property was confiscated, and prisoners were even subjected to excruciating tortures.

No unseemly deed was left undone until, about fifty years after the death of Gracchus, Cornelius Sulla, one of these chiefs of factions, doctoring one evil with another, made himself sole master of the state for a very long time. Such officials were formerly called dictators — an office created in the most perilous emergencies for six months only, and long since fallen into disuse. But Sulla, although nominally elected, became dictator for life by force and compulsion. Nevertheless he became satiated with power and was the first man, so far as I know, holding supreme power, who had the courage to lay it down voluntarily and to declare that he would render an account of his stewardship to any who were dissatisfied with it. And so, for a considerable period, he walked to the forum as a private citizen in the sight of all and returned home unmolested, so great was the awe of his government still remaining in the minds of the onlookers, or their amazement at his laying it down. Perhaps they were ashamed to call him to account, or entertained other good feeling toward him, or a belief that his despotism had been beneficial to the state.

Thus there was a cessation of factions for a short time while Sulla lived, and a compensation for the evils which he had wrought, but after his death similar troubles broke out and continued until Gaius Caesar, who had held the command in Gaul by election for some years, when ordered by the Senate to lay down his command, excused himself on the ground that this was not the wish of the Senate, but of Pompey, his enemy, who had command of an army in Italy, and was scheming to depose him. So he sent proposals that either both should retain their armies, so neither need fear the other's enmity, or that Pompey also should dismiss his forces and live as a private citizen under the laws in like manner with himself. Both suggestions being refused, he marched from Gaul against Pompey into Roman territory, entered Rome, and finding Pompey fled, pursued him into Thessaly, won a brilliant victory over him in a great battle, and followed him to Egypt. After Pompey had been slain by certain Egyptians Caesar set to work on Egyptian affairs and remained there until he could settle the dynasty of that country. Then he returned to Rome. Having overpowered by war his principal rival, who had been surnamed the Great on account of his brilliant military exploits, he now ruled without disguise, nobody daring any longer to dispute with him about anything, and was chosen, next after Sulla, dictator for life. Again all civil dissensions ceased until Brutus and Cassius, envious of his great power and desiring to restore the government of their fathers, slew in the Senate-house one who had proved himself truly popular, and most experienced in the art of government. The people certainly mourned for him greatly. They scoured the city in pursuit of his murderers, buried him in the middle of the forum, built a temple on the site of his funeral pyre, and offer sacrifice to him as a god.

And now civil discord broke out again worse than ever and increased enormously. Massacres, banishments, and proscriptions of both senators and knights took place straightway, including great numbers of both classes, the chiefs of factions surrendering their enemies to each other, and for this purpose not sparing even their friends and brothers; so much did animosity toward rivals overpower the love of kindred. So in the course of events the Roman empire was partitioned, as though it had been their private property, by these three men: Antony, Lepidus, and the one who was first called Octavius, but afterwards Caesar from his relationship to the other Caesar and adoption in his will. Shortly after this division they fell to quarrelling among themselves, as was natural, and Octavius, who was the superior in understanding and skill, first deprived Lepidus of Africa, which had fallen to his lot, and afterward, as the result of the battle of Actium, took from Antony all the provinces lying between Syria and the Adriatic gulf. Thereupon, while all the world was filled with astonishment at these wonderful displays of power, he sailed to Egypt and took that country, which was the oldest and at that time the strongest possession of the successors of Alexander, and the only one wanting to complete the Roman empire as it now stands. In immediate consequence of these exploits he was, while still living, the first to be regarded by the Romans as 'august,' and to be called by them "Augustus." He assumed to himself an authority like Caesar's over the country and the subject nations, and even greater than Caesar's, no longer needing any form of election, or authorization, or even the pretence of it. His government proved both lasting and masterful, and being himself successful in all things and dreaded by all, he left a lineage and succession that held the supreme power in like manner after him.

Thus, out of multifarious civil commotions, the Roman state passed into harmony and monarchy. To show how these things came about I have written and compiled this narrative, which is well worth the study of those who wish to know the measureless ambition of men, their dreadful lust of power, their unwearying perseverance, and the countless forms of evil. And it is especially necessary for me to describe these things beforehand since they are the preliminaries of my Egyptian history, and will end where that begins, for Egypt was seized in consequence of this last civil commotion, Cleopatra having joined forces with Antony. On account of its magnitude I have divided the work, first taking up the events that occurred from the time of Sempronius Gracchus to that of Cornelius Sulla; next, those that followed to the death of Caesar. The remaining books of the civil wars treat of those waged by the triumvirs against each other and the Roman people, up to the grand climax of these conflicts, the battle of Actium fought by Octavius Caesar against Antony and Cleopatra together, which will be the beginning of the Egyptian history.

The Romans, as they subdued the Italian peoples successively in war, used to seize a part of their lands and build towns there, or enrol colonists of their own to occupy those already existing, and their idea was to use these as outposts; but of the land acquired by war they assigned the cultivated part forthwith to the colonists, or sold or leased it. Since they had no leisure as yet to allot the part which then lay desolated by war (this was generally the greater part), they made proclamation that in the meantime those who were willing to work it might do so for a toll of the yearly crops, a tenth of the grain and a fifth of the fruit. From those who kept flocks was required a toll of the animals, both oxen and small cattle. They did these things in order to multiply the Italian race, which they considered the most laborious of peoples, so that they might have plenty of allies at home. But the very opposite thing happened; for the rich, getting possession of the greater part of the undistributed lands, and being emboldened by the lapse of time to believe that they would never be dispossessed, absorbing any adjacent strips and their poor neighbours' allotments, partly by purchase under persuasion and partly by force, came to cultivate vast tracts instead of single estates, using slaves as labourers and herdsmen, lest free labourers should be drawn from agriculture into the army. At the same time the ownership of slaves brought them great gain from the multitude of their progeny, who increased because they were exempt from military service. Thus certain powerful men became extremely rich and the race of slaves multiplied throughout the country, while the Italian people dwindled in numbers and strength, being oppressed by penury, taxes, and military service. If they had any respite from these evils they passed their time in idleness, because the land was held by the rich, who employed slaves instead of freemen as cultivators.

For these reasons the people became troubled lest they should no longer have sufficient allies of the Italian stock, and lest the government itself should be endangered by such a vast number of slaves. As they did not perceive any remedy, for it was not easy, nor in any way just, to deprive men of so many possessions they had held so long, including their own trees, buildings, and fixtures, a law was at last passed with difficulty at the instance of the tribunes, that nobody should hold more than 500 jugera of this land, or pasture on it more than 100 cattle or 500 sheep. To ensure the observance of this law it was provided also that there should be a certain number of freemen employed on the farms, whose business it should be to watch and report what was going on.

Having thus comprehended all this in a law, they took an oath over and above the law, and fixed penalties for violating it, and it was supposed that the remaining land would soon be divided among the poor in small parcels. But there was not the smallest consideration shown for the law or the oaths. The few who seemed to pay some respect to them conveyed their lands to their relations fraudulently, but the greater part disregarded it altogether, till at last Tiberius Sempronius Gracchus, an illustrious man, eager for glory, a most powerful speaker, and for these reasons well known to all, delivered an eloquent discourse, while serving as tribune, concerning the Italian race, lamenting that a people so valiant in war, and related in blood to the Romans, were declining little by little into pauperism and paucity of numbers without any hope of remedy. He inveighed against the multitude of slaves as useless in war and never faithful to their masters, and adduced the recent calamity brought upon the masters by their slaves in Sicily, where the demands of agriculture had greatly increased the number of the latter; recalling also the war waged against them by the Romans, which was neither easy nor short, but long-protracted and full of vicissitudes and dangers. After speaking thus he again brought forward the law, providing that nobody should hold more than the 500 jugera of the public domain. But he added a provision to the former law, that the sons of the occupiers might each hold one-half of that amount, and that the remainder should be divided among the poor by three elected commissioners, who should be changed annually.

This was extremely disturbing to the rich because, on account of the triumvirs, they could no longer disregard the law as they had done before; nor could they buy the allotments of others, because Gracchus had provided against this by forbidding sales. They collected together in groups, and made lamentation, and accused the poor of appropriating the results of their tillage, their vineyards, and their dwellings. Some said that they had paid the price of the land to their neighbours. Were they to lose the money with their land? Others said that the graves of their ancestors were in the ground, which had been allotted to them in the division of their fathers' estates. Others said that their wives' dowries had been expended on the estates, or that the land had been given to their own daughters as dowry. Money-lenders could show loans made on this security. All kinds of wailing and expressions of indignation were heard at once. On the other side were heard the lamentations of the poor — that they were being reduced from competence to extreme penury, and from that to childlessness, because they were unable to rear their offspring. They recounted the military services they had rendered, by which this very land had been acquired, and were angry that they should be robbed of their share of the common property. They reproached the rich for employing slaves, who were always faithless and ill-disposed and for that reason unserviceable in war, instead of freemen, citizens, and soldiers. While these classes were thus lamenting and indulging in mutual accusations, a great number of others, composed of colonists, or inhabitants of the free towns, or persons otherwise interested in the lands and who were under like apprehensions, flocked in and took sides with their respective factions. Emboldened by numbers and exasperated against each other they kindled considerable disturbances, and waited eagerly for the voting on the new law, some intending to prevent its enactment by all means, and others to enact it at all costs. In addition to personal interest the spirit of rivalry spurred both sides in the preparations they were making against each other for the appointed day.

What Gracchus had in his mind in proposing the measure was not money, but men. Inspired greatly by the usefulness of the work, and believing that nothing more advantageous or admirable could ever happen to Italy, he took no account of the difficulties surrounding it. When the time for voting came he advanced many other arguments at considerable length and also asked them whether it was not just to let the commons divide the common property; whether a citizen was not worthy of more consideration at all times than a slave; whether a man who served in the army was not more useful than one who did not; and whether one who had a share in the country was not more likely to be devoted to the public interests. He did not dwell long on this comparison between freemen and slaves, which he considered degrading, but proceeded at once to a review of their hopes and fears for the country, saying that the Romans possessed most of their territory by conquest, and that they had hopes of occupying the rest of the habitable world; but now the question of greatest hazard was, whether they should gain the rest by having plenty of brave men, or whether, through their weakness and mutual jealousy, their enemies should take away what they already possessed. After exaggerating the glory and riches on the one side and the danger and fear on the other, he admonished the rich to take heed, and said that for the realization of these hopes they ought to bestow this very land as a free gift, if necessary, on men who would rear children, and not, by contending about small things, overlook larger ones; especially since for any labour they had spent they were receiving ample compensation in the undisputed title to 500 jugera each of free land, in a high state of cultivation, without cost, and half as much more for each son in the case of those who had sons. After saying much more to the same purport and exciting the poor, as well as others who were moved by reason rather than by the desire for gain, he ordered the clerk to read the proposed law.

Marcus Octavius, however, another tribune, who had been induced by those in possession of the lands to interpose his veto (for among the Romans the negative veto always defeats an affirmative proposal), ordered the clerk to keep silence. Thereupon Gracchus reproached him severely and adjourned the comitia to the following day. Then he stationed near himself a sufficient guard, as if to force Octavius against his will, and ordered the clerk with threats to read the proposed law to the multitude. He began to read, but when Octavius again forbade he stopped. Then the tribunes fell to wrangling with each other, and a considerable tumult arose among the people. The leading citizens besought the tribunes to submit their controversy to the Senate for decision. Gracchus seized on the suggestion, believing that the law was acceptable to all well-disposed persons, and hastened to the senate-house. But, as he had only a few followers there and was upbraided by the rich, he ran back to the forum and said that he would take the vote at the comitia of the following day, both on the law and on the official rights of Octavius, to determine whether a tribune who was acting contrary to the people's interest could continue to hold office. And this Gracchus did; for when Octavius, nothing daunted, again interposed, Gracchus proposed to take the vote on him first.

When the first tribe voted to abrogate the magistracy of Octavius, Gracchus turned to him and begged him to desist from his veto. As he would not yield, he took the votes of the other tribes. There were thirty-five tribes at that time. The seventeen that voted first passionately supported the motion. If the eighteenth should do the same it would make a majority. Again did Gracchus, in the sight of the people, urgently importune Octavius in his present extreme danger not to prevent a work which was most righteous and useful to all Italy, and not to frustrate the wishes so earnestly entertained by the people, whose desires he ought rather to share in his character of tribune, and not to risk the loss of his office by public condemnation. After speaking thus he called the gods to witness that he did not willingly do any despite to his colleague. As Octavius was still unyielding he went on taking the vote. Octavius was forthwith reduced to the rank of a private citizen and slunk away unobserved. Quintus Mummius was chosen tribune in his place, and the agrarian law was enacted.

The first triumvirs appointed to divide the land were Gracchus himself, the proposer of the law, his brother of the same name, and his father-in-law, Appius Claudius, since the people still feared that the law might fail of execution unless Gracchus should take the lead with his whole family. Gracchus became immensely popular by reason of the law and was escorted home by the multitude as though he were the founder, not of a single city or race, but of all the nations of Italy. After this the victorious party returned to the fields from which they had come to attend to this business. The defeated ones remained in the city and talked the matter over, feeling aggrieved, and saying that as soon as Gracchus should become a private citizen he would be sorry that he had done despite to the sacred and inviolable office of tribune, and had sown in Italy so many seeds of future strife.

一 文献出处

Appian of Alexandria, *Histories of Rome, The Civil War*, Loeb Classical Library, trans. by Horace White, Harvard University Press, 1913.

二 文献导读

希腊人阿庇安（Appian of Alexandria, 约公元 95~165 年），是亚历山大里亚杰出历史作家。虽然他生活在罗马帝国早期，但他撰写的主要是记载罗马共和国晚期的断代史著作。阿庇安在亚历山大里亚担任公职期间曾经目睹过公元 116 年犹太人反对罗马统治的起义。获得罗马公民权以后，他曾迁居罗马做律师。壮年后又到埃及行省做过代理总督。

阿庇安的中青年时代正是安敦尼王朝图拉真、哈德良统治时代，是罗马帝国的"黄金时代"，同时也是各种社会危机隐孕待发，罗马帝国开始由极盛而转衰的时期。生逢盛世的阿庇安对罗马国家的发展史充满了感慨。他说："亚述人……的延续年代合并起来也不到九百年，而罗马此时已经达到了同样长的时期。"从他的这段感慨中可以推断：阿庇安开始写作《罗马史》的时间大约是在公元 147 年以后，完成时间却不得而知。

《罗马史》共有 24 卷，是用希腊文写成的，直到 1452 年才第一次被翻译成拉丁文。留传至今的《罗马史》11 卷，即第 6~9 卷和第 11~17 卷，有 10 卷是完整的，另外 1 卷属于基本完整，其余部分则是由从他人著作的引文中辑录出来的片断汇编而成的（其中主要来源是公元 950 年编纂的拜占庭的两部著作——《使节》和《美德与恶行》）。现在存留下来的部分大约是原书比较重要的一半，尤其是关于格拉古兄弟改革时代到第二次"三雄同盟"为止的记载（第 13~17 卷），可以说是这部《罗马史》最有价值和最重要的部分。

阿庇安的《罗马史》从王政时代写起，止于公元 2 世纪初的图拉真统治时期，涉及的时间跨度将近 900 年，堪称"罗马通史"。然而，阿庇安并没有按照罗马历史发展的年代顺序来写。他对自己著作的编纂体例有过明确的说明："把每个国家有关的那部分历史分别叙述，略去其他国家中所同时发生的事情，留到其他适当的地方再去叙述"，"国外战争是按照各民族分卷，国内战争是按照主要司令官分卷"。这样一来，尽管《罗马史》所涉及的内容非常庞杂，但主要内容却是记载罗马历史上的各次重大战争，可以清楚地分为两大部分，即罗马人与各民族的对外战争史和罗马内战史。通过对这些战争过程的叙述，作者勾勒出了罗马国家逐渐形成和发展演变的全部历史。这种按照民族或重大历史事件分门别类、每卷自成体系、分别叙述各自历史进程及其前因后果的编纂形式，类似于我国史书中的纪事本末体，因而阿庇安也就成为西方史学中纪事本末体的创始者。

第6~9卷是"内战史"，几乎包括了内战时期的全部基本史料。它记载的斯巴达克斯奴隶起义比同时期的著名历史作家撒鲁斯特记载得更全面。对格拉古兄弟的改革过程记载全面，因果分析深入。阿庇安不但在他的著作中为我们保存了今已失传的第一手材料，他还十分注意考察历史事件发生的社会经济背景。第11~17卷叙述了西班牙战争、汉尼拔（Hannibal）战争、迦太基战争、伊利里亚（Illyria）战争、叙利亚战争和米特拉达梯战争等6次战争。阿庇安既揭露了罗马对外征服掠夺的暴行，又介绍了各族人民的反抗斗争。

上文节选自《罗马史》第6卷。

三　延伸阅读

Breed, Brian W., and Andreola Cynthia Pamon, ed., *Citizens of Discord: Rome and Its Civil War*, New York, 2010.

Golden, G.K., *Crisis Management during the Roman Republic*, Cambridge, 2013.

P. C. Tacitus: The Annals [*]

Book I - (A.D. 14-15)

ROME at the beginning was ruled by kings. Freedom and the consulship were established by Lucius Brutus. Dictatorships were held for a temporary crisis. The power of the decemvirs did not last beyond two years, nor was the consular jurisdiction of the military tribunes of long duration. The despotisms of Cinna and Sulla were brief; the rule of Pompeius and of Crassus soon yielded before Caesar; the arms of Lepidus and Antonius before Augustus; who, when the world was wearied by civil strife, subjected it to empire under the title of "Prince." But the successes and reverses of the old Roman people have been recorded by famous historians; and fine intellects were not wanting to describe the times of Augustus, till growing sycophancy scared them away. The histories of Tiberius, Caius, Claudius, and Nero, while they were in power, were falsified through terror, and after their death were written under the irritation of a recent hatred. Hence my purpose is to relate a few facts about Augustus-more particularly his last acts, then the reign of Tiberius, and all which follows, without either bitterness or partiality, from any motives to which I am far

---

* 塔西佗《编年史》第 1 卷节选。

removed.

When after the destruction of Brutus and Cassius there was no longer any army of the Commonwealth, when Pompeius was crushed in Sicily, and when, with Lepidus pushed aside and Antonius slain, even the Julian faction had only Caesar left to lead it, then, dropping the title of triumvir, and giving out that he was a Consul, and was satisfied with a tribune's authority for the protection of the people, Augustus won over the soldiers with gifts, the populace with cheap corn, and all men with the sweets of repose, and so grew greater by degrees, while he concentrated in himself the functions of the Senate, the magistrates, and the laws. He was wholly unopposed, for the boldest spirits had fallen in battle, or in the proscription, while the remaining nobles, the readier they were to be slaves, were raised the higher by wealth and promotion, so that, aggrandised by revolution, they preferred the safety of the present to the dangerous past. Nor did the provinces dislike that condition of affairs, for they distrusted the government of the Senate and the people, because of the rivalries between the leading men and the rapacity of the officials, while the protection of the laws was unavailing, as they were continually deranged by violence, intrigue, and finally by corruption.

Augustus meanwhile, as supports to his despotism, raised to the pontificate and curule aedileship Claudius Marcellus, his sister's son, while a mere stripling, and Marcus Agrippa, of humble birth, a good soldier, and one who had shared his victory, to two consecutive consulships, and as Marcellus soon afterwards died, he also accepted him as his son-in-law. Tiberius Nero and Claudius Drusus, his stepsons, he honored with imperial tides, although his own family was as yet undiminished. For he had admitted the children of Agrippa, Caius and Lucius, into the house of the Caesars; and before they had yet laid aside the dress of boyhood he had most fervently desired, with an outward show of reluctance, that they should be entitled "princes of the youth, " and be consuls-elect. When Agrippa died, and Lucius Caesar as he was on his way to our armies in Spain, and Caius while returning from Armenia, still suffering from a wound, were prematurely cut off by destiny, or by their step-mother Livia's treachery, Drusus too having long been dead, Nero remained alone of the stepsons, and in him everything tended to centre. He was adopted as a son, as a colleague in empire and a partner in the tribunitian power, and paraded through all the armies, no longer through his mother's secret intrigues, but at her open suggestion. For she had gained such a hold on the aged Augustus that he drove out as an exile into the island of Planasia, his only grandson, Agrippa Postumus, who, though devoid of worthy qualities, and having only the brute courage of physical strength, had not been convicted of any gross offence. And yet Augustus had appointed Germanicus, Drusus's offspring, to the command of eight legions on the Rhine, and required Tiberius to adopt him, although Tiberius had a son, now a young man, in his house; but he did it that he might have several safeguards to rest on. He had no war at the time on his hands except against the Germans, which was rather to wipe out the disgrace of the loss of Quintilius Varus and his army than out of an ambition to extend the empire, or for any adequate recompense. At home all was tranquil, and there were magistrates with the same titles; there was a younger generation, sprung up since the victory of Actium, and even many of the older men had been born during the civil wars. How few were left who had seen the republic!

Thus the State had been revolutionised, and there was not a vestige left of the old sound morality. Stript of equality, all looked up to the commands of a sovereign without the least apprehension for the present, while Augustus in the vigour of life, could maintain his own position, that of his house, and the general tranquillity. When in advanced old age, he was worn out by a sickly frame, and the end was near and new prospects opened, a few spoke in vain of the blessings of freedom, but most people dreaded and some longed for war. The popular gossip of the large majority fastened itself variously on their future masters. "Agrippa was savage, and had been exasperated by insult, and neither from age nor experience in affairs was equal to so great a burden. Tiberius Nero was of mature years, and had established his fame in war, but he had the old arrogance inbred in the Claudian family, and many symptoms of a cruel temper, though they were repressed, now and then broke out. He had also from earliest infancy been reared in an imperial house; consulships and triumphs had been heaped on him in his younger days; even in the years which, on the pretext of seclusion he spent in exile at Rhodes, he had had no thoughts but of wrath, hypocrisy, and secret sensuality. There was his mother too with a woman caprice. They must, it seemed, be subject to a female and to two striplings besides, who for a while would burden, and some day rend asunder the State."

While these and like topics were discussed, the infirmities of Augustus increased, and some suspected guilt on his wife's part. For a rumour had gone abroad that a few months before he had sailed to Planasia on a visit to Agrippa, with the knowledge of some chosen friends, and with one companion, Fabius Maximus; that many tears were shed on both sides, with expressions of affection, and that thus there was a hope of the young man being restored to the home of his grandfather. This, it was said, Maximus had divulged to his wife Marcia, she again to Livia. All was known to Caesar, and when Maximus soon afterwards died, by a death some thought to be self-inflicted, there were heard at his funeral wailings from Marcia, in which she reproached herself for having been the cause of her husband's destruction. Whatever the fact was, Tiberius as he was just entering Illyria was summoned home by an urgent letter from his mother, and it has not been thoroughly ascertained whether at the city of Nola he found Augustus still breathing or quite lifeless. For Livia had surrounded the house and its approaches with a strict watch, and favourable bulletins were published from time to time, till, provision having been made for the demands of the crisis, one and the same report told men that Augustus was dead and that Tiberius Nero was master of the State.

The first crime of the new reign was the murder of Postumus Agrippa. Though he was surprised and unarmed, a centurion of the firmest resolution despatched him with difficulty. Tiberius gave no explanation of the matter to the Senate; he pretended that there were directions from his father ordering the tribune in charge of the prisoner not to delay the slaughter of Agrippa, whenever he should himself have breathed his last. Beyond a doubt, Augustus had often complained of the young man's character, and had thus succeeded in obtaining the sanction of a decree of the Senate for his banishment. But he never was hard-hearted enough to destroy any of his kinsfolk, nor was it credible that death was to be the sentence of the grandson in order that the stepson might feel secure. It was more probable that Tiberius and Livia, the one from fear the other from a stepmother's enmity, hurried on the destruction of a youth whom they suspected and hated. When the centurion reported, according to military custom, that he had executed the command, Tiberius replied that he had not given the command, and that the act must be justified to the Senate. As soon as Sallustius Crispus who shared the secret (he had, in fact, sent the written order to the tribune) knew this, fearing that the charge would be shifted on himself, and that his peril would be the same whether he uttered fiction or truth, he advised Livia not to divulge the secrets of her house or the counsels of friends, or any services performed by the soldiers, nor to let Tiberius weaken the strength of imperial power by referring everything to the Senate, for "the condition," he said, "of holding empire is that an account cannot be balanced unless it be rendered to one person."

Meanwhile at Rome people plunged into slavery-consuls, senators, knights. The higher a man's rank, the more eager his hypocrisy, and his looks the more carefully studied, so as neither to betray joy at the decease of one emperor nor sorrow at the rise of another, while he mingled delight and lamentations with his flattery. Sextus Pompeius and Sextus Apuleius, the consuls, were the first to swear allegiance to Tiberius Caesar, and in their presence the oath was taken by Seius Strabo and Caius Turranius, respectively the commander of the praetorian cohorts and the superintendent of the corn supplies. Then the Senate, the soldiers and the people did the same. Tiberius would inaugurate everything with the consuls, as though the ancient constitution remained, and he hesitated about being emperor. Even the proclamation by which he summoned the senators to their chamber, he issued merely with the title of Tribune, which he had received under Augustus. The wording of the proclamation was brief, and in a very modest tone. "He would," it said, "provide for the honors due to his father, and not leave the lifeless body, and this was the only public duty he now claimed." As soon, however, as Augustus was dead, he had given the watchword to the praetorian cohorts, as commander-in-chief. He had the guard under arms, with all the other adjuncts of a court; soldiers attended him to the forum; soldiers went with him to the Senate House. He sent letters to the different armies, as though supreme power was now his, and showed hesitation only when he spoke in the Senate. His chief motive was fear that Germanicus, who had at his disposal so many legions, such vast auxiliary forces of the allies, and such wonderful popularity, might prefer the possession to the expectation of empire. He looked also at public opinion, wishing to have the credit of having been called and elected by the State rather than of having crept into power through the intrigues of a wife and a dotard's adoption. It was subsequently understood that he assumed a wavering attitude, to test likewise the temper of the nobles. For he would twist a word or a look into a crime and treasure it up in his memory.

On the first day of the Senate he allowed nothing to be discussed but the funeral of Augustus, whose will, which was brought in by the Vestal Virgins, named as his heirs Tiberius and Livia. The latter was to be admitted into the Julian family with the name of Augusta; next in expectation were the grand and great-grandchildren. In the third place, he had named the chief men of the State, most of whom he hated, simply out of ostentation and to win credit with posterity. His legacies were not beyond the scale of a private citizen, except a bequest of forty-three million five hundred thousand sesterces "to the people and populace of Rome," of one thousand to every praetorian soldier, and of three hundred to every man in the legionary cohorts composed of Roman citizens. Next following a deliberation about funeral honors. Of these the most imposing were thought fitting. The procession was to be conducted through "the gate of triumph," on the motion of Gallus Asinius; the titles of the laws passed, the names of the nations conquered by Augustus were to be borne in front, on that of Lucius Arruntius. Messala Valerius further proposed that the oath of allegiance to Tiberius should be yearly renewed, and when Tiberius asked him whether it was at his bidding that he had brought forward this motion, he replied that he had proposed it spontaneously, and that in whatever concerned the State he would use only his own discretion, even at the risk of offending. This was the only style of adulation which yet remained. The Senators unanimously exclaimed that the body ought to be borne on their shoulders to the funeral pile. The emperor left the point to them with disdainful moderation; he then admonished the people by a proclamation not to indulge in that tumultuous enthusiasm which had distracted the funeral of the Divine Julius, or express a wish that Augustus should be burnt in the Forum instead of in his appointed resting-place in the Campus Martius. On the day of the funeral soldiers stood round as a guard, amid much ridicule from those who had either themselves witnessed or who had heard from their parents of the famous day when slavery was still something fresh, and freedom had been resought in vain, when the slaying of Caesar, the Dictator, seemed to some the vilest, to others, the most glorious of deeds. "Now," they said, "an aged sovereign, whose power had lasted long, who had provided his heirs with abundant means to coerce the State, requires forsooth the defense of soldiers that his burial may be undisturbed."

Then followed much talk about Augustus himself, and many expressed an idle wonder that the same day marked the beginning of his assumption of empire and the close of his life, and, again, that he had ended his days at Nola in the same house and room as his father Octavius. People extolled too the number of his consulships, in which he had equalled Valerius Corvus and Caius Marius combined, the continuance for thirty-seven years of the tribunitian power, the title of Imperator twenty-one times earned, and his other honours which had either frequently repeated or were wholly new. Sensible men, however, spoke variously of his life with praise and censure. Some said "that dutiful feeling towards a father, and the necessities of the State in which laws had then no place, drove him into civil war, which can neither be planned nor conducted on any right principles. He had often yielded to Antonius, while he was taking vengeance on his father's murderers, often also to Lepidus. When the latter sank into feeble dotage and the former had been ruined by his profligacy, the only remedy for his distracted country was the rule of a single man. Yet the State had been organized under the name neither of a kingdom nor a dictatorship, but under that of a prince. The ocean and remote rivers were the boundaries of the empire; the legions, provinces, fleets, all things were linked together; there was law for the citizens; there was respect shown to the allies. The capital had been embellished on a grand scale; only in a few instances had he resorted to force, simply to secure general tranquillity."

It was said, on the other hand, "that filial duty and State necessity were merely assumed as a mask. It was really from a lust of sovereignty that he had excited the veterans by bribery, had, when a young man and a subject, raised an army, tampered with the Consul's legions, and feigned an attachment to the faction of Pompeius. Then, when by a decree of the Senate he had usurped the high functions and authority of Praetor when Hirtius and Pansa were slain - whether they were destroyed by the enemy, or Pansa by poison infused into a wound, Hirtius by his own soldiers and Caesar's treacherous machinations - he at once possessed himself of both their armies, wrested the consulate from a reluctant Senate, and turned against the State the arms with which he had been intrusted against Antonius. Citizens were proscribed, lands divided, without as much as the approval of those who executed these deeds. Even granting that the deaths of Cassius and of the Bruti were sacrifices to a hereditary enmity (though duty requires us to waive private feuds for the sake of the public welfare), still Pompeius had been deluded by the phantom of peace, and Lepidus by the mask of friendship. Subsequently, Antonius had been lured on by the treaties of Tarentum and Brundisium, and by his marriage with the sister, and paid by his death the penalty of a treacherous alliance. No doubt, there was peace after all this, but it was a peace stained with blood; there were the disasters of Lollius and Varus, the murders at Rome of the Varros, Egnatii, and Juli." The domestic life too of Augustus was not spared. "Nero's wife had been taken from him, and there had been the farce of consulting the pontiffs, whether, with a child conceived and not yet born, she could properly marry. There were the excesses of Quintus Tedius and Vedius Pollio; last of all, there was Livia, terrible to the State as a mother, terrible to the house of the Caesars as a stepmother. No honour was left for the gods, when Augustus chose to be himself worshipped with temples and statues, like those of the deities, and with flamens and priests. He had not even adopted Tiberius as his successor out of affection or any regard to the State, but, having thoroughly seen his arrogant and savage temper, he had sought glory for himself by a contrast of extreme wickedness." For, in fact, Augustus, a few years before, when he was a second time asking from the Senate the tribunitian power for Tiberius, though his speech was complimentary, had thrown out certain hints as to his manners, style, and habits of life, which he meant as reproaches, while he seemed to excuse. However, when his obsequies had been duly performed, a temple with a religious ritual was decreed him.

After this all prayers were addressed to Tiberius. He, on his part, urged various considerations, the greatness of the empire, and his distrust of himself. "Only", he said, "the intellect of the Divine Augustus was equal to such a burden. Called as he had been by him to share his anxieties, he had learnt by experience how exposed to fortune's caprices was the task of universal rule. Consequently, in a state which had the support of so many great men, they should not put everything on one man, as many, by uniting their efforts would more easily discharge public functions." There was more grand sentiment than good faith in such words. Tiberius's language even in matters which he did not care to conceal, either from nature or habit, was always hesitating and obscure, and now that he was struggling to hide his feelings completely, it was all the more involved in uncertainty and doubt. The Senators, however, whose only fear was lest they might seem to understand him, burst into complaints, tears, and prayers. They raised their hands to the gods, to the statue of Augustus, and to the knees of Tiberius, when he ordered a document to be produced and read. This contained a description of the resources of the State, of the number of citizens and allies under arms, of the fleets, subject kingdoms, provinces, taxes, direct and indirect, necessary expenses and customary bounties. All these details Augustus had written with his own hand, and had added a counsel, that the empire should be confined to its present limits, either from fear or out of jealousy.

Meantime, while the Senate stooped to the most abject supplication, Tiberius happened to say that although he was not equal to the whole burden of the State, yet he would undertake the charge of whatever part of it might be intrusted to him. Thereupon Asinius Gallus said, "I ask you, Caesar, what part of the State you wish to have intrusted to you?" Confounded by the sudden inquiry he was silent for a few moments; then, recovering his presence of mind, he replied that it would by no means become his modesty to choose or to avoid in a case where he would prefer to be wholly excused. Then Gallus again, who had inferred anger from his looks, said that the question had not been asked with the intention of dividing what could not be separated, but to convince him by his own admission that the body of the State was one, and must be directed by a single mind. He further spoke in praise of Augustus, and reminded Tiberius himself of his victories and of his admirable deeds for many years as a civilian. Still, he did not thereby soften the emperor's resentment, for he had long been detested from an impression that, as he had married Vipsania, daughter of Marcus Agrippa, who had once been the wife of Tiberius, he aspired to be more than a citizen, and kept up the arrogant tone of his father, Asinius Pollio.

Next, Lucius Arruntius, who differed but little from the speech of Gallus, gave like offence, though Tiberius had no old grudge against him, but simply mistrusted him, because he was rich and daring, had brilliant accomplishments, and corresponding popularity. For Augustus, when in his last conversations he was discussing who would refuse the highest place, though sufficiently capable, who would aspire to it without being equal to it, and who would unite both the ability and ambition, had described Marcus Lepidus as able but contemptuously indifferent, Gallus Asinius as ambitious and incapable, Lucius Arruntius as not unworthy of it, and, should the chance be given him, sure to make the venture. About the two first there is a general agreement, but instead of Arruntius some have mentioned Cneius Piso, and all these men, except Lepidus, were soon afterwards destroyed by various charges through the contrivance of Tiberius. Quintus Haterius too and Mamercus Scaurus ruffled his suspicious temper, Haterius by having said—"How long, Caesar, will you suffer the State to be without a head?" Scaurus by the remark that there was a hope that the Senate's prayers would not be fruitless, seeing that he had not used his right as Tribune to negative the motion of the Consuls. Tiberius instantly broke out into invective against Haterius; Scaurus, with whom he was far more deeply displeased, he passed over in silence. Wearied at last by the assembly's clamorous importunity and the urgent demands of individual Senators, he gave way by degrees, not admitting that he undertook empire, but yet ceasing to refuse it and to be entreated. It is known that Haterius having entered the palace to ask pardon, and thrown himself at the knees of Tiberius as he was walking, was almost killed by the soldiers, because Tiberius fell forward, accidentally or from being entangled by the suppliant's hands. Yet the peril of so great a man did not make him relent, till Haterius went with entreaties to Augusta, and was saved by her very earnest intercessions.

Great too was the Senate's sycophancy to Augusta. Some would have her styled "parent"; others "mother of the country, " and a majority proposed that to the name of Caesar should be added "son of Julia." The emperor repeatedly asserted that there must be a limit to the honours paid to women, and that he would observe similar moderation in those bestowed on himself, but annoyed at the invidious proposal, and indeed regarding a woman's elevation as a slight to himself, he would not allow so much as a lictor to be assigned her, and forbade the erection of an altar in memory of her adoption, and any like distinction. But for Germanicus Caesar he asked pro-consular powers, and envoys were despatched to confer them on him, and also to express sympathy with his grief at the death of Augustus. The same request was not made for Drusus, because he was consul elect and present at Rome. Twelve candidates were named for the praetorship, the number which Augustus had handed down, and when the Senate urged Tiberius to increase it, he bound himself by an oath not to exceed it.

It was the first time that the elections were transferred from the Campus Martius to the Senate. For up to that day, though the most important rested with the emperor's choice, some were settled by the partialities of the tribes. Nor did the people complain of having the right taken from them, except in mere idle talk, and the Senate, being now released from the necessity of bribery and of degrading solicitations, gladly upheld the change, Tiberius confining himself to the recommendation of only four candidates who were to be nominated without rejection or canvass. Meanwhile the tribunes of the people asked leave to exhibit at their own expense games to be named after Augustus and added to the Calendar as the Augustales. Money was, however, voted from the exchequer, and though the use of the triumphal robe in the circus was prescribed, it was not allowed them to ride in a chariot. Soon the annual celebration was transferred to the praetor, to whose lot fell the administration of justice between citizens and foreigners.

This was the state of affairs at Rome when a mutiny broke out in the legions of

Pannonia, which could be traced to no fresh cause except the change of emperors and the prospect it held out of license in tumult and of profit from a civil war. In the summer camp three legions were quartered, under the command of Junius Blaesus, who on hearing of the death of Augustus and the accession of Tiberius, had allowed his men a rest from military duties, either for mourning or rejoicing. This was the beginning of demoralization among the troops, of quarreling, of listening to the talk of every pestilent fellow, in short, of craving for luxury and idleness and loathing discipline and toil. In the camp was one Percennius, who had once been a leader of one of the theatrical factions, then became a common soldier, had a saucy tongue, and had learnt from his applause of actors how to stir up a crowd. By working on ignorant minds, which doubted as to what would be the terms of military service after Augustus, this man gradually influenced them in conversations at night or at nightfall, and when the better men had dispersed, he gathered round him all the worst spirits.

At last, when there were others ready to be abettors of a mutiny, he asked, in the tone of a demagogue, why, like slaves, they submitted to a few centurions and still fewer tribunes. "When", he said, "will you dare to demand relief, if you do not go with your prayers or arms to a new and yet tottering throne? We have blundered enough by our tameness for so many years, in having to endure thirty or forty campaigns till we grow old, most of us with bodies maimed by wounds. Even dismissal is not the end of our service, but, quartered under a legion's standard we toil through the same hardships under another title. If a soldier survives so many risks, he is still dragged into remote regions where, under the name of lands, he receives soaking swamps or mountainous wastes. Assuredly, military service itself is burdensome and unprofitable; ten ases a day is the value set on life and limb; out of this, clothing, arms, tents, as well as the mercy of centurions and exemptions from duty have to be purchased. But indeed of floggings and wounds, of hard winters, wearisome summers, of terrible war, or barren peace, there is no end. Our only relief can come from military life being entered on under fixed conditions, from receiving each the pay of a denarius, and from the sixteenth year terminating our service. We must be retained no longer under a standard, but in the same camp compensation in money must be paid us. Do the praetorian cohorts, which have just got their two denarii per man, and which after sixteen years are restored to their homes, encounter more perils? We do not disparage the guards of the capital; still, here amid barbarous tribes we have to face the enemy from our tents."

The throng applauded from various motives, some pointing with indignation to the marks of the lash, others to their grey locks, and most of them to their threadbare garments and naked limbs. At, last, in their fury they went so far as to propose to combine the three legions into one. Driven from their purpose by the jealousy with which every one sought the chief honor for his own legion, they turned to other thoughts, and set up in one spot the three eagles, with the ensigns of the cohorts. At the same time, they piled up turf and raised a mound, that they might have a more conspicuous meeting-place. Amid the bustle Blaesus came up. He upbraided them and held back man after man with the exclamation, "Better imbrue your hands in my blood: it will be less guilt to slay your commander than it is to be in revolt from the emperor. Either living I will uphold the loyalty of the legions, or pierced to the heart I will hasten on your repentance."

None the less however was the mound piled up, and it was quite breast high when, at last overcome by his persistency, they gave up their purpose. Blaesus, with the consummate tact of an orator, said, "It is not through mutiny and tumult that the desires of the army ought to be communicated to Caesar, nor did our soldiers of old ever ask so novel a boon of ancient commanders, nor have you yourselves asked it of the Divine Augustus. It is far from opportune that the emperor's cares, now in their first beginning, should be aggravated. If, however, you are bent upon attempting in peace what even after your victory in the civil wars you did not demand, why, contrary to the habit of obedience, contrary to the law of discipline, do you meditate violence? Decide on sending envoys, and give them instructions in your presence." It was carried by acclamation that the son of Blaesus, one of the tribunes, should undertake the mission, and demand for the soldiers release from service after sixteen years. He was to have the rest of their message when the first part had been successful. After the young man departure there was comparative quiet, but there was an arrogant tone among the soldiers, to whom the fact that their commander's son was pleading their common cause clearly showed that they had wrested by compulsion what they had failed to obtain by good behaviour.

Meanwhile the companies which previous to the mutiny had been sent to Nauportus to make roads and bridges and for other purposes, when they heard of the tumult in the camp, tore up the standards, and having plundered the neighboring villages and Nauportus itself, which was like a town, assailed the centurions who restrained them with jeers and insults, last of all, with blows. Their chief rage was against Aufidienus Rufus, the camp-prefect, whom they dragged from a waggon, loaded with baggage, and drove on at the head of the column, asking him in ridicule whether he liked to bear such huge burdens and such long marches. Rufus, who had long been a common soldier, then a centurion, and subsequently camp-prefect, tried to revive the old severe discipline, inured as he was to work and toil, and all the sterner because he had endured.

On the arrival of these troops the mutiny broke out afresh, and straggling from the camp they plundered the neighbourhood. Blaesus ordered a few who had conspicuously loaded themselves with spoil to be scourged and imprisoned as a terror to the rest; for, even as it then was, the commander was still obeyed by the centurions and by all the best men among the soldiers. As the men were dragged off, they struggled violently, clasped the knees of the bystanders, called to their comrades by name, or to the company, cohort, or legion to which they respectively belonged, exclaiming that all were threatened with the same fate. At the same time they heaped abuse on the commander; they appealed to heaven and to the gods, and left nothing undone by which they might excite resentment and pity, alarm and rage. They all rushed to the spot, broke open the guardhouse, unbound the prisoners, and were in a moment fraternizing with deserters and men convicted on capital charges.

Thence arose a more furious outbreak, with more leaders of the mutiny. Vibulenus, a common soldier, was hoisted in front of the general's tribunal on the shoulders of the bystanders and addressed the excited throng, who eagerly awaited his intentions. "You have indeed, " he said, "restored light and air to these innocent and most unhappy men, but who restores to my brother his life, or my brother to myself? Sent to you by the German army in our common cause, he was last night butchered by the gladiators whom the general keeps and arms for the destruction of his soldiers. Answer, Blaesus, where you have flung aside the corpse? Even an enemy grudges not burial. When, with embraces and tears, I have sated my grief, order me also to be slain, provided only that when we have been destroyed for no crime, but only because we consulted the good of the legions, we may be buried by these men around me."

He inflamed their excitement by weeping and smiting his breast and face with his hands. Then, hurling aside those who bore him on their shoulders, and impetuously flinging himself at the feet of one man after another, he roused such dismay and indignation that some of the soldiers put fetters on the gladiators who were among the number of Blaesus's slaves, others did the like to the rest of his household, while a third party hurried out to look for the corpse. And had it not quickly been known that no corpse was found, that the slaves, when tortures were applied, denied the murder, and that the man never had a brother, they would have been on the point of destroying the general. As it was, they thrust out the tribunes and the camp-prefect; they plundered the baggage of the fugitives, and they killed a centurion, Lucilius, to whom, with soldiers' humour, they had given the name "Bring another, " because when he had broken one vine-stick on a man's back, he would call in a loud voice for another and another. The rest sheltered themselves in concealment, and one only was detained, Clemens Julius, whom the soldiers considered a fit person to carry messages, from his ready wit. Two legions, the eighth and the fifteenth, were actually drawing swords against each other, the former demanding the death of a centurion, whom they nicknamed Sirpicus, while the men of the fifteenth defended him, but the soldiers of the ninth interposed their entreaties, and when these were disregarded, their menaces.

This intelligence had such an effect on Tiberius, close as he was, and most careful to hush up every very serious disaster, that he despatched his son Drusus with the leading men of the State and with two praetorian cohorts, without any definite instructions, to take suitable measures. The cohorts were strengthened beyond their usual force with some picked troops. There was in addition a considerable part of the Praetorian cavalry, and the flower of the German soldiery, which was then the emperor's guard. With them too was the commander of the praetorians, Aelius Sejanus, who had been associated with his own father, Strabo, had great influence with Tiberius, and was to advise and direct the young prince, and to hold out punishment or reward to the soldiers. When Drusus approached, the legions, as a mark of respect, met him, not as usual, with glad looks or the glitter of military decorations, but in unsightly squalor, and face which, though they simulated grief, rather expressed defiance.

As soon as he entered the entrenchments, they secured the gates with sentries, and ordered bodies of armed men to be in readiness at certain points of the camp. The rest crowded round the general's tribunal in a dense mass. Drusus stood there, and with a gesture of his hand demanded silence. As often as they turned their eyes back on the throng, they broke into savage exclamations, then looking up to Drusus they trembled. There was a confused hum, a fierce shouting, and a sudden lull. Urged by conflicting emotions, they felt panic and they caused the like. At last, in an interval of the uproar, Drusus read his father's letter, in which it was fully stated that he had a special care for the brave legions with which he had endured a number of campaigns; that, as soon as his mind had recovered from its grief, he would lay their demands before the Senators; that meanwhile he had sent his son to concede unhesitatingly what could be immediately granted, and that the rest must be reserved for the Senate, which ought to have a voice in showing either favor or severity.

The crowd replied that they had delivered their instructions to Clemens, one of the centurions, which he was to convey to Rome. He began to speak of the soldiers' discharge after sixteen years, of the rewards of completed service, of the daily pay being a denarius, and of the veterans not being detained under a standard. When Drusus pleaded in answer reference to the Senate and to his father, he was interrupted by a tumultuous shout. "Why had he come, neither to increase the soldiers' pay, nor to alleviate their hardships, in a word, with no power to better their lot? Yet heaven knew that all were allowed to scourge and to execute. Tiberius used formerly in the name of Augustus to frustrate the wishes of the legions, and the same tricks were now revived by Drusus. Was it only sons who were to visit them? Certainly, it was a new thing for the emperor to refer to the Senate merely what concerned the soldier's interests. Was then the same Senate to be consulted whenever notice was given of an execution or of a battle? Were their rewards to be at the discretion of absolute rulers, their punishments to be without appeal?"

At last they deserted the general's tribunal, and to any praetorian soldier or friend of Caesar's who met them, they used those threatening gestures which are the cause of strife and the beginning of a conflict, with special rage against Cneius Lentulus, because they thought that he above all others, by his age and warlike renown, encouraged Drusus, and was the first to scorn such blots on military discipline. Soon after, as he was leaving with Drusus to betake himself in foresight of his danger to the winter camp, they surrounded him, and asked him again and again whither he was going; was it to the emperor or to the Senate, there also to oppose the interests of the legions. At the same moment they menaced him savagely and flung stones. And now, bleeding from a blow, and feeling destruction certain, he was rescued by the hurried arrival of the throng which had accompanied Drusus.

That terrible night which threatened an explosion of crime was tranquillised by a mere accident. Suddenly in a clear sky the moon's radiance seemed to die away. This the soldiers in their ignorance of the cause regarded as an omen of their condition, comparing the failure of her light to their own efforts, and imagining that their attempts would end prosperously should her brightness and splendour be restored to the goddess. And so they raised a din with brazen instruments and the combined notes of trumpets and horns, with joy or sorrow, as she brightened or grew dark. When clouds arose and obstructed their sight, and it was thought she was buried in the gloom, with that proneness to superstition which steals over minds once thoroughly cowed, they lamented that this was a portent of never-ending hardship, and that heaven frowned on their deeds. Drusus, thinking that he ought to avail himself of this change in their temper and turn what chance had offered to a wise account, ordered the tents to be visited. Clemens, the centurion was summoned with all others who for their good qualities were liked by the common soldiers. These men made their way among the patrols, sentries and guards of the camp-gates, suggesting hope or holding out threats. "How long will you besiege the emperor's son? What is to be the end of our strifes? Will Percennius and Vibulenus give pay to the soldiers and land to those who have earned their discharge? In a word, are they, instead of the Neros and the Drusi, to control the empire of the Roman people? Why are we not rather first in our repentance as we were last in the offence? Demands made in common are granted slowly; a separate favour you may deserve and receive at the same moment." With minds affected by these words and growing mutually suspicious, they divided off the new troops from the old, and one legion from another. Then by degrees the instinct of obedience returned. They quitted the gates and restored to their places the standards which at the beginning of the mutiny they had grouped into one spot.

At daybreak Drusus called them to an assembly, and, though not a practiced speaker, yet with natural dignity upbraided them for their past and commended their present behaviors. He was not, he said, to be conquered by terror or by threats. Were he to see them inclining to submission and hear the language of entreaty, he would write to his father, that he might be merciful and receive the legions' petition. At their prayer, Blaesus and Lucius Apronius, a Roman knight on Drusus's staff, with Justus Catonius, a first-rank centurion, were again sent to Tiberius. Then ensued a conflict of opinion among them, some maintaining that it was best to wait the envoys' return and meanwhile humor the soldiers, others, that stronger measures ought to be used, inasmuch as the rabble knows no mean, and inspires fear, unless they are afraid, though when they have once been overawed, they can be safely despised. "While superstition still swayed them, the general should apply terror by removing the leaders of the mutiny." Drusus's temper was inclined to harsh measures. He summoned Vibulenus and Percennius and ordered them to be put to death. The common account is that they were buried in the general's tent, though according to some their bodies were flung outside the entrenchments for all to see.

Search was then made for all the chief mutineers. Some as they roamed outside the camp were cut down by the centurions or by soldiers of the praetorian cohorts. Some even the companies gave up in proof of their loyalty. The men's troubles were increased by an early winter with continuous storms so violent that they could not go beyond their tents or meet together or keep the standards in their places, from which they were perpetually torn by hurricane and rain. And there still lingered the dread of the divine wrath; nor was it without meaning, they thought, that, hostile to an impious host, the stars grew dim and storms burst over them. Their only relief from misery was to quit an ill-omened and polluted camp, and, having purged themselves of their guilt, to betake themselves again every one to his winterquarters. First the eighth, then the fifteenth legion returned; the ninth cried again and again that they ought to wait for the letter from Tiberius, but soon finding themselves isolated by the departure of the rest, they voluntarily forestalled their inevitable fate. Drusus, without awaiting the envoys' return, as for the present all was quiet, went back to Rome.

About the same time, from the same causes, the legions of Germany rose in mutiny, with a fury proportioned to their greater numbers, in the confident hope that Germanicus Caesar would not be able to endure another's supremacy and offer himself to the legions, whose strength would carry everything before it. There were two armies on the bank of the Rhine; that named the upper army had Caius Silius for general; the lower was under the charge of Aulus Caecina. The supreme direction rested with Germanicus, then busily employed in conducting the assessment of Gaul. The troops under the control of Silius, with minds yet in suspense, watched the issue of mutiny elsewhere; but the soldiers of the lower army fell into a frenzy, which had its beginning in the men of the twenty-first and fifth legions, and into which the first and twentieth were also drawn. For they were all quartered in the same summer-camp, in the territory of the Ubii, enjoying ease or having only light duties. Accordingly on hearing of the death of Augustus, a rabble of city slaves, who had been enlisted under a recent levy at Rome, habituated to laxity and impatient of hardship, filled the ignorant minds of the other soldiers with notions that the time had come when the veteran might demand a timely discharge, the young, more liberal pay, all, an end of their miseries, and vengeance on the cruelty of centurions. It was not one alone who spoke thus, as did Percennius among the legions of Pannonia, nor was it in the ears of trembling soldiers, who looked with apprehension to other and mightier armies, but there was sedition in many a face and voice. "The Roman world," they said, "was in their hand; their victories aggrandised the State; it was from them that emperors received their titles."

Nor did their commander check them. Indeed, the blind rage of so many had robbed him of his resolution., In a sudden frenzy they rushed with drawn swords on the centurions, the immemorial object of the soldiers' resentment and the first cause of savage fury. They threw them to the earth and beat them sorely, sixty to one, so as to correspond with the number of centurions. Then tearing them from the ground, mangled, and some lifeless, they flung them outside the entrenchments or into the river Rhine. One Septimius, who fled to the tribunal and was grovelling at Caecina's feet, was persistently demanded till he was given up to destruction. Cassius Chaerea, who won for himself a memory with posterity by the murder of Caius Caesar, being then a youth of high spirit, cleared a passage with his sword through the armed and opposing throng. Neither tribune nor camp-prefect maintained authority any longer. Patrols, sentries, and whatever else the needs of the time required, were distributed by the men themselves. To those who could guess the temper of soldiers with some penetration, the strongest symptom of a wide-spread and intractable commotion, was the fact that, instead of being divided or instigated by a few persons, they were unanimous in their fury and equally unanimous in their composure, with so uniform a consistency that one would have thought them to be under command.

Meantime Germanicus, while, as I have related, he was collecting the taxes of Gaul, receiving news of the death of Augustus. He was married to the granddaughter of Augustus, Agrippina, by whom he had several children, and though he was himself the son of Drusus, brother of Tiberius, and grandson of Augusta, he was troubled by the secret hatred of his uncle and grandmother, the motives for which were the more venomous because unjust. For the memory of Drusus was held in honor of the Roman people, they believed that had he obtained empire, he would have restored freedom. Hence they regarded Germanicus with favour and with the same hope. He was indeed a young man of unaspiring temper, and of wonderful kindliness, contrasting strongly with the proud and mysterious reserve that marked the conversation and the features of Tiberius. Then, there were feminine jealousies, Livia feeling a stepmother's bitterness towards Agrippina, and Agrippina herself too being rather excitable, only her purity and love of her husband gave a right direction to her otherwise imperious disposition.

But the nearer Germanicus was to the highest hope, the more laboriously did he exert himself for Tiberius, and he made the neighbouring Sequani and all the Belgic states swear obedience to him. On hearing of the mutiny in the legions, he instantly went to the spot, and met them outside the camp, eyes fixed on the ground, and seemingly repentant. As soon as he entered the entrenchments, confused murmurs became audible. Some men, seizing his hand under pretence of kissing it, thrust his fingers into their mouths, that he might touch their toothless gums; others showed him their limbs bowed with age. He ordered the throng which stood near him, as it seemed a promiscuous gathering, to separate itself into its military companies. They replied that they would hear better as they were. The standards were then to be advanced, so that thus at least the cohorts might be distinguished. The soldiers obeyed reluctantly. Then beginning with a reverent mention of Augustus, he passed on to the victories and triumphs of Tiberius, dwelling with especial praise on his glorious achievements with those legions in Germany. Next, he extolled the unity of Italy, the loyalty of Gaul, the entire absence of turbulence or strife. He was heard in silence or with but a slight murmur.

As soon as he touched on the mutiny and asked what had become of soldierly obedience, of the glory of ancient discipline, whither they had driven their tribunes and centurions, they all bared their bodies and taunted him with the scars of their wounds and the marks of the lash. And then with confused exclamations they spoke bitterly of the prices of exemptions, of their scanty pay, of the severity of their tasks, with special mention of the entrenchment, the fosse, the conveyance of fodder, building-timber, firewood, and whatever else had to be procured from necessity, or as a check on idleness in the camp. The fiercest clamour arose from the veteran soldiers, who, as they counted their thirty campaigns or more, implored him to relieve worn-out men, and not let them die under the same hardships, but have an end of such harassing service, and repose without beggary. Some even claimed the legacy of the Divine Augustus, with words of good omen for Germanicus, and, should he wish for empire, they showed themselves abundantly willing. Thereupon, as though he were contracting the pollution of guilt, he leapt impetuously from the tribunal. The men opposed his departure with their weapons, threatening him repeatedly if he would not go back. But Germanicus protesting that he would die rather than cast off his loyalty, plucked his sword from his side, raised it aloft and was plunging it into his breast, when those nearest him seized his hand and held it by force. The remotest and most densely crowded part of the throng, and, what almost passes belief, some, who came close up to him, urged him to strike the blow, and a soldier, by name Calusidius, offered him a drawn sword, saying that it was sharper than his own. Even in their fury, this seemed to them a savage act and one of evil precedent, and there was a pause during which Caesar's friends hurried him into his tent.

There they took counsel how to heal matters. For news was also brought that the soldiers were preparing the despatch of envoys who were to draw the upper army into their cause; that the capital of the Ubii was marked out for destruction, and that hands with the stain of plunder on them would soon be daring enough for the pillage of Gaul. The alarm was heightened by the knowledge that the enemy was aware of the Roman mutiny, and would certainly attack if the Rhine bank were undefended. Yet if the auxiliary troops and allies were to be armed against the retiring legions, civil war was in fact begun. Severity would be dangerous; profuse liberality would be scandalous. Whether all or nothing were conceded to the soldiery, the State was equally in jeopardy. Accordingly, having weighed their plans one against each other, they decided that a letter should be written in the prince's name, to the effect that full discharge was granted to those who had served in twenty campaigns; that there was a conditional release for those who had served sixteen, and that they were to be retained under a standard with immunity from everything except actually keeping off the enemy; that the legacies which they had asked, were to be paid and doubled.

The soldiers perceived that all this was invented for the occasion, and instantly pressed their demands. The discharge from service was quickly arranged by the tribunes. Payment was put off till they reached their respective winter quarters. The men of the fifth and twenty-first legions refused to go till in the summer-camp where they stood the money was made up out of the purses of Germanicus himself and his friends, and paid in full. The first and twentieth legions were led back by their officer Caecina to the canton of the Ubii, marching in disgrace, since sums of money which had been extorted from the general were carried among the eagles and standards. Germanicus went to the Upper Army, and the second, thirteenth, and sixteenth legions, without any delay, accepted from him the oath of allegiance. The fourteenth hesitated a little, but their money and the discharge were offered even without their demanding it.

Meanwhile there was an outbreak among the Chauci, begun by some veterans of the mutinous legions on garrison duty. They were quelled for a time by the instant execution of two soldiers. Such was the order of Mennius, the camp-prefect, more as a salutary warning than as a legal act. Then, when the commotion increased, he fled and having been discovered, as his hiding place was now unsafe, he borrowed a resource from audacity. "It was not," he told them, "the camp-prefect, it was Germanicus, their general, it was Tiberius, their emperor, whom they were insulting." At the same moment, overawing all resistance, he seized the standard, faced round towards the river-bank, and exclaiming that whoever left the ranks, he would hold as a deserter, he led them back into their winter-quarters, disaffected indeed, but cowed.

Meanwhile envoys from the Senate had an interview with Germanicus, who had now returned, at the Altar of the Ubii. Two legions, the first and twentieth, with veterans discharged and serving under a standard, were there in winter-quarters. In the bewilderment of terror and conscious guilt they were penetrated by an apprehension that persons had come at the Senate's orders to cancel the concessions they had extorted by mutiny. And as it is the way with a mob to fix any charge, however groundless, on some particular person, they reproached Manatius Plancus, an ex-consul and the chief envoy, with being the author of the Senate's decree. At midnight they began to demand the imperial standard kept in Germanicus's quarters, and having rushed together to the entrance, burst the door, dragged Caesar from his bed, and forced him by menaces of death to give up the standard. Then roaming through the camp-streets, they met the envoys, who on hearing of the tumult were hastening to Germanicus. They oaded them with insults, and were on the point of murdering them, Plancus especially, whose high rank had deterred him from flight. In his peril he found safety only in the camp of the first legion. There clasping the standards and the eagle, he sought to protect himself under their sanctity. And had not the eagle-bearer, Calpurnius, saved him from the worst violence, the blood of an envoy of the Roman people, an occurrence rare even among our foes, would in a Roman camp have stained the altars of the gods. At last, with the light of day, when the general and the soldiers and the whole affair were clearly recognised, Germanicus entered the camp, ordered Plancus to be conducted to him, and received him on the tribunal. He then upbraided them with their fatal infatuation, revived not so much by the anger of the soldiers as by that of heaven, and explained the reasons of the envoys' arrival. On the rights of ambassadors, on the dreadful and undeserved peril of Plancus, and also on the disgrace into which the legion had brought itself, he dwelt with the eloquence of pity, and while the throng was confounded rather than appeased, he dismissed the envoys with an escort of auxiliary cavalry.

Amid the alarm all condemned Germanicus for not going to the Upper Army, where he might find obedience and help against the rebels. "Enough and more than enough blunders," they said, "had been made by granting discharges and money, indeed, by conciliatory measures. Even if Germanicus held his own life cheap, why should he keep a little son and a pregnant wife among madmen who outraged every human right? Let these, at least, be restored safely to their grandsire and to the State." When his wife spurned the notion, protesting that she was a descendant of the Divine Augustus and could face peril with no degenerate spirit, he at last embraced her and the son of their love with many tears, and after long delay compelled her to depart. Slowly moved along a pitiable procession of women, a general's fugitive wife with a little son in her bosom, her friends' wives weeping round her, as with her they were dragging themselves from the camp. Not less sorrowful were those who remained.

一 文献出处

P. C. Tacitus, *The Annals*, translated by Alfred John Church and William Jackson Brodribb, Nabu Press, 2010.

二 文献导读

塔西佗（P. Cornelius Tacitus, 公元 56~120 年）是最早记载罗马帝国早期断代史的历史作家、文学家，出身于旧贵族家庭。在罗马帝国屡任要职，公元 97 年任执政官，公元 112~113 年任亚细亚行省总督。代表作《编年史》（*The Annals*）涵盖公元 14~68 年史事，《历史》（*Historiae*）涵盖公元 69~96 年史事；《编年史》和《历史》连在一起，就是一部从朱利亚-克劳迪乌斯王朝的开国皇帝提比略到弗拉维王朝的末帝图密善的历史。可惜两部著作都没有完整保存下来。共 18 卷的《编年史》现大体留存第 1~6 卷（主要是公元 14~37 年提比略时代的历史）、第 11~16 卷（主要是公元 47~66 年克劳迪乌斯和尼禄时代的历史）。共 12 卷的《历史》保存下来的只有第 1~4 卷和第 5 卷的一部分，记述了从公元 69 年初到公元 70 年 8 月，朱利亚-克劳迪乌斯王朝最后三个皇帝与弗拉维王朝开国皇帝韦斯帕芗争夺帝位的史事以及韦斯帕芗及其儿子提图斯的胜利。《历史》中有关弗拉维王朝的部分已经全部失传。塔西佗属于贵族共和派，既承认帝制不可避免，又憎恨专制君主。《编年史》和《历史》都无情揭露了元老们奴颜婢膝、两面三刀的丑恶嘴脸，对帝国下层也极尽嘲讽。

塔西佗的另外两部著作是《日耳曼尼亚志》《阿古利可拉传》。《日耳曼尼亚志》（De origine et situ Germanorum）是现存关于公元 1~2 世纪日耳曼社会的唯一详细的史料；《阿古利可拉传》（De vita Julii Agricolae）是塔西佗为其征服不列颠的岳父阿古利可拉写的传记，对研究不列颠早期历史具有重要价值。塔西佗的传世著作还有《演说家对话录》，论述演说术衰落的原因。

上文节选自《编年史》第 1 卷。《编年史》原名《塔西佗撰写神圣奥古斯都逝世以来史》（Cornelii Taciti ab excessu divi Augusti），大概于公元 115 年到 120 年间出版，共 18 卷，现存第 1~4 卷全部，第 5、6 卷的局部以及第 11~16 卷的内容。塔西佗仔细地研究过前辈历史学家的著作，例如修昔底德、撒鲁斯特，引用了一些老普林尼《自然史》的资料，并参考了罗马的官方档案。该书覆盖了从公元 14 年（奥古斯都逝世）到公元 68 年这一时期；第 16 卷在尼禄皇帝去世之前突然中断。换言之，其内容包括提比略皇帝（公元 37 年去世）、卡利古拉皇帝（公元 41 年去世）、克劳迪乌斯皇帝（公元 54 年去世）以及尼禄皇帝（公元 68 年去世），其中对提比略在位期间的历史描述最详细，作者用晦涩的文笔描绘了这个皇帝的多疑与狡猾。作者阐述了罗马在朱利亚－克劳迪王朝皇帝们领导下的发展，并试图阐明这种发展的内在原因和动力。塔西佗特别注重罗马城的政治问题，忽视经济、文化因素和外省的影响，只有当外省的事件直接影响到罗马时，他才提及罗马以外的地区。

三　延伸阅读：

O'Gorman, E., *Irony and Misreading in the Annals of Tacitus*, Cambridge, 2000.

Pagan, V.E., ed., *A Companion to Tacitus*, Chichester, 2012.

Suetonius: Lives of the Caesars [*]

In the course of his sixteenth year [c. 85/84 B.C.] he lost his father. In the
next consulate, having previously been nominated priest of Jupiter [by Marius
and Cinna, Cos. 86], he broke his engagement with Cossutia, a lady of only
equestrian rank, but very wealthy, who had been betrothed to him before he
assumed the gown of manhood, and married Cornelia, daughter of that Cinna
who was four times consul, by whom he afterwards had a daughter Julia; and
the dictator Sulla could by no means force him to put away his wife. Therefore
besides being punished by the loss of his priesthood, his wife's dowry, and his
family inheritances, Caesar was held to be one of the opposite party. He was
accordingly forced to go into hiding, and though suffering from a severe attack
of quartan ague, to change from one covert to another almost every night, and
save himself from Sulla's detectives by bribes. But at last, through the good
offices of the Vestal virgins and of his near kinsmen, Mamercus Aemilius and
Aurelius Cotta, he obtained forgiveness. Everyone knows that when Sulla
had long held out against the most devoted and eminent men of his party who
interceded for Caesar, and they obstinately persisted, he at last gave way and
cried, either by divine inspiration or a shrewd forecast: 'Have your way and take

* 苏维托纽斯《凯撒传》节选，出自《罗马十二帝王传》。

him; only bear in mind that the man you are so eager to save will one day deal the death blow to the cause of the aristocracy, which you have joined with me in upholding; for in this Caesar there is more than one Marius.'

He served his first campaign in Asia on the personal staff of Marcus. Thermus, governor of the province [81 B.C.]. Being sent by Thermus to Bithynia, to fetch a fleet, he dawdled so long at the court of Nicomedes that he was suspected of improper relations with the king; and he lent color to this scandal by going back to Bithynia a few days after his return, with the alleged purpose of collecting a debt for a freedman, one of his dependents. During the rest of the campaign he enjoyed a better reputation, and at the storming of Mytilene [80 B.C.] Thermus awarded him the civic crown [a chaplet of oak leaves, given for saving the life of a fellow-citizen, the highest military award of the Roman state].

He served too under Servilius Isauricus in Cilicia, but only for a short time; for learning of the death of Sulla, and at the same time hoping to profit by a counter-revolution which Marcus Lepidus was setting on foot, he hurriedly returned to Rome [78 B.C.]. But he did not make common cause with Lepidus, although he was offered highly favorable terms, through lack of confidence both in that leader's capacity and in the outlook, which he found less promising than he had expected.

Then, after the civil disturbance had been quieted, he brought a charge of extortion against Cornelius Dolabella, an ex-consul who had been honored with a triumph [77 B.C.]. On the acquittal of Dolabella, Caesar determined to withdraw to Rhodes, to escape from the ill-will which he had incurred, and at the same time to rest and have leisure to study under Apollonius Molo, the most eminent teacher of oratory of that time. While crossing to Rhodes [74 B.C.], after the winter season had already begun, he was taken by pirates near the island of Pharmacussa and remained in their custody for nearly forty days in a state of intense vexation, attended only by a single physician and two body-servants; for he had sent off his travelling companions and the rest of his attendants at the outset, to raise money for his ransom. Once he was set on shore on payment of fifty talents, he did not delay then and there to launch a fleet and pursue the departing pirates, and the moment they were in his power to inflict on them the punishment which he had often threatened when joking with them. He then proceeded to Rhodes, but as Mithridates was devastating the neighboring regions, he crossed over into Asia, to avoid the appearance of inaction when the allies of the Roman people were in danger. There he levied a band of auxiliaries and drove the king's prefect from the province, thus holding the wavering and irresolute states to their allegiance.

While serving as military tribune, the first office which was conferred on him by vote of the people after his return to Rome, he ardently supported the leaders in the attempt to re-establish the authority of the tribunes of the commons, the extent of which Sulla had curtailed. Furthermore, through a bill proposed by one Plotius [70 B.C.], he effected the recall of his wife's brother Lucius Cinna, as well as of the others who had taken part with Lepidus in his revolution and after the consul's death had fled to Sertorius; and he personally spoke in favor of the measure.

When quaestor [67 B.C.], he pronounced the customary orations from the rostra in praise of his aunt Julia and his wife Cornelia, who had both died. And in the eulogy of his aunt he spoke in the following terms of her paternal and maternal ancestry and that of his own father: "The family of my aunt Julia is descended by her mother from the kings, and on her father's side is akin to the immortal Gods; for the Marcii Reges (her mother's family name) go back to Ancus Marcius, and the Julii, the family of which ours is a branch, to Venus. Our stock therefore has at once the sanctity of kings, whose power is supreme among mortal men, and the claim to reverence which attaches to the Gods, who hold sway over kings themselves." In place of Cornelia he took to wife Pompeia, daughter of Quintus Pompeius and granddaughter of Lucius Sulla. But he afterward divorced her [62 B.C.], suspecting her of adultery with Publius

Clodius; and in fact the report that Clodius had gained access to her in woman's garb during a public religious ceremony was so persistent, that the senate decreed that the pollution of the sacred rites be judicially investigated.

As quaestor it fell to his lot to serve in Hispania Ulterior. When he was there, while making the circuit of the towns, to hold court under commission from the praetor, he came to Gades, and noticing a statue of Alexander the Great in the temple of Hercules, he heaved a sigh, and as if out of patience with his own incapacity in having as yet done nothing noteworthy at a time of life when Alexander had already brought the world to his feet, he straightway asked for his discharge, to grasp the first opportunity for greater enterprises at Rome. Furthermore, when he was dismayed by a dream the following night (for he thought that he had offered violence to his mother) the soothsayers inspired him with high hopes by their interpretation, which was that he was destined to rule the world, since the mother whom he had seen in his power was none other than the earth, which is regarded as the common parent of all mankind.

Departing therefore before his term was over, he went to the Latin colonies which were in a state of unrest and meditating a demand for citizenship [those towns beyond the Po River, such as Verona, Comum, and Cremona, wished to obtain the rights of citizenship, which had been given to many of the Italian towns at the close of the Social War of 90-88 B.C.] and he might have spurred them on to some rash act, had not the consuls, in anticipation of that very danger, detained there for a time the legions which had been enrolled for service in Cilicia.

For all that he presently made a more daring attempt at Rome; for a few days before he entered upon his aedileship he was suspected of having made a conspiracy with Marcus Crassus, an ex-consul, and likewise with Publius Sulla and Lucius Autronius, who, after their election to the consulship, had been found guilty of corrupt practices [65 B.C.]. The design was to set upon the senate at the opening of the year and put to the sword as many as they thought good; then

Crassus was to usurp the dictatorship, naming Caesar as his master of horse, and when they had organized the state according to their pleasure, the consulship was to be restored to Sulla and Autronius. This plot is mentioned by Tanusius Geminus in his History, by Marcus Bibulus in his edicts, and by Gaius Curio the elder in his speeches. Cicero too seems to hint at it in a letter to Axius, where he says that Caesar in his consulship established the despotism which he had had in mind when he was aedile. Tanusius adds that Crassus, either conscience-stricken or moved by fear, did not appear on the day appointed for the massacre, and that therefore Caesar did not give the signal which it had been agreed that he should give; and Curio says that the arrangement was that Caesar should let his toga fall from his shoulder. Not only Curio, but Marcus Actorius Naso as well declare that Caesar made another plot with Gnaeus Piso, a young man to whom the province of Hispania had been assigned unasked and out of the regular order, because he was suspected of political intrigues at Rome; that they agreed to rise in revolt at the same time, Piso abroad and Caesar at Rome, aided by the Ambrani and the peoples beyond the Po; but that Piso's death brought both their designs to naught.

When aedile [65 B.C.], Caesar decorated not only the Comitium and the Forum with its adjacent basilicas, but the Capitol as well, building temporary colonnades for the display of a part of his material. He exhibited combats with wild beasts and stageplays too, both with his colleague and independently. The result was that Caesar alone took all the credit even for what they spent in common, and his colleague Marcus Bibulus openly said that his was the fate of Pollux: "For," said he, "just as the temple erected in the Forum to the twin brethren, bears only the name of Castor, so the joint liberality of Caesar and myself is credited to Caesar alone." Caesar gave a gladiatorial show besides, but with somewhat fewer pairs of combatants than he had purposed; for the huge band which he assembled from all quarters so terrified his opponents, that a bill was passed limiting the number of gladiators which anyone was to be allowed to keep in the city.

Having won the goodwill of the masses, Caesar made an attempt through some of the tribunes to have the charge of Egypt given him by a decree of the commons, seizing the opportunity to ask for so irregular an appointment because the citizens of Alexandria had deposed their king, who had been named by the senate an ally and friend of the Roman people, and their action was generally condemned. He failed however because of the opposition of the Optimates [a political faction among the Roman nobles]; wishing therefore to impair their prestige in every way he could, he restored the trophies commemorating the victories of Gaius Marius over Jugurtha and over the Cimbri and Teutoni, which Sulla had long since demolished. Furthermore in conducting prosecutions for murder, he included in the number of murderers even those who had received moneys from the public treasury during the proscriptions for bringing in the heads of Roman citizens, although they were expressly exempted by the Cornelian laws.

He also bribed a man to bring a charge of high treason against Gaius Rabirius, who some years before, had rendered conspicuous service to the senate in repressing the seditious designs of the tribune Lucius Saturninus; and when he had been selected by lot to sentence the accused, he did so with such eagerness, that when Rabirius appealed to the people, nothing was so much in his favor as the bitter hostility of his judge.

After giving up hope of the special commission, he announced his candidacy for the office of pontifex maximus, resorting to the most lavish bribery. Thinking on the enormous debt which he had thus contracted, he is said to have declared to his mother on the morning of the election, as she kissed him when he was starting for the polls, that he would never return except as pontifex. And in fact he so decisively defeated two very strong competitors (for they were greatly his superiors in age and rank), that he polled more votes in their tribes than were cast for both of them in all the tribes.

When the conspiracy of Catiline was detected [63 B.C.], and all the rest of the senate favored inflicting the extreme penalty on those implicated in the plot, Caesar, who was now praetor elect, alone proposed that their goods be confiscated and that they be imprisoned each in a separate town. Nay, more, he inspired such fear in those who favored severer measures, by picturing the hatred which the Roman commons would feel for them for all future time, that Decimus Silanus, consul elect, was not ashamed to give a milder interpretation to his proposal (since it would have been humiliating to change it) alleging that it had been understood in a harsher sense than he intended. Caesar would have prevailed too, for a number had already gone over to him, including Cicero, the consul's brother, had not the address of Marcus Cato kept the wavering senate in line. Yet not even then did he cease to delay the proceedings, but only when an armed troop of Roman knights that stood on guard about the place threatened him with death as he persisted in his headstrong opposition. They even drew their swords and made such passes at him that his friends who sat next him forsook him, while a few had much ado to shield him in their embrace or with their robes. Then, in evident fear, he not only yielded the point, but for the rest of the year kept aloof from the House.

On the first day of his praetorship [62 B.C.] he called upon Quintus Catulus to render an account to the people touching the restoration of the Capitol, proposing a bill for turning over the commission to another [namely, Gnaeus Pompeius]. But he withdrew the measure, since he could not cope with the united opposition of the optimates, seeing that they had at once dropped their attendance on the newly elected consuls and hastily gathered in throngs, resolved on an obstinate resistance.

Nevertheless, when Caecilius Metellus, tribune of the commons, brought forward some bills of a highly seditious nature in spite of the veto of his colleagues, Caesar abetted him and espoused his cause in the stubbornest fashion, until at last both were suspended from the exercise of their public functions by a decree of the senate. Yet in spite of this Caesar had the audacity to continue in office and to hold court, but when he learned that some were ready to stop him by force of arms, he dismissed his lictors, laid aside his robe of office, and slipped off privily to his house, intending to remain in retirement because of the state of the times. Indeed, when the populace on the following day flocked to him quite of their own accord, and with riotous demonstrations offered him their aid in recovering his position, he held them in check. Since this action of his was wholly unexpected, the senate, which had been hurriedly convoked to take action about that very gathering, publicly thanked him through its leading men; then summoning him to the House and lauding him in the strongest terms, they rescinded their former decree and restored him to his rank.

He again fell into danger by being named among the accomplices of Catiline, both before the commissioner [quaesitor] Novius Niger by an informer called Lucius Vettius and in the senate by Quintus Curius, who had been voted a sum of money from the public funds as the first to disclose the plans of the conspirators. Curius alleged that his information came directly from Catiline, while Vettius actually offered to produce a letter to Catiline in Caesar's hand writing. But Caesar, thinking that such an indignity could in no wise be endured, showed by appealing to Cicero's testimony that he had of his own accord reported to the consul certain details of the plot, and thus prevented Curius from getting the reward. As for Vettius, after his bond was declared forfeit and his goods seized, he was roughly handled by the populace assembled before the rostra, and all but torn to pieces. Caesar then put him in prison, and Novius the commissioner went there too, for allowing an official of superior rank to be arraigned before his tribunal.

Being allotted the province of Hispania Ulterior [61 B.C.] after his praetorship, Caesar got rid of his creditors, who tried to detain him, by means of sureties and contrary both to precedent and law was on his way before the provinces were provided for [i.e., without waiting for the decrees of the senate which formally confirmed the appointments of the new governors, and provided them with funds and equipment]; possibly through fear of a private impeachment or perhaps to respond more promptly to the entreaties of our allies for help. After restoring order in his province, he made off with equal haste, and without waiting for the arrival of his successor, to sue at the same time for a triumph and the consulship. But inasmuch as the day for the elections had already been announced and no account could be taken of Caesar's candidacy unless he entered the city as a private citizen, and since his intrigues to gain exemption from the laws met with general protest, he was forced to forgo the triumph, to avoid losing the consulship.

[60 B.C.] Of the two other candidates for this office, Lucius Lucceius and Marcus Bibulus, Caesar joined forces with the former, making a bargain with him that since Lucceius had less influence but more funds, he should in their common name promise largess to the electors from his own pocket. When this became known, the optimates authorized Bibulus to promise the same amount, being seized with fear that Caesar would stick at nothing when he became ohief magistrate, if he had a colleague who was heart and soul with him. Many of them contributed to the fund, and even Cato did not deny that bribery under such circumstances was for the good of the commonwealth. So Caesar was chosen consul with Bibulus. With the same motives the optimates took care that provinces of the smallest importance should be assigned to the newly elected consuls; that is, mere woods and pastures [It seems to designate provinces where the duties of the governor would be confined to guarding the mountain-pastures and keeping the woods free from bandits. The senate would not run the risk of letting Caesar secure a province involving the command of an army]. Thereupon Caesar, especially incensed by this slight, by every possible attention courted the goodwill of Gnaeus Pompeius, who was at odds with the senate because of its tardiness in ratifying his acts after his victory over king Mithridates [in the Third Mithridatic War]. He also patched up a peace between Pompeius and Marcus

Crassus, who had been enemies since their consulship, which had been one of constant wrangling. Then [60 B.C.] he so made a compact with both of them, that no step should be taken in public affairs which did not suit any one of the three.

Caesar's very first enactment after becoming consul was, that the proceedings both of the senate and of the people should day by day be compiled and published. He also revived a by-gone custom, that during the months when he did not have the fasces an orderly should walk before him, while the lictors followed him. He brought forward an agrarian law too, and when his colleague announced adverse omens [Business could be interrupted or postponed at Rome by the announcement of an augur or a magistrate that he had seen a flash of lightning or some other adverse sign; sometimes an opponent merely announced that he would 'watch the skies' for such omens], he resorted to arms and drove him from the Forum; and when next day Bibulus made complaint in the senate and no one could be found who ventured to make a motion, or even to express an opinion about so high-handed a proceeding (although decrees had often been passed touching less serious breaches of the peace), Caesar's conduct drove him to such a pitch of desperation, that from that time until the end of his term he did not leave his house, but merely issued proclamations announcing adverse omens. From that time on Caesar managed all the affairs of state alone and after his own pleasure; so that sundry witty fellows, pretending by way of jest to sign and seal testamentary documents, wrote "Done in the consulship of Julius and Caesar, " instead of "Bibulus and Caesar," writing down the same man twice, by name and by surname. Presently too the following verses were on everyone's lips:

"In Caesar's year, not Bibulus', an act took place of late;

For naught do I remember done in Bibulus' consulate."

The plain called Stellas, which had been devoted to public uses by the men of by-gone days, and the Campanian territory, which had been reserved to pay revenues for the aid of the government, he divided without casting lots [through a special commission of twenty men] among twenty thousand citizens who had three or more children each. When the publicans asked for relief, he freed them from a third part of their obligation, and openly warned them in contracting for taxes in the future not to bid too recklessly. He freely granted everything else that anyone took it into his head to ask, either without opposition or by intimidating anyone who tried to object. Marcus Cato, who tried to delay proceedings [by making a speech of several hours' duration; Gell. 4.10.8. The senate arose in a body and escorted Cato to prison, and Caesar was forced to release him], was dragged from the House by a lictor at Caesar's command and taken off to prison. When Lucius Lucullus was somewhat too outspoken in his opposition, he filled him with such fear of malicious prosecution [for his conduct during the Third Mithridatic War] that Lucullus actually fell on his knees before him. Because Cicero, while pleading in court, deplored the state of the times, Caesar transferred the orator's enemy Publius Clodius that very same day from the patricians to the plebeians [59 B.C.], a thing for which Clodius had for a long time been vainly striving; and that too at the ninth hour [That is, after the close of the business day, an indication of the haste with which the adoption was rushed through]. Finally taking action against all the opposition in a body, he bribed an informer to declare that he had been egged on by certain men to murder Gnaeus Pompeius, and to come out upon the rostra and name the guilty parties according to a pre-arranged plot. But when the informer had named one or two to no purpose and not without suspicion of double-dealing, Caesar, hopeless of the success of his over-hasty attempt, is supposed to have had him taken off by poison.

At about the same time he took to wife Calpurnia, daughter of Lucius Piso, who was to succeed him in the consulship, and affianced his own daughter Julia to Gnaeus Pompeius, breaking a previous engagement with Servilius Caepio, although the latter had shortly before rendered him conspicuous service in his contest with Bibulus. And after this new alliance he began to call upon Pompeius first to give his opinion in the senate, although it had been his habit to begin with Crassus, and it was the rule for the consul in calling for opinions to continue throughout the year the order which he had established on the Kalends of January.

Backed therefore by his father-in-law and son-in-law, out of all the numerous provinces he made Gallia his choice, as the most likely to enrich him and furnish suitable material for triumphs. At first, it is true, by the bill of Vatinius he received only Gallia Cisalpina with the addition of Illyricum; but presently he was assigned Gallia Comata as well by the senate, since the members feared that even if they should refuse it, the people would give him this also. Transported with joy at this success, he could not keep from boasting a few days later before a crowded house, that having gained his heart's desire to the grief and lamentation of his opponents, he would therefore from that time mount on their heads [used in a double sense, one sexual]; and when someone insultingly remarked that that would be no easy matter for any woman, he replied in the same vein that Semiramis too had been ueen in Syria and the Amazons in days of old had held sway over a great part of Asia.

When at the close of his consulship the praetors Gaius Memmius and Lucius Domitius moved an inquiry into his conduct during the previous year, Caesar laid the matter before the senate; and when they failed to take it up, and three days had been wasted in fruitless wrangling, went off to his province. Whereupon his quaestor was at once arraigned on several counts, as a preliminary to his own impeachment. Presently he himself too was prosecuted by Lucius Antistius, tribune of the commons, and it was only by appealing to the whole college that he contrived not to be brought to trial, on the ground that he was absent on public service. Then to secure himself for the future, he took great pains always to put the magistrates for the year under personal obligation, and not to aid any candidates or suffer any to be elected, save such as guaranteed to defend him in his absence. And he did not hesitate in some cases to exact an oath to keep this pledge or even a written contract.

[55 B.C.] When, however, Lucius Domitius, candidate for the consulship, openly threatened to effect as consul what he had been unable to do as praetor, and to take his armies from him, Caesar compelled Pompeius and Crassus to come to Luca, a city in his province, where he prevailed on them to stand for a second consulship, to defeat Domitius; and he also succeeded through their influence in having his term as governor of Gallia made five years longer. Encouraged by this, he added to the legions which he had received from the state others at his own cost, one actually composed of men of Gallia Transalpina and bearing a Gallic name too (for it was called Alauda [A Celtic word meaning a crested lark (Plin. N.H. 11.37) which was the device on the helmets of the legion]), which he trained in the Roman tactics and equipped with Roman arms; and later on he gave every man of it citizenship. After that he did not let slip any pretext for war, however unjust and dangerous it might be, picking quarrels as well with allied, as with hostile and barbarous nations; so that once the senate decreed that a commission be sent to inquire into the condition of the Gallic provinces, and some even recommended that Caesar be handed over to the enemy. But as his enterprises prospered, thanksgivings were appointed in his honor oftener and for longer periods than for anyone before his time.

[58-49 B.C.] During the nine years of his command this is in substance what he did. All that part of Gallia which is bounded by the Pyrenees, the Alps and the Cévennes, and by the Rhine and Rhone rivers, a circuit of some 3, 200 miles [Roman measure, about 3, 106 English miles], with the exception of some allied states which had rendered him good service, he reduced to the form of a province; and imposed upon it a yearly tribute of 40, 000, 000 sesterces. He was the first Roman to build a bridge and attack the Germans beyond the Rhine; and he inflicted heavy losses upon them. He invaded the Britons too, a people unknown before, vanquished them, and exacted moneys and hostages. Amid all these successes he met with adverse fortune but three times in all: in Britannia, where his fleet narrowly escaped destruction in a violent storm; in Gallia, when one of his legions was routed at Gergovia; and on the borders of Germania, when his lieutenants Titurius and Aurunculeius were ambushed and slain.

Within this same space of time he lost first his mother, then his daughter, and soon afterwards his grandchild. Meanwhile, as the community was aghast at the murder of Publius Clodius, the senate had voted that only one consul should be chosen, and expressly named Gnaeus Pompeius. When the tribunes planned to make him Pompeius' colleague, Caesar urged them rather to propose to the people that he be permitted to stand for a second consulship without coming to Rome, when the term of his governorship drew near its end, to prevent his being forced for the sake of the office to leave his province prematurely and without finishing the war. On the granting of this, aiming still higher and flushed with hope, he neglected nothing in the way of lavish expenditure or of favors to anyone, either in his public capacity or privately. He began a forum with the proceeds of his spoils, the ground for which cost more than a hundred million sesterces. He announced a combat of gladiators and a feast for the people in memory of his daughter, a thing quite without precedent. To raise the expectation of these events to the highest possible pitch, he had the material for the banquet prepared in part by his own household, although he had let contracts to the markets as well. He gave orders too that whenever famous gladiators fought without winning the favor of the people [when ordinarily they would be put to death], they should be rescued by force and kept for him. He had the novices trained, not in a gladiatorial school by professionals, but in private houses by Roman knights and even by senators who were skilled in arms, earnestly beseeching them, as is shown by his own letters, to give the recruits individual attention and personally direct their exercises. He doubled the pay of the legions for all time. Whenever grain was plentiful, he distributed it to them without stint or measure, and now and then gave each man a slave from among the captives.

Moreover, to retain his relationship and friendship with Pompeius, Caesar offered him his sister's granddaughter Octavia in marriage, although she was already the wife of Gaius Marcellus, and asked for the hand of Pompeius' daughter, who was promised to Faustus Sulla. When he had put all Pompeius' friends under obligation, as well as the great part of the senate, through loans made without interest or at a low rate, he lavished gifts on men of all other classes, both those whom he invited to accept his bounty and those who applied to him unasked, including even freedmen and slaves who were special favorites of their masters or patrons. In short, he was the sole and ever ready help of all who were in legal difficulties or in debt and of young spendthrifts, excepting only those whose burden of guilt or of poverty was so heavy, or who were so given up to riotous living, that even he could not save them; and to these he declared in the plainest terms that what they needed was a civil war.

He took no less pains to win the devotion of princes and provinces all over the world, offering prisoners to some by the thousand as a gift, and sending auxiliary troops to the aid of others whenever they wished, and as often as they wished, without the sanction of the senate or people, besides adorning the principal cities of Asia and Graecia with magnificent public works, as well as those of Italia and the provinces of Gallia and Hispania. At last [51 B.C.], when all were thunderstruck at his actions and wondered what their purpose could be, the consul Marcus Claudius Marcellus, after first making proclamation that he purposed to bring before the senate a matter of the highest public moment, proposed that a successor to Caesar be appointed before the end of his term, on the ground that the war was ended, peace was established, and the victorious army ought to be disbanded; also that no account be taken of Caesar at the elections, unless he were present, since Pompeius' subsequent action [i.e., in correcting the bill after it had been passed and filed, as explained in the following sentence] had not annulled the decree of the people. And it was true that when Pompeius proposed a bill touching the privileges of officials, in the clause where he debarred absentees from candidacy for office he forgot to make a special exception in Caesar's case, and did not correct the oversight until the law had been inscribed on a tablet of bronze and deposited in the treasury. Not content with depriving Caesar of his provinces and his privilege, Marcellus also moved that the colonists whom Caesar had settled in Novum Comum by the bill of Vatinius should lose their citizenship, on the ground that it had been given from political motives and was not authorized by the law.

Greatly troubled by these measures, and thinking, as they say he was often heard to remark, that now that he was the leading man of the state, it was harder to push him down from the first place to the second than it would be from the second to the lowest, Caesar stoutly resisted Marcellus, partly through vetoes of the tribunes and partly through the other consul, Servius Sulpicius. When next year Gaius Marcellus, who had succeeded his cousin Marcus as consul, tried the same thing, Caesar by a heavy bribe secured the support of the other consul, Aemilius Paulus, and of Gaius Curio, the most reckless of the tribunes. But seeing that everything was being pushed most persistently, and that even the consuls elect were among the opposition, he sent a written appeal to the senate, not to take from him the privilege which the people had granted, or else to compel the others in command of armies to resign also; feeling sure, it was thought, that he could more readily muster his veterans as soon as he wished, than Pompeius his newly levied troops. He further proposed a compromise to his opponents, that after giving up eight legions and Gallia Transalpina, he be allowed to keep two legions and Gallia Cisalpina, or at least one legion and Illyricum, until he was elected consul.

But when the senate declined to interfere, and his opponents declared that they would accept no compromise in a matter affecting the public welfare, he crossed to Gallia Citerior, and after hearing all the legal cases, halted at Ravenna, intending to resort to war if the senate took any drastic action against the tribunes of the commons who interposed vetoes in his behalf. Now this was his excuse for the civil war, but it is believed that he had other motives. Gnaeus Pompeius used to declare that since Caesar's own means were not sufficient to complete the works which he had planned, nor to do all that he had led the people to expect on his return, he desired a state of general unrest and turmoil. Others say that he dreaded the necessity of rendering an account for what he had done in his first consulship contrary to the auspices and the laws, and regardless of vetoes; for Marcus Cato often declared, and took oath too, that he would impeach Caesar the moment he had disbanded his army. It was openly said too that if he was out of office on his return, he would be obliged, like Milo [who had been accused and tried for the murder of Publius Clodius], to make his defence in a court hedged about by armed men. The latter opinion is the more credible one in view of the assertion of Asinius Pollio, that when Caesar at the battle of Pharsalus saw his enemies slain or in flight, he said, word for word: "They would have it so. Even I, Gaius Caesar, after so many great deeds, should have been found guilty, if I had not turned to my army for help." Some think that habit had given him a love of power, and that weighing the strength of his adversaries against his own, he grasped the opportunity of usurping the despotism which had been his heart's desire from early youth. Cicero too was seemingly of this opinion, when he wrote in the third book of his De Officiis [3.82; cf. 1.26] that Caesar ever had upon his lips these lines of Euripides [Phoenissae, 524 ff.], of which Cicero himself adds a version:

'If wrong may e'er be right, for a throne's sake

Were wrong most right: —be God in all else feared.'

[49 B.C.] Accordingly, when word came that the veto of the tribunes had been set aside and they themselves had left the city, he at once sent on a few cohorts with all secrecy, and then, to disarm suspicion, concealed his purpose by appearing at a public show, inspecting the plans of a gladiatorial school which he intended building, and joining as usual in a banquet with a large company. It was not until after sunset that he set out very privily with a small company, taking the mules from a bakeshop hard by and harnessing them to a carriage; and when his lights went out and he lost his way, he was astray for some time, but at last found a guide at dawn and got back to the road on foot by narrow bypaths. Then, overtaking his cohorts at the river Rubicon, which was the boundary of his province, he paused for a while, and realizing what a step he was taking, he turned to those about him and said: "Even yet we may draw back; but once cross yon little bridge, and the whole issue is with the sword."

As he stood in doubt, this sign was given him. On a sudden there appeared hard by a being of wondrous stature and beauty, who sat and played upon a reed; and when not only the shepherds flocked to hear him, but many of the soldiers left their posts, and among them some of the trumpeters, the apparition snatched a trumpet from one of them, rushed to the river, and sounding the war-note with mighty blast, strode to the opposite bank. Then Caesar cried: " Take we the course which the signs of the gods and the false dealing of our foes point out. The die is cast [A>Iacta alea est,' inquit']."

Accordingly, crossing with his army, and welcoming the tribunes of the plebeians, who had come to him after being driven from Rome, he harangued the soldiers with tears, and rending his robe from his breast besought their faithful service. It is even thought that he promised every man the estate of an eques, but that came of a misunderstanding; for since he often pointed to the finger of his left hand as he addressed them and urged them on, declaring that to satisfy all those who helped him to defend his honor he would gladly tear his very ring from his hand, those on the edge of the assembly, who could see him better than they could hear his words, assumed that he said what his gesture seemed to mean; and so the report went about that he had promised them the right of the ring and four hundred thousand sesterces as well [The equites as well as senators had the privilege of wearing a gold ring, and must possess an estate of 400, 000 sesterces].

The sum total of his movements after that is, in their order, as follows: He overran Umbria, Picenum, and Etruria, took prisoner Lucius Domitius, who had been irregularly named his successor, and was holding Corfinium with a garrison, let him go free, and then proceeded along the Adriatic to Brundisium, where Pompeius and the consuls had taken refuge, intending to cross the sea as soon as might be. After vainly trying by every kind of hindrance to prevent their sailing, he marched off to Rome, and after calling the senate together to discuss public business, went to attack Pompeius' strongest forces, which were in Hispania under command of three of his lieutenants—Marcus Petreius, Lucius Afranius, and Marcus Varro—saying to his friends before he left "I go to meet an army without a leader, and I shall return to meet a leader without an army." And in fact, though his advance was delayed by the siege of Massilia, which had shut its gates against him, and by extreme scarcity of supplies, he nevertheless quickly gained a complete victory.

[48 B.C.] Returning thence to Rome, he crossed into Macedonia, and after blockading Pompeius for almost four months behind mighty ramparts, finally routed him in the battle at Pharsalus, followed him in his flight to Alexandria, and when he learned that his rival had been slain, made war on King Ptolemy, whom he perceived to be plotting against his own safety as well; a war in truth of great difficulty, convenient neither in time nor place, but carried on during the winter season, within the walls of a well-provisioned and crafty foeman, while Caesar himself was without supplies of any kind and ill-prepared. Victor in spite of all, he turned over the rule of Egypt to Cleopatra and her younger brother [47 B.C.], fearing that if he made a province of it, it might one day under a headstrong governor be a source of revolution. From Alexandria he crossed to Syria, and from there went to Pontus, spurred on by the news that Pharnaces, son of Mithridates the Great, had taken advantage of the situation to make war, and was already flushed with numerous successes; but Caesar vanquished him in a single battle within five days after his arrival and four hours after getting sight of him, often remarking on Pompeius' good luck in gaining his principal fame as a general by victories over such feeble foemen. Then he overcame Scipio and Juba [46 B.C.], who were patching up the remnants of their party in Africa, and the sons of Pompeius in Spain [45 B C.].

In all the civil wars he suffered not a single disaster except through his lieutenants, of whom Gaius Curio perished in Africa, Gaius Antonius fell into the hands of the enemy in Illyricum, Publius Dolabella lost a fleet also off Illyricum, and Gnaeus Domitius Calvinus an army in Pontus. Personally he always fought with the utmost success, and the issue was never even in doubt save twice: once at Dyrrachium, where he was put to flight, and said of Pompeius, who failed to follow up his success, that he did not know how to use a victory; again in Spain, in the final struggle, when, believing the battle lost, he actually thought of suicide.

Having ended the wars, he celebrated five triumphs, four in a single month, but at intervals of a few days, after vanquishing Scipio; and another on defeating Pompeius' sons. The first and most splendid was the Gallic triumph, the next the Alexandrian, then the Pontic, after that the African, and finally the Hispanic, each differing from the rest in its equipment and display of spoils. As he rode through the Velabrum on the day of his Gallic triumph, the axle of his chariot broke, and he was all but thrown out; and he mounted the Capitol by torchlight, with forty elephants bearing lamps on his right and his left. In his Pontic triumph he displayed among the show-pieces of the procession an inscription of but three words, "I came, I saw, I conquered, " ['Veni, vidi, vici'] not indicating the events of the war, as the others did, but the speed with which it was finished.

To each and every foot-soldier of his veteran legions he gave twenty-four thousand sesterces by way of plunder, over and above the two thousand apiece which he had paid them at the beginning of the civil strife. He also assigned them lands, but not side by side, to avoid dispossessing any of the former owners. To every man of the people, besides ten pecks of grain and the same number of pounds of oil, he distributed the three hundred sesterces which he had

promised at first, and one hundred apiece because of the delay. He also remitted
a year's rent in Rome to tenants who paid two thousand sesterces or less, and in
Italy up to five hundred sesterces. He added a banquet and a dole of meat, and
after his Hispanic victory two dinners; for deeming that the former of these had
not been served with a liberality creditable to his generosity, he gave another five
days later on a most lavish scale.

He gave entertainments of divers kinds: a combat of gladiators and also stageplays in every ward all over the city, performed too by actors of all languages,
as well as races in the circus, athletic contests, and a sham sea-fight. In the
gladiatorial contest in the Forum Furius Leptinus, a man of praetorian stock,
and Quintus Calpenus, a former senator and pleader at the bar, fought to a
finish. A Pyrrhic dance was performed by the sons of the princes of Asia and
Bithynia. During the plays Decimus Laberius, a Roman eques, acted a farce of
his own composition, and having been presented with five hundred thousand
sesterces and a gold ring [in token of his restoration to the rank of eques,
which he forfeited by appearing on the stage], passed from the stage through
the orchestra and took his place in the fourteen rows [the first fourteen rows
above the orchestra, reserved for the equites by the law of L. Roscius Otho,
tribune of the plebeians, in 67 B.C.]. For the races the circus was lengthened
at either end and a broad canal was dug all about it; then young men of
the highest rank drove four-horse and two-horse chariots and rode pairs of
horses, vaulting from one to the other. The game called Troy was performed
by two troops, of younger and of older boys. Combats with wild beasts were
presented on five successive days, and last of all there was a battle between two
opposing armies, in which five hundred foot-soldiers, twenty elephants, and
thirty horsemen engaged on each side. To make room for this, the goals were
taken down and in their place two camps were pitched over against each other.
The athletic competitions lasted for three days in a temporary stadium built for
the purpose in the region of the Campus Martius. For the naval battle a pool

was dug in the lesser Codeta and there was a contest of ships of two, three, and four banks of oars, belonging to the Tyrian and Egyptian fleets, manned by a large force of fighting men. Such a throng flocked to all these shows from every quarter, that many strangers had to lodge in tents pitched in the streets or along the roads, and the press was often such that many were crushed to death, including two senators.

Then turning his attention to the reorganisation of the state, he reformed the calendar, which the negligence of the pontiffs had long since so disordered, through their privilege of adding months or days at pleasure, that the harvest festivals did not come in summer nor those of the vintage in the autumn; and he adjusted the year to the sun's course by making it consist of three hundred and sixty-five days, abolishing the intercalary month, and adding one day every fourth year [the year had previously consisted of 355 days, and the deficiency of about eleven days was made up by inserting an intercalary month of twenty-two or twenty-three days after February]. Furthermore, that the correct reckoning of seasons might begin with the next Kalends of January, he inserted two other months between those of November and December; hence the year in which these arrangements were made was one of fifteen months, including the intercalary month, which belonged to that year according to the former custom.

He filled the vacancies in the senate, enrolled additional patricians, and increased the number of praetors, aediles, and quaestors, as well as of the minor officials; he reinstated those who had been degraded by official action of the censors or found guilty of bribery by verdict of the jurors. He shared the elections with the people on this basis: that except in the case of the consulship, half of the magistrates should be appointed by the people's choice, while the rest should be those whom he had personally nominated. And these he announced in brief notes like the following, circulated in each tribe: "Caesar the Dictator to this or that tribe. I commend to you so and so, to hold their positions by your votes." He admitted to office even the sons of those who had been proscribed.

He limited the right of serving as jurors to two classes, the equestrian and senatorial orders, disqualifying the third class, the tribunes of the treasury. He made the enumeration of the people neither in the usual manner nor place, but from street to street aided by the owners of blocks of houses, and reduced the number of those who received grain at public expense from three hundred and twenty thousand to one hundred and fifty thousand. And to prevent the calling of additional meetings at any future time for purposes of enrolment, he provided that the places of such as died should be filled each year by the praetors from those who were not on the list.

Moreover, to keep up the population of the city, depleted as it was by the assignment of eighty thousand citizens to colonies across the sea, he made a law that no citizen older than twenty or younger than forty, who was not detained by service in the army, should be absent from Italia for more than three successive years; that no senator's son should go abroad except as the companion of a magistrate or on his staff; and that those who made a business of grazing should have among their herdsmen at least one-third who were men of free birth. He conferred citizenship on all who practiced medicine at Rome, and on all teachers of the liberal arts, to make them more desirous of living in the city and to induce others to resort to it. As to debts, he disappointed those who looked for their cancellation, which was often agitated, but finally decreed that the debtors should satisfy their creditors according to a valuation of their possessions at the price which they had paid for them before the civil war, deducting from the principal whatever interest had been paid in cash or pledged through bankers; an arrangement which wiped out about a fourth part of their indebtedness. He dissolved all collegii [associations], except those of ancient foundation. He increased the penalties for crimes; and inasmuch as the rich involved themselves in guilt with less hesitation because they merely suffered exile, without any loss of property, he punished murderers of freemen by the confiscation of all their goods, as Cicero writes, and others by the loss of one-half.

He administered justice with the utmost conscientiousness and strictness. Those convicted of extortion he even dismissed from the senatorial order. He annulled the marriage of an ex-praetor, who had married a woman the very day after her divorce, although there was no suspicion of adultery. He imposed duties on foreign wares. He denied the use of litters and the wearing of scarlet robes or pearls to all except to those of a designated position and age, and on set days. In particular, he enforced the law against extravagance, setting watchmen in various parts of the market, to seize and bring to him dainties which were exposed for sale in violation of the law; and sometimes he sent his lictors and soldiers to take from a dining-room any articles which had escaped the vigilance of his watchmen, even after they had been served.

In particular, for the adornment and convenience of the city, also for the protection and extension of the Empire, he formed more projects and more extensive ones every day; first of all, to rear a temple to Mars, greater than any in existence, filling up and levelling the pool in which he had exhibited the sea-fight, and to build a theater of vast size, sloping down from the Tarpeian Rock; to reduce the civil code to fixed limites, and of the vast and prolix mass of statutes to include only the best and most essential in a limited number of volumes; to open to the public the greatest possible libraries of Greek and Latin books, assigning to Marcus Varro the charge of procuring and classifying them; to drain the Pomptine marshes; to let out the water from Lake Fucinus; to make a highway from the Adriatic across the summit of the Apennines as far as the Tiber; to cut a canal through the Isthmus; to check the Dacians, who had poured into Pontus and Thrace; then to make war on the Parthians by way of Lesser Armenia, but not to risk a battle with them until he had first tested their mettle. All these enterprises and plans were cut short by his death. But before I speak of that, it will not be amiss to describe briefly his personal appearance, his dress, his mode of life, and his character, as well as his conduct in civil and military life.

一 文献出处

Suetonius, *Lives of the Caesars*, trans. by J. C. Rolfe, Cambridge, Mass.: Harvard University Press; London: William Henemann, 1920.

二 文献导读

苏维托纽斯（C. Suetonius Tranquillus, 公元 69~122 年？）是罗马帝国早期的历史作家，政要小普林尼的挚友。苏维托纽斯出身于罗马骑士家庭，青年时代短时间做过律师。公元 117 年，皇帝哈德良登基，苏维托纽斯也随之被小普林尼等人推荐进入宫廷，担任兼管皇家图书和档案的小官。公元 121 年擢升为皇帝侍从秘书，次年因疏忽宫廷礼节被解职，旋即埋头著书。

他的著作虽然很多，但大多数已经失传。作品中近乎完整地保存下来的只有公元 120 年发表的 8 卷构成的《罗马十二帝王传》。《罗马十二帝王传》是苏维托纽斯的代表作，它叙述了罗马 12 个元首／皇帝从凯撒（Caesar, 公元前 100~前 44 年）到图密善（Domitian, 公元 51~96 年）的生平事迹。现在通行的本子缺了《凯撒传》最前面的少数几节，还有几处不重要的脱漏。

12 部传记的共同结构是时间顺序和分类叙述交替进行：先按时间顺序叙述，从皇帝的祖先家世开始追溯，然后写他的诞生地点和时间，再后描述他的童年、青年、仕途履历，一直写到成为皇帝那一天。描写对象登基以后，作者就改为按主题分类描述。每一位皇帝的事迹按类别分为以下范畴：社会生活和私人生活、战争、与军队的关系、居所或公共设施的建设、对宗教和法律的态度、庆祝活动或表演、对制度和改革的贡献。关于皇帝私人生活，突出描述了其家庭生活、与朋友的关系以及休闲生活。最后又回到按时间顺序叙述，叙述皇帝临终、葬礼和遗嘱。作者虽然也重视论述皇帝们的美德或缺点，但没有结合历史背景进行深刻的分析，而是过分热衷于奇闻轶事，尽管其中有很多有趣的细节写得栩栩如生，但部分是不可靠的。

虽然罗马人在文学艺术的创作或哲学的深刻思维方面不及希腊人有天赋，但是在历史散文著作方面则名家辈出、各领风骚。公元前1世纪，除了传统编年史学之外，奈波斯开创了新的传记体史学形式。公元1~2世纪间，苏维托纽斯的《罗马十二帝王传》与普鲁塔克的《希腊罗马名人传》、塔西佗的《阿古利可拉传》共同代表了罗马传记史学的最高水平。《罗马十二帝王传》问世后，曾受到广泛的喜爱、传播，许多作家模仿它。

诚然，与同时代的其他两位传记大家相比，用严肃史学的成就来衡量，苏维托纽斯确实比不上塔西佗和普鲁塔克。但我们如能不拘一格看人才，那么应该说《罗马十二帝王传》也不失为一部别具特色的作品。《罗马十二帝王传》提供了极其丰富的史料，弥补了塔西佗著作的不足，极大地丰富了后人对于公元1世纪罗马帝国宫廷生活的了解。

此外，《罗马十二帝王传》也有很高的文学价值，因其文风简洁流畅，不事浮华雕饰，对后世产生了广泛而持久的影响。后世的许多作家都从此寻找资料，并借鉴方法。

上文节选自《罗马十二帝王传》中的《凯撒传》。

三　延伸阅读

Suetonius, *Nero*, ed. by B.H. Warmington, London: Bristol Classical Press, 1999.

Suetonius, *The Twelve Caesars (Titus)*, London: Penguin, 1979.

Wallace-Hadrill, A., *Suetonius: The Scholar and his Caesars*, London: Duckworth, 1983.

Wardle, D., *Suetonius' Life of Caligula: A Commentary*, Brussels: Latomus, 1994.

后 记

五卷本的《西方历史文献选读》即将付梓问世，我们在如释重负之际，难免有几分感慨！

五年前，为了切实改进世界史专业的教学，提升各个层次学生培养的质量，中国人民大学历史学院世界史专业教师团队申报并承担了学校的这一"九八五工程"项目的子课题。为了很好地完成任务，我们先后多次召开研讨会，对文献选编的内容、标准与体例反复磋商，交流意见，达成共识。同时，负责各卷的人员，在编选过程中悉心挑选篇目，并在文后作出尽可能精准的解析。通过艰苦的劳动与紧密协作，最终将任务顺利完成。

中国人民大学历史学院前任院长孙家洲教授，现任院长黄兴涛教授、副院长刘后滨教授与夏明方教授等对这项课题从立项到完成都给予了热诚支持。国内史学前辈和同仁也十分关心这套丛书的选编，并提出了不少有益的建议。对此，我们深表谢忱！社会科学文献出版社人文分社宋月华社长、张晓莉总编辑对本成果的出版提供了很多帮助，我们也在此深切致谢。

本卷的希腊史部分由王大庆副教授完成，罗马史部分由米辰峰副教授完成。在编选文献的过程中，我们本着实事求是的态度，尽可能遴选具有代表性的资料，并对相关文献做到尽可能接近历史真实的解析。在这些方面，史学界当然会仁者见仁、智者见智，不可能有众所认同的统一标准与看法。同时，由于视野与水平有限，丛书难免存在着这样那样的不足。我们真诚地希望听到史界同仁及广大读者的建议与批评。

编　者
2014 年冬于中国人民大学

图书在版编目（CIP）数据

西方历史文献选读. 古代卷 / 孟广林主编；王大庆，
米辰峰选编. —北京：社会科学文献出版社，2015.6（2023.8重印）
ISBN 978-7-5097-7340-6

Ⅰ.①西… Ⅱ.①孟… ②王… ③米… Ⅲ.①西方
国家－历史－文献－选编－古代 Ⅳ.①K106

中国版本图书馆CIP数据核字（2015）第069786号

西方历史文献选读（古代卷）

主　　编 / 孟广林
选　　编 / 王大庆　米辰峰

出 版 人 / 冀祥德
项目统筹 / 宋月华　张晓莉
责任编辑 / 张晓莉　李邦文

出　　版 / 社会科学文献出版社·人文分社（010）59367215
　　　　　 地址：北京市北三环中路甲29号院华龙大厦　邮编：100029
　　　　　 网址：www.ssap.com.cn
发　　行 / 社会科学文献出版社（010）59367028
印　　装 / 北京虎彩文化传播有限公司

规　　格 / 开　本：787mm×1092mm 1/16
　　　　　 印　张：24.75　字　数：389千字
版　　次 / 2015年6月第1版　2023年8月第4次印刷
书　　号 / ISBN 978-7-5097-7340-6
定　　价 / 89.00元

读者服务电话：4008918866